CORNUCOPIA OF CRIME

CORNUCOPIA OF CRIME

Francis M. Nevins

RAMBLE HOUSE

©2010 by Francis M. Nevins

ISBN 13: 978-1-60543-458-2

ISBN 10: 1-60543-458-2

Cover Art: Gavin L. O'Keefe
Preparation: Fender Tucker

For Jon L. Breen

TABLE OF CONTENTS

I. INTRODUCTION 13
II. TITANS 21
   Erle Stanley Gardner 23
   Cornell Woolrich 53
   Ellery Queen 72
   Anthony Boucher 92
III. COLD CASES 105
   Anthony Abbot 107
   Cleve F. Adams 114
   John Lawrence 130
   Milton Propper 147
   William Ard 161
IV. PROFILES 181
   Michael Avallone 183
   Edward D. Hoch 189
   Harry Stephen Keeler 201
   John Lutz 209
   John D. MacDonald 214
   Jack Ritchie 222
V. BROTHER AGENTS 229
   James Atlee Phillips 231
   David Atlee Phillips 249
VI. PLEASE READ BEFORE THE LIGHTS DIM 273
VII. POETIC PUZZLEMENT 353
VIII. MEDIA 369
   Point Blank 371
   Bernard Herrmann 379
   Boucher and Sherlock Holmes 382
   Notes on Crime Shows of TV's Golden Age 385
IX. BITS AND PIECES 389
X. FOR THE ABSENT 401
   Christianna Brand 403
   Ray B. Browne 404
   Joe L. Hensley 406
   Edward D. Hoch 407
   Stuart M. Kaminsky 409
   Joseph H. Lewis 411
   Aaron Marc Stein 414
   Two Women 416

CORNUCOPIA OF CRIME

INTRODUCTION

If you leave out the accident of having been born, the first step that led to this book happened when, at around age four, I somehow learned to read. In one of the last conversations I had with my mother before her death she insisted she hadn't taught me. Her best guess was that somehow I had taught myself by playing with a set of alphabet blocks. I have no recollection of the process but I was reading before I first set my little feet in the kindergarten class of Sherman School in Roselle Park, New Jersey.

I never saw my father reading much except the New York *Daily News* but he must have been an avid reader when he was young. One of the books on his shelves was *The Benson Murder Case* (1926), first of S.S. Van Dine's once hugely popular Philo Vance detective novels. At age nine or ten I had no idea what detective fiction was but I remember trying to read that book and giving up after one or two chapters, skunked by Van Dine's sesquipedalian ponderosity. But when I turned 13 and was given access to the adult sections of the Roselle Park Public Library, chance or fate brought me to the mystery fiction shelves where I discovered Sherlock Holmes and Charlie Chan and was hooked for life.

Throughout my high school and college years I kept discovering new mystery writers and characters and worlds: Agatha Christie, John Dickson Carr, Erle Stanley Gardner, Rex Stout, Leslie Charteris, Ellery Queen. I can still see myself sitting in a creaky old green-painted rocking chair in front of my grandmother's house during the heat of the 1957 summer, lost in ecstasy as I wandered with Ellery through the labyrinths of *The Greek Coffin Mystery*. I remember the all but orgasmic excitement that shot through me when I reached the last chapter of Christie's *Murder in the Calais Coach*. Back in the Fifties the academic consensus was that mystery fiction was escapist trash; there was no secondary literature about the genre and one discovered interesting authors by trial and error or not at all. The best help I had came from a secondhand bookstore I had to pass every afternoon on the way home from school, a dusty old place with bare floorboards and naked light bulbs and books and magazines piled to the rafters, owned by a nasty old man and his kindly wife.

Most afternoons I would look in the window as I passed that store. If the man was there I'd move on but if his wife was in charge I'd step in and buy some mysteries. Hardcovers cost a quarter, paperbacks a nickel or a dime. Even on a high-school kid's allowance one could build up quite a nice library of crime fiction at those prices. I knew nothing about most of the stuff I bought but by the law of averages I picked up lots of books that later came to prove quite valuable, like the paperback originals by David Goodis and Jim Thompson and John D. MacDonald. I can still see in my mind's eye some treasures that I found in that store but in my ignorance passed up, like that first edition of Graham Greene's 1931 *Rumour at Nightfall*, one of the two novels Greene would never allow to be reprinted after he'd become rich and famous. That copy is probably worth a mint today. If only I had invested a quarter in it back in 1958! But at age fifteen who knew from Graham Greene?

In college I got into the habit of buying the New York *Times* every Sunday just for the pleasure of reading Anthony Boucher's Criminals at Large column. Between classes I haunted the college library's microfilm room, poring over Boucher's columns from years before in back issues of the *Times*. Every few weeks I would hop across the Hudson River to Manhattan and make the rounds of the secondhand bookstores that in the early Sixties filled Fourth Avenue between Ninth and Fourteenth Streets. Once I picked up a first edition of the earliest Cornell Woolrich story collection (*I Wouldn't Be in Your Shoes*, 1943) for a dollar. One Saturday morning my father drove me into New York so I could pick up twenty or thirty Rex Stouts (book club editions, but I didn't know the difference back then) at three—or was it four?—for a buck.

In college I concentrated on what I recently heard someone call literature-philosophy-and-do-you-want-fries-with-that. I was a bookish nerd but in senior year a little voice began whispering to me that it was time I learned something practical. I took the Graduate Record Examination in philosophy and, if memory serves, wound up with two points short of a perfect score so that I could have gone anywhere in the country, I suppose, and spent a few years studying Hume or Hegel or whoever. But I also took the Law School Admission Test, and did well enough to get scholarship offers from some prestigious institutions. The one I accepted was from NYU.

Going to law school was a blind leap in the dark. There were no attorneys in my family, I didn't know a single person with a law degree, and all I knew about the subject came from having read most of the Perry Mason novels three or four times apiece in high school and college. That's why I like to say that law school disappointed me because I thought I was going to learn how to solve murders. But diving into the sea of legal education turned out to be a smart move. Keeping up with the work took me every waking moment and I literally had to stop reading mysteries, although I still bought the Sunday *Times* each week and saved the Book Review sections with Boucher's columns. Even with that sacrifice I didn't excel at legal studies to quite the degree I had in high school and college but I did manage to graduate in the top ten percent of my class.

With law school and the bar examination and two decades of life as a student behind me I began feeling the urge to write. Since I didn't believe I had the talent to write mysteries, I began writing about them. The periodical that published my stuff most often was *The Armchair Detective*, a quarterly founded in 1967 by Allen J. Hubin, who soon became a close friend and who took over the Criminals at Large column for the *Times* after Tony Boucher's death of cancer at the unbearably early age of 56.

I first heard about *TAD* shortly after taking the New Jersey bar examination. The results were still a few months away and I was marking time with a job as assistant to the editor in chief at a law publishing house. I lived in a tiny Greenwich Village apartment furnished along the lines of the Kramdens' dump on *The Honeymooners*, slept in a Murphy bed, often found a roach or three in the bathroom or micro-kitchen. But the place was close to school and my job and just a few blocks from the Hudson Tubes that connected New York with New Jersey, and the rent was cheap. Somehow I heard about a fellow named Hubin in White Bear Lake, Minnesota who was planning to launch a journal devoted to the entire field of mystery fiction. I wrote asking for more information and soon got back a much longer letter, the first exchange in a correspondence whose total wordage eventually surpassed *War and Peace*. Not only did I subscribe, which cost the lordly sum of $2.00 a year in those mesozoic days, but I soon got into the habit of offering material for publication: letters of comment, essays on favorite authors like Harry Stephen Keeler and Cornell Woolrich, whatever I felt like tackling. Much of this was published in *TAD*. Other small journals devoted to mystery fiction began appearing, and I did some writing for most of them too. Eventually I was asked to write entries for reference books on the genre, to edit and write introductions to collections of stories by various mystery writers, to review for newspapers and magazines, to serve on the boards of various crime-fiction publishing projects and as a consultant to the estates of the some of the authors I had most admired, notably to the trustees handling the estate of Cornell Woolrich, which, as I like to tell my students, raises every problem known in copyright law plus some others.

By the end of the turbulent Sixties, academic and other journals were regularly publishing commentary on mystery fiction and a growing number of colleges were offering courses on the genre. There was need for a book of readings that could be used in such courses, and Ray Browne of Bowling Green University Popular Press asked me to put together that book. The result was *The Mystery Writer's Art* (1970), a hodgepodge that somehow stayed in print for more than twenty years, long after I thought it had outlived its usefulness.

While I was working on that anthology and other projects I came to meet the author who more than any other single individual changed my life. His name was Frederic Dannay but he was much better known as Ellery Queen, the byline under which he and his first cousin Manfred B. Lee had been collaborating on brilliant detective novels and stories since 1929. Forty years after the publication of the first Queen novel, I stepped off a New Haven Railroad commuter train at Larchmont, about forty-five minutes from midtown Manhattan, and was shaking hands for the first time with Fred and his then wife Hilda and riding in their car to the Dannay home. One of the long-term projects I had been considering was a book-length study of the Queen novels and stories. Fred, it turned out, was not only willing to cooperate but flattered that someone was writing a book about Queen, and over the next few years he helped me with that book in countless ways. By the time it was published (in 1974, as *Royal Bloodline: Ellery Queen, Author and Detective*), he had made a mystery writer out of me.

In the fall of 1941 Fred had founded *Ellery Queen's Mystery Magazine*, which he continued to edit actively for almost forty years. One of Fred's abiding concerns was bringing new blood into the genre, and every month he would publish at least one short story by an author who had never written a mystery before. He must have encouraged almost everyone he met to try writing for him. After we had come to know each other he certainly encouraged me. I slaved over a story for more than two months and finally mailed it to him. Another few months of rethinking and rewriting and that hunk of junk became my first published story, "Open Letter to Survivors" (*Ellery Queen's Mystery Magazine*, May 1972).

At the time Fred bought that tale I was working at Middlesex County Legal Services Corporation, practicing law by the seat of my pants on behalf of that New Jersey county's poor. I and several other young lawyers shared a disorganized office above a downtown New Brunswick storefront, its waiting room overflowing with clients whose problems we had no time to research as we made an endless round of appearances before various judges and bureaucrats. We were expected to be able to handle any type of legal situation that was thrown at us. I might be arguing an appeal in the New Jersey Supreme Court one day and trying to get some penniless family on welfare the next morning. In rapid order I was storing up a huge variety of experiences that wouldn't have come to me in five years of private practice, but it was a hectic way to live and I had virtually no time to do any writing of my own. By the time my first story was published I had exchanged that pressure-cooker environment for another lifestyle entirely—far less tension, much higher salary, much lower cost of living, summers free, plenty of time for writing—by migrating to the Midwest and becoming a professor at St. Louis University School of Law.

I also became something of a writing fool. Since the move to St. Louis I've turned out 40-odd more stories, a thick cross-section of them recently collected in *Night Forms* (2010). Plus six mystery novels. Plus two Edgar-winning biographical-critical books. Plus a pile of articles for law journals. Plus a mountain of nonfiction writing about some of my fellow mystery writers and their work. A thick cross-section of *that* material, written over five decades, is collected here.

One point on which I want to be perfectly clear I can best make by going back to 1997 when a St. Louis magazine asked me, or more precisely leaned on me, to crank out a short essay naming my top ten mystery writers. Damn you, Letterman! I *hate* that kind of list! Probably I should have refused, but instead I insisted on simplifying the impossible task by limiting myself to authors who were (1) American, (2) male and (3) dead.

~ ~ ~ ~ ~

DASHIELL HAMMETT (1894-1961) in a very real sense invented American crime fiction. Not only is he one of the founding fathers of the private eye story but his three major novels—*Red Harvest* (1929), *The Maltese Falcon* (1930) and *The Glass Key* (1931)—are the first classics of the dark downbeat kind of fiction we call *noir*. He was also a master at devising plots of labyrinth complexity.

RAYMOND CHANDLER (1888-1959) tended to get lost in his

own plots, but his private eye Philip Marlowe is such a vivid character and his style is so richly evocative that his finest novels—*The Big Sleep* (1939), *Farewell, My Lovely* (1940) and *The Long Goodbye* (1954)—are endlessly rereadable.

ERLE STANLEY GARDNER (1889-1970) was a born-again social Darwinian who saw life and law practice as forms of combat, and in the dozens of Perry Mason novels published between 1933 and his death he turned the trial into a form of art: martial art. Virtually every line of dialogue in his novels, whether in or out of court, is a thrust or parry in a never-ending duel. He wrote the simplest business English, but with his whirlwind pace and zest for courtroom pyrotechnics and tight control of involuted plots he hardly needed literary grace.

CORNELL WOOLRICH (1903-1968), the Poe of the 20th century and the poet of its shadows, was a reclusive loner who in a little under fifteen years (1934-48) wrote more than a dozen novels and over two hundred shorter works of crime fiction so full of anguish and nail-biting suspense that he's revered today as one of the literary origins of *film noir* and as the Hitchcock of the written word. Hitchcock, by the way, based several of his films on Woolrich tales, the best known being *Rear Window* (1954).

DAVID GOODIS (1917-1967), another *noir* poet, wrote even more bleakly than Woolrich by eliminating the Woolrich hallmark: suspense. Woolrich stories sometimes end happily, sometimes in despair, and since he used no series characters the reader could never tell in advance whether a particular tale would be light or dark, *allegre* or *noir*. In Goodis, whose novels are hard to take but unremittingly powerful, there is no suspense and we are compelled to watch his anguished characters slide inevitably to doom.

JOHN DICKSON CARR (1906-1977), supreme master of the detective novel featuring crimes committed in locked rooms or other impossible circumstances, was born in Pennsylvania but set most of his books in England where he lived for many years. His literary idol G.K. Chesterton was the model for his detective character Dr. Gideon Fell but his haunting style owes more to Poe.

ELLERY QUEEN (the joint byline of first cousins Frederic Dannay, 1905-1982, and Manfred B. Lee, 1905-1971) practiced the classic detective novel with devilish cunning and complete fairness to the reader (at least if the reader was a genius) from 1929 until Manny Lee's death more than forty years later. Fred Dannay, the scholar and bibliophile of the duo, also founded *Ellery Queen's Mystery Magazine* and served as editor in chief from its creation in 1941 until the

Introduction

last year of his life, launching the careers of several topflight mystery writers and countless minor talents including me.

REX STOUT (1886-1975) gave American detective fiction a potent shot in the arm in 1934 when he began his long-running series about the obese intellectual sleuth Nero Wolfe and that great American wiseass Archie Goodwin. His plots are nothing special but the superb interaction of these two characters and the vivid evocation of their ménage on New York's West 35th Street represent the closest any American has ever come to capturing the magic of Sherlock Holmes, Dr. Watson and 221-B Baker Street. If only there had been a Nero-and-Archie movie starring the middle-aged Orson Welles and the young James Garner!

ANTHONY BOUCHER (1911-1968) wrote mystery novels and short stories, science-fiction tales, mountains of essays and book reviews, mainly for the San Francisco *Chronicle* and the New York *Times*. He also edited countless mystery and s-f anthologies, wrote up to three radio scripts a week, and was an aficionado of everything from football to limericks to opera to gourmet cooking to politics. He was the Renaissance man *par excellence* and his multiple enthusiasms enliven everything he wrote.

HARRY STEPHEN KEELER (1890-1967) wrote the wackiest, most bizarre books I've ever read, almost a hundred of them, the last few dozen so eccentric they were published only in Portugal or Spain if at all. If ever there was a real-world original of Vonnegut's Kilgore Trout and Kesey's R.P. MacMurphy it's the indescribable HSK. *The Spectacles of Mr. Cagliostro, The Skull of the Waltzing Clown, Y. Cheung—Business Detective, The Case of the Barking Clock, The Case of the Two-Headed Idiot,* the mathematically constructed madness goes on and on. Check him out on the Web.

~ ~ ~ ~ ~

That was the list I put together late last century. Over the 40-odd years since I began commenting on mystery writers I've written quite a bit about five of the ten, and four of the five can be found here in the Titans section. But I've had very few occasions to express myself on the subjects of Hammett, Chandler, Goodis, Carr or Stout, who are titans one and all. My list might well look different if I were idiot enough to do it over again today, for the simple reason that several excellent writers whom I ruled out for being alive have died in the last few years: Donald E. Westlake, Stuart M. Kaminsky, Robert B. Parker, Michael Collins (Dennis Lynds) and Ed McBain (Evan

Hunter), just to name a few. But again, I've had very few occasions to write about most of these. Nor should we forget the first-rate English authors of both sexes and Europeans and American women, Conan Doyle and Chesterton and Michael Innes and Nicholas Blake and Graham Greene and John Le Carré, Georges Simenon, Agatha Christie and Dorothy L. Sayers and Margery Allingham and Christianna Brand and Ruth Rendell and P.D. James. As chance would have it, I happen to have written little or nothing about most of them. On the other hand, few besides me have ever become absorbed in almost forgotten writers like Cleve F. Adams and John Lawrence and Milton Propper, all of whom are covered here.

This is a personal book. It makes no claim to discuss the finest mystery writers of all time or any time. It's about a few, by no means most or all, of the writers whose novels and stories in this genre have meant something to me. There's also material on some other subjects: detective and suspense films, radio, TV, even music. But everything is linked to the world I first discovered on that frabjous day when I was first allowed into the adult section of the Roselle Park Public Library and happened upon the exploits of Sherlock Holmes and Charlie Chan.

Francis M. Nevins
St. Louis, Missouri
March 20, 2010

TITANS

ERLE STANLEY GARDNER

He's been dead forty years but what he accomplished in his eight decades on the planet still survives. Beginning in the middle 1920s he wrote hundreds of tales—many the length of short novels—for the pulp magazines whose lurid covers filled the nation's newsstands in the time between world wars. In his first full-length novel, *The Case of the Velvet Claws* (1933), he created Perry Mason, fiction's most celebrated attorney, the courtroom dynamo who was to become the protagonist of 82 books (1933-71), a movie series (1934-37), a long-running radio series (1943-55), a legendary television series (1957-66), and a cycle of two-hour TV movies (1986-93). As if that weren't enough for one lifetime, Gardner also created several other book-length series including one (1937-49) about a prosecuting attorney and another (1939-70) about a disbarred lawyer turned private detective and his irascible female partner. Small wonder that he liked to refer to himself as "the fiction factory."

Gardner was born on July 17, 1889 in the small town of Malden, Massachusetts to a mother whose ancestors came over on the Mayflower and a civil-engineer father descended from a long line of sea captains. This boy whose earliest years coincided with the golden age of social Darwinism was a born combatant, with a boundless zest for competition and an unstoppable drive to succeed. In 1899, while in fourth grade, he wrote a school essay on the Greek myth of Atalanta, the theme of which is that whoever doesn't win the race dies. Later that year his family moved west, settling in 1902 in a prosperous California mining town. Wander though he did throughout his life, Gardner called the Golden State his home from that day forward.

He spent his early teens traveling with his father through remote stretches of California, Oregon and the Klondike, developing a zest for outdoor living that was to become a hallmark of his fiction. In school he was a maverick and a troublemaker, earning pocket money by boxing in unlicensed matches, and his interest in the law seems to have grown out of hunting for loopholes in the California statutes that made prizefighting illegal. After completing high school in 1909 he was admitted to Valparaiso University in Indiana but was soon expelled for slugging a professor. He went back to California, apprenticed himself to one established attorney after another and, in

1911, passed the state bar. Over the next twenty years he discovered that litigation was a form of combat at which he could excel, and he earned a reputation as one of the state's most flamboyant trial lawyers.

Many of his clients came from the Chinese community of Oxnard, and in *The Case of Erle Stanley Gardner* (1947) journalist Alva Johnston reconstructed a number of the forensic scams he perpetrated on their behalf. During one of the city's periodic anti-lottery crusades, Gardner was representing twenty Chinese accused of selling lottery tickets. While all the defendants were out on bail and just before the first batch was to be brought in for trial, Gardner made some secret arrangements with the leader of the local Asian community. The next day a plainclothesman "picked up a Chinese who was booked as Ah Lee . . . At the station the Chinese prisoner gave a friendly greeting to a deputy sheriff." When the deputy learned that the prisoner had been booked as Ah Lee, he told the detective: "That's not Ah Lee." Detective: "That certainly is Ah Lee . . . I bought a ticket from him a week ago, and I just arrested him at Ah Lee's laundry." Deputy: "I've known Ah Lee for ten years. He does my Sunday shirts. This is Wong Duck, the butcher." Detective: "But I tell you he was running the laundry . . . He was bossing the others around. What would a butcher be doing running a laundry?" Deputy: "Who knows why a Chinaman does anything?" Next the detective identified another defendant from whom he had purchased a lottery ticket as Ho Ling, the grocer. Deputy: "He's Ong Hai Foo, the druggist . . . the biggest dealer in dried-lizard medicine in Southern California." Detective: "But I tell you he was running Ho Ling's grocery when we arrested him . . . He was waiting on customers. Why would a druggist be selling vegetables?" The answer of course is that Gardner had had dozens of Asian merchants exchange identities so that each would be booked under another's name. After it became clear that the key prosecution witness had wrongly identified several defendants, all twenty cases were quietly dismissed. This is simply one specimen from the bag of courtroom tricks and fireworks which, when he began writing novels, Gardner handed over to his alter ego Perry Mason.

Since the practice of law could not contain his energies, Gardner launched a number of sales businesses as a sideline. But he was a born wanderer, to whom the four walls of a law office or courtroom were like the walls of a prison cell, and the only way he could think of to make decent money and still enjoy a free-ranging lifestyle was to establish himself as a professional writer. But he quickly discovered that writing fiction wasn't the same as writing briefs. "It was like trying to sign my name with my left hand," he said many years later. "I knew what I wanted to do but for the life of me I couldn't do it." He collected a drawerful of rejection slips but his Can Do spirit never flagged and as soon as one magazine had bounced a story he'd mail it out to another. In the spring of 1921, as he put it, "Glory be, I clicked!" His first sales were a pair of humorous skits for which the pulp magazine *Breezy Stories* paid him ten or fifteen dollars apiece.

For the next two years he sold hardly a word. "I wrote the worst stories that ever hit New York," he said near the end of his life. "I have the word of an editor for that, and he hadn't seen my worst stories because the worst ones I wrote under a pen name." Finally thanks to sheer persistence he sold one of those pseudonymous tales ("The Shrieking Skeleton", as by Charles M. Green, *Black Mask*, December 1923), and from then on he appeared with mind-boggling frequency in the so-called pulps that made up most Americans' entertainment in the days before radio and TV. *Black Mask, Top-Notch, Argosy, West, Clues, Air Adventure, Detective Fiction Weekly, Three Star, Prize Detective, Detective Action Stories, Gangland Stories, Western Trails, Gang World, Dime Detective*—the entire list of magazines in which he published would fill most of a page.

How did he keep up this pace without coming apart? "For a period of several years," he said, "I pounded out stories on the typewriter at the rate of a novelette every third day, and at the same time practiced law, much of it trying cases in front of juries, which I can testify is a very exhausting occupation." After a full day at the office or in court and an evening at home dictating legal memoranda and correspondence, Gardner would sit down at the typewriter around 10:00 P.M. and start work on a story. "I would work until one, one-thirty, or two o'clock in the morning when I would be so dog-tired that whenever I would stop to rest I would fall asleep in the chair and have nightmares, dreaming for the most part about the characters in the story, waking up a few seconds later all confused as to what had been in the story and what had been in my dream. At that time I would go to bed. I would sleep about three hours a night, waking up around five or five-thirty in the morning. Then I would take a shower, shave, pull up my typewriter and write until it came time to go to the office. It's a wonder that I didn't kill myself with overwork. If I finished one story at twelve-thirty at night, I couldn't go to bed without starting another." Night after night he would pound away at those typewriter keys until his fingers bled. Eventually he switched to a primitive dictating machine and set himself a fiction quota of 100,000 words a month.

The genre pulps in which Gardner appeared were flimsily bound and stapled and printed on dirt-cheap paper which the years have turned dirt-brown, but copies today are hard to come by and often command astronomical prices. Even if you had the time and fortune to assemble a complete library of the pulps that featured Gardner stories, whenever you opened the pages of an issue to enjoy his contribution you'd run the risk that the magazine might fall apart in your hands. And frankly, many of those early tales don't hold up all that well so many decades later. They were uniformly written in a fiendish hurry and some of them wind up with plot complications not only unexplained but beyond explicability. Yet even the weaker stories are often filled with the kind of raw vivid inventiveness and taut immediacy that have long since vanished from fiction, and the outstanding ones are as readable today as they were when Hoover and FDR sat in the White House.

As his friend Freeman Lewis wrote shortly after Gardner's death: "He was a born story-teller. In over forty years as a publisher, I never met a writer so generously endowed with that quality. In an evening's conversation (perhaps monologue would be a better word) he would produce more ideas and plots for books than most writers come by in a lifetime." Writing as much and at such white-hot speed as he did, it's small wonder that he often lost track of various elements in his plots. In his defense he argued that "[e]very mystery story ever written has some loose threads" and claimed that the breakneck pace of his novels and stories made it all but impossible for readers to catch the plot flubs. "After all, on a trotting horse who is going to see the difference? The main thing is to keep the horse trotting and the pace fast and furious."

The number of series characters Gardner created for the pulps defies belief. In the Western genre alone he wrote ten stories for *Black Mask* (1924-32) about Bob Larkin, an adventurous juggler who uses a billiard cue instead of a gun; eight tales for the same magazine (1925-35) featuring Black Barr, a gunfighter who considers himself an instrument of God's justice; three stories apiece about The Old Walrus (1926-27) and Buck Riley (1927-28) and two apiece about Fish Mouth McGinnis (1926-31) and Sheriff Billy Bales (1928). The 21 Whispering Sands tales he wrote for *Argosy* (1930-34) are perhaps his finest work in this genre, with their rich descriptions reflecting his lifelong love of the desert, and after his death a substantial number of these stories were collected by editors Charles G. Waugh and Martin H. Greenberg in *Whispering Sands: Stories of Gold Fever and the Western Desert* (1981) and *Pay Dirt and Other Whispering Sands Stories* (1983). Gardner also wrote a surprising number of science-fiction tales without any series characters, collected by the same editors in *The Human Zero* (1981).

The majority of his pulp stories, however, were contemporary crime thrillers, most of them with protagonists somewhat reminiscent of the "good badman" characters of the sort that were portrayed again and again by silent Western film star William S. Hart. The longest running and best known of his series characters in this vein is Ed Jenkins, the Phantom Crook, who appeared in 72 stories for *Black Mask* between 1925 and 1943 and whose adventures can be sampled in the posthumous collections *The Blonde in Lower Six* and *Dead Men's Letters*, both published in 1990. Not far behind Jenkins in durability is Lester Leith, an aristocratic thief and amateur sleuth whose butler is really an undercover cop assigned to nail him. A total of 66 stories about this character were published in various pulps between 1929 and 1943, and some of the finest were collected in *The Amazing Adventures of Lester Leith* (1981). Also in the running are Speed Dash, the Human Fly (20 stories for *Top-Notch*, 1925-30); Sidney Zoom (17 stories for *Detective Fiction Weekly*, 1930-34), an aloof and godlike sleuth who, like his creator, "aided misfortune, but detested weakness" and whose only friend is a police dog; Dan Seller, the Patent Leather Kid (14 stories, 1930-34); Senor Arnaz de Lobo (23 stories, 1930-34), a sort of Zorro figure without the cape and mask; and Paul Pry (27 stories, 1930-39), another gentleman thief and amateur detective, sidekicked by a one-armed hulk with the improbable name of Mugs Magoo. Then there's a small army of shorter-lived series characters including Major Copely Brane (8 stories for *Argosy*, 1931-34), Rex Kane (3 tales for *Detective Action Stories*, 1931-32), Steve Raney (7 stories for *Clues*, 1932-33), El Paisano (5 stories for *Argosy*, 1933-35), Stan Wider, The Man in the Silver Mask (3 tales for *Detective Fiction Weekly*, 1935), Barney Killigen (4 stories for *Clues*, 1938-39), Ed Migrane, the Headache (3 tales for *Detective Fiction Weekly*, 1939-40), and several more to boot. Random samplings in these series suggest that legal elements appear in them sometimes but not to an overwhelming extent. What almost all Gardner protagonists have in common is that they're scam artists.

Take, for example, Paul Pry, the impossibly debonair young adventurer who debuted in the October 1930 issue of *Gang World* and, after appearing in all but four of the magazine's 25 issues, continued his career in the pages of *Dime Detective*. Pry makes his living hijacking stolen goods from the underworld and then collecting huge rewards from the rightful owners. In each of his early exploits he concocts an elaborate scam to frustrate the latest crime coup of gangster mastermind Big Front Gilvray; and if you can ignore Gardner's graceless and verbose style and just enjoy the clever plotting, these episodes can be almost as much fun as a brace of Roadrunner cartoons, with "A Double Deal in Diamonds" (*Gang World*, February 1931) having special appeal thanks to vivid action scenes on board an interurban tramcar. A selection of these early *Gang World* tales can be found in *The Adventures of Paul Pry* (1989).

After awhile the duels with Gilvray vanish and each later story in the series is a self-standing unit. In "Dressed to Kill" (*Dime Detective*, 1 September 1933), Pry and his sidekick Mugs Magoo are having supper at a nightclub when Mugs, who has a photographic memory for faces and an encyclopedic knowledge of the underworld, pieces together information he happens to have about several fellow diners and tells Pry they're about to witness the surreptitious delivery of a letter from a certain imprisoned gem thief to his lawyer. Sniffing stolen jewels in the air, Pry deftly snatches the letter before it can be delivered and takes it back to his table, only to find sitting there a lovely lady who allows him to seduce her in record time, then tells him she's being blackmailed and asks him to accompany her to a masquerade ball and steal back for her some compromising letters. It's hardly a surprise when we learn that the indiscreet letters and the stolen jewels are connected, but it's still fun to watch Pry walk into the lion's mouth, tweak the noses of the ungodly and emerge with all the boodle in sight.

"The Finishing Touch" (*Dime Detective*, August 1938) also opens with Paul and Mugs enjoying dinner at a night spot. Two jewel-cases containing identical gems happen providentially to be in Pry's pocket. Mugs spots a certain lovely lady in the club and tells Paul she's an ex-convict whose underworld bosses are forcing her to work the badger game on amorous males. The scheme Pry devises on the spot is never explained to his partner or us but calls for him to allow the woman to work the badger game on him and steal one of the twin jewels while at the same time Mugs flashes the other stone around the nightclub's bar. When the scheme goes haywire, Pry instantly concocts another, this time trying to convince the thieves that he has a geiger counter that can locate stolen jewels.

In the twenty-seventh and last tale in the series, "It's the McCoy" (*Dime Detective*, January 1939), Paul and Mugs are relaxing at a baseball game when Magoo intercepts code signals between a jewel thief and a master fence. Pry instantly cracks the code, audaciously breaks into the signaled conversation and waits for the crooks' reaction, which is not long in coming. A young woman steps in front of his car as he's leaving the ballfield parking lot. Her "doctor" tells Pry that she has an incurable disease that will kill her in a few weeks and asks him to take her out every night and make her last hours happy. (How many defendants in auto negligence suits must wish they had hit so forgiving a victim!) Paul then sends Mugs to the city's best hotel disguised as a visiting rajah, complete with a fake ruby in his turban and some out-of-work black showgirls as his harem. The argument between Magoo and a bad-tempered belly dancer is one of the funniest scenes Gardner ever wrote. When Pry tells his dying girlfriend that he's a professional thief with designs on the rajah's ruby, she breaks out in gales of enthusiasm for the scheme, saying "I don't think it's exactly a crime to rob the very rich" and "After all, the world owes you a living." Once again Pry's master plan is never explained but it works perfectly and our heroes come out of the climactic bloody battle unscathed and the richer by two suitcases full of jewelry while the poor dying maiden gets stuck with the red glass from Mugs' turban.

At around the same time he created Paul Pry, Gardner also launched an even longer-running series about the light-fingered larcenist Lester Leith, whose forte is solving crimes by analysis of newspaper reports and then hijacking the loot before he exposes the criminal to the stupid police. Lead-witted Sergeant Ackley has planted an agent in Leith's palatial penthouse but Lester has long been aware that his valet is a spy and delights in twisting poor Scuttle into a pretzel each time the game is afoot: sending him out on humiliating wild goose chases, ridiculing his every word, almost but never quite letting the servant know that his cover is blown, manipulating events so that Scuttle and Ackley slam into each other full tilt while he nimbly slips between them with the boodle. Most of Leith's 66 adventures are hastily assembled and prone to loose plot threads but unfailingly rich in verve and zip and bounce and sheer readability. One of the finest in the series is "The Candy Kid" (*Detective Fiction Weekly*, 14 March 1931), a walloping bamboozler of a tale in which Leith leads the forces of law and order around by their noses as everyone searches for the rajah's rubies which an unlucky stickup artist had snatched and then apparently hidden somewhere in a candy factory moments before being swiss-cheesed by police bullets. Before he's finished Lester finds uses for fifty dollars' worth of chocolate, an electric soldering iron, a string of firecrackers, a police siren, a blowtorch, and a mad scheme to save heat by pretending November is July.

The tales at the end of the cycle are just as wild and crazy as the early entries in the series. In "Something Like a Pelican" (*Flynn's Detective Fiction Magazine*, January 1943), Leith happens to be on the sidewalk below when a mysterious woman throws a silver fox cape out of a furrier's window to the accompaniment of screams for the police. Puzzled, he returns to the neighborhood that night just in time to witness the abduction of a secretary in the precision instrument company across the street from the furrier's. It soon develops that the blueprints for a new invention were stolen from the company's vault during the fur-tossing diversion and the caper turns into a race for the plans between Leith and the police and a fight between Leith and the company over the innocent secretary's claim for damages. The plot would have been killed in its tracks by a thorough police search at the get-go but this is a fun story, paced like a rocket, spiced with laconic wit and boasting the added dividends of satire on amateur authors and expert-sounding shotgun lore. In "The Black Feather" (*Flynn's Detective Fiction*, July 1943), the police spy Scuttle is replaced as Leith's valet by Singra Bhat, who pretends to be a Burmese detective but is actually a Japanese spy planning to steal a secret treaty from a sick diplomat in a hotel and pin the blame on Lester. Meanwhile Leith becomes interested in a jewel theft and sets out to hijack the loot with the help of a siren-equipped baby carriage, some smoke bombs, and a wacky scheme to produce 16mm movies for home viewing. With this 66th and last caper the series ended.

~ ~ ~ ~ ~

Of more immediate interest to us here are those of Gardner's magazine stories that deal directly with law, lawyers, lawyering and justice. His first series of direct relevance to these subjects lasted for six separate but thematically connected stories, written (or more likely dictated) and published in *Black Mask* during the period when he was making the transition from pulp magazines to hardcover novels, and collected after his death by editors Greenberg and Waugh in *Honest Money* (1991). Protagonist of these tales is Ken Corning, a young man fresh out of law school who, for no particular reason except that it's a Darwinian challenge, sets up practice in a metropolis which for sheer corruption rivals (and no doubt was strongly influenced by) the poisonvilles in Dashiell Hammett's *Red Harvest* (1929) and *The*

Glass Key (1931). Hardly is the paint dry on Corning's office door when he begins to run afoul of the politicians in control of the York City government. In each tale he represents a far from admirable person who's being framed on a criminal charge by some of the local powers that be and in each tale he clears his client not by any lawyerly skills but by getting out into the streets and concocting an imaginative scam that flushes out the truth. Assisting him in these schemes is his secretary Helen Vail, who is the prototype of Della Street as Gardner first drew her: a tough-talking but good-hearted dame who gladly takes risks from which the most loyal secretary in the real world would run screaming. Corning's ultimate adversary, political boss Carl Dwight, comes onstage only in the first tale and has vanished down the memory hole long before the last.

In "Honest Money" (November 1932) the client is speakeasy proprietor Esther Parks, who's been locked up on a phony charge of attempting to bribe Sergeant Perkins of the local Prohibition squad. A few hours after he's retained Corning to handle the case, Mrs. Parks' obese husband is shot down on the street. Corning goes into action and soon discovers that she's being railroaded because she had inadvertently discovered too much about corruption in the city water department. The tale ends with a gunbattle and the release of Corning's client but, in a touch of truly Hammett-like cynicism, nothing happens to the murderers.

In "The Top Comes Off" (December 1932) Corning gets involved in what seems a private matter as a mysterious woman hires him to represent George Colton, who's in jail charged with the murder of his wife's lover, politically connected realtor Harry Ladue. Corning quickly realizes that the woman is Mrs. Colton, and that she's on the brink of suicide. This time the murderer turns out to be Sergeant Perkins, the corrupt cop from the first Corning story, who, being relatively low on the political food chain, winds up having to pay for his crime.

The client in "Close Call" (January 1933) is Amos Dangerfield, a politically ambitious businessman who has gone into hiding at Corning's suggestion after being accused of the hit-and-run murder of hostile newspaper publisher Walter Copley. Once again it's a political frameup, which Corning explodes by setting a trap that proves the man who claims to have witnessed the killing is actually the assassin for hire who did it. Neither he nor his higher-ups is arrested for the crime.

"Making the Breaks" (June 1933) opens with Helen Vail coming to Corning in the middle of the night after having money planted on her that is tied to a murder case her boss is defending. Clearly the powers that be are out to discourage Corning from representing ex-convict and small-time burglar Fred Parkett, who's been charged with a street killing on evidence he claimed the arresting officer planted on him. With the help of an undercover Federal agent, Corning establishes that the real killers were the men who claimed they witnessed the murder and the police detective.

"Devil's Fire" (July 1933) begins in medias res with Corning at the scene of another street murder, this one apparently the result of a violent argument between underworld bosses Frank Glover, who wound up dead, and George Pyle, who's charged with the murder. A sniveling small-time crook by the name of Henry Lampson buttonholes Corning on the street, claims he saw the murder and offers to testify in Pyle's favor if he's paid off. When Corning refuses to give a bribe, Lampson goes to the police and makes a deal to frame the lawyer for suborning perjured testimony. Eventually Corning sets up a scam involving a rigged target-shooting competition to lure the real killer out of the woodwork.

"Blackmail with Lead" (August 1933) brings the series to an end of sorts. Corning is retained by small-time criminal Sam Driver, who's accused of killing his partner Harry Green, and soon finds that the case is linked to the murder of wealthy George Bixel in a lonely mountain cabin several months before. When a rapacious slattern who knows some of the truth is bought off and sent packing, Corning gets Helen Vail to impersonate the woman and rigs a charade that exposes the facts.

~ ~ ~ ~ ~

In 1931, when most of the country was in the pit of the Depression, Gardner made over $20,000 from pulp writing, in addition to his income as a lawyer, but his success almost killed him. He decided that the only way to free himself for the nomadic life he wanted to live was to phase himself out as a lawyer, cut back his torrent of wordage for the pulps and start writing, or rather dictating, novels for hardcover publication. The result was Perry Mason, who debuted in *The Case of the Velvet Claws* (1933) and eventually made his creator one of the wealthiest and most widely read authors in the history of the world.

What accounts for the mind-boggling success of the Mason novels? Gardner himself never claimed they were written with any grace. His characterizations and descriptions tend to be perfunctory and are often reduced to a handful of lines that he recycled in book after book. Indeed virtually every word not within quotation marks could be left out of any Perry Mason exploit and little would be lost. For what vivifies these novels is the sheer readability, the breakneck pacing, the involuted plotting, the fireworks displays of courtroom tactics based in large part on Gardner's own law practice in Oxnard, and the dialogue, that inimitable Gardner dialogue whose every line, whether spoken in or out of court, is a jab in a complex form of oral combat.

The first nine Mason books, published between 1933 and 1936, are set in the dog-eat-dog milieu of the free enterprise system in the depths of its worst depression, and Gardner, born scrapper that he was, revels in it. The Mason of these novels is a tiger in the social Darwinian jungle, totally self-reliant, asking no favors, despising the weaklings who want society to care for them, willing to take any risk for a client no matter how unfairly the client plays the game with him. On the first page of *The Case of the Velvet Claws* we are told of Mason: "He gave the impression of being a thinker and a fighter, a man who could work with infinite patience to jockey an adversary into just the right position, and then finish him with one terrific punch." A few pages later there is this telling exchange between Mason and the beautiful treacherous woman who has consulted him. Mason: ". . . Nobody ever called on me to organize a corporation, and I've never yet probated an estate. I haven't drawn up over a dozen contracts in my life, and I wouldn't know how to go about foreclosing a mortgage. People that come to me don't come to me because they like the looks of my eyes, or the way my office is furnished, or because they've known me at a club. They come to me because they need me. They come to me because they want to hire me for what I can do." Woman: "Just what is it that you do, Mr. Mason?" Mason: "I fight!"

Variations on this scene recur throughout Gardner's early novels, in which Mason again and again says of himself: "I am a paid gladiator." If Gardner had wanted to connect back with his Western stories he might have had Mason describe himself as a hired gun; if his affinity had been for Japanese rather than Chinese culture he would probably have called his character a samurai. In the last analysis all three formulations have the same meaning. And Della Street in her first incarnation is cut from the same cloth: in the words of Gardner's publisher Thayer Hobson, "a gal who would poison her mother, eat unslaked lime, and twist a baby's wrist for the man she cared for."

Any doubts that these characters clearly reflect their creator are dispelled by a glance at Gardner's voluminous correspondence. At the outset of his career as a novelist he wrote his publisher: "I want to make my hero a fighter, not by having him be ruthless with women and underlings, but by having him wade into the opposition and battle his way through to victory . . . More than that, I want to establish a style of swift motion. I want to have characters who start from scratch and sprint the whole darned way to a goal line . . ." The letter he wrote his publisher at the end of 1934 is full of similar imagery: "Let's plant our feet firmly on the ground, double our right fists, measure the distance with a nice left lead, and sock all competitors right between the eyes. Yours for a belligerently successful 1935."

In *The Case of the Velvet Claws* Mason outlines his creed to private detective Paul Drake. "I'm a lawyer. I take people who are in trouble, and I try to get them out of trouble. I'm not presenting the people's side of the case, I'm only presenting the defendant's side. The District Attorney represents the people, and he makes the strongest kind of a case he can. It's my duty to make the strongest kind of a case I can on the other side, and then it's up to the jury to decide. That's the way we get justice. If the District Attorney would be fair, then I could be fair. But the District Attorney uses everything he can in order to get a conviction. I use everything I can in order to get an acquittal. It's like two teams playing football. One of them tries to go in one direction just as hard as it can, and the other tries to go in the other direction just as hard as it can . . . My clients aren't blameless. Many of them are crooks. Probably a lot of them are guilty. That's not for me to determine. That's for the jury to determine."

Perry Mason as Gardner first created him does indeed use everything he can, and usually his tools are the little people whose financial desperation in the pit of the Depression forces them to accept almost any risk in return for a little money. In *The Case of the Velvet Claws* Mason pays twenty dollars to a hotel switchboard operator to tell him what number a certain person called and then with twenty-five bucks bribes a policeman who lost his shirt at poker the previous night to get confidential information from the phone company as to who has that number. Later in the same novel he loosens the tongue of a hostile witness by pretending to frame him for a murder, and at the climax he manipulates estate funds to prevent a murderer who is not his client from obtaining money for his defense. In *The Case of the Counterfeit Eye* (1935) Mason is searching for a woman to impersonate a prosecution witness. Mason: "Go to an employment agency and find a young woman [of a certain description] who is hungry . . . Be damn sure she's hungry." Della Street: "How hungry?" Mason: "Hungry enough so she won't argue with cash." Della: "Will she go to jail?" Mason: "She may, but she won't stay there, and she'll be paid for it if she does . . ." Della brings back a young woman and Mason's talk with her goes in part as follows. Mason: "Been out of a job long?" Woman: "Yes." Mason: "Ready to do anything that's offered?" Woman: "That depends on what it is." Mason says nothing. Woman: "I don't give a damn what it is." Mason: "That's better."

Indeed Mason in his original incarnation will even twist evidence to get a guilty client acquitted, and does so in *The Case of the Howling Dog* (1934). "I've told you before, and I'm telling you again, that I'm not a judge and I'm not a jury. I'm a lawyer. The district attorney does everything he can to build up a strong case against the defendant. It's up to the lawyer for the defendant to do everything he can to break down the case for the district attorney . . . [A defense lawyer is] a partisan, a representative hired by the defendant, with the sanction of the state, whose solemn duty it is to present the case of the defendant in its strongest light. That's my creed and that's what I try to do." At the end of this powerful novel, after Mason has twisted the evidence so that the client he knew to be guilty has been acquitted by a jury and can never be tried again, an ambivalent Della Street says to him: "You are a cross between a saint and a devil." "All men are," he replies.

If the original Mason seems an amoral and unattractive character, from Gardner's perspective this was already a sanitized version of what he wanted to present. Chapter X of *The Case of the Counterfeit Eye* (1935) contains a fascinating dialogue between Mason and the newly elected district attorney Hamilton Burger. "You've got a reputation for being tricky," Burger says, "and I find that you *are* tricky, but I think they're legitimate tricks . . . I think an attorney has a right to work any legitimate trick in order to bring out the truth . . . I notice that your tricks aren't for the purpose of confusing a witness, but for the purpose of blasting preconceived notions out of his head, so that he can tell the truth . . . District attorneys have a habit of wanting to get convictions. That's natural. The police work up a case and dump it in the lap of the district attorney. It's up to him to get a conviction. In fact, the reputation of a district attorney is predicated on the percentage of convictions he gets on the number of cases tried . . . When I took this job . . . I wanted to be conscientious. I have a horror of prosecuting an innocent person . . . Your courtroom technique is clever, but it's all of it founded on having first reached a correct solution of the case. When you resort to unorthodox tricks as a part of your courtroom technique I'm opposed to them, but when you use those tricks to bring about a correct solution of a mystery I'm for them. My hands are tied. I can't resort to unorthodox, spectacular tactics. Sometimes I wish I could . . ." Mason replies: " . . . I don't ask a man if he's guilty or innocent. When I start to represent him, I take his money and handle his case. Guilty or innocent, he's entitled to his day in court, *but* if I should find one of my clients was really guilty of murder and wasn't legally or morally justified, I'd make that client plead guilty and trust to the mercy of the Court . . . If a person is morally justified in killing, I'll save that person from the legal penalty if it's possible to do so." The last sentence clearly refers to what Mason did for the guilty client in *The Case of the Howling Dog*. However, in a letter to his publishers from the same period Gardner said that he had toned down his conception of Mason "in order to make it appear that he wouldn't defend a man and try to get him off if he thought that person was guilty of cold-blooded murder without any moral justification." But he bitterly resented having to water down his Darwinian notion of law practice and would have preferred his books to reflect the real-world fact "that the burning question which confronts a man accused of crime who enters the office of any reputable criminal attorney is not the question of his guilt or innocence but the question of whether he has the necessary retainer available in the form of spot cash."

Love him or hate him, he told the truth as he knew it.

For Perry Mason as Gardner first created him, the core value is loyalty to his client, despite the client's despicable character and acts, regardless of how unfairly the client deals with him. In *The Case of the Velvet Claws* Mason is retained by a seductive blonde who initially conceals her identity from him but turns out to be Eva Belter, a predatory and promiscuous woman whose wealthy husband owns a scandal magazine. When George Belter is shot to death, Eva tries to force Mason to keep her out of trouble by telling lies that make Mason himself seem to be the murderer. At what seems to be the climax of the novel, Mason—emulating the climactic scene between Sam Spade and Brigid O'Shaughnessy in Dashiell Hammett's classic *The Maltese Falcon* (1930)—accuses Eva of the murder and, when she confesses her guilt, turns her and the evidence to convict her over to the police. This apparent betrayal of a client causes Mason's secretary to lose faith in him, as Gardner explained to his publisher, "until the very last, when she suddenly realizes he was working for his client all the time instead of against her, and . . . they get back to a basis of Della Street worshipping Mason's fighting loyalty." Describing exactly how Gardner pulled off this feat would ruin a fascinating novel for those who haven't read it, but his strategy is a brilliant creative variation on the often slavishly imitated *Maltese Falcon* denouement.

If Mason the samurai stands for Gardner's ideal of good lawyering, what is his notion of a bad lawyer? In *The Case of the Caretaker's Cat* (1935) Mason is consulted by a crippled servant at the mansion of the late Peter Laxter, whose grandsons and testamentary legatees are trying to make the man get rid of his beloved cat. Mason sends a letter claiming without any firm legal basis that the provision in Laxter's will requiring the caretaker's continued employment impliedly allows him to keep the cat, and that any action against the animal would breach that condition and lead to the forfeiture of their bequests. The grandsons consult Nathaniel Shuster, whom Mason holds in absolute contempt. "He poses as a big trial lawyer, but he's a bigger crook than the people he defends. Any damn fool can win a case if he has the jury bribed." "If there's anything in reincarnation, he must have been a Chinese laundryman in a prior existence. Every time he snickers, he sprays his audience, like a Chinese laundryman sprinkling clothes." "He's a disgrace to the profession, and he gets us all into disrepute." "Shuster will try to egg his clients into a fight, and I'll either have to back up or play into his hands. If I back up, he makes his clients believe he's browbeaten me into submission, and charges them a good fee. If I don't back up, he tells them their whole inheritance is involved and soaks them a percentage. That's what I get for running that bluff about a forfeiture of the inheritance." Sure enough Mason's adversary is the shyster his name unsubtly suggests. "It's going to be a hard fight; it's going to be a bitter fight. I've warned my clients of that. You're a resourceful man. You're a sly man. If you don't mind the expression, I'll say you're a cunning man. Lots of us would take that as a compliment; I take that as a compliment myself. Lots of times my clients say, 'Shuster is cunning.' Do I get sore? I don't! I say that's a compliment . . . I warned my clients that Winifred [Peter Laxter's disinherited granddaughter] was going to try to break the will. I knew she'd try it by every means in her power, but she couldn't claim the grandfather was of unsound mind, and there's no question of undue influence. So . . . she picked on Ashton and his cat." Shuster refuses to settle the dispute unless "Winifred signs an agreement that she won't contest the will . . ." Mason: "I don't know anything about Winifred. I've never met her and haven't talked with her. I can't ask *her* to sign anything." Shuster, rubbing his hands gleefully: "We couldn't settle on any other basis. It's a matter of principle with us . . ." Mason, finally losing his temper: "You know damn well I'm not representing Winifred. You knew that that letter of mine meant exactly what it said, but you knew you couldn't kid your clients into paying big fees over a cat, so you dragged in this will-contest business . . . You've frightened your clients into believing they've got to get Winifred's signature on a release. That's laying the foundation for a nice fat fee for you." Shuster screams: "That's slander!" Mason, to the grandsons: " . . . I'm not your guardian. I'm not going to break my neck trying to save your money. If you two want to give that cat a home, say so now; that's all there'll be to it. If you don't, I'll make Shuster earn his fees by dragging you into the damndest fight you've ever been in . . ." The moral is clear: a good lawyer will do almost anything for a client but will not generate a dispute for the lawyer's own profit.

How did the original Mason mutate into the radically different character whom younger audiences are familiar with from TV? As we've seen, the process began as early as 1935 with the initial dialogue between Mason and Hamilton Burger in *The Case of the Counterfeit Eye*. It accelerated around 1937 when the *Saturday Evening Post*, which had previously published many a lawyer story by Melville Davisson Post and Arthur Train, began offering huge sums of money for the right to serialize Perry Mason novels before their appearance in hardcover. But Gardner in return had to tone down the series even more, in order to satisfy the magazine's requirements. He did so in a way that was nothing short of brilliant. I will guarantee you in advance, he said in effect to his readers, that Mason's clients will always be innocent, so that you can enjoy the way I have him skate on the thin edge of the law and pull all sorts of sneaky courtroom tricks without being bothered by any moral qualms about the cause he is serving. We might call this Gardner's personal contract with America, a contract which he kept from the late 1930s until his death.

At first Gardner was ambivalent about what he must have regarded as a Faustian bargain. In December 1936, just after completing the first Mason novel that the *Post* accepted for serialization, he described the book to his publisher as a case "with lame canaries and moving vans and silenced rifles and firebugs and trick garages and substituted amnesia victims and what the hell have we . . . No real life lawyer would ever have been mixed up in a mess like that." But only a few years later, in *The Case of the Perjured Parrot* (1939),

Gardner denounced precisely the kind of lawyer he had told his publishers he had originally wanted to portray as a hero. Mason, reading his mail, says to Della Street: "Oh, Lord, here's another one. A man, who's swindled a bunch of people into buying worthless stock, wants me to prove that he was within the letter of the law." The echo of Melville Davisson Post's early tales about lawyer Randolph Mason, who had no qualms about advising clients how to commit any crime, even murder, without running afoul of the law, resounds loud and clear for those with ears. "You know, Della," Mason continues, "I wish people would learn to differentiate between the reputable lawyer who represents persons accused of crime, and the criminal lawyer who becomes a silent partner in the profits of crime . . . I never take a case unless I'm convinced my client was incapable of committing the crime charged . . ."

In the Mason novels published between the late 1930s and the late 1950s, not only are the clients always innocent but the ruthlessness is muted, "love interest" plays a stronger role, and Mason becomes increasingly more stodgy, to the point that by the end of this middle period he refuses even to drive above the speed limit. But the oral combat remains as breathlessly exciting as ever, the pace as frantic and the plots as twisty, the best of them centering on various sharp-witted and greedy people battling over control of capital. Mason of course is still Gardner's alter ego but in several novels of these years he creates a second surrogate in the person of a philosophic old entrepreneur who delights in living on his own in the wilderness, as Gardner did himself.

One of the most interesting of these stand-ins is Fremont C. Sabin, whose obituary is summarized in the first chapter of *The Case of the Perjured Parrot* (1939).

> "Just touching sixty, he represented a strange figure of man; one who had wrung from life all that it offered in the way of material success; a man who literally had more money than he knew what to do with . . . [F]or the most part he did not believe in philanthropy, thinking that the ultimate purpose of life was to develop character; that the more a person came to depend on outside assistance, the more his character was weakened.
>
> " . . . Sabin had believed that life was a struggle and had purposely been made a struggle; that competition developed

character; that victory was of value only as it marked the goal of achievement . . .

"[He] had placed something over a million dollars in trust funds for charitable uses, but he had stipulated that the money was to go only to those who had been incapacitated in life's battles: the crippled, the aged, the infirm. To those who could still struggle on, Sabin offered nothing. The privilege of struggling for achievement was the privilege of living, and to take away that right to struggle was equivalent to taking away life itself."

Gardner's admiration for this man is so obvious that it comes as no great surprise when later in the book he turns out not to be dead at all.

Most of the Perry Mason novels Gardner wrote during the roughly twenty years that constitute his middle period are still highly readable today and a few offer rewards out of the ordinary. *The Case of the Rolling Bones* (1939) features two courtroom scenes, a wild complex plot, subtly planted clues to the truth and a pair of first-rate Mason scams, one on the street when a cop tries to give him a speeding ticket and another in court when he uses his office switchboard operator to play mind games with a hostile witness. A full-blown jury trial complete with closing arguments is the centerpiece of *The Case of the Careless Kitten* (1942), in which Della Street is charged with helping to hide a key prosecution witness. *The Case of the Crooked Candle* (1944) is considered in some quarters the finest pure detective novel in the Gardner canon, with its exceptionally long trial sequence, diagram, timetable, and detailed technical testimony about tides. In *The Case of the Half-Wakened Wife* (1945) the sky falls in on Mason more thunderously than in almost any other novel: not only is he fired by his client in mid-trial but gets sued for defamation of character by someone he wrongly accused of the murder his client is being tried for. *The Case of the Fiery Fingers* (1951) features two jury trials with separate defendants and one of Mason's longest and most sustained cross-examinations of a hostile witness. There are many other gems in the canon awaiting rediscovery by readers with the good sense to overlook the formulaic elements that even in the best of Mason's cases are repeated endlessly, and such readers will find tightly compressed but well-informed and accurate summaries of most of Gardner's books in Jon L. Breen's *Novel Verdicts: A Guide to Courtroom Fiction* (2nd ed. 1999).

~ ~ ~ ~ ~

At around the same time he was reinventing Perry Mason for the benefit of the *Saturday Evening Post*, Gardner created another fictional world which in many respects was closer to his heart. The setting is Madison City, county seat of a farm district in rural California a couple of hours' drive from Los Angeles. The protagonists are Doug Selby, an idealistic young man who has just been elected District Attorney, and Rex Brandon, a crusty middle-aged former rancher turned sheriff who is clearly something of a stand-in for Gardner himself. There is also a large supporting cast of recurring small-town characters who, according to Gardner's friend Dean John H. Wigmore, "give the [series] a solid permanence in good literature."

For our purposes the most important of these is criminal lawyer A.B. Carr, who "looked more like a successful actor than a practicing attorney . . ." and (although by this time Gardner hated Hollywood) seems tailor made to be played by John Carradine or some other preternaturally slim purveyor of movie menace. The fascination of the nine-volume D.A. series (1937-48) is that here Gardner reversed the polarities of the Perry Masons: the prosecutor and sheriff are the heroes and the defense lawyer a shyster of the first water, whose highest priority is (in Gardner's own words of a few years before) whether his client "has the necessary retainer in the form of spot cash . . ." and whose cunning tricks on behalf of the guilty are confounded again and again like those of Squire Mason in Arthur Train's Mr. Tutt stories. But there's a fundamental difference between Gardner's series and Train's. In the latter's tales the duel is typically legalistic, with Squire Mason wielding some arcane rule of law in order to assist his evil client and Ephraim Tutt, following in the footsteps of Shakespeare's Portia in *The Merchant of Venice*, countering with an even more arcane rule of law. Carr in the D.A. series typically serves his odorous clients by hocusing evidence and Selby defeats him by detective work that ferrets out the truth.

Carr first appears in the third and perhaps finest Selby book, *The D.A. Draws a Circle* (1939), when he buys a house in Madison City, claiming he wants a retreat from the hurly-burly of Los Angeles criminal practice. Hardly has he moved in when a nude corpse is found in the barranca between Carr's house and that of lovely Rita Artrim, who was so outraged at the prospect of a shyster neighbor that she'd consulted Selby about legal means of forcing him out. Lying side by side in the body are two bullets from different guns. Whichever bullet entered the man first killed him instantly, and Selby soon suspects that Carr has covered for the murderer by himself shooting into the corpse just so as to be able to create a reasonable doubt if his client is brought to trial. At the climax it's revealed that Carr's plot was even more devious than suspected, but this is typical of the tactics Selby confronts in subsequent books. By the time the series ends, with *The D.A. Takes a Chance* (1949), Carr has been forced to marry a woman who knows too much about one of these schemes and is rooting about for a way of divorcing her without freeing her to testify against him.

~ ~ ~ ~ ~

In the same year that saw the sanitized Perry Mason debut in the *Saturday Evening Post* and the first Doug Selby novel appear in hardcover, Gardner took us back into the social Darwinian jungle when he launched yet another lawyer series for *Black Mask*, the pulp in which he had his roots. In the firm of Jonathan & Boniface there works a young man named Peter Wennick who plays six roles to the hilt: apprentice lawyer, ardent lover, wheeler-dealer, flim-flam man, snappy sleuth, and lively first-person narrator. To call the relations between him and the senior partners unorthodox is like calling King Kong a cute little monk. On the surface Pete is a law student with a sideline of chasing the secretaries, and only the surface is visible to Cedric L. Boniface, the plump, smug, precedent-spouting academician who has "bluish-white eyes, looking like two peeled hard-boiled eggs" and gives the firm its image of conservative respectability. In reality Pete doesn't have the slightest interest in law. "Who wants to talk intelligently with lawyers? They don't even talk intelligently among themselves." He works directly and solely for E.B. Jonathan, an amoral old Machiavellian with eyes "as smoothly moist as a snake's tongue" and a voice "as smooth as butter on hotcakes," and his true function is to go outside the law to crack cases for the firm without cracking the firm's image.

Pete makes his first appearance in "Among Thieves" (September 1937) when the firm is retained to defend a young man named James Raymore who is charged with the cold-blooded murder of his lover's husband. Hardly has he set foot in the small city of Loma Vista where the crime took place than Pete learns he's in a hub of political corruption that has been cloned, as it were, from York City in Gardner's Ken Corning series, and suspects that Raymore was the victim of an official frame-up. Posing as a real-estate sharpshooter ready to pay whatever bribes it takes to get a certain piece of property rezoned, Pete is put in touch with the slimeballs who run the city and begins playing them against each other in the tradition of the Continental Op in Hammett's *Red Harvest* (1929). He uses a worthless check to open an account in the local bank under a phony name but then discovers that the name he's chosen for himself happens to be that of a wealthy investor, which means he's inadvertently committed the crime of forgery. Before this long and lightning-paced tale is over he gets trapped in the middle of a gun duel between political gangsters, extracts a confession from a wounded conspirator by pretending to be a doctor ("The anterior sclerosis shows symptoms of a traumatic regurgitation in the cardiac reflexes") and falsely telling the man he's dying, endures a flogging with rubber hoses in the back room of police headquarters, and sues the city's political boss for assault and false arrest.

In "Leg Man" (February 1938) the firm is retained by Mrs. Olive Pemberton to keep a certain red-headed golddigger from starting a lawsuit against her husband Harvey. Posing as Olive's long-lost brother, Pete visits the Pemberton residence, wangles an invitation to stay on for a few days, and that evening begins spying on Harvey's brokerage business from the adjoining office suite which helpful Olive has conveniently rented and bugged. Then Pete conjures up a noble scam to recover Harvey's passionate love letters from the redhead—a plan that calls for him to impersonate in rapid succession a masked burglar, a cop and a second cop—but the con game is interrupted when Harvey is found murdered and helpful Olive tries to frame Pete for the crime. An inspired combination of speed, luck, bluff, fast talk and nimble brainwork pull Pete out of the fire in this wonderful mini-novel.

In "Take It Or Leave It" (March 1939) the firm becomes entangled in another web of politics and murder reminiscent of Gardner's earlier *Black Mask* tales about Ken Corning. With Mayor Layton Spred and the municipal council of the city of Marlin facing a recall election after the exposure of massive corruption, the editor of the leading anti-administration newspaper is found shot to death on Spred's doorstep. The mayor claims he acted in self-defense, shooting at what he thought was a prowler, but when the ballistic evidence makes him out a liar, he and his lovely daughter Millicent retain J&B for the defense. Pete visits Marlin posing as a slot-machine racketeer, edges into the smoke-filled back rooms where the city's crooked politics is conducted, charms all the females and hocuses all the evidence in sight, and figures out the real murderer while Cedric L. Boniface sits in the law library researching precedents. Pete's solution is of arguable fairness but the story is briskly paced and with a beautifully simple and ironic key gimmick.

One of the many strengths of the short-lived Wennick series is its sardonic treatment of sacred cows. In these tales as in many Gardner novels, sex and marriage are economic weapons and combat over money is the order of the day in both home and office. There's a wonderful exchange between Wennick and E.B. Jonathan when the old man discovers Pete has been chasing one of the secretaries. Jonathan: "How are you going to play with fire without getting your fingers burnt?" Wennick: "How the hell am I going to warm my hands over a cold stove?" Jonathan (who is paying alimony to two much younger ex-wives): "You don't need to warm your hands . . . [Women] will get you in the long run . . . After the fighting begins, your home will seem like hell . . . [A]limony, eating into your salary like a cancer . . . When they see the infatuation waning, they try to find some way of capitalizing." In both "Among Thieves" and "Take It Or Leave It" the police are tools of the politicians who wallow like pigs in graft and corruption and violence. But all the social criticism in the Wennick series is only marginally more important than their legal component. First and foremost is that they're grand tales, told by a superb natural storyteller at the top of his form.

~ ~ ~ ~ ~

Gardner's last series of novels began a few years after the debut of the D.A. series and ran until his death almost a third of a century later. The protagonists of the 29 books he wrote under the byline of A.A. Fair are an obese irascible private investigator and a savvy young leg man, perhaps vaguely suggestive of Rex Stout's Nero Wolfe and Archie Goodwin but with the difference that fat foul-mouthed money-mad Bertha Cool is a woman and small street-smart Donald Lam is a former lawyer. With his eye for female beauty, genius for constructing elaborate scams, detective skill and zippy first-person narrative style, Donald is not so much an Archie Goodwin clone as Peter Wennick under an alias. And, like virtually every Gardner series character before him, he revels in the Darwinian struggle, seeming (in the words of Frank E. Robbins) "to take chances simply because of the urge to beat the opposition and come out on top."

Gardner was no expert on the history of the kind of fiction he wrote but he clearly knew Melville Davisson Post's "The Corpus Delicti" (1896) and, with full acknowledgment of his source, developed the heart of that story—the lawyer's ability and willingness to advise a client how to commit a cold-blooded murder, admit the deed in open court and walk away free—into *The Bigger They Come* (1939), first and one of the finest of the Cool and Lam novels. Here's the crucial conversation between Lam and his new employer. Cool: "Donald, . . . I know all about your trouble. You were disbarred for violating professional ethics." Lam: "I wasn't disbarred and I didn't violate professional ethics." Cool: "The grievance committee reported that you did." Lam: "The grievance committee were a lot of stuffed shirts. I talked too much, that's all." Cool: "What about, Donald?" Lam: "I did some work for a client. We got to talking about the law. I told him a man could break any law and get away with it if he went about it right." Cool: "That's nothing. Anyone knows that." Lam: "The trouble is I didn't stop there . . . I don't figure knowledge is any good unless you can apply it. I'd studied out a lot of legal tricks. I knew how to apply them." Cool: "Go on from there. What happened?" Lam: "I told this man it would be possible to commit a murder so there was nothing anyone could do about it. He said I was wrong. I got mad and offered to bet him five hundred dollars I was right, and could prove it. He said he was ready to put up the money any time I'd put up my five hundred bucks. I told him to come back the next day. That night he was arrested. He turned out to be a small-time gangster. He babbled everything he knew to the police. Among other things, he told them that I had agreed to tell him how he could commit a murder and get off scot-free. That he was to pay me five hundred dollars for the information, and then if it looked good to him, he had planned to bump off a rival gangster." Cool: "What happened?" Lam: "The grievance committee went after me hammer and tongs. They revoked my license for a year. They thought I was some sort of a shyster. I told them it was an argument and a bet. Under the circumstances, they didn't believe me. And, naturally, they took the other side of the question—that a man couldn't commit deliberate murder and go unpunished." Cool: "Could he, Donald?" Lam: "Yes." "Cool: "And you know how?" Lam: "Yes . . ." Cool: "And locked inside that head of yours is a plan by which I could kill someone and the law couldn't do a damn thing about it?" Lam: "Yes." Cool: "You mean if I was smart enough so I didn't get caught." Lam: "I don't mean anything of the sort. You'd have to put yourself in my hands and do just as I told you." Cool: "You don't mean that old gag about fixing it so they couldn't find the body?" Lam: "That is the bunk. I'm talking about a loophole in the law itself, something a man could take advantage of to commit a murder." Cool: "Tell me, Donald." Lam [laughing]: "Remember, I've been through that once." At the climax Lam demonstrates his own thesis by getting up in a courtroom, confessing to a murder (which in fact he didn't commit) and daring the legal system to touch him for it.

A detailed description of the ploy provides a vivid picture of Gardner's legal mind in action. X commits a murder in California, then drives across the state line into Arizona where he proceeds to frame himself on a charge of obtaining property under false pretenses, although leaving a legal escape hatch open for himself. He then drives back to California, runs through the quarantine station at the border, is chased and caught by California policemen and locked up in the border town of El Centro. In due course he is legally extradited to Arizona to face the false pretenses charge. Once he clears himself and that charge is officially dropped, he confesses to the California murder. But when California moves to extradite him, he files a writ of habeas corpus, arguing that on these facts he can't be compelled to return. "The only authority which one state has to take prisoners from another state comes from the organic law which provides that fugitives from justice may be extradited from one sovereign state to another. I am not a fugitive from justice . . . [A] man is not a fugitive from a state unless he flees from that state. He doesn't flee the state unless he does so voluntarily and in order to avoid arrest. I did not flee from California. I was dragged from California. I was taken out under legal process to answer for a crime of which I was innocent. I claimed that I was innocent. I came to Arizona and established my innocence. Any time I get good and ready to go back to California, California can arrest me for murder. Until I get good and ready to go back, I can stay here and no power on earth can make me budge." In support of his position Donald Lam cited two California judicial decisions, *In re Whittington* (1917) and *People v. Jones* (1921). Gardner's friend Dean Wigmore scoffed at this device but, after ESG had literally written a brief for him on the issue, admitted that the gimmick was more plausible than he had at first thought. *Jones* involved a man who had fled to Mexico after being convicted of manslaughter in Oklahoma. Mexican officials later took him forcibly across the border to California, where he was arrested by California authorities and held for extradition to Oklahoma. The court held that Jones' contention of an illegal conspiracy between Mexican and U.S. authorities was unsupported by any evidence and that, even if his removal from Mexico were irregular under Mexican law, he couldn't challenge that procedure in the courts of California. This case is easily distinguishable from the situation in *The Bigger They Come. Whittington*, which is much closer to the situation in the novel, was all but overruled by the California Supreme Court in *In re Patterson* (1966).

The ambience of the Cool & Lam series gave Gardner the opportunity to build novels around the sort of grand scams that previously he had confined to magazine stories. Only rarely does a Lam novel deal centrally with lawyer characters and legal themes, but on those occasions Gardner is at his most Darwinian. In *Beware the Curves* (1956) Lam winds up in Orange County, masterminding the strategy of law school classmate Barney Quinn who is defense counsel at the trial of John Ansel for the six-year-old murder of his employer Karl Endicott. Detective work has convinced Lam that the real murderer was banker Cooper Hale but he has no evidence to prove it. The defense rests without putting on a case. Closing arguments begin and, following Lam's script, Barney Quinn manipulates the district attorney into committing himself to an unequivocal theory of what had happened. "He sketched Ansel, emotionally upset, blowing hot and cold. First he intended to kill Endicott then he intended not to. He had thrown his gun away and had intended to leave [Endicott's] house. Then opportunity had presented itself and he had snatched [a second] gun from the bureau and had killed Endicott." The judge instructs the jury that they can find Ansel guilty of first-degree murder, second-degree murder or manslaughter. Conferring with Quinn after the jury has retired, Lam explains his strategy. "The district attorney walked into the trap . . . If the killing was committed with the gun lying on the dresser . . . it had to be manslaughter." Quinn: "And suppose the jury convicts him of manslaughter?" Lam:" . . . [T]hen come to the rail for a whispered consultation with me." The jury indeed returns a manslaughter verdict and after the whispered conference with Lam comes a scene reminiscent of Melville Davisson Post's earliest Randolph Mason tales as Quinn moves to set aside the verdict. "The crime of manslaughter outlaws within a period of three years. In other words, there can be no prosecution or conviction for manslaughter after a period of three years has elapsed from the date of the crime . . . [S]ince the defendant has now been convicted of a manslaughter which was perpetrated more than three years ago, the Court has no alternative but to release him . . ." The novel ends with the innocent man convicted but released on a technicality and the guilty man, untouchable for the crime he committed, implausibly sentenced to life without parole after being framed by a woman on the periphery of the plot who has a penchant for having sex with men and then charging them with rape. Such breathtaking cynicism would have been unthinkable in a contemporaneous adventure of Perry Mason.

~ ~ ~ ~ ~

In the final years of his middle period as a novelist, Gardner was still living up to the contract with America he had imposed on himself almost twenty years earlier, allowing millions of readers to thrill to Mason's lawyerly hocus-pocus without moral twinges. Indeed he created some of the most ingenious variations on his standard themes in his novels of the early and middle Nineteen Fifties. *The Case of the Hesitant Hostess* (1953) begins in mid-trial and is built almost entirely around Mason's desperate attempts to demolish the testimony of the chief witness against the derelict defendant. In *The Case of the Terrified Typist* (1956) Gardner turns handsprings to keep to his contract despite a jury verdict against Mason's client and despite the fact that the defendant is indeed both guilty and without moral justification.

One of the finest demonstrations of the Gardner contract at work is found in one of the last novels of the period. In *The Case of the Lucky Loser* (1957) an anonymous woman hires Mason over the phone to sit in court during a trial and let her know his conclusions. Wealthy young Ted Balfour is charged with involuntary manslaughter after allegedly getting drunk at a party and driving his car over an unidentifiable drifter whose "skull was smashed like an eggshell." A day of testimony convinces Mason that the chief prosecution witness is lying and that there will probably be a hung jury. In the next morning's paper he reads that the jury had indeed split and that Ted's attorney had then agreed to accept the verdict of the trial judge provided the penalty be limited to a fine and suspended sentence. (This sounds obscene in today's post-MADD era but was not all that shocking in the Fifties.) Later that day Mason is retained by the seductive young wife of Ted's uncle to visit the palatial home of Addison Balfour, the dying tyrant who rules the family with an iron hand, and convince the old man that his grandson is indeed innocent. Addison offers Mason a huge fee if he'll take over Ted's defense from the attorney who brokered the plea bargain. "You're not like most of these criminal lawyers. You don't want just to get a client off. You try to dig out the truth. I like that . . ." Next the police find a bullet in the crushed skull of the drifter and, concluding that Ted deliberately shot the man and then faked the hit-and-run to mutilate the man's face and body, charge him with Murder One. Mason goes into court and argues, with full citation to several California appellate decisions, that Ted can't be tried because, having been found guilty of involuntary manslaughter in the same matter, he's already been once in jeopardy and any further prosecution would violate the Fifth Amendment. This move would remind us irresistibly of how Melville Davisson Post's satanic lawyer Randolph Mason defended the guilty murderer in "The Corpus Delicti"—except that Gardner has made a solemn contract with us and we know Mason is not exerting his wiles on behalf of someone we don't want to see beat the system. Like the jurists in Post's early tales, Judge Cadwell is taken aback by the apparently outrageous legal result demanded by the lawyer named Mason who's arguing before him. "It comes as a shock to the Court to think that a defendant could place himself behind such a barricade of legal technicality." Unlike Post's trial-level judges, Gardner's refuses to let law trump justice. " . . . I feel a higher court should pass on this matter . . . If I hold the defendant for trial . . . , the matter can be taken to a higher court on a plea of once in jeopardy." Eventually of course Mason sees the truth and exposes one of the most convoluted plots his creator ever dreamed up.

~ ~ ~ ~ ~

A few months after *Lucky Loser* was published, the Perry Mason TV series began its long prime-time run on CBS. The company that made the series, Paisano Productions, was named after Gardner's Rancho del Paisano in Temecula, which in turn was named for El Paisano, one of the dozens of characters Gardner had created for the pulps. Not only did Gardner own a controlling interest in the company, but between 1957 and 1966 he put in long hours closely supervising the scripts.

There is no better index of how far his concept of lawyering had changed since the early 1930s than the memoranda he dictated in his capacity as adviser to the TV series. "[O]ne of the first things to do is to start with some character who is to become Perry Mason's client and to make the audience like that character . . . Therefore when I see these scripts come in [where apparently Mason represented guilty clients and used his legal skills to get them off] I feel that we are selling our character down the river. I want to vomit at the idea of the great Perry Mason with his sense of justice, his basic faith in human nature, descending so low as to be hired to represent a person of that caliber . . . [I]t is a basic rule of the Perry Mason stories that the audience must want the character to be represented by Perry Mason to come out on top."

During the program's decade-long run Gardner somehow found time to dictate new Perry Mason novels, but to an increasing extent he came to think of them as fodder for the TV series and they soon began showing the marks of the medium's infantile restrictions. The courtroom tiger of the earlier books, evolved into the kinder, gentler lawyer of the middle period, now mutated into a close cousin of the character Raymond Burr was portraying every week on the small screen, a ponderous bureaucrat mindful of the law's niceties. The last ten or twelve years' worth of Mason novels are as chaotic as most of the episodes of the weekly TV episodes. Plot holes left unplugged, ludicrous motivations, mush-witted reasoning, characters who know things they couldn't possibly have known, solutions that don't begin to explain who did what to whom, daisy chains of multiple coincidence, all are found abundantly in late Masons. Even the courtroom sequences are often as wretchedly constructed as their TV-series counterparts: in *The Case of the Daring Divorcee* (1964) Hamilton Burger introduces totally irrelevant evidence just so that certain story elements can be furthered, and in *The Case of the Worried Waitress* (1966) he forgets to present evidence that a crime was even committed.

But even in these sad last years there are a few highlights. *The Case of the Bigamous Spouse* (1961) has a beautifully mounted plot and a variety of sharp comments on everything from sales technique and modern marriage to police lawlessness and the undertaking business. Much of *The Case of the Ice-Cold Hands* (1962) deals not with murder but with an intriguing civil issue: who owns the proceeds when a winning bet at the racetrack is made with embezzled funds? In *The Case of the Phantom Fortune* (1964) Mason all but reverts to his original incarnation, playing fast and loose with the penal law while protecting his client's wife from a blackmailer, then finding himself suspected of trying to hang a felony charge on an innocent party. Mason is given superb cross-examination scenes in *The Case of the Shapely Shadow* (1960), *The Case of the Reluctant Model* (1961), *The Case of the Mischievous Doll* (1963), and *The Case of the Amorous Aunt* (1964), while *The Case of the Troubled Trustee* (1965) is distinguished by Hamilton Burger's savage cross-examination of Mason's client.

At age 75 Gardner seems to have become painfully aware of the ease with which, before subsequent reforms in civil commitment law, unscrupulous relatives with a hired doctor and lawyer in their pockets could railroad a mentally sound senior into a death-trap sanitarium. The result of his concerns was *The Case of the Beautiful Beggar* (1965), the most excitingly inventive and deeply personal of all his late novels. A young woman who claims to be the niece of a wealthy 75-year-old entrepreneur (another Gardner self-portrait?) begs Mason to rescue her uncle from greedy relatives who have had the old man institutionalized and themselves appointed conservators of his property. Mason's conduct of the proceeding over the old man's competency and his gorgeous banking gimmick to get some of the client's money back occupy the first half of the book. Late in the game comes the inevitable murder-and-trial complex which, as in so many late Gardner books, is routine, boring, and punctuated by incredible runs of lucky guesswork on Mason's part.

By the time the Mason TV series ended its run (with a case where the judge was played by Gardner himself), the decisions of the Supreme Court under Earl Warren had almost completely undermined what had always been the premise of the Mason novels: that a defendant menaced by the underhanded tactics of police and prosecutors needed a pyrotechnician like Mason in his or her corner. Once the so-called theory of trial by ambush had become obsolete, once the Court had ruled that convictions obtained by such tactics were unconstitutional and had to be reversed, Mason lost his *raison d'etre*.

The new wave of Court decisions roughly coincided with Gardner's discovery that he had cancer. He responded to both threats in the same way: by carrying on as if nothing had happened. No changes in the American legal system or within his slowly dying body could keep him from doing what he wanted with his own life or the life of the universe he had created. When Mason in *The Case of the Velvet Claws* said: "I fight!" he was speaking for Gardner too. What he had written in *The Case of the Lucky Loser* about Addison Balfour he lived in his own flesh. "Despite the sentence of death which had been pronounced upon him, he continued to be the same old irascible, unpredictable fighter. Disease had ravaged his body, but the belligerency of the man's mind remained unimpaired." The sole concession Gardner made to the mood of the times was in *The Case of the Fabulous Fake* (1969), which includes a sequence unconnected with the main plot where Mason defends his only minority client, a young black man falsely accused of a pawnshop robbery. On

March 11, 1970, less than a year after that novel's publication, Gardner's fight came to an end.

~ ~ ~ ~ ~

I discovered Perry Mason when I was thirteen and read most of his cases three or four times apiece during my eight years in high school and college. In my senior year, when I signed up to take the Law School Admission Test, it was a blind leap in the dark: all I knew about law I had learned from Gardner's novels. As chance or fate would have it, I performed well enough to receive scholarship offers I couldn't refuse. A year and a half after graduating from New York University School of Law, chance or fate stepped in again and I began corresponding with Gardner, having no idea that he was dying. Near the end of his first and longest letter to me, dated January 22, 1969, he mentioned his declining output of fiction and blamed it on "the terrific influx of mail. I just don't know how to handle this mail. I feel that letters should be answered but there are times when it seems an impossible task. My secretaries counted up one day (which was exceptional) and found I had dictated more than twenty thousand words of correspondence on that day and I was still far from being caught up." We exchanged a number of letters afterwards but I never got around to explaining how in effect he had turned me into a lawyer, or to thank him.

Now I've done both.

CORNELL WOOLRICH

Of all the authors whose forte was turning our spines to columns of ice, this man was the supreme master of the art, the Hitchcock of the written word. The honors he received on his centenary in 2003 were richly deserved, but if he had been alive and well he wouldn't have enjoyed a moment of the events that celebrated him and probably wouldn't have shown up for them.

His full name was Cornell George Hopley-Woolrich. His mother, born Claire Attalie Tarler, was the daughter of George Tarler, a Russian Jewish émigré who had made his fortune in the import trade with Mexico and Central America. His father, Genaro Hopley-Woolrich, was of Canadian and Mexican descent, an adventurous macho who was both attractive and susceptible to women. Genaro's half-nephew Carlos Burlingham, who as a teen-ager in the early 1940s lived with him for a year, described him as "a very good-looking man with deep blue eyes . . . But you would never see him to smile. He always had a very narrow smile." Around 1901 or 1902, while in the U.S. and working on the construction of New York City's infant subway system, Genaro met Claire Tarler and soon married her. Their only child was born on December 4, 1903. In 1907 they left New York with three-year-old Cornell to resettle in Mexico but the marriage did not long survive the move. Claire returned to the Tarler household on West 113th Street near Morningside Park and the child stayed with Genaro below the border. His schooling was punctuated by holidays whenever another revolutionary leader captured the town where they lived, and as a hobby he collected the spent rifle cartridges that littered the streets beneath his windows.

When he was eight Grandfather Tarler took him to Mexico City's Palace of Fine Arts to see a traveling French company perform Puccini's then new opera *Madama Butterfly*, an experience that gave the boy a sudden sharp insight into color and drama and his first sense of tragedy. Three years later, on a night when he looked up at the low-hanging stars from the valley of Anahuac, he understood that someday like Cio-Cio-San he too would have to die. From that moment he was haunted by a sense of doom. "I had that trapped feeling," he wrote, "like some sort of a poor insect that you've put inside a down-turned glass, and it tries to climb up the sides, and it can't, and it can't, and it can't."

During his adolescence he returned to New York City and lived with his grandfather and aunt and mother in George Tarler's house on 113th Street. In 1921 he enrolled in Columbia College, a short walk from home, choosing journalism as his major but dreaming of a more romantic occupation, like being an author or a professional dancer. In his junior year, while immobilized with either an infected foot or a bad case of jaundice (his own accounts of the incident are at odds), he began the first draft of a novel. When it sold a few months later, he quit Columbia to pursue the dream of bright lights.

The main influence on Woolrich's early work was F. Scott Fitzgerald, the literary idol of the Twenties, and his first novel, *Cover Charge* (1926), chronicles the lives and loves of the Jazz Age's gilded youth, child-people flitting from thrill to thrill, conversing in a mannered slang which reads today like a foreign language. But several motifs from his earlier and later life and his later suspense fiction can be detected in this rather amateurish debut. The fascination with dance halls and movie palaces. The use of popular song lyrics to convey mood. Touches of vibrantly colorful description. A long interlude in Mexico City complete with performance of *Madama Butterfly*. Romance between Alan Walker, the ballroom-dancer protagonist, and two women each of whom is old enough to be his mother. An extravaganza of coincidence to keep the story moving. And a despairing climax with Alan alone in a cheap hotel room, his legs all but useless after an auto smashup, abandoned by the women he at various times loved, contemplating suicide. "I hate this world. Everything comes into it so clean and goes out so dirty."

Woolrich's second novel was *Children of the Ritz* (1927), a frothy concoction about a spoiled heiress who impulsively marries her chauffeur. The book won first prize of $10,000 in a contest cosponsored by *College Humor* magazine, which serialized it, and First National Pictures, which filmed the story in 1929. Woolrich was invited to Hollywood to help with the adaptation and stayed on as a staff writer, although he never received screen credit for whatever contributions he made. One of First National's dialogue and title writers at this time was named William Irish.

With novels, movie chores and an occasional article or story for magazines like *College Humor, College Life, McClure's* and *Smart Set*, Woolrich must have been a busy young man indeed. By the time of his gritty and cynical third book, *Times Square* (1929), he had begun to develop the headlong storytelling drive and the concern with the torments and the maniacal power of love which were to mark his later suspense fiction. The first half of his semi-autobiographical novel *A Young Man's Heart* (1930) is set in Mexico around 1910 and the viewpoint is that of a young boy during and after the collapse of his parents' marriage.

In December 1930, while still working in Hollywood, Woolrich suddenly married 20-year-old Gloria Blackton, a daughter of pioneer movie producer J. Stuart Blackton, who had founded Vitagraph Studios in 1897. The marriage was never consummated. A graphic diary that Gloria eventually found and read but later returned to Woolrich (who destroyed it) indicates that he had been homosexual for some time prior to the marriage, which he had entered as a sort of sick joke, or perhaps for cover. In the middle of the night he would put on a sailor outfit that he kept in a locked suitcase and prowl the waterfront for partners. The marriage soon ended and Woolrich fled to New York and mother. "I was born to be solitary," he said in his autobiography, "and I liked it that way." But the pages of his novels and stories are haunted by the shadow of his desperate need for a relationship with a woman who never was and never could have been.

After the breakup of his marriage, Woolrich and his mother traveled extensively in Europe. His sixth novel, *Manhattan Love Song* (1932), is the best of his youthful books and the only one that, if published a few decades later, would have been called a crime novel. It begins with a quintessential Woolrich moment.

> First she was just a figure moving toward me in the distance, among a great many others doing the same thing. A second later she was a girl. Then she became a pretty girl, exquisitely dressed. Next a responsive girl, whose eyes said "Are you lonely?", whose shadow of a smile said, "Then speak." And by that time we had reached and were almost passing one another. Our glances seemed to strike a spark between us in mid-air.

Wade, the narrator, soon becomes a helpless slave to his passion for the enigmatic Bernice. Under her spell he abandons his job, assaults and robs a homosexual actor for money to spend on her, abuses his wife Maxine who still loves him desperately. Bernice in some mysterious way is controlled by unseen powers in the city but responds so passionately to Wade's abject passion for her that she's ready to sacrifice everything and risk the powers' vengeance to start life over again with him. But as usual in Woolrich, love opens the door to horror and those who manage to survive have nothing left but to wait for the merciful release of death.

For the next two years Woolrich sold next to nothing. He had moved out of the house on 113th Street and into a cheap hotel, determined to make it as a writer without his mother's help, but was soon deep in debt and reduced to sneaking into movie houses by the fire doors for entertainment. Frantically he tried to complete and find a publisher for a novel he'd begun two years earlier, a story of ballroom dancers in 1912 Paris for which he hoped some Hollywood studio would pay him enough to liberate him from the Depression. No one was interested in the book and finally Woolrich tossed the entire manuscript of *I Love You, Paris* into the garbage. But at that moment he was on the brink of a new life as a writer, one so different from his earlier literary career that decades later he said it would have been better if all his pre-suspense fiction "had been written in invisible ink and the reagent had been thrown away." He was about to become the Poe of the twentieth century and the poet of its shadows.

~ ~ ~ ~ ~

"There was another patient ahead of me in the waiting room. He was sitting there quietly, humbly, with all the terrible resignation of the very poor." Woolrich's first crime story, "Death Sits in the Dentist's Chair" (*Detective Fiction Weekly*, August 4, 1934), offers a vivid picture of New York City during the worst of the Depression, a bizarre murder method (cyanide in a temporary filling), and a race against the clock to save the poisoned protagonist—elements which would soon become Woolrich hallmarks.

In his next dozen tales (all of them plus his debut story included in my 1985 collection *Darkness at Dawn*) we find the invasion of nightmare into the viewpoint character's workaday existence, a Hollywood movie-making background, first-person narration by a woman, casual police brutality, intuition passed off as reasoning, terror in a milieu of jazz musicians, the use of Manhattan landmarks as settings, inexplicable evil powers that prey on man, set-pieces of nail-biting suspense, whirlwind physical action, the James M. Cain theme of the guy who gets away with the murder he did commit but is nailed for one he didn't—in short, the first appearances of countless motifs and beliefs and devices that would recur throughout his later fiction.

Between 1936 and 1939 Woolrich sold at least 105 more stories as well as two book-length magazine serials, and by the end of the decade he had become a fixture in mystery pulps of all levels of quality from *Black Mask* and *Detective Fiction Weekly* to cheapies like *Thrilling Mystery* and *Black Book Detective* and had also appeared in Whit Burnett's prestigious general fiction magazine *Story*. His stories of this period—historical adventures, Runyonesque comedies, gems of Grand Guignol, even an occasional tale of pure detection—range in quality from magnificent to abysmal but very few lack the unique Woolrich mood, tone and preoccupations. A look at twelve of his finest stories from these years gives us a vivid picture of his development.

One of the most characteristic types of Woolrich story is the oscillation thriller. Two central characters share a close relationship—lovers, husband and wife, father and son, roommates. A crime is committed, slowly mounting evidence compels or comes within an inch of compelling one of the two to believe that the other is guilty, and the suspense builds as the viewpoint character oscillates between doubt and trust and doubt again. In "The Night Reveals" (*Story*, April 1936) Woolrich makes us undergo this dark night of the soul with insurance investigator Harry Jordan as he learns that his wife Marie has been slipping out of their Lexington Avenue apartment in the hours before dawn. He begins following her through the ghostly city streets and soon comes to suspect that something has turned her into a pyromaniac. Is he right? In some oscillation stories the suspected person is innocent and the damning evidence comes from wild coincidence or a frameup, but in others the person is indeed guilty, and in still others neither the characters nor the reader ever learn the truth. Since Woolrich has no series characters or ground rules, the suspense is real and our own uncertainty matches that of the people on the page.

Another Woolrich specialty was the heart-in-the-throat *noir* thriller with a race against time and death. "Johnny on the Spot" (*Detective Fiction Weekly*, May 2, 1936) is set in the depth of New York's night. Hunted by the mob because he knows too much and wants out, Johnny Donovan is cornered in an all-night cafeteria and about to be taken away for torture and death when his 18-year-old wife Jean comes into the hash joint for a furtive rendezvous with him and sees that the hit men have him. For the rest of the story we race with Jean through the darkness on a mad quest to kidnap the top mobster's wife and swap her for Johnny—or, if it's too late for that, to kill her too.

Among Woolrich's fast-action whizbangs one of the most suspenseful is "You Pays Your Nickel" (*Argosy*, August 22, 1936). Subway guard Delaney is bored stiff at his job until one morning when his train is taken over by a homicidal maniac and he's suddenly part of a hair-raising underground duel as the cars carrying the two of them and hundreds of screaming commuters and a bag with $50,000 in stolen money careen out of control through the tunnels. This superb action story, usually reprinted as "Subway," is so vividly written you are thrust into the volcano and trapped there until Woolrich has melted you.

In "The Corpse Next Door" (*Detective Fiction Weekly*, January 23, 1937) Woolrich pushes us into the skin of a man with a guilt-flayed conscience and, as in Poe's "The Tell-Tale Heart," makes us live his torments. A faceless nonentity scratching out a bare white-collar existence amid the quiet despair of the Depression is driven mad with fury by the invisible thief who's been stealing his bottle of milk from the stoop of his drab apartment before he and his wife get up in the morning. He sets a trap for the thief, kills the man in a fit of wrath, hides the body inside the closeted Murphy bed in the vacant apartment next door, and slowly but inevitably is driven over the edge.

"Murder at the Automat" (*Dime Detective*, August 1937) offers not only a vivid picture of 1930s New York but a lovely puzzle resolved with total fairness to the reader. Homicide detective Nelson tackles the case of Leo Avram, an old skinflint who came into the Automat every night for coffee and a bologna sandwich, until the night the sandwich behind the coin slot he chose turned out to be laced with cyanide and killed him. Woolrich powerfully evokes the Automat and the seedy night people who call it home. It's typical in his world that when the police can't figure out how anyone could have poisoned precisely the sandwich Avram selected, they threaten to frame the prime suspect.

"Goodbye, New York" (*Story*, October 1937) takes place in Manhattan's streets, subways and railroad tunnels and is told in first person from the viewpoint of a young woman whose husband has killed his corrupt ex-boss and stolen just enough to let the couple start life over. This edgy, feverish heartbreaker of a tale follows their frantic attempts to evade the police net closing around them and get out of the city. "Two doomed things, running away. From nothingness, into nothingness . . . Turn back we dare not, stand still they wouldn't let us, and to go forward was destruction at our own hands." A perfect image of life in the Woolrich world.

In "Dusk to Dawn" (*Black Mask,* December 1937) we live with yet another hunted and doomed protagonist running headlong through the nightscape. Jobless and penniless Lew Stahl sneaks into a New York movie palace without a ticket as Woolrich had often done in the lean years. He tries to lift the wallet of a sleeper in the deserted mezzanine and take out one dollar to buy a meal with but discovers that the man isn't asleep but dead, with a knife in his back. A woman several rows behind them in the dark is convinced she saw Lew wield the knife and runs for the police. Stalked and desperate, fleeing through the nightbound city, he steals a gun, then uses it, and his fate is sealed. Woolrich tales like this one apparently had a profound influence on Richard Wright, who is known to have read countless pulp detective magazines during the late Thirties and whose classic first novel *Native Son* (1940) follows the young black fugitive Bigger Thomas, also wrongly accused of a murder, as he flees through a Woolrich-like nightscape made even more perilous for him by his race.

"Dime a Dance" (*Black Mask*, February 1938) is the first of several Woolrich tales in which a female first-person narrator is staked out as bait to trap a psychotic murderer of women. Taxi dancer Ginger Allen is taken from work one night by homicide cop Nick Ballestier and told that her only friend among the dancers has been strangled and then stabbed repeatedly by a serial killer who dances with his victims' corpses (as in "Dead on Her Feet") to the jazz tune "Poor Butterfly" (as in Puccini's opera). A month later a strange new customer shows up at Joyland and asks Ginger to dance with him. The climax is a suspense classic.

"I Wouldn't Be in Your Shoes" (*Detective Fiction Weekly*, March 12, 1938) combines a powerful picture of scratching for survival with a dark picture of the human condition. We enter the quietly wretched life of Tom Flynn, who works for a miserable salary and every day dreads being laid off. One stifling August night he loses control and throws a pair of his shoes out the open bedroom window at a pair of cats yowling on the back fence. Months later those shoes lead to his arrest, conviction and death sentence for the murder of an old miser in a shack a few blocks away. The haunted and lonely plainclothesman Bob White meets Quinn's wife Ann and the two of them race the clock to find another murderer. The man they track down, however, insists that he's innocent too, and it seems impossible that either he or Quinn is guilty. But one of them must be, and by the story's end both are left in ruin. Life is a trap, malevolent and beyond reason. To anyone unlucky enough to be born, Woolrich says: "I wouldn't be in your shoes, buddy," knowing he's in them too.

"Mystery in Room 913" (*Detective Fiction Weekly*, June 4, 1938) is an episodic novelet taking place in a New York hotel. Over a long stretch of the Depression, three different men check into Room 913 and unaccountably jump out the window into the street during the night. House detective Striker refuses to accept the deaths as coincidental suicides and becomes obsessed to the point of psychosis with proving they were something else. He finds a Bowery derelict, sets him up in 913 as bait and becomes responsible for the man's death, then goes jobless for months and changes his appearance until he can check into 913 himself without being recognized and force a confrontation with the spectre which is the naked face of death, and of the world's malevolence.

The protagonist of "Three O'Clock" (*Detective Fiction Weekly*, October 1, 1938) is Paul Stapp, the nondescript owner of a small clock and watch repair shop, who after an unexplained concussion has become convinced that his wife Fran is entertaining a lover in their house while he's at work. Rather than confront her he decides to blow up both her, the lover, the house and everything in it. Over time he smuggles into his basement the raw materials for a bomb. Then one afternoon at the hour when Fran is shopping he comes home, goes down to the basement and sets the bomb to explode at three. But this is the same afternoon two moronic daylight burglars have picked to break into Stapp's house. When he encounters them on his way out they knock him unconscious, bind and gag him in the basement, tie him to a thick pipe and make their getaway, unaware that they've immobilized him within a few feet of a bomb set to explode in ninety minutes. For those minutes Woolrich makes us live in Stapp's flesh, unable to speak or move or make a sound anyone can hear, his frozen eyes fixed on the clock as its hands plunge towards three. The suspense and anguish are so intense in this quintessential Woolrich story that one can hardly read it without dying a little.

"Men Must Die" (*Black Mask*, August 1939), better known under its reprint title "Guillotine" is set in France and broken down into a large number of short scenes. The events of the present, as condemned murderer Robert Lamont is ritually prepared for execution, alternate with chronologically ordered flashbacks so that we see what Lamont did and why he hopes he won't have to die for it. His lover Babette has contrived to meet the headsman, an old loner whose pride is his status as the only man in France with a license to kill. Babette dines with M. de Paris on the night before he is to decapitate

Lamont, hoping desperately that she'll be able to slip poison into his meal and thus invoke the national tradition (which Woolrich apparently invented) that when the executioner dies the next one set to be guillotined receives a pardon. The narration is so objective and detached that we get no hint which of these two, the private murderer or the state murderer, we're supposed to wish dead. And by the time the flashback scenes have caught up to the present and Lamont is brought step by step closer to the scaffold while the old man is journeying across predawn Paris with the guillotine blade in his bag and his own death churning inside him, the tension in this grotesque classic has become all but unbearable.

What was the man like who spun out these bleak visions? The best physical description comes from Woolrich's pulp contemporary Steve Fisher (1912-1980), who used him as the model for the brutal and love-tormented homicide detective Cornell in *I Wake Up Screaming* (1941). "He had red hair and thin white skin and red eyebrows and blue eyes. He looked sick. He looked like a corpse. His clothes didn't fit him . . . He was frail, grey-faced and bitter. He was possessed with a macabre humor. His voice was nasal. You'd think he was crying. He might have had T.B. He looked like he couldn't stand up in a wind." Imagine a painfully introverted man, living in hotels with his mother, going out almost never, the torments of his fictional characters mirroring his own. That in a nutshell is Woolrich.

~ ~ ~ ~ ~

In 1940 he joined the migration of pulp detective writers from luridcovered magazines to hardcover books. In his first overt crime novel, *The Bride Wore Black* (1940), he writes in cool unemotional prose of a mysterious woman named Julie who enters the lives of various men and, for reasons never explained until the climax, murders them. Woolrich divides the book into five free-standing episodes, each built around a symbolic three-step dance. First a chapter showing Julie, each time in a new persona, preparing the trap for her current target; then the execution of her plan, each victim being ensnared in his own romantic image of the perfect woman; finally some pages dealing with the faceless homicide cop who's stalking the huntress through the years.

This first in Woolrich's so-called Black Series was followed by *The Black Curtain* (1941), the masterpiece on the overworked subject of amnesia. Frank Townsend recovers from a three years' loss of memory, becomes obsessed with learning who and what he was during those missing years, and finds love, hate and a murder charge waiting for him behind the curtain.

Black Alibi (1942) is a terror novel about a killer jaguar menacing a South American city while a lone Anglo hunts a human murderer who may be hiding behind the jaguar's claws. This time Woolrich dropped his quintessential themes of loneliness and despair and concentrated on pure suspense, and the result is a thriller with menace breathing on every page.

The Black Angel (1943) deals with a terrified young wife's race against time to prove that her convicted husband did not murder his girlfriend and that some other man in the dead woman's life is guilty. Like Julie in *The Bride Wore Black*, she enters the lives of several such men, of whom one at most is the killer she's looking for, and in one way or another destroys them all and herself too. Writing in first person from the wife's viewpoint—a huge risk for an introverted loner who never knew a woman intimately—Woolrich makes us feel her love and anguish, her terror and desperation, her obsessions that grow to madness inside her like a cancer as she flails the world like a destroying angel to save her man from Mister Death.

The Black Path of Fear (1944) tells of a man who runs away to Havana with an American gangster's wife, followed by the vengeful husband, who kills the woman and frames her lover, leaving him a stranger in a strange land, menaced on all sides and fighting for his life. The earlier chapters, with their evocations of love discovered and love destroyed, their sense of what it must be like to be alone and hunted through a nightmare city of the mind, demonstrate vividly Woolrich's claim to be called the Hitchcock of the written word.

In *Rendezvous in Black* (1948) grief-crazed Johnny Marr holds one among a small group of people responsible for his fiancée's death and devotes his life to entering the lives of each of that group in turn, finding out whom each one most loves and murdering these loved ones so that the person who killed his fiancée will live the grief he lives. This is *The Bride Wore Black* with the sexes reversed and the structure as it should have been: with the explanation of the serial murders at the beginning so that we have some clue how to respond; with a genuine noir cop instead of a cipher in the role of hunter stalking the killer through the years; with a wealth of heart-stopping suspense and anguish instead of cool objective narration; with the forces of chance and fate kept in perfect balance; with a strong climax lacking *The Bride*'s monkey tricks of plot manipulation. Woolrich as usual punches ridiculous holes in the continuity, but on the visceral level where his work stands or falls this is a masterpiece.

Among his finest shorter crime fiction of the early 1940s are the annihilation stories "All at Once, No Alice" (*Argosy*, March 22, 1940) and "Finger of Doom" (*Detective Fiction Weekly*, June 22, 1940), which share one of the most powerful premises in *noir* literature. A lonely young man has miraculously found the one right woman but just before they are to marry she vanishes into nothingness. Everyone who apparently had known or seen the woman denies she ever existed, and the police to whom the man frantically appeals for help can't find the slightest proof she walked the earth. Convinced that she's a figment of his lunatic imagination, they kick him out with contempt and abandon him to despair—all but one lone-wolf cop who's willing to believe that the young man just might be telling the truth. The living nightmare stories "C-Jag" (*Black Mask*, October 1940) and "And So to Death" (*Argosy*, March 1, 1941), better known respectively under their reprint titles "Cocaine" and "Nightmare", form another matched pair of *noir* classics. The protagonist comes to after a blackout episode of one sort or another and is haunted by the memory of having done something horrible while out of himself. Back in the waking world he tries to shrug off the memory as the residue of a bad dream, hangover, drug dose or whatever. Then he finds on his person an objective fragment from the nightmare, and then another, and before long he's on the edge of madness. Desperately he appeals to his brother-in-law, who is a cop and, like most Woolrich cops, as ready to hang those in need of aid as to help them. The two men go back together into the shadows, hunting for the answer.

In the early Forties the entrepreneurs of dramatic radio discovered that countless Woolrich stories were naturals for audio adaptation and began buying from him the rights to adapt his tales for broadcast on series like *Suspense* and *Mollé Mystery Theatre*. The 30-minute version of *The Black Curtain* (*Suspense*, CBS, December 3, 1943, starring Cary Grant), which may have been scripted by Woolrich himself, ranks among the most powerful radio dramas ever written. "I tried to put it all behind me, to resume my life where it left off over three years ago . . . I don't want to find out anything anymore. I want it all to die away and be still. And it will. All except Ruth. *Because somewhere behind that black curtain I was loved, and loved someone!* We must have known a love I'll never know again."

Woolrich continued to write more novels—too many for publication under a single byline—and soon needed to come up with a pseudonym. The name that he and *Story* magazine editor Whit Burnett hit upon was William Irish. Had Woolrich known that obscure First National title writer back in the Twenties, and had he been carrying the man's name in the back of his mind ever since? The first novel published under the Irish byline was *Phantom Lady* (1942). Scott Henderson quarrels with his wife, goes out and picks up a woman in a bar, spends the evening with her, and comes home to find his wife dead and himself accused of her murder. All the evidence is against him and his only hope is to find the woman who was with him when his wife was killed. But she seems to have vanished into thin air, and everyone in a position to know swears that no such woman ever existed. He is sentenced to die, and as the hours rush towards execution day, the woman who loves him and his best friend race the clock to find the phantom. The plot is so involuted that final explanations require two dozen closely printed and none too plausible pages, but the emotional torment and suspense are unforgettable.

Deadline at Dawn (1944) takes place on a single night in the bleak streets and concrete caves of New York as we follow a desperate young couple who have until sunrise to clear themselves of a murder charge and escape the web of the city. The storyline is loose and relaxed, with many characters and incidents in no way connected to the main plot. But the cliffhanger crosscutting between Quinn's and Bricky's searches through the night streets keeps tension high, and the two-pronged quest is punctuated by touches of the deepest *noir*. Woolrich evokes New York after dark and the despair of those who walk its streets with a pathos unmatched in the genre.

Of all his novels the one most completely dominated by death and fate is *Night Has a Thousand Eyes* (1945), which was published as by George Hopley (Woolrich's middle names). A simple-minded recluse with apparently uncanny powers predicts that millionaire Harlan Reid will die in three weeks, precisely at midnight, at the jaws of a lion, and the tension rises to unbearable pitch as the doomed man's daughter and a sympathetic cop struggle to avert a destiny which they suspect and soon come to hope was conceived by a human power. Woolrich makes us live the emotional torment of this waking nightmare until we are literally shivering in our seats.

Waltz into Darkness (1947), again as by Irish, is set in New Orleans around 1880 and begins as much of Woolrich begins, with a man being eaten alive by loneliness. "Any love, from anywhere, on any terms. Quick, before it was too late! Only not to be alone any longer." Enter *la femme fatale*, the nameless woman who is Louis Durand's destiny, whom he comes to love with such maniacal intensity that for her he will degrade himself to any extent, cheat, kill, endure torture and even death. Like several Woolrich men before him,

Louis is an acolyte worshipping at the altar of love, and the woman is his goddess. Woolrich describes her in overwhelmingly religious and maternal language. She is God the Mother, unknowable and cruel as life. Louis is caught in her as in a whirlpool and we are trapped in his skin. In the cold light of reason the book is ludicrous, but no one can read Woolrich and be reasonable.

In *I Married a Dead Man* (1948) a woman with nothing to live for and in flight from her sadistic husband is injured in a train wreck. She wakes up in a hospital bed surrounded by luxuries because, as she eventually realizes, she's been wrongly identified as another woman, one who had had everything to live for but had died in the train disaster. Helen grasps what seems to be a heaven-sent chance to start over and even falls in love again, but her new life proves to be a gift from the dark god who rules the Woolrich world. At the climax she and we are confronted with two and only two possibilities, neither of which makes the least sense, each of which will destroy innocent lives. "I don't know what the game was ... I only know we must have played it wrong, somewhere along the way ... We've lost. That's all I know. We've lost. And now the game is through." Woolrich's last major novel is one of the finest and bleakest of his works.

The success of his novels led to publication of several collections of his shorter work in hardcover and paperback volumes which are extremely rare today. His stories were staple items in the endless anthologies of short mystery fiction published during the Forties. In addition to the dozens of radio plays adapted from his work, fifteen movies were made from Woolrich material between 1942 and 1950 alone. And his influence pervaded the culture of the Forties so extensively that many *film noir* classics of that period give the sense of having been adapted from his work even though he had nothing to do with them.

~ ~ ~ ~ ~

Woolrich published little new after 1948, apparently because his long absent father's death and his mother's prolonged illnesses paralyzed his ability to write. That he was remembered during the Fifties is largely due to Ellery Queen (Frederic Dannay), who reprinted in his magazine a host of Woolrich pulp tales, and to Alfred Hitchcock, whose *Rear Window* (1954) was based on a Woolrich story. His magazine work proved as adaptable to television as it had to radio a decade earlier, and series like *Mirror Theater, Ford Theater, Alfred Hitchcock Presents* and *Schlitz Playhouse of Stars* frequently presented 30-minute filmed versions of his material. Even the prestigious *Playhouse 90* made use of Woolrich, presenting a 90-minute adaptation of *Rendezvous in Black* (CBS, October 25, 1956), directed by John Frankenheimer and starring Franchot Tone, Laraine Day and Boris Karloff. The finest adaptation of Woolrich in any form is Hitchcock's 60-minute version of "Three O'Clock", starring E.G. Marshall and broadcast on the series *Suspicion* (NBC, September 30, 1957) as *Four O'Clock*. It's pure Hitchcock, pure Woolrich and perhaps the most totally suspenseful film the master ever directed.

Woolrich's personal situation remained wretched, and more than once he sank to passing off slightly updated old stories as new work, fooling book and magazine publishers as well as readers. Not long after his mother's death in 1957 came *Hotel Room* (1958), a collection of tales set in a single room of a New York City hotel at various times from the building's years of sumptuous fashionableness to the last days before its demolition. The St. Anselm was an amalgam of the desiccated residential hotels in which mother and son had lived and the stories set there mark the beginning of Woolrich's end. Yet once in a while he could still conjure up the old power. "The Penny-a-Worder" (*Ellery Queen's Mystery Magazine*, September 1958) is a wry downbeat tale of a pulp mystery writer of the 1930s desperately trying to crank out a complete novelet overnight. And "The Number's Up" (in *Beyond the Night*, 1959) is a bitter little account of gangland executioners mistakenly taking an innocent couple out to be shot.

Diabetic, alcoholic, wracked by self-contempt and alone, Woolrich dragged out his life. He would come to a party, bringing his own bottle of cheap wine in a paper bag, and stand in a corner the whole evening. If someone approached and tried to tell him how much he or she admired his work, he would growl "You don't mean that" and find another corner. In 1965 he moved into a spartan suite of rooms on the second floor of the Sheraton Russell, at Park Avenue and 37th Street, and continued the slow process of dying by inches. He wrote a little, left unfinished much more than he completed, but publishers continued to issue collections of his stories. The last such book published in his lifetime was *The Dark Side of Love* (1965), which brought together eight of his recent "tales of love and despair," among them that dark gem "Too Nice a Day to Die." A desperately lonely woman turns on the gas in her apartment one morning, ready to end her life. The phone rings. From force of habit she picks up the receiver. It's a wrong number, someone wanting Schultz's Delicatessen. The absurdity gives her the will to live one day longer. She goes out, walks about the city and, thanks to the long arm of chance or fate, meets in Rockefeller Plaza a man who seems to be as right for her as she seems to be for him. As they're on their way to her place for dinner, she's run down while crossing the street and dies. The world according to Woolrich has rarely been rendered in such fitting form.

During 1967 his slow march to the grave quickened into a fast walk. He developed a bad case of gangrene in one leg but put off seeing a doctor for so long that, in January 1968, it had to be amputated above the knee. He returned to the Sheraton-Russell with an artificial leg on which he could never learn to walk and spent his final months in a wheelchair, alone and immobilized much like the protagonist of his 1926 novel *Cover Charge*. But the best of his late stories still hold the magic touch that chills the heart, and his last two suspense tales are among his finest. "For the Rest of Her Life" (*Ellery Queen's Mystery Magazine*, May 1968) follows a young woman whose husband has turned out to be a sadistic abuser of women. She meets another man, confesses the truth, and together they try to escape. Every move they make throughout this excruciating story is precisely the wrong thing to do, and Woolrich keeps tightening the screws until we're screaming at them to change their course before it's too late. But each wrong move has also been foreordained in the womb of destiny, and Linda and Garry are the last of the doomed couples whose shattered remains fill the Woolrich world.

In the late Sixties Woolrich had plenty of money and his critical reputation was secure not only in America but in Europe, where François Truffaut had recently filmed both *The Bride Wore Black* and *Waltz into Darkness*, but his physical and emotional condition remained hopeless. He died of a stroke on September 25, 1968, leaving unfinished two novels (*Into the Night* and *Tonight, Somewhere in New York*, also known as *The Loser*), an autobiography (*Blues of a Lifetime*), a collection of short stories (*I Was Waiting for You*), and a long list of titles for stories he had never begun, one of which captures his bleak world in a single phrase: *First You Dream, Then You Die*. He left no survivors and only a handful of people attended his funeral. His estate was willed in trust to Columbia University for the establishment of a scholarship fund for students of creative writing. The fund is named for Woolrich's mother.

~ ~ ~ ~ ~

In Woolrich's crime fiction there is a gradual development from pulp to *noir*. The earlier a story, the more likely it stresses pulp elements: one-dimensional macho protagonists, preposterous methods of murder, hordes of cardboard gangsters, dialogue full of whiny insults, blistering fast action. But even in some of his earliest crime stories one finds aspects of *noir*, and over time the stream works itself pure.

In mature Woolrich the world is an incomprehensible place where beams happen to fall, and are predestined to fall, and are toppled over by malevolent powers; a world ruled by chance, fate and God the malign thug. But the everyday life he portrays is just as terrifying and treacherous. The dominant economic reality is the Depression, which for Woolrich usually means a frightened little guy in a rundown apartment with a hungry wife and children, no money, no job and desperation eating him like a cancer. The dominant political reality is a police force made up of a few decent cops and a horde of sociopaths licensed to torture and kill, whose outrages are casually accepted by all concerned, not least by the victims. The prevailing emotional states are loneliness and fear. Events take place in darkness, menace breathes out of every corner of the night, the bleak cityscape comes alive on the page and in our hearts.

Woolrich had a genius for creating types of story perfectly consonant with his world: the noir cop story, the clock race story, the waking nightmare, the oscillation thriller, the headlong through the night story, the annihilation story, the last hours story. These situations, and variations on them, and others like them, are paradigms of our position in the world as Woolrich sees it. His mastery of suspense, his genius (like that of his spiritual brother Alfred Hitchcock) for keeping us on the edge of our seats and gasping with fright, stems not only from the nightmarish situations he conjured up but from his prose, which is compulsively readable, cinematically vivid, highstrung almost to the point of hysteria, forcing us into the skins of the hunted and doomed where we live their agonies and die with them a thousand small deaths. In his finest work every detail serves this purpose, even the chapter headings. Chapter 1 of *Phantom Lady* is entitled "The Hundred and Fiftieth Day Before the Execution" so that even before Marcella Henderson is strangled the countdown to the day of her innocent husband's electrocution for the murder has begun. In *Deadline at Dawn* Woolrich replaces the customary chapter titles or numbers with clock faces so that like Quinn and Bricky we feel in our bones the coming of the dreaded sunrise.

But suspense presupposes uncertainty. No matter how nightmarish the situation, real suspense is impossible when we know in advance that the protagonist will prevail (as we would if Woolrich had used series characters) or will be destroyed. This is why, despite his congenital pessimism, Woolrich manages any number of times to squeeze out an upbeat resolution. Precisely because we can never know whether a particular novel or story will be light or dark, *allegre* or *noir*, his work remains hauntingly suspenseful.

The viewpoint character in each story is usually someone trapped in a living nightmare, but this doesn't guarantee that we and the protagonist are at one. In fact Woolrich often makes us pull away from the person at the center of the storm, splitting our reaction in two, stripping his protagonist of moral authority, denying us the luxury of unequivocal identification, drawing characters so psychologically warped and sometimes so despicable that a part of us wants to see them suffer. Woolrich also denies us the luxury of total disidentification with all sorts of sociopaths, especially those who wear badges. His Noir Cop tales are crammed with acts of police sadism, usually committed or at least endorsed by the detective protagonist. These monstrosities are explicitly condemned almost never and the moral outrage we feel has no internal support in the stories except the objective horror of what is shown, so that one might almost believe that a part of Woolrich wants us to enjoy the spectacles. If so, it's yet another instance of how his most powerful novels and stories are divided against themselves so as to evoke in us a divided response that mirrors his own self-division.

Even on the subject of love he tends to divide our reaction. Often of course he identifies unambiguously with whoever is lonely, whoever is in love, or needs love or has lost it. From the absence of love in his own life springs much of the poignancy with which he portrayed its power and joys and risks and pains and much of the piercing sadness with which he described its corrosion and loss. There's a haunting moment in *Phantom Lady* when the morgue attendants are carrying out the body of Scott Henderson's wife. "Hands riveted to him, holding him there. The outer door closed muffledly. A little sachet came drifting out of the empty bedroom, seeming to whisper: 'Remember? Remember when I was your love? Remember?' " On the other hand, several Woolrich classics are precisely about protagonists—Julie in *The Bride Wore Black*, Alberta in *The Black Angel*, Johnny Marr in *Rendezvous in Black*—who destroy their own lives and the lives of others in a mad quest to save a loved one from death or avenge one who has already died.

Woolrich does invariably unite himself and us with his people at one moment. In the face of the specter of Anahuac nothing matters anymore: saint or beast, sane or mad, if any person is on the brink of death Woolrich becomes that person and makes us do likewise. In "Three O'Clock" we sit bound and gagged and paralyzed with the morally warped Stapp while the bomb ticks closer and closer to the moment of destruction, and Woolrich punctuates the unbearable suspense with language and imagery clearly echoing the story of the crucifixion of Jesus, whose agony also ended (according to some traditions) at three o'clock. During the brief electrocution scene of "Three Kills for One", the cold steel hood falls over the head of the murderer Gates and he whispers: "Helen, I love you." No character named Helen ever appears in the story. At the point of death we are forgiven much, and if we love we are forgiven everything.

The intense, feverish, irrational nature of the Woolrich world is mirrored in his literary faults. His plots are full of outlandish contrivances, outrageous coincidences, "surprise" developments that require us to suspend not only our disbelief but our knowledge of elementary real-world facts, chains of so-called reasoning that a two-year-old could pull apart. But in his most powerful work these are not gaffes but functional elements that enable him to integrate contradiction and existential absurdity into his dark fabric. Long before the Theater of the Absurd, Woolrich discovered that an incomprehensible universe is best reflected in an incomprehensible story. The same holds true for his style, which is often undisciplined, hysterical, sprawling with phrases and clauses crying out to be cut and sentences without subjects or predicates or rhyme or reason and words that simply don't mean what Woolrich guesses they mean. But many (by no means all) of these features are functional in Woolrich's doom-shrouded world, just like many (by no means all) of his plot flubs. Without the sentences rushing out of control across the page like his hunted characters across the nightscape, without the manic emotionalism and indifference to grammatical niceties, the form and content of the Woolrich world would be at odds. Between his style and his substance Woolrich achieved the perfect union that he never came within a mile of in his private life.

"I was only trying to cheat death," he wrote in a fragment found among his papers. "I was only trying to surmount for a little while the darkness that all my life I surely knew was going to come rolling in on me some day and obliterate me. I was only trying to stay alive a little brief while longer, after I was already gone." Trapped in a wretched psychological environment and gifted or cursed with an understanding that being trapped is *par excellence* the human condition, he took his decades of solitude and shaped them into a haunting body of work. He tried to escape the spectre of Anahuac, and he couldn't, and he couldn't, and he couldn't. The world he imagined, will.

ELLERY QUEEN

We need to begin with a glossary. Throughout this chapter "Ellery" means the detective protagonist of the Ellery Queen novels and stories. "Queen" means the byline on each of Ellery's adventures in deduction and the joint pseudonym of the men who in their early twenties created both Ellery and Queen.

The first cousins who called themselves Frederic Dannay and Manfred B. Lee and called each other Manny and Danny were born in Brooklyn's Brownsville district, nine months and five blocks apart. Lee was born Manford Lepofsky on January 11, 1905, and Dannay was born Daniel Nathan on October 20 of the same year. The Nathans moved upstate to Elmira when Danny was a baby and he spent his childhood in a Mark Twainish rural environment where he roamed the woods and fields and concocted elaborate schemes like charging playmates two cents apiece to see the ghost of Long John Silver. His best friend during the Elmira years was named Ellery. The Lepofskys remained in Brooklyn but Manny would visit cousin Danny in Elmira every summer and the boys would spend their time playing games of oneupmanship with each other which in altered forms they continued to play during more than forty years of collaboration. In 1917 the Nathans moved back to Brooklyn and that winter, while 12-year-old Danny was in bed with an ear infection, one of his aunts loaned him a copy of Conan Doyle's *Adventures of Sherlock Holmes*. The book so fired the boy's imagination that the next morning he got a public library card and stripped the shelves of every Holmes book he saw.

During their teens the boys became best friends. "We were cousins," Dannay said more than sixty years later, "but we were closer than brothers." One of the interests that drew and kept them together was a common passion for detective fiction, and as early as 1920, while walking or riding the streetcar to and from Boys' High, they began, Dannay said, "to experiment with ideas, to play with the strings of plot." Manny Lee went on from high school to NYU but Prohibition put an end to Meyer Nathan's liquor business and forced his son to quit Boys' High after third year and go to work. In 1926 Dannay married the first of his three wives and two years later he was working as copywriter and art director for a New York advertising agency. Lee graduated from NYU in 1926, married for the first time in 1928, and found work in the Manhattan publicity department of the Pathé movie studio. The cousins' offices were only a few blocks apart and they met for lunch almost every day.

American detective fiction in the late 1920s was dominated by the best-selling Philo Vance novels, written by art critic Willard Huntington Wright (1888-1939) under the pseudonym of S.S. Van Dine, and over their lunches Dannay and Lee discussed the idea of collaborating on a detective novel of their own in the same manner, complete with hyperintellectual sleuth and reams of erudite deduction. The announcement of a $7500 prize contest, sponsored jointly by *McClure's Magazine* and the publisher Frederick A. Stokes, catalyzed them into serious action, and over the next several months they worked frantically on evenings, weekends and vacation time to complete a novel before the deadline. "I remember Manny Lee had to go to a wedding in Philadelphia during the time we were writing it," Fred Dannay said in 1979. "And I had to go with him, to the wedding of a complete stranger, just so we wouldn't lose the time it took to get there and back on the train." With their backgrounds in advertising and publicity they took great pains to give their protagonist a name that would be slightly unusual, easy to remember and rhythmic in sound, and after a few false starts they hit upon Ellery Queen. To comply with the contest rule that every entry be submitted under a pseudonym, the cousins made the brilliant decision to use Ellery Queen not only for their protagonist—who is himself a detective novelist, presumably under his own name—but also for their joint byline. Didn't I say we needed to begin with a glossary?

The early months of 1929 put the cousins on an emotional rollercoaster. The literary agency running the contest unofficially informed them that their submission had won, then a few days later told them that *McClure's* had gone bankrupt and its new owners had decided to award the prize to another entry. But Stokes liked their manuscript enough to make an offer for it anyway, though with a much smaller advance, and the result was the publication in August 1929 of *The Roman Hat Mystery*, under the byline of and starring Ellery Queen. In 1931, the pit of the Depression, after selling two more Queen books, Dannay and Lee gave up their day jobs and devoted full time to turning out a 90,000-word detective novel every three months for the next few years.

What was each cousin's function in the Queen partnership? Through most of their long collaboration Dannay and Lee were asked this question countless times and always replied enigmatically, drawing a veil of secrecy over their division of labor as a sort of advertising stunt to keep readers intrigued. The truth in capsule form: Dannay created the skeletons and Lee put flesh on the bones. Each Ellery Queen novel began with a plot synopsis of about 25,000 words in which Dannay would set forth the book's themes, plot, characters, clues and deductions. As soon as Lee finished absorbing that synopsis the fur would begin to fly between the cousins. After one heated argument over the phone, Lee's son Rand said, "Dad threw down a plot outline and exclaimed, 'He gives me the most ridiculous characters to work with and expects me to make them realistic!' " When the quarrels were settled, Lee would expand Dannay's synopsis into a novel of around 100,000 words and then the fighting would begin all over. "We are competitors and always have been," Dannay said. "We are always trying to out-top each other." And Lee once described a time when he and Dannay were working briefly as Hollywood screenwriters with an office directly under the studio's mimeograph department, whose duplicating machines clattered constantly. *"They* complained about the noise *we* were making!"

The cousins' first period runs from *The Roman Hat Mystery* (1929) through *The Spanish Cape Mystery* (1935) and encompasses nine novels as by and starring Ellery Queen, four more as by Barnaby Ross, and a number of short stories most of which were collected as *The Adventures of Ellery Queen* (1934)—a title deliberately echoing that first book of Sherlock Holmes tales which had so changed young Dannay's life. Although superior in plotting, characterization and style, the Queen novels of the first period were heavily influenced by the Van Dine blockbusters. The strict pattern of the titles, *The* Adjective-of-Nationality *Noun Mystery*, comes from Van Dine's pattern, *The* Six-Letter-Word *Murder Case*. Each running character in early Queen has a counterpart in Van Dine, with blockheaded Sergeant Velie for instance stemming from dumb Sergeant Heath in the Vance cases. Ellery's father, Inspector Richard Queen of the NYPD, calls on his brilliant son for help in abstruse crime puzzles much as District Attorney Markham called on that insufferable mandarin Philo Vance. Most important, it was from Van Dine that Dannay and Lee borrowed the concept of the detective as polysyllabic literatus, full of scholarly quotations, detached from people and the world, interested only in abstract problems, a Harvard-educated dilettante bibliophile who usually calls his father "pater" or "Inspector darling." Here is Ellery I as he walks on stage in *Roman Hat*: "There was a square cut to his shoulders and an agreeable swing to his body as he walked. He was dressed in oxford grey and carried a light stick. On his nose perched what seemed an incongruous note in so athletic a man—a pince-nez. But the brow above, the long delicate lines of the face, the bright eyes were those of a man of thought rather than action." In their twilight years the cousins came to hate this version of their character, whom Manny Lee derided as "the biggest prig that ever came down the pike." But those early novels are among the most richly plotted Golden Age deductive puzzles, bursting with bizarre circumstances, conflicting testimony, enigmatic clues (including that Queenian hallmark the dying message), alternative solutions, fireworks displays of virtuoso reasoning, and a constant crackle of intellectual excitement.

What makes Queen's novels stand out from the other detective fiction of the time was the cousins' insistence on playing fair. In Dannay's words, "the reader had to know everything that the detective knew, and therefore had an even chance of beating the detective before the solution was given . . ." And they did play the game with scrupulous fairness, not only presenting all the facts (albeit quite trickily on occasion) but stopping most of the novels at a certain point to issue a formal "Challenge to the Reader" to solve the puzzle ahead of Ellery. The odds of course were stacked in favor of the house, and when Dannay once boasted to an interviewer that Queen was always "completely fair to the reader," Lee cut in: "We are fair to the reader only if he is a genius."

Among the early Queen novels perhaps the finest is *The Greek Coffin Mystery* (1932). Blind art dealer Georg Khalkis dies of heart failure in the library of his West 54th Street brownstone. Three days later the coffin is taken to the church graveyard next door and lowered into the family crypt. When the burial party returns to the house, the attorney for the estate discovers that the steel box with Khalkis' will is missing from the wall safe. The police are summoned but after two days the box is still missing. At a conference called to discuss the case are Inspector Richard Queen and a young and cocksure Ellery, who deduces that the box must be in Khalkis' coffin. An exhumation order is obtained, the coffin is opened, and inside is not the will but the decaying corpse of a second man, strangled, lying atop Khalkis' body. Inspector Queen and his men soon unearth a cornucopia of counterplots inside the Khalkis household and an assortment of intrigues outside, many rooted in the theft of a Leonardo from a British museum. After about 130 pages Ellery proposes a devilishly ingenious solution based on the amount of tea water in a percolator and the color of a dead man's tie, but he soon learns that this version of events was prepared for him to find by "the player on the other side." This is the first of four solutions to the Khalkis case, each one radiating outward from those that went before and accounting for more of the total picture. The fourth and last explanation alone embraces the entire brain-boggling web of plot and counterplot (described by Ellery as "a complex plan which requires assiduous concentration for complete comprehension") and reveals, with total fairness to the superhumanly alert reader, a stunning surprise murderer. Although not flawless, *The Greek Coffin Mystery* is probably the most involuted, brain-crushing, meticulously constructed detective novel published in the United States during the genre's golden age.

The cousins next introduced a second joint byline, Barnaby Ross, and a new detective in the person of retired Shakespearean actor Drury Lane. Driven from the stage by total deafness, Lane has recreated an Elizabethan village community on his acreage above the Hudson, populating it with down-and-out theater people who earn their keep by sporting period costumes and Shakespearean names. But this power-driven tyrant wants more: "From obeying the jerk of the master's strings, I now have the impulse to pull the strings myself, in a greater authorship than created drama." In a mad oedipal rivalry with Shakespeare's shade, Lane turns to intervening in real-world stories and in a sense rewriting them.

The Tragedy of X (1932) opens with a biographical sketch of Lane and his letter to the NYPD offering the solution to an unsolved murder case. When his deductions prove right, Inspector Thumm and District Attorney Bruno visit and thank the old man and ask his help on a problem even more bewildering. We flash back to four days earlier and eavesdrop on a cocktail party thrown by sadistic and lecherous stockbroker Harley Longstreet to celebrate his engagement to a much younger woman and make his guests squirm. Among those invited are Longstreet's browbeaten partner, his former mistress, a man who's in love with the woman he wants as his next mistress, a former lover of his present fiancée, and a corrupt politician who blames the brokers for ruinous losses in the market. After cocktails Longstreet insists that everyone go along with him to a dinner party in new Jersey. When a sudden thunderstorm makes it impossible to get a taxi for the trip to the ferry, they all board a crosstown trolley. The packed streetcar is lurching west towards the ferry slip when Longstreet reaches into his pocket and suddenly falls into the aisle, his hand pricked and bleeding in a dozen places. Once on the scene, Inspector Thumm searches the dead man's pockets and finds a cork ball riddled with needles, each one coated at both ends with pure nicotine poison. But there are too many suspects with motive and opportunity and his investigation founders. When Thumm and Bruno have recounted these facts, Drury Lane announces that he believes he knows the murderer but, due in roughly equal parts to his analysis of the situation and his lust to exercise power, refuses to say more. The next evening there's a second murder, the victim thrown from the upper deck of a ferry and crushed to pulp as the boat pulls into the Weehawken slip. Later come a spectacular murder trial, a disturbing conversation aboard a New Jersey commuter train, a third murder committed within a few feet of Lane himself, and finally, during another train ride, the unmasking.

The Tragedy of X introduced into the cousins' repertoire two motifs that were to become hallmarks. One, which they borrowed from Conan Doyle's *The Valley of Fear* (1915) and recycled throughout the novels of their first period, can't be revealed here without ruining several of those novels for those not yet familiar with them. The other, on which Dannay and Lee played variations for the rest of their careers, is the dying message clue. During a night journey on the Weehawken local which one commuter will not live to complete, Drury Lane and others involved in the case have a conversation about the last moments before death which is as central to Queen as is the locked room lecture in *The Three Coffins* (1935) to the works of John Dickson Carr. "There are no limits to which the human mind cannot soar," Lane declares, "in this unique, godlike instant before the end of life." Not only does *The Tragedy of X* offer a superb plot-puzzle and the rationale for dozens of future dying message stories, it recreates vividly a vanished time when American cities and suburbs were linked by streetcars, ferries, electric interurban lines, commuter trains—by a mass transit system that worked, and in this novel lives again.

In *The Tragedy of Y* (1932) Drury Lane visits Washington Square to probe a series of bizarre and imbecilic crimes in the doom-haunted Hatter household which for the cousins seems to be a paradigm of American society, its members rotting with greed, sadism and inertia, consenting for the sake of expected inheritances to be dehumanized in love-hate relationships with each other and with the bitch goddess of wealth and property who rules the roost. The identity of the murderer—a stunning surprise in the early Thirties but far less so today—combines with the themes of Iagoesque manipulation and despair of human nature to make this one of the darkest detective novels ever written. Lane tackled his third puzzle in *The Tragedy of Z* (1933) and died at the end of his fourth, which is aptly titled *Drury Lane's Last Case* (1933).

Ellery Queen remained active as both pseudonym and sleuth during the Drury Lane years. In *The Egyptian Cross Mystery* (1932), which may be the bloodiest pure detective novel ever, Ellery and his father spend months on the trail of a multiple murderer who beheads and crucifies victims so as to turn them into embodiments of the letter T. As usual in Golden Age whodunits with a serial killer, the crimes are not random but connected. In *The American Gun Mystery* (1933) Ellery and Inspector Queen are among the twenty thousand spectators who have piled into the New York Colosseum for the opening night of a rodeo whose main attraction is the aging silent Western film star Buck Horne, a character clearly modeled on William S. Hart. While Horne is supposed to be leading forty wild-shooting riders in a chase around the arena, someone fires a shot not in the script and the aged horseman falls to the tanbark where he's trampled to death. *The Siamese Twin Mystery* (1933) leaves Ellery and his father and the members of the household of Dr. John Xavier trapped by a forest fire in a mountaintop mansion, so that when Xavier is found shot to death in his study with a game of solitaire laid out in front of him and the torn half of the six of spades clenched between his fingers, the Queens have to tackle the crime with no outside help. The climax deftly blends nobility and lunacy: the fire reaches the house, everyone left alive holes up in the cellar, and Ellery undertakes the absurd act of exposing the murderer while they're all waiting for a horrible death. *The Chinese Orange Mystery* (1934) begins when an excruciatingly ordinary man is shown into a waiting room in the office suite of wealthy young publisher and stamp collector Donald Kirk, who happens to be a friend of Ellery's. An hour later when Kirk and Ellery enter the waiting room, it's been transformed into something out of Lewis Carroll: the rug turned upside down, pictures and clock facing the walls, floor lamps standing on their shades. Lying on the overturned rug with his brains splattered and two African spears thrust up through his pants legs and under his jacket is Mr. Nobody from Nowhere, whose every article of clothing—collar, shirt, coat, trousers, shoes—is on him backwards. The opening situation is so outré it's a shame the plot turns out neither credible nor all that complex.

Among the short stories collected in *The Adventures of Ellery Queen* (1934) "The Glass-Domed Clock" and "The Bearded Lady" are notable for complex plotting and subtle dying-message clues. In "The Mad Tea Party", Dannay's favorite short tale from this period and another proof of his fondness for Lewis Carroll, Ellery is invited to a Long Island house party that is to feature a private performance of *Alice in Wonderland,* but festive spirits are dampened when the host vanishes the morning after Ellery arrives. Then comes the delivery of a series of packages containing pairs of shoes, cabbages, chessmen and other bizarre objects. The tale indeed owes much to Carroll but Ellery's psychological war against his adversary is inspired by Poe's "Thou Art the Man".

At the tail end of Queen's first period came "The Lamp of God", one of the finest of all detective novelets. A desperate phone call from an attorney friend takes Ellery to the raw January snowscape of Long Island. The patriarch of the maniacal Mayhew family is believed to have hidden a fortune in gold somewhere in the Poesque old mansion where he had lived and recently died, and attorney Thorne suspects that certain of the old tyrant's relatives are bent on finding and taking the treasure before it can be turned over to the old man's long-lost daughter. After a raw-nerved evening with an obese doctor, a demented old lady and an enigmatic young hired man, Ellery and the others go to bed but awaken to an event that convinces them the world has gone mad. The entire huge black house of old Sylvester Mayhew, next door to where they've been sleeping, has vanished in the night. This is one of the finest pieces of atmospheric writing in the genre, evoking chills that rise off the page into our bones. With imagery of light against darkness, sun against cold, reason against the absurd, Queen summons up the terror of a universe abandoned to the demonic, then exorcises it through the rigorous use of the instrument given us by "chance, cosmos, God, whatever you may choose to call it": the enlightening human mind.

By the mid-1930s Dannay and Lee were making excellent money not just from books but from two lucrative media which had begun to buy their work: the slick-paper magazines like *Redbook* and *Cosmopolitan* and the movies. The demands of these markets led the cousins to reconfigure their principal character into Ellery II. In second-period Queen (1936-40) the Van Dine patterned titles vanish and Ellery gradually trades in his intellectual priggishness for humanity. In Dannay's words: "We loosened the construction . . . ; we put more emphasis on character development and background; we put more emphasis on human-interest situations . . . We turned to commercialism because we frankly wanted to make more money." Compared with the classics of period one, much of the cousins' output of the late 1930s suffers from thin plots, overdoses of tedious boy-meets-girl byplay, and characters tailored to please story editors at the slick magazine suites and the studios. But in the longer view the exploits of Ellery II served at least in part to open up the deductive puzzle and make room within its cerebral rigor for more of the virtues of mainstream storytelling. In several short tales and in the novels *The Devil to Pay* and *The Four of Hearts* (both 1938) Ellery works as a Hollywood screenwriter, paralleling the cousins' brief stints at Columbia, Paramount and MGM. Hoping to make their character more appealing to the mass media, Dannay and Lee had Ellery become involved with lovely gossip columnist Paula Paris, a prose amalgam of the heroines from Hollywood's screwball comedies of the time. And perhaps screwball is the best one-word description of Queen's take on movieland. "The place was filled with crazy people," Dannay said in 1979. "I told Manny even if I had to dig ditches for the rest of my life, I wasn't coming back." *The New Adventures of Ellery Queen* (1940), which brought together all the short cases of Ellery II plus "The Lamp of God" and a few others from the early years, concluded this phase of the saga.

By 1940 Fred and Mary Dannay and their sons were living the suburban life in Great Neck, Long Island and Fred was close to reaching his goal as a book collector: owning a copy of every volume of detective-crime short stories ever published. Manny Lee, divorced from his first wife, was sharing a Park Avenue apartment with his daughters. The cousins put in 12-hour workdays at their respective homes and met once a week at a rented office to consolidate their material. Both men were chain smokers and their workplace atmosphere tended to be on the thick side. On the office floor they kept a tattered brown envelope labeled IDEAS.

And at that time they needed every idea they could conjure up. Since June of 1939, when *The Adventures of Ellery Queen* series had debuted on the CBS radio network, they had had to turn out a 60-minute script every week. Among the most complex of the early audio adventures is "The Last Man Club" (June 25, 1939), in which Ellery (Hugh Marlowe) and his secretary and love interest Nikki Porter (Marian Shockley), a new character created by the cousins to attract female listeners, witness a hit-and-run and are propelled by the victim's dying words into the affairs of a survivor-take-all group to which the dead man belonged—the first but far from the last death-plagued tontine in the Queen canon. Some of the best Queen radio plays were collected in *The Adventure of the Murdered Moths* (2005).

Radio work gave Dannay and Lee a steady income but left them no time for any other writing. In September 1940 the show left the air, and the next fifteen months were among the most fruitful in the cousins' lives. Dannay, the historian and bibliophile of the duo, used his library of detective-crime short story collections as the basis for editing *101 Years' Entertainment* (1941), the definitive anthology of short mystery fiction between Poe and Pearl Harbor. When he found countless first-rate tales for which that mammoth volume had no room, he persuaded publisher Lawrence E. Spivak to launch *Ellery Queen's Mystery Magazine (EQMM)*, the genre's premier periodical, which Dannay actively edited from its first issue (Fall 1941) until shortly before his death more than forty years later. It was also during these fifteen months that the cousins commenced their third and richest period as writers. Ellery III is no longer a detached Philo Vance clone but a human being sCarréd by the horrors he encounters, and the Queen novels are no longer problems in deduction but much closer to mainstream fiction.

Calamity Town (1942) opens on the afternoon of August 6, 1940, when Ellery steps off the train and into Wrightsville, a small tight-knit vividly portrayed community that with the outbreak of war in Europe has become a boomtown. He needs a place to stay while writing his next novel but no hotel rooms or furnished houses are available except for one which has developed a reputation as a jinx. John F. and Hermione Wright had built a house next to their own as a wedding present for their daughter Nora and her fiancé Jim Haight, but Jim had disappeared the day before the wedding and later a prospective purchaser had died of a heart attack in the house. Ellery rents the place and quickly bonds with the entire Wright family, especially with youngest daughter Pat, whose steady is the county prosecutor. Then Jim Haight returns to town, reconciles with and marries Nora. The newlyweds move into the house built for them three years before and day by day over months the marriage goes sour and the atmosphere thickens with hints that Jim is planning to kill his wife. At the Wrights' New Year's Eve party one of the drinks raised to toast the beginning of 1941 turns out to be poisoned, and Wrightsville's first homicide in years tears apart both the family and the town. The investigation, public reactions, a sensational trial and what happens afterward are not just pieces of a puzzle (though a neat plot is hidden among them) but nightmares happening to people one cares about, with Ellery no longer the controlling mind but a man in a muddle, powerless to affect events and contributing nothing until the final chapter.

Calamity Town, Dannay said, was "the best book that we thought we had written up to that time." But no national magazine made the offer for serialization rights that the cousins had expected and no editor could explain why not. "We'd better find another basket for our eggs," Dannay told Lee. "If you can be turned down with no reason apparent on the best book you've ever written . . . then you've got to do something else." The obvious contender for "something else" was radio, and the cousins' agent soon found a new network and sponsor for the continuing audio exploits of Ellery Queen. In January 1942 the series returned to the air and Dannay and Lee to the old grind of a script a week, although several of the "new" adventures were tighter rewrites of 60-minute dramas from the program's first months. Manny Lee happened to visit the NBC studio during a rehearsal on April 1 and met actress Kaye Brinker, who was featured in the week's story. They began dating at once, were married on July 4, and stayed together until Lee's death almost 29 years later. Except for summer rerun cycles and several hiatus periods the series was heard weekly on one network or another until the spring of 1948. "A new plot every week knocked me out," Dannay said. Even after mid-1945 when his function of providing a weekly plot outline was taken over by others, notably Anthony Boucher, the demands of *EQMM* left him little time for Ellery Queen novels.

The cousins had taken such care and pains over the creation of Wrightsville that it's no wonder they had Ellery go back in *The Murderer Is a Fox* (1945). In the summer of 1944 a nerve-shattered war hero returns home after receiving some anonymous letters intimating that his wife was unfaithful during his service as a fighter pilot in Asia. Twelve years earlier Captain Davy Fox's mother had been murdered and his father sentenced to life imprisonment for the crime, and the boy's adolescence had been a nightmare of failed attempts to escape the stigma and the fear of his own "tainted blood." As Davy wrestles with a growing compulsion to kill his wife, she goes for help to Ellery, who concludes that the only way to release Davy from the trap in which the past holds him is to reopen the old case and try to prove that his father did not kill his mother. Ellery's meticulous reconstruction of exactly what happened in the house of Bayard and Jessica Fox on June 14, 1932 is carried out with the intellectual tools of the historian and generates the sort of excitement that every conscientious historian feels while on the hunt for the truth of the past. Like many Queen novels to come, this one ends with a false or partial solution followed by a second solution that is both final and shattering.

"In the beginning it was without form, a darkness that kept shifting like dancers." With that echo from Genesis I:2 we return yet again to Wrightsville in *Ten Days' Wonder* (1948). Howard Van Horn, sculptor son of a multimillionaire, comes in desperation to Ellery after a series of amnesic blackouts that began on the night of his father Diedrich's marriage to the beautiful Sally whom Diedrich had raised from childhood. Psychiatrists have failed to free Howard from his obsessive fear that he has done or will do something horrible during a blackout. Ellery agrees to stay at the Van Horn mansion in Wrightsville and watch over this tormented young man but before long he finds himself drawn into the hopeless trap in which Howard and Sally are caught. He reluctantly agrees to act as their go-between with an anonymous blackmailer and comes close to being jailed for grand theft. A missing necklace, a midnight chase through a storm-tossed graveyard and a night-prowling religious fanatic combine with less theatrical elements to sustain the sense of menace among a cast of (excluding Ellery himself) only four central characters. In the final quarter of the novel there is a murder, followed by Ellery's virtuoso reconstruction of the crime, capped by an even more thunderous solution, revealed by Ellery to no one but the murderer, who will remind some of Drury Lane, others of Iago, and a great many of the biblical God. Beneath the mind-boggling plot which Dannay spent years working out, *Ten Days' Wonder* is an audacious, ambitious attempt to recreate the cosmic drama of Western culture since the Enlightenment: the penetration through the facade of infinite knowledge and love to the sadistic beast beneath, the demand of reason and decency for God's death.

At the start of the next and perhaps finest Queen novel, *Cat of Many Tails* (1949), Ellery has renounced his habit of intervening in others' lives. "Just let me be . . . I've given all that up. I'm not interested any longer." Racked with guilt over his responsibility for others' deaths and perhaps over his deicide victory in the Van Horn tragedy, he has detached himself. It's a scorching Manhattan summer a few years after the end of World War II, and the reminders of Hiroshima, the Nazi death camps, the Cold War, the division of Vienna, the first Arab-Israeli conflict, the anti-Communist witch hunts and the threat of nuclear annihilation generate an atmosphere thick with impending holocaust. But the world and national news headlines are dwarfed by local headlines that convey the same message of mortality. A serial killer is loose in the city. Six people strangled in less than three months, each victim totally different from fellow victims in ethnic roots, economic worth, social position, neighborhood of residence and every other way. The faceless bachelor from the Gramercy Park district, the aging prostitute living above Times Square, the struggling shoe salesman from Chelsea, the madcap heiress who loved the subways, the bitter paralytic of East 102nd Street, the black girl from Harlem and the later victims of the Cat share only the cord of Indian tussah silk knotted about each one's neck. The bait of involvement is dangled before Ellery again with all its pain and risk and once again he snaps at it, immersing himself in the Cat hunt until like his father and the police commissioner and the mayor and everyone else he's ready to drop in his tracks from the exhaustion and frustration of strategy conferences, press releases, radio addresses, coordination among agencies, liaison with psychiatrists, confrontations with neighborhood self-defense committees, endless reviewing of files and plodding up blind alleys until, suddenly and beyond human expectation, the obvious yet subtle link connecting all the victims and making sense of the carnage leaps into sight. Once again the apparent solution is topped by another and once again Ellery is left shattered.

In key scenes at the beginning, middle and end of this powerful novel, Ellery receives instruction from a father figure: first from Inspector Queen who spurs him to involve himself again, then in a dream from the titan Prometheus who in Greek mythology was the father of civilization, finally from the Viennese psychiatrist Dr. Seligmann, the "grandfather of the tribe," who has seen all the terrors in the world and the human heart. "I do not read newspapers since the war begins. I, I do not like to suffer. . . . For me there is today this room, tomorrow cremation, unless the authorities cannot agree to allow it, in which case they may stuff me and place me in the clock tower of the *Rathaus* and I shall keep reminding them of the time." Queen in *Cat of Many Tails* shows a fastidious contempt for humanity in the abstract but infuses life into countless individual people including the Cat's victims, who are never seen alive but are resurrected, as it were, in the words of others. From the interweaving of victims and survivors and bystanders and investigators, from the vivid pictures of where and how each one lives and what he or she thinks and hopes and fears, there emerges a portrait of the city as a living character itself. Queen encompasses countless aspects of urban life from the racial turmoil to the struggle against the heat, from the chaos of a full-scale riot to the simple delights of radio programs like *The Shadow* and *Stella Dallas*. It's the most abundant book in the canon, offering permanent testimony to the potential of mystery fiction.

No Queen novel of the 1950s quite equals these two masterpieces but many are worth exploring. In *The Origin of Evil* (1951) Ellery returns to Hollywood, no longer the goofy madhouse of the Thirties but a grim place whose movie industry is under siege from television. His attempt to finish a novel is frustrated when 19-year-old

Laurel Hill knocks on his door with the claim that her wealthy foster father was literally frightened to death two weeks earlier upon finding a dead dog on his doorstep. Roger Priam, the dead man's partner in the jewelry business, has also been sent some strange objects, and Priam's lush exotic wife quickly entangles Ellery in a household that includes an enigmatic secretary, a wandering philatelist and a young man who lives in a treehouse. As Ellery probes more deeply into the Hill and Priam households, the bizarre objects—a mess of dead frogs, an empty wallet, a portfolio of worthless stock certificates—keep popping up. Eventually he discerns the pattern and his solution, followed as usual by a second even more breathtaking, ties plot and theme into an organic whole. The leitmotif of the book is Darwinian biology and the answer to the implied question in its title is Humankind. "People mean trouble . . . There's too much trouble in this world."

As an editor Dannay had long believed that a mystery anthology should be held together by a central concept or theme, and he and Lee extended this tenet to their third collection of Ellery Queen short stories. Each of the twelve tales in *Calendar of Crime* (1952) had begun life as a script for the Queen radio series which Manny Lee later rewrote in prose form for publication in *EQMM,* and each adventure centers on an event associated with a particular month of the year, from New Year's Day through Washington's Birthday and Memorial Day and Hallowe'en to (of course) Thanksgiving and Christmas. The finest of the dozen are "The Inner Circle," in which Ellery investigates the deaths of several members of a survivor-take-all tontine among the 1913 graduating class of Eastern University, and "The Dauphin's Doll", an impossible-crime puzzle with Ellery trying to protect a 49-carat diamond crown from a master thief who's boasted that he'll steal it while it's on display at a department store on the day before Christmas.

Those tales, stemming as they do from radio plays of the middle Forties, are rather light and amusing in tone. That the Queen novels from the late Forties and early Fifties are so much darker stems largely from events in the life of Fred Dannay. His first wife had died of cancer in 1945. Two years later he married again and bought a colonial house in Larchmont, a suburb forty minutes by train from Manhattan, and in 1948 Hilda Dannay gave birth to their first and only child. "[Stephen] was born prematurely at seven months and weighing less than two pounds. He was the miracle baby of Doctors Hospital in New York City. We didn't realize for about a year that he—that the boy had had brain damage at birth . . . so severe that the child, who had an absolutely angelic face, never walked and never talked... I was aware long before my wife that one of these days the tragedy would be capped by the death of that child. Actually he lived till he was six years old." It is to the short unhappy life of Stephen Dannay that we owe the pervasive birth-death themes in several Queen novels beginning with *Cat of Many Tails*, which grew out of an anecdote told to Fred by one of the infant's doctors over dinner in the hospital cafeteria. And in a sense it's Stephen who inspired the only novel Dannay wrote without a collaborator.

The Golden Summer (1953), published under his birth name Daniel Nathan, was written as a kind of therapy against his son's impending death, a nostalgic reenactment of his own vanished childhood and an exorcism of his anguished middle life. The scene is Elmira in the summer of 1915 and the storyline deals with the business adventures of 10-year-old Danny Nathan, a skinny bespectacled physical weakling who's shrewd and nimble-witted enough to talk himself out of any spot and to manipulate his playmates out of their loose change. He displays the ghost of Long John Silver for a two-cent admission fee, raffles off a damaged copy of the latest Sherlock Holmes novel, and even adds a dime to his hoard through a splendiferous one-upmanship contest with his city cousin "Telford." *The Golden Summer* is at root a book-length *double entendre*: the season of innocent security and peace, the season when Danny tricked his contemporaries out of $4.73. Fred's brutally honest self-portrait provides the key to countless features of the Ellery Queen world, including the image of Ellery I as the weak-eyed young genius who dominates his environment by the force of his mind and perhaps the Iagoesque quality of so many of the murderers exposed by Ellery in all his incarnations.

The Glass Village (1954) is doubly unusual: one of only two Queen novels without Ellery and the other familiar series characters, and the only Queen book set in the midst of the cultural terror that marked the years of Joe McCarthy and HUAC and the blacklist. In the withered New England hamlet of Shinn Corners live exactly 36 people, most of them embittered puritanical bigots. Judge Lewis Shinn is spending a week at his vacation home in the village where he was born, bonding with his nephew Johnny, a war veteran who had witnessed Hiroshima and was sexually mutilated in Korea and calls himself "a vegetable" and "the missing link between the flora and the fauna." What precipitates Johnny's slow journey back to the human race is the bludgeoning to death of 91-year-old artist Fanny Adams in her studio one rainy afternoon. A foreign-looking tramp who had passed through the village shortly before the murder is instantly tagged as the perpetrator, hunted down, beaten and almost lynched by the outraged citizens of Shinn Corners, who refuse to turn over their prey to the state police and insist on trying him themselves. To avert a gun battle Judge Shinn agrees to preside at that trial, a proceeding aswarm with legal gaffes, designed to placate the townspeople for now and be reversed by an appellate court later. Among the jurors is Johnny Shinn. Ten of the other jurors admit under oath that they're already certain the tramp is guilty. The bailiff, the court reporter, most of the jurors and even the judge testify for the prosecution. Judge Shinn takes over as prosecutor while the prosecutor testifies against the defendant. Defense counsel fails to object to gross violations of his client's rights but fights loudly over the admissibility of trivia. The judge bangs the darning egg he's using as a gavel and hands down legal rulings he knows are dead wrong. This study in due process on the other side of the rabbit hole is also one of the finest Queen novels of the Fifties, replete with bizarre clues and inspired misdirection and even a sort of dying message, and with dark overtones like Johnny's reflection that "man was a chaos without rhyme or reason; that he blundered about like a maddened animal in the delicate balance of the world, smashing and disrupting, eager only for his own destruction."

In *Q.B.I.: Queen's Bureau of Investigation* (1955) the cousins brought together most of the Ellery Queen short-short stories (several based on scripts from the Queen radio series) which had been published regularly in *This Week* since 1949 and reprinted just as regularly in *EQMM*. Among the best tales in the collection are "My Queer Dean!", in which an academic's linguistic spoonerisms help Ellery solve the theft of $10,000 from a university administration building, and "Snowball in July," where an entire train apparently vanishes one summer morning on a straight stretch of track between two upstate New York whistlestops six minutes apart.

Queen's third period ended with *The Finishing Stroke* (1958), in which the cousins nostalgically recreated Ellery's young manhood and their own. It's December 1929, shortly after publication of the author-detective's first novel (titled, of course, *The Roman Hat Mystery)*, and Ellery is one of the guests invited to a 12-day house party at the estate of his publisher's former partner. The holiday mood begins to dissolve when a costumed Santa distributes gifts and then vanishes. Next some bizarre objects start popping up—a sandalwood ox, a toy house, a tiny lead camel—each accompanied by a piece of doggerel derived from "The Twelve Days of Christmas". Then an unidentified body is discovered in the library, more weird gifts turn up, blackmail and a love quadrangle and a second murder enter the picture, and young Ellery can shed no light until chance again throws the case in his path 28 years later. The characters in *The Finishing Stroke* are little more than line drawings, the prose is simple and unadorned, the plot elements deadeningly overfamiliar—the snowbound house-party, the thirteenth guest, murder with an antique dagger in the lordly mansion's library, a seance, identical twins, mysterious clues dropped by an unseen hand—and the signals are clear all through this reduction of the mystery genre to its bare fundamentals that after completing their elegy to "the lovely past" Dannay and Lee would write no more.

And for the next several years they didn't. Manny Lee, who had moved his family to a 63-acre farm in Roxbury, Connecticut, became active in civic affairs, served a term as Justice of the Peace and beat his playwright neighbor Arthur Miller in an election for a seat on the library board. Fred Dannay sold his huge collection of detective story volumes to the University of Texas and spent two semesters on campus as a professor of creative writing.

If Dannay wanted to work on more Ellery Queen books he was stymied by the fact that Lee was suffering from a prolonged case of writer's block and could no longer do his share of the collaborations. In 1960 the cousins' literary agent came up with a scheme to expand Queen's readership beyond the slowly fading genre of pure detective fiction and into the booming field of original softcover crime novels without detection. Contingent on Dannay's and Lee's approval, the Scott Meredith literary agency arranged for a cycle of non-series paperback suspensers, to be ghost-written by other Meredith clients for a flat fee of around $2,000 per book and published as by Ellery Queen, with royalties to be split by Dannay and Lee after the agency took its commission. Lee, who had eight children to support and was still plagued by writer's block, favored the proposal. Dannay was violently against it but felt that his cousin's financial and creative problems left him little choice but to go along. The manuscripts written by the various ghosts were submitted to Manny, who edited and sometimes heavily revised them as Fred edited and sometimes heavily revised the stories he bought for *EQMM*. But Dannay refused to read any of the books published under this scheme and terminated the arrangement soon after his cousin's death.

Five years after publication of *The Finishing Stroke*, the Meredith agency signed other writers, with no credits in the mystery field but high reputations in science fiction, to assume Lee's function and turn

Dannay's complex synopses into new hardcover exploits of Ellery Queen. The Queen novels of this fourth and final period are marked by a zest for experiment within the strict deductive tradition and by a retreat from all semblance of plausibility into what Dannay liked to call "fun and games," i.e. a potpourri of stylized plots and characters and dozens of motifs lifted from earlier Queen material.

First and finest of the fourth-period novels was *The Player on the Other Side* (1963), written by Theodore Sturgeon from Dannay's lengthy outline. The setting is York Square, in Manhattan but surely not of it, an isolated pocket of the past at each corner of which stands a castle inhabited by one of four cousins, with a diamond-shaped park in the square's center. The unifying image of course is chess: York Square is the board, each dwelling in the position of a rook, or castle, at the start of a game. The cousins are required to live in these castles by the terms of Nathaniel York Senior's will, which leaves them his millions in equal shares after ten years of residence, with the share of any cousin who dies during the decade to be split among the survivors—our old friend the tontine redux. This time however we know the murderer from the outset. The person who's sending a paper polygon stamped with a cryptic initial to each York in turn before killing them is Walt, the weak-brained and zombie-like handyman who serves a caretaker for all four cousins. But Walt is a simple soldier following orders, carrying out the detailed written instructions of someone signing himself Y, who is using Walt the way Iago used Othello, as a living murder weapon. In *Cat of Many Tails* Inspector Queen had prodded Ellery out of guilt-haunted detachment by dangling the bait of involvement with the real world, but in *Player* he goads his son out of the real world onto the chessboard of York Square. As the murders continue, as Ellery several times comes achingly close to the part of the truth we have known from the beginning, as possibilities multiply and secrets are bared, the pattern of the web slowly becomes clearer until at least Ellery encounters the player on the other side—who is revealed to be not just a human being but symbolically the primal Y, YHWH, God. Whose death, as in *Ten Days' Wonder*, is witnessed by Ellery at the climax.

The next Queen novel, probably the most controversial book in the canon, was written from Dannay's outline by Avram Davidson. *And On the Eighth Day* (1964) is set in the war-ravaged spring of 1944. Ellery gets lost driving across the Western desert, chances upon a religious-socialist community in the wilderness, and soon discovers that his coming had been foretold by the community's sacred book. All property in the valley of Quenan is held in common, no act of violence has been committed for generations, the word war is not in the lexicon, no one is alienated from the work he or she performs, the earth and humankind are in natural harmony—clearly this is Eden before the fall. Ellery's coming marks the beginning of a time of troubles foretold in the sacred book, and on the third night of his visit there is a murder. The plot doesn't and under the circumstances can't be expected to generate much intellectual excitement, but Queen structures his religious and historical analogies so as to create a sense of "the recurrence of the great and the famous across the shifting planes of space-time" and to generate an intuition of the presence of something that the human mind can never fathom. "It is too much . . . it's more than reason can bear. Too much, an infinite complexity beyond the grasp of man. Acknowledge. Acknowledge and depart."

After a few more books with Avram Davidson performing the Manny Lee function, Lee overcame his writer's block and collaborated with Dannay on such late Ellery Queen novels as the excellent *Face to Face* (1967) and the well-meaning but awkward *The Last Woman in His Life* (1970). Most of Ellery's as yet uncollected short cases were assembled in *Q.E.D.: Queen's Experiments in Detection* (1968). The book's last and finest tale is "Abraham Lincoln's Clue," which brings together bibliomania, philately, history and the art of the riddle as Ellery tries to locate a lost first printing of Poe's "The Purloined Letter" autographed by both the author and our sixteenth president.

In the late 1960s Manny Lee suffered several heart attacks and, on doctor's orders, lost a great deal of weight. It didn't save him. On April 2, 1971, the 65-year-old Lee had another attack and died on the way to the Waterbury hospital. He never saw a copy of the last Ellery Queen novel. In *A Fine and Private Place* (1971) Ellery investigates a series of bizarre crimes in the household of the squat and bestial tycoon Nino Importuna, who was born on September 9, 1899 and lives in a 9-story building at 99 East 99th Street and in countless ways is obsessed with the number 9. The orgy of variations on this theme—including links between the conception and development of the murderer's Byzantine scheme and the conception and development of a baby—is almost enough to make one overlook the unlikeliness of the plot.

At first Dannay planned to continue the series, either alone or with a new partner, but in 1972 his second wife died of cancer like his first 27 years before, and with her death he began dying by inches. The only thing that kept him functioning was the inexorable work schedule that *EQMM* and the anthologies he continued to edit demanded of him. He abandoned all thought of writing more Ellery Queen novels, saying it would be disloyal to Manny's memory. Photographs of him taken in 1973 show the empty, devastated face of a man waiting for the dark to claim him.

In November 1975 he married for the third time, and it is not too much to say that Rose Koppel Dannay saved Fred's life. He had always been such a private person that after almost thirty years many of his closest Larchmont neighbors had no idea what he did for a living. Rose made it possible for him to enjoy the role of the genre's elder statesman that time and the deaths of his peers like Carr, Christie and Stout had bestowed on him.

In his eighth decade Dannay received more media exposure than in all his previous life. First came the 60-minute TV series (NBC, 1975-76) starring Jim Hutton and David Wayne as Ellery and Inspector Queen. This was followed by guest lectures at the University of California, two appearances on the Dick Cavett show, superstar treatment at the 1978 International Crime Writers Congress, interviews with *Playboy* and *People* magazine and countless other periodicals, a testimonial dinner celebrating the 50th anniversary of *The Roman Hat Mystery*, an invitation to Tokyo for the premiere of a Japanese movie based on *Calamity Town*—it was a miracle he got any work done at all. But after he turned 75 failing health forced him to curtail more and more activities. He was hospitalized three times and, over the Labor Day weekend of 1982, his heart stopped.

His death meant more than the end of a great tradition in detective fiction. Both separately and together, Frederic Dannay and Manfred B. Lee contributed so abundantly to so many different aspects of the genre—novels, novelets, short stories, radio dramas, anthologies, magazines, bibliographic and scholarly studies—that Anthony Boucher, the founding father of intelligent and informed commentary on the field, needed just one short sentence to sum up their accomplishments: "Ellery Queen *is* the American detective story."

ANTHONY BOUCHER

An Anthony Boucher walks the earth but once. He treated every day of his adult life as the bountiful universe's invitation to create, to enjoy and help others enjoy creations, to care. Whatever he touched he made come alive with his informed love. He excelled at all he did, and what he did best no one will ever do better.

He was a native Californian, born in Oakland on August 21, 1911 with the rather ordinary name of William Anthony Parker White. Both his parents were doctors but his father died seven months after the boy was born and his grandfather, a lawyer and Civil War veteran, helped William's mother raise him. "His grandfather... meant a lot to him," Boucher's widow said a few years before her own death. "He had come to America from Scotland, where he had been an iron worker in Glasgow. I think there was an arrangement for men to get free passage if they would fight in the Civil War. I doubt he could have afforded it otherwise. I gathered he was something of a rake. Quite an old rogue. My husband enjoyed that in people."

Asthma and other ills kept William bedridden for half his childhood and made him a voracious reader and writer even in youth. Despite missing school so often, he was a bright and precocious boy—so gifted in fact that Stanford University researchers included him in a special group of California children whose future careers were to be studied for clues to the origins of genius.

Early vocational aptitude testing indicated that he should become an architect, and his first intellectual interests were scientific in nature, but in his mid-teens he turned decisively to language and literature. At age 15 he made his first fiction sale, a short spoof he called "Ye Goode Olde Ghoste Storie" (*Weird Tales*, January 1927) and later described as "so abominably written . . . that the editor who bought it must have had a sadistic grudge against his readers." His health improved in high school and college so that he was able not only to keep up with his studies but to immerse himself in dramatics and journalism, to go regularly to plays and concerts and movies, to start collecting stamps, coins and phonograph records, and to write—stories, plays, book reviews, translations, poetry in Spanish and German. He graduated from Pasadena High in 1928 and from the

University of Southern California in 1932, taking with him from USC a Bachelor of Arts degree, a Phi Beta Kappa key and a fellowship to the University of California at Berkeley. While studying there for his M.A. he met Phyllis Mary Price (1915-2000), who was in her first year of college and a few years later was to become his wife.

"I met my husband at a student party at my parents' house," Phyllis White recalled. "My father was Lawrence Marsden Price, of the University of California German Department, and my parents often entertained students. I remember the first time he came to our house he addressed just one remark to me. He asked whether I knew what became of the cookies. After he had been to a couple of parties at my parents' house, he invited us all to dinner at an apartment he had near the campus with his mother. At the end of the dinner he made a date with me to go to the theater with him.

"His mother was an unusual woman because in her time there weren't so many woman doctors. And what was also pretty unusual for her time, she smoked and drank too. She was about average height with white hair and blue eyes. She was very intelligent and very opinionated. We used to have lively discussions. She was a Republican and we were Democrats. The fact that we were to her left made us personally responsible for everything the Communists did.

"My first date with my future husband was the first date I ever had. I never dated in high school. One of the things we talked about was how much we liked the old theater stock companies. That was a great institution but it had died by the time we met. There was at that time an attempt to revive it in Oakland and we went to check it out." The play they saw, at the old Fulton Theater, was called *Gambling, Gambling!* "It was a bit disappointing. It wasn't like the real old-time stock companies at all."

William Anthony Parker White was one of those brilliant students who never needed to study. Despite a courseload in German, Spanish, Portuguese, Russian and Sanskrit, he spent most of his time writing, acting and directing in the little theater movement, and continued to attend as many plays, movies, concerts and football games as he could squeeze in. He had concentrated heavily on language courses with the original aim of becoming a teacher but decided early in his two-year stint at graduate school that academia was not for him. "One reason," said Phyllis White, "was that he felt he didn't have the patience to make it as a teacher. Another thing that bothered him was that he was surrounded by people who took no interest in contemporary popular literature but at the same time were trying to research the popular literature of a few centuries back." Rejecting the professorial life, he resolved instead to become a writer. In 1934, after completing his Master of Arts thesis ("The Duality of Impressionism in the Recent German Drama") and receiving his graduate degree, he returned to Los Angeles in the hope of launching a literary career. Discovering that the Library of Congress catalogues already listed 75 authors named William White, he adopted the byline of Anthony Boucher (his own second name plus the maiden name of his maternal grandmother, which rhymes with voucher) and wrote stories and poems and plays and translations with concentrated fury. And sold not a word.

His only published work during this period was the theater and music criticism he wrote for a political weekly, the Los Angeles *United Progressive News*, beginning in 1935. He was paid in the form of free tickets to plays and concerts, no cash. As for the quality of his unpublished stories and dramas of those years, he said in 1952, "when in morbid moments I now go back and reread them, I'm ashamed of my exceedingly slow development as a writer ... I, a dull and muddy-mettled rascal, went on well into my middle twenties producing stuff for which unprofessional is the kindest epithet."

In 1936 he tried his hand at a classical detective novel, because of the discipline a strict form would impose on him and out of admiration for puzzlemasters like John Dickson Carr, Agatha Christie and Ellery Queen. The manuscript was sent out to eight publishers and rejected by each. Then one day early in 1937 Lee Wright, mystery editor at Simon & Schuster, picked that submission at random out of the slush pile and took it home to read. At two the next morning she woke up her husband with the excited cry that she'd just found the first unsolicited manuscript she ever wanted to publish.

The Case of the Seven of Calvary (1937) is set on the Berkeley campus and features as amateur detectives the erudite professor of Sanskrit Dr. Ashwin and his eager young graduate student Martin Lamb, who's a transparent stand-in for Boucher himself. The model for Ashwin was Professor Arthur William Ryder (1877-1938), who had taught Boucher Sanskrit at Berkeley. "I never met Dr. Ryder," Phyllis White recalled, "but I used to hear a lot about him. Tony was studying with him when we met. A pleasant habit of Dr. Ryder was to invite my husband over for an evening of talk occasionally, and he would have on hand a bottle of Scotch. At the end of the evening he would present him with what was left to take away with him." No wonder Boucher felt inclined to say thanks by making his mentor the model for the detective character in his first novel. *Ashwin* is a Sanskrit word meaning a rider. The plot of *The Case of the Seven of Cal-*

vary hinges on a fairly obvious alibi gimmick but Lee Wright's excitement over the manuscript was well justified. No other mystery so lovingly evokes the academic atmosphere and the joys of learning and thinking as this whodunit debut.

In May of 1938 and on the strength of first success Boucher married Phyllis Price, who meanwhile had graduated from the University of California's Library School. "He was a Catholic so the wedding was at Newman Hall. That was the old Newman Hall, which has been torn down for parking." The newlyweds moved to Los Angeles, where Phyllis worked as a librarian until the birth of their first child. While hoping for a screenwriter's contract at a movie studio, Boucher wrote and sold six more detective novels. Four of these deal with amateur of crime Fergus O'Breen, a sort of Southern California Ellery Queen with brogue, and/or his LAPD counterpart, Lieutenant Jackson. The other pair, published under the byline of H.H. Holmes (the real-life pseudonym of 19th-century mass murderer Herman W. Mudgett), star Sister Ursula of the Order of Martha of Bethany, a nun variant on G.K. Chesterton's immortal Father Brown. All of Boucher's seven novels hold up well today as specimens of the grand deductive tradition, full of locked-room puzzles and bizarre clues and intellectual fireworks, enlivened by the author's love of language and literature and theater and opera and Sherlock Holmes and science fiction and bawdy humor and the tolerant, socially concerned wing of the Catholic church. Like his idols Doyle and Chesterton and Carr and Queen, Boucher infused the classical detective form with his own multifarious enthusiasms, and enriched the genre in the process.

His career as a novelist ended when he found work at which he was even better, writing about the novels of others. In early 1942 the family moved back to Berkeley, which was to be Boucher's home base for the rest of his life. "Larry, our first son, was with us," Phyllis White said, "and we were soon joined by his brother James [Marsden White]. For the first five years we lived in a rented house on Ellsworth Street. Then we moved to our own house on Dana Street and we never moved again. Berkeley suited my husband just fine as a place to live. He liked being near the University, where he could use the library and attend the sporting events and the concerts. He particularly liked being near San Francisco."

Between October 1942 and the summer of 1947 Boucher spent much of his time writing articles and reviews covering mysteries, fantasies, science fiction and other books for the San Francisco *Chronicle*. As a result he had to cut back his own imaginative output to an average of four or five magazine stories a year, either mysteries or fantasy-science fiction or, like most of the short exploits of Fergus O'Breen, both at once. Perhaps his most fondly remembered "pure" detective stories of the period are the cases of alcoholic ex-cop Nick Noble which appeared in *Ellery Queen's Mystery Magazine* (*EQMM*), but there were others as well—Sister Ursula stories, O'Breen exploits and non-series tales—and all are represented in *Exeunt Murderers* (1983), a collection I was privileged to edit.

Boucher's short mystery stories, like his mystery novels and science fiction, reflect all the interests and enthusiasms that filled his life, with religion, opera, football, politics, movies, true crime, record collecting and an abundance of good food and wine alongside the clues and puzzles and deductions. His stories are further enhanced by a dimension whose value has increased with the passing years. "He used to say," Phyllis White remarked, "that the heresy of our age is the perceived dichotomy between art and entertainment: if something is one, it cannot be the other. Things that are now being studied in school were in their own time great popular successes. The public avidly awaited the next installment of a current Dickens novel. There was a popular following of the Elizabethan theater and of the Greek theater. He used to say you could get a better idea of just what it was like to be alive in that time from reading the fiction of an earlier period than you could from reading a factual history." In his critical writing Boucher stressed again and again the function of mysteries as (in Hamlet's words to Polonius about the players) the abstracts and brief chronicles of the time. The whodunits of any period bear witness to later generations about the way we lived then, and Boucher's tales of the early and middle 1940s, with their ambience of rationed consumer goods and gung-ho patriotism and defense plants and rumor mills and returning combat heroes, capture the sensibility of the American home front during World War II like nothing else in the genre.

In those years the tradition of the amateur mastersleuth whose brilliance solves crimes where police work failed was still vital and flourishing, and to devotees of that tradition the roots of Boucher's protagonists will be evident. In Nick Noble for instance there is quite clearly a bit of the historic Poe and even more of Baroness Orczy's Old Man in the Corner. Boucher created the character in 1942 for the then infant *EQMM*, which is still happily with us (if only Boucher were himself!) almost seventy years later. The Screwball Division was a translation into colloquial American of *The Department of Queer Complaints* in Carter Dickson/John Dickson Carr's 1940 collection of that title. The Chula Negra was based on a little Mexican café on Second Street in Los Angeles where in the mid-1930s Boucher and other *United Progressive News* journalists "used to gather to talk about the stories we were going to write and eat the best *lengua en mole* I've ever tasted and drink sherry . . . at ten cents per water-glassful." Sister Ursula, as we've seen, derives from Father Brown and Fergus O'Breen, as the cadence of his name suggests, from Ellery Queen.

During the years he wrote most of his short detective stories he also edited his first two anthologies, *The Pocket Book of True Crime Stories* (1943) and *Great American Detective Stories* (1945), both of them prized collector's items today. In addition he translated several Georges Simenon stories for publication in *EQMM* and did other translations from the Spanish and Portuguese. On one of his regular business trips to New York he became a charter member of the Mystery Writers of America organization (MWA). "He was always proud of carrying card number five," Phyllis said. Along with fellow *Chronicle* reviewer Joseph Henry Jackson, he took the lead in forming a San Francisco scion society of the Baker Street Irregulars, giving himself the designation Brother Scanlon of the Scowrers. "My husband was rather ahead of his time in his views as to the equality of women. The Baker Street Irregulars was a stag organization. He insisted that there must be not only Scowrers but also Mollies." (For the benefit of tyros in the literature of Sherlock Holmes I should mention that both the Scowrers and the Molly Maguires figure prominently in the 1915 novel *The Valley of Fear*, fourth and last of Sir Arthur Conan Doyle's book-length Holmes tales.)

In collaboration respectively with Denis Green and Manfred B. Lee, Boucher wrote scripts for the *Sherlock Holmes* and *Ellery Queen* radio programs. *The Case Book of Gregory Hood*, a detective series heard irregularly on the Mutual radio network between 1946 and 1950, was created and scripted by Boucher and Green and at various times starred Gale Gordon, Elliot Lewis and Martin Gabel as the San Francisco importer-sleuth. "Even during the period when his main occupation was writing radio plays," said Phyllis White, "shows that emanated from Los Angeles and New York, he stayed in Berkeley and commuted. He was on a schedule of Hollywood roughly every six weeks and New York every six months." While juggling all these activities, Boucher also found time to teach a writing class once a week in his home. Among his students who went on to professional careers were the science-fiction writers Ron Goulart and Philip K. Dick and the novelists David Duncan and Jean Backus. "For a while," Phyllis added, "he was in the Berkeley Lawn Bowling

Club. And for a while there was a group of serious students and collectors of the limerick . . . Then there was a group of people who got together once a month to drink wine, and I am sure there are many other things that I am not thinking of."

What was it like to live with Boucher while he was working and playing so intensely? The most vivid account we are ever likely to have is that of his older son, Lawrence White. "As I remember, a typical work day for my father would begin with the sound of the alarm clock somewhere around eight o'clock in the morning. The purpose of the alarm clock was to notify anyone else who was awake, usually my brother or myself, to start giving wake-up calls every few minutes. If that didn't work, we had to escalate the wake-up shakes and deliveries of hot coffee passed under the nose until he could finally get himself out of bed. After he got up it was quite a while before he could work himself into a normal breathing pattern. He was a lifelong asthmatic. He never had what most of us consider a healthy day in his life. The period right after waking up was the worst for him. After a considerable breathing stabilization period and some coffee, he would be ready to repair to his study for his first workshift of the day, usually around nine or ten o'clock.

"His study was on the top floor of our large split-level house, on the side where he got the sun in the morning. This was nice because our cat gravitated toward the sun, and so he would have his muse there in the corner by the window, lying there saying, 'Yes, it is time to get to work.' So the door was shut, and he was doing whatever he did. He might emerge around midday to come down to the kitchen, fix himself a nice tartare steak, and return to his study until about four o'clock in the afternoon. At this point he would try to nap for a couple of hours until dinner time. Then we went through the whole waking up ritual again between six and seven o'clock; usually he'd go through a review copy while he was waking up.

"We always had dinner together in the evenings, which I remember as a very pleasant time. We were all on our own for the other meals. Dinner was the one time of the day when everyone was together, but after dinner he was back to his study for another four or five hours of work. After my brother and I were in bed, at eleven or twelve o'clock, we could often hear my father and mother playing records from their large opera collection and talking animatedly. They both liked to stay up until two or three o'clock in the morning. But generally my father's schedule was to put in two shifts on a normal, full workday. We had to go through this terrible waking up period twice a day.

"The actual process of his work was not really visible to me. I saw a lot of reading. He seldom went anywhere without a review copy under his arm or in front of his face. I could hear a lot of one finger typing and the occasional slap of cards from some solitaire breaks. I couldn't hear him working the cyphers or cryptograms and double-crostics and other forms of what he called relaxation that he would sometimes do for breaks. Occasionally large envelopes would be passed out of the study to be taken to the nearest mailbox. His level of concentration I am sure was quite high when he was in there. He didn't care too much to be disturbed . . .

"The study was a large room, I guess about twelve by twenty feet, maybe even larger because it was lined with books all the way around. The windows were not covered but every other part of the wall was. The main type of bookcase was an orange crate, which was nice because it is modular and you could stack books two deep. In his study he had his mystery collection, his science fiction collection, his Sherlock Holmes collection, his true crime collection, his limerick collection, his pornography collection (very small—it mostly overlapped the limerick collection), and a lot of reference books. They were mostly books on words and dictionaries in many languages. There wasn't much of what you would call office equipment—a typewriter, a few rubber stamps.

"It seemed to us as children that our father was kind of a rationed commodity because he was around so much, but yet he was off limits so much of the time. From my perspective now I see we probably had more time with him than most kids do with fathers who go to work and have golf and a bunch of other things; they're not home very much. There was a lot of play time, which kind of had its own schedule, but competed very strongly with the work schedule and the deadlines. No matter how bad the pressures, among the entertainments were: going to plays (musical comedies were big on the agenda); opera (they didn't drag us kids along to that); a lot of fine dining; a lot of sports spectating, which my mother didn't participate in; and lots of home table games. There were lots of parties involving the local writing crowd, and we went at least once per year to Playland at the Beach.

"My father got involved in so many things. He went to all the football games, the Cal basketball games, track meets, rugby games, gymnastics. He was doing all this just on the side."

Perhaps Boucher's most lasting contribution to world literature came in the months after he'd left the *Chronicle* and was supporting himself and his family with periodical and radio work. Scholar of

Latin American mystery fiction that he was, Boucher translated from Spanish, and persuaded his colleague in crime Frederic Dannay (Ellery Queen) to publish, the first story by Jorge Luis Borges to appear in the English language ("The Garden of Forking Paths", *EQMM*, August 1948). But his most important editorial and critical accomplishments still lay ahead of him.

During the late 1940s, while his science-fiction reviews were appearing in the Chicago *Sun-Times*, Boucher's reviews of current mystery fiction were being published in occasional *EQMM* columns and in odd corners of the Sunday *New York Times Book Review*. Beginning July 1, 1951, he took over as the *Times*' regular mystery critic, and his "Criminals at Large" column graced every issue of the *Book Review* for just short of the next seventeen years. Although his primary allegiance was to the fair-play detective novels of the sort he used to write himself, he was so eclectic in taste as to appreciate all kinds of crime fiction—suspense, Gothic, espionage, psychological, farce, private eye, police procedural, high adventure—and he insisted in his first *Times* column that "the important distinction is not between the schools of the whodunit but between the good and bad books whatever the school."

By practicing that credo Boucher brought mystery criticism to a perfection it will never see again. Six or eight times a week for almost seventeen years, he would tell us whether a book was good of its kind, whether the author succeeded within the chosen framework or formula. When a whodunit was truly excellent his praise would ring to the sky, as when he reviewed 23-year-old Ira Levin's first novel, *A Kiss Before Dying* (*NYTBR*, October 25, 1953): " . . . superlatively enviable sheer professionalism . . . Levin combines great talent for pure novel writing—full-bodied characterization, subtle psychological exploration, vivid evocation of locale—with strict technical whodunit tricks as dazzling as anything ever brought off by Carr, Rawson, Queen or Christie." If the book was a weak effort with some saving grace, he'd pinpoint the flaws precisely and take pains to note the good side: " . . . a slow-moving routine plot, weakly detected, but partially redeemed by a convincing first-hand picture of northernmost Alaska." To the hopelessly shoddy or inept work he'd give short shrift but usually with a dash of wit, as when he called a particularly boring John Rhode novel "the dreariest Rhode I have yet traversed." He never wrote maliciously.

Did I say never? Well, *hardly* ever! On the occasions when he encountered a book so atrocious it should never have been published at all, he didn't hesitate to say so bluntly. And during the early 1950s, the evil days of McCarthyism and HUAC, his single *bete noire* was Mickey Spillane, whose best-selling thrillers Boucher despised for their neo-fascist political slant, joy in sadism, sniggering approach to sex and slapdash prose and plots, all the antitheses to Boucher's own values which were rooted in Christian intellectualism and the liberal humanist tradition. In the 1960s when Spillane's influence had faded, Boucher mellowed toward the creator of Mike Hammer and began to see in him the last of the old pulp storytellers.

Boucher was an awesomely rapid reader, capable of finishing and fully comprehending a novel in two to three hours. After the reading he'd arrange all the relevant information about the book, from bibliographic details to a plot summary to any factual errors he'd caught, on one or both sides of a 3x5 card. The space limitation led him to employ his own system of abbreviations on these cards: OH, for instance, stood for Our Hero, and IH for Idiot Heroine, a creature he must have encountered hundreds of times in so-called novels of romantic suspense. On completing the file card he'd write his review of the book, a process that generally took him thirty minutes or less. Even though most of the titles Boucher reviewed are long forgotten, his thousands of *Chronicle* and *Times* critiques are so full of wit and insight and infectious readability as to defy being laid down. I am proud to have collected his earlier literary journalism in *The Anthony Boucher Chronicles* (2001-02). If someday a publisher is found with the sense and tenacity to assemble his *Times* work in book form, that volume (or more likely that set of volumes) when combined with the *Chronicles* will have given us the definitive critical history of the genre during one of its richest quarter centuries.

Boucher lived and worked at 78 rpm while the rest of the world revolved lazily at 33. His speed-reading gift left him many hours for a legion of other activities during his years with the *Times*. Through most of the 1950s Boucher and his colleague J. Francis McComas co-edited the monthly *Magazine of Fantasy and Science Fiction* and the annual *Best of Fantasy and Science Fiction* anthologies culled from the magazine. One of Boucher's duties was to check the scientific accuracy of submitted manuscripts, and thanks to his boyhood interest in science, he said, a bell would ring in his head whenever he read a questionable statement of technical fact. Boucher, McComas wrote years later, "combined an unerring sense of what was 'commercial' with excellent literary taste . . . He was essentially a *kind* editor . . . especially gentle with beginning writers . . . If a submission showed any merit at all, he was ever ready to take the time for written encouragement, with detailed suggestions for plot revision, or character strengthening, or style polishing... His proudest boast was the number of first stories he had bought."

And somehow he *still* found time for other work. He and McComas co-edited the excellent but commercially unsuccessful magazine *True Crime Detective* during the last year (Fall 1952-Fall 1953) of its brief life. He wrote a monthly review column in *EQMM* for much of his tenure with the *Times*. He and several other members of the Northern California chapter of MWA turned out a collaborative suspense novel, *The Marble Forest* (1951), which was adapted into director William Castle's 1958 movie chiller *Macabre*. His science-fiction reviews as H.H. Holmes migrated east from the Chicago *Sun-Times* to the New York *Herald-Tribune*. He wrote entries on Dashiell Hammett and Erle Stanley Gardner for a new edition of the *Encyclopaedia Britannica*. From 1962 through 1967 he edited the annual *Best Detective Stories of the Year* anthologies, supplying not only warm and thoughtful introductions to each tale he selected but also an invaluable "Yearbook of the Detective Story" appendix listing the year's short story collections, anthologies, prize-winning crime novels, and sad but necessary notes on the mystery writers who had died during the year. For Pacifica's public radio station KPFA he conducted a regular mystery-review program. He served as regional vice-president and eventually as national president of MWA and won three richly deserved Edgar awards from the organization for his criticism. He selected and wrote introductions for the novels in several series of quality paperback mystery reprints. And to every piece of work he brought such enthusiasm and knowledge and love that he seemed not to be working at all but just having fun.

Superficially he might have resembled the hopeless workaholic but Boucher's lives as writer, editor and critic were never the alpha and omega of his existence. He had enough hobbies for a small army—gourmet cooking, wine culture, football and basketball, Gilbert & Sullivan, theology, limericks, multilingual Scrabble, poker—and gave time and attention to each. Indeed his kitchen skills were such that for a period during World War II when his wife had her hands full with two small children, Boucher took over as the family cook, and despite wartime rationing and food shortages did better than satisfactorily.

"Another development," Phyllis White said, "was his turning pro with what had been a lifelong hobby. He had always been an opera buff and a collector of records. As a boy he laid the foundation for his record collection back in the Twenties when the new orthophonic records were introduced and the old acoustic records were sold off for a dime. He acquired quantities of records of the great singers of the so-called golden age of opera. In later years he kept haunting thrift shops and got on the mailing lists of specialist dealers . . . After his death, his record collection was acquired by the University of California for their music library at the Santa Barbara campus." Around that collection of more than nine thousand old operatic discs he built his public radio series *Golden Voices*, which ran on KPFA every Sunday evening from 1949 until his death. "Each week he would take up a different singer, talk about the career, and play illustrations from his collection. This led to television work at KQED—programs about the San Francisco Opera and interviews of singers." An opera buff *par excellence*, he loved to put on top hat and white tie and tails once a year for the San Francisco Opera's gala first nights. He wrote countless notes for the company's printed programs and, from 1961 until his death, served as local correspondent for the Metropolitan Opera's magazine *Opera News*, arguing for increased attention to the form's dramatic aspects. "He served one term as president of the Berkeley Democratic Club," said Phyllis, "and two terms on the State Central Committee." After giving up political activity on doctors' orders he remained in constant demand as a speaker on campuses, at liberal and labor fund-raisers, at conventions of science-fiction fans. And overarching all his work and all his play (the two for him being indistinguishable) were family and faith. He was committed to Catholicism with all his fervor and learning and love, donating time to the weekends of spiritual renewal sponsored by his parish church, volunteering as a lay reader at Sunday Mass in the mid-1960s following the liturgical reforms of Vatican Council II, helping to translate some of the liturgy from Latin into contemporary English.

What makes Boucher's many-lives-in-one even more astounding is that he so rarely enjoyed a day of truly robust health. Although he compared himself to the sundial with the motto "I count only the sunny hours" in his ability to blot out weakness and pain, he and Fred Dannay often said to each other only half in jest "that if both of us had been blessed with good health, how much more we could have accomplished!" Bouts of illness often forced Boucher to scrap or postpone projects to which he'd made commitments. But his spirit outfought his body and he kept working with courage, gusto and relentless intelligence. Until the spring of 1968.

That was when he was admitted to Kaiser Foundation Hospital and diagnosed as suffering from advanced lung cancer—too late for surgery to do any good. "He never knew about the cancer," Phyllis

White said, "because it was very hard to diagnose him and by the time that they figured it out, he was out of it and couldn't be told anything." On April 29, at the unbearably early age of 56, he died. What he did with his life would have been staggering if he'd lived ten times as long.

The eulogy at his funeral was read by Father Brian Joyce, his closest friend among the clergy. "He had that quality so characteristic of the truly Christian and of the fully human life," the priest said, "the quality of joy." Like the two other deeply religious major figures in crime fiction, G.K. Chesterton and Dorothy L. Sayers, Boucher taught with his life a lesson of inspiration to people of his own faith and of another and of none: that living creatively is itself a sacrament, ennobling and liberating those who live that way, so that they relate to their lives as God is said to relate to the universe. He was one of those who make us proud we are of his species, who give us ideals for our own lives. We'll never see his like again. An Anthony Boucher walks the earth but once.

COLD CASES

ANTHONY ABBOT

He didn't live to a ripe old age but surely left his mark before he died. Under his own name Fulton Oursler (1893-1952) he was well known as a novelist and the editor of *Liberty* magazine, not to mention as an amateur magician and a close friend of Franklin Delano Roosevelt. In the late 1940s he reached the highest peaks of popular acclaim as senior editor of *Reader's Digest* and author of that religioso blockbuster *The Greatest Story Ever Told* (1949). Our concern here however is with the detective novels he (and, apparently for the last two, another man) wrote during the Thirties and early Forties as Anthony Abbot.

He seems to have chosen the Abbot byline for the same reason he used titles beginning with *About the Murder of . . .*: in order to get top billing on library lists whether they were arranged by the author's name or the book's. The eight novels in the series deal with the adventures of New York City police commissioner Thatcher Colt and are narrated by Colt's faceless secretary and Watson. The patterned titles and the use of the same name for narrator and byline come of course from the best-selling Philo Vance mysteries, narrated and supposedly written by Vance's factotum S.S. Van Dine. Colt is tall, solidly built, probably in his early forties, a World War I hero, a wealthy man who turned to criminology and police science as John F. Kennedy later turned to politics. He's a brilliant thinker but tends to assume a cold ultra-logical manner and to talk like a book—or like a less insufferable version of Philo Vance—but, unlike Vance, is deeply and compassionately aware that many of the people he deals with are caught in private traps from which they can't escape. Abbot's more obnoxious but also more vivid version of Van Dine's John F.X. Markham is Merle K. Dougherty, the obese blundering red-faced District Attorney of New York County, forever demanding the arrest of suspects Colt is convinced are innocent. Abbot's Dr. Jeremiah Multooler, the crusty cigar-smoking Medical Examiner, is somewhat harder to tell apart from his Van Dine counterpart Dr. Doremus, both men constantly griping about being hauled out of bed at ungodly hours to examine the latest corpse. Visitors are ushered into

Colt's office at the north end of the second floor of the old Headquarters building on Centre Street by stern-faced Captain Israel Henry, and those who are invited into Colt's vast library on the third floor of his graystone mansion on West 70th Street are shown in by the dusky Jamaican butler Arthur, clearly Abbot's version of Philo Vance's veddy British butler Currie. Disc-faced Neal O'Brien pilots Colt's official limousine through any weather and at any hour. Abbot's version of Van Dine's Van Dine is of course Tony Abbot, Colt's secretary, always one step behind his adored boss physically and several logically.

Although heavily influenced by Van Dine and perhaps by the earliest Ellery Queen novels, Abbot's possess their own distinctive flavor. The first body is generally found in bizarre circumstances, each of the abundant and tantalizing clues points in a different direction, the trail leads to several suspects who are shown in due course to have had ample motive and means and opportunity. Eventually comes a conference among the officials, often between two and five in the morning, with Arthur serving highballs, creamed chicken on toast and delicious coffee as Colt, Dougherty and the others argue alternative theories and reconstructions of the crime, electrifying the atmosphere with intellectual excitement. Usually about two-thirds of the way through the book there's another murder or violent incident which offers Colt the clues he needs to solve the puzzle. Abbot departs from Queen (though not from Van Dine) in often failing to lay all the evidence before the reader. But he's so skillful in other respects that I for one don't object to the unfairness too loudly.

The series begins with *About the Murder of Geraldine Foster* (1930), which is dedicated "TO THE STANDING ARMY OF THE CITY OF NEW YORK—*The Police Department.*" According to Oursler's posthumously published autobiography *Behold This Dreamer!* (1964): "I became one of the first apologists for the police in detective fiction. To get my facts right, I dawdled around the old Headquarters Building in Center Street and got my facts straight from the source; and for a fee, the secretary of the police commissioner read the scripts and checked every detail. The books were meticulously accurate." Well, this I doubt, but they do sound a bit more procedurally accurate than most Golden Age detective novels. In *Geraldine Foster* we follow the step-by-step investigation into the disappearance and later the brutal axe-murder of an enigmatic physician's secretary. The solution is reasonably fair to the reader and exposes one of the most complicated frame-up schemes in the genre but somehow seems less impressive than the problem itself. Some florid dialogue and wooden exposition don't detract too much from this debut.

Midway through the novel comes a marrow-chilling sequence whose accuracy, as we've seen, Oursler has guaranteed. Dr. Maskell, prime suspect in his secretary's murder, claims to have a perfect alibi. "Good!" says Colt. "You have the rest of the night to prove it." "The third degree for me, eh?" Maskell asks, and goes on:

> "I am familiar with the confessions extorted by the French methods—the Parisian third degree. In fact, I have seen innocent men, at the Paris *Sûreté*, collapse into confession in the room that is called the Chamber of Spontaneous Avowals. The spontaneity of the avowals is accelerated by beating the soles of the bare feet of the unfortunate suspects with long staves. That is called the bastinado. Very well. The New York equivalent is probably a fist on the jaw. Nevertheless you will get nothing from me. I have an alibi. I did not kill Geraldine Foster."

A moment later he asks: "And if I [tell the truth] I have nothing to fear?" "Except what you just said—a sock in the jaw," replies Detective Hogan, who then refuses food to the doctor, who's had nothing to eat since breakfast, and growls: "Step lively. There's a gang waiting for you in the room downstairs, and it's been a long time since they had any exercise."

The next chapter, fittingly titled "A Long, Long Night," describes how "Doctor Maskell was subjected to the ordeal of a third degree that is still considered a classic in Headquarters." Before treating us to the details, Abbot offers a vigorous defense of police thuggery:

> Of course, a man of Maskell's standing was in no danger of beating from the police. Nor by this do I mean to pretend that physical violence is no longer practised. It is still practised, although not as much as before. But such treatment is reserved for men who will respond to nothing else, who are themselves violent creatures intimidated by nothing except violent physical pain. Moreover, the results from such manhandling are no longer so effective in court. A prisoner roughly treated in the third degree can call his lawyer the

next day, exhibit his bruises, have them photographed, and the pictures of his wounds will be shown at the trial to discredit his enforced revelations. The chief value lies in getting a confession that can be substantiated by confirming details subsequently checked up. With men of the stamp of Doctor Maskell, the police have more subtle methods; before the night was over Doctor Maskell was sure to wish that physical violence was all he had to face.

Through the night the ordeal goes on: incessant questioning by a dozen detectives "bully[ing] and harass[ing] the man with trick questions," forcing him to repeat his story over and over and pouncing on every slightest variation in detail, compelling him to go the morgue and look at his secretary's mutilated body, shouting vivid descriptions of the death agonies of the electric chair into his face. Only the arrival of the doctor's brother, who happens to be a noted civil liberties lawyer, prevents the inquisition from going on beyond dawn of the next morning. In case it makes any difference, Dr. Maskell didn't kill Geraldine Foster. This novel is required reading for anyone who still wonders why the U.S. Supreme Court imposed the exclusionary rule on the states more than thirty years later.

In *About the Murder of the Clergyman's Mistress* (1931) Abbot shows amazing dexterity keeping control of dozens of strands in a fiendishly complex plot. The novel is loosely based on the famous Hall-Mills murder case of the Twenties and opens with the discovery of the bodies of a respected Episcopal minister and of a singer in his choir, floating down the East River in a rowboat. No reader will anticipate Colt's solution but every lover of early Queen and Carr will enjoy this lavish formal problem, complete with a sardonic portrait of the WASP clergy.

About the Murder of the Night Club Lady (1931) deals with a lovely but greedy socialite who is murdered by untraceable means at exactly 3:00 A.M. on New Year's morning while ensconced in her penthouse and surrounded by Colt and a cordon of police. It's a fascinating premise but Abbot cheats without mercy in this one. He suppresses from our view evidence long known to Colt, he leaves us scratching our heads over how the murderer could possibly have done what Colt proves must have been done, he keeps the interrelations of the suspects in a frustrating muddle that never gets resolved. You must be a rabid devotee indeed to admire this book. But at the time it clearly impressed someone in Hollywood:

before the end of the year it became the basis of *The Night Club Lady* (Columbia, 1932), directed by Irving Cummings from a screenplay by Robert Riskin, frequent collaborator of Frank Capra. Colt was played by Adolphe Menjou and the titular lady by Mayo Methot, who offscreen was Humphrey Bogart's first wife.

About the Murder of the Circus Queen (1932) finds Colt in Madison Square Garden for the opening night of a circus which has been plagued by a disastrous series of "accidents." When the star trapeze artist falls to her death from the high rings before a crowd of thousands, Colt begins to suspect something more fiendish than chance. The plot and backstage atmosphere are fascinating and the presence of a Ubangi tribe in the circus gives rise to a wealth of candid racial material, but once again Abbot allows Colt to put vital evidence in his pocket before the reader sees it. This novel was adapted into the second and last of Columbia's Thatcher Colt movies. *The Circus Queen Murder* (1933) again starred Adolphe Menjou but this one was directed by Roy William Neill, who is famous in the mystery world for having helmed most of Universal's Sherlock Holmes films with Basil Rathbone and Nigel Bruce.

About the Murder of a Startled Lady (1935) begins eerily enough with a seance in Colt's office. A demonstrably phony female medium claims to have received genuine messages from a young woman named Madeline who says she was murdered, dismembered and sunk in the river near Jones Beach Park. In due course a box full of human bones is found in the specified place. Systematically Colt and the police discover the dead woman's identity and unearth suspects: her abused mother, her father and wheelchair-bound grandfather (a pair of disgusting religious maniacs if ever there were two), a violent-tempered medical student and a political kingmaker. Too bad that this exciting whodunit culminates in one of the genre's hokiest denouements.

In *Startled Lady* as in *Geraldine Foster*, one of the suspects is subjected to the third degree, which once again Oursler defends.

> Alfred Keplinger came to us, fresh, or rather, wilted, from a three hour third degree—a very short ordeal, as police practice goes. I know the third degree is a cruel institution. I cannot argue with its detractors on that point; I can only say that those in police work have not learned how to succeed without it in some cases. No one had struck Alfred Keplinger. Physical violence is used only on the lowest of crimi-

nals, creatures who respond to pain and to nothing else; sentimentalists to the contrary, there are such creatures in our work; we meet them every day. For men like Alfred Keplinger, there is instead a mental third degree—long hours of questioning, without physical punishment of any kind. Keplinger was not denied food or water or attention to his bodily wants. Tales of such practices are generally lies. But all night long, Keplinger would have to go on, listening to questions and giving answers. Often they would be questions that he had already answered, not once but several times. Everything he said would be taken down by stenographers, typed immediately and studied by relays of two or three detectives—fresh, vigorous, steamed-up men who would go after him with more questions when others were finished with him. Meanwhile every verifiable statement he made was being checked. Every contradiction, every variation in his testimony, was noticed and he was confronted with it, unsympathetically and skeptically. More, he was subjected to emotional attacks. Some of his inquisitors were bullies; others soft-spoken and friendly. All were there to trap him if they could. This I know and say was cruel—but it was necessary. Already Alfred Keplinger showed the strain of those last few hours, with their incessant barrage. The pale-faced, goggle-eyed young medical student stood before us, his hair tousled because he had run his hands through it so many times; he was tired out and listless and he looked at Thatcher Colt as a man might look at death, after a long and painful illness.

About the Murder of a Man Afraid of Women (1937) opens with Colt searching for a naked man who vanished in freezing weather, continues with the titular murder and some adroit time-table maneuvering, and closes with a solution that is both beautifully surprising and fair to the reader. On the negative side, Abbot once again leaves a few loose ends of plot dangling and hasn't the foggiest notion of what a crime syndicate is like.

In a sense the series comes to an end here except for two short stories. In "About the Disappearance of Agatha King" (*Cosmopolitan*, June 1932) Colt looks into the disappearance of a high-society bride just before her wedding, finding the answer in a pair of dyed shoes. In "About the Perfect Crime of Mr. Digberry" (*Cosmopolitan*, October 1940) he encounters a staggeringly complex situation involving a wigmaker found exiting a cemetery in the middle of the night and the corpse of an opera singer in a Murphy bed. This excellent tale became the basis of the third and last Thatcher Colt movie, *The Panther's Claw* (PRC, 1943), a low-budget throwaway directed by William Beaudine, with Sidney Blackmer as Colt and that dithering milquetoast Byron Foulger as Digberry.

The two final novels about Colt are so different from the earlier six that even if Fred Dannay hadn't told me that they were written by a different author (Oscar Schisgall, 1901-1984, a super-prolific contributor to magazines Oursler edited and countless other publications), one would sense the presence of a ghost. In *The Creeps* (1939) Colt has gotten married, and the Manhattan milieu and intricate intellectual fireworks of the earlier cases are replaced with a hackneyed tale of a murder at a house party during a snowstorm, one of the suspects being a devilish hypnotist obviously made in the image of Bela Lugosi. Colt is still the main character in *The Shudders* (1943) but everything else about the book makes us feel we've wandered into a Sax Rohmer novel with strong overtones of Conan Doyle's "The Final Problem." Here Colt's adversary is yet another Lugosiesque mad scientist, who has devised an untraceable means of murder and is using it seriatim on all the parties to a three-year-old electrocution, among whom was Colt himself. The author sustains the mood of eerie tension and horror but the denouement is based on the flimsiest of evidence and made possible by blatant deception of the reader.

In the same year his detective character made his last bow, Fulton Oursler was formally received into the Catholic Church. Six years later came *The Greatest Story Ever Told*, which probably made him far more money than all eight Thatcher Colt novels together. Three of the octet were reprinted in paperback between 1945 and 1950, but for the past sixty years the series has been forgotten except perhaps by the creators of the NBC Mystery Movie series *McMillan and Wife* (1971-77), who resurrected the premise of the police commissioner as mastersleuth. But for anyone who wishes there were more whodunits in the manner of the early Ellery Queen, Abbot's are the books to read.

CLEVE F. ADAMS

Here is one of mystery fiction's shadow figures: little read today, mentioned only in passing if at all by most commentators on the genre, dismissed as a talentless hack on the basis of scanty acquaintance. On page 213 of Howard Haycraft's *Murder for Pleasure* (1941), the first comprehensive history of the literature of crime, we are told that Adams is a follower of Dashiell Hammett and that his detective's name is Rex McBride. In an editorial note to his superb anthology of critical writings *The Art of the Mystery Story* (1946) Haycraft commends Adams' novel *Sabotage* as worthy of our attention. Anthony Boucher, the genre's finest critic ever, has an essay in the same anthology which warns us away from Adams' *Up Jumped the Devil*. Adams' name pops up in *Raymond Chandler Speaking* (1963) and *Selected Letters of Raymond Chandler* (1981) but we learn from those collections of Chandler's correspondence nothing more than that Chandler wrote him some letters. In *A Catalogue of Crime* (1972) Jacques Barzun and Wendell Hertig Taylor describe Adams as a "prolific author of low-tension, low-credibility stories on the margin of espionage, private-eye detection, and international intrigue." In William Ruehlmann's *Saint with a Gun: The Unlawful American Private Eye* (1974), the first book-length study of the private eye novel, Adams isn't even mentioned despite the fact that he fits Ruehlmann's thesis about the fascistic tendencies of the genre better than many authors Ruehlmann cites as examples. There are entries on Adams in reference books like the *Encyclopedia of Mystery and Detection* (1976), 20th *Century Crime and Mystery Writers* (1980, 1985) and *1001 Midnights* (1986), but such interest in him as still exists has done nothing to return his work to print and as a practical matter he's been long forgotten.

He deserves better. No sane reader would rank Adams beside Hammett and Chandler but he was a fascinating minor talent who might have developed into a major contender if he'd lived longer. In any event he's ripe for rediscovery.

~~~~~

His full name is replete (to use one of his favorite words) with American history: Cleveland Franklin Adams. He was born in Chicago in 1895, moved to the west coast in 1919, and spent much of his young adulthood drifting from job to job, including a stint as a Montana copper miner that was to inspire his last and perhaps finest novel. By 1931 he was managing a chain candy store in Culver City, California. But his dream was to become a writer, and that year he met another young man with the same dream.

Willis Todhunter Ballard (1903-1980) had already sold a few pulp stories here and there but he was far from an established professional at the time he and Adams met and became friends. Eventually he became a prolific writer of Westerns and hardboiled mysteries and later of TV scripts. A few years before his death, in an interview with pulp fan Stephen Mertz (*The Armchair Detective*, Winter 1979), he described how he and Adams and another aspiring writer named Glen Wichman organized about twenty young people with similar ambitions into a club they called The Fictioneers.

> "It was an entirely social group with neither rules nor by-laws. Cleve ran it through the first few years as secretary, the only office we had, sending out notices of where and when the next meeting would be held. We paid for cards and postage. I have no idea how many members there were, for we kept no records and charged no dues, but I would say the number ran into the hundreds. Any writer, fixed or just passing through, was welcome if he cared to join, and at times we had more members than the Authors League. However, our monthly dinners seldom turned out more than thirty or forty at any one gathering."

The group held together until World War II, when many of its members went into the military, and the several postwar attempts to revive it "were largely unsuccessful," Ballard said, "because most of us had moved into the slick markets and the book field, and had scattered."

Adams seems to have considered himself a first-rate talent even before he became a hardboiled hit. "He had an exalted regard for his own ability," Ballard recalled, "and seldom discussed his work with anyone, including family." He wasn't at all reticent, however, about discussing in negative terms the work of other Fictioneers.

"Cleve was a father figure to the fiction writing group, much loved but a porcupine nevertheless." Often after reading a manuscript by a colleague he'd remark: "It's a beautiful typing job."

Early in the 1940s Adams summarized his life to date:

> "I have been, not necessarily in the order named, a soda jerker; a copper miner; a section hand; a motion picture art director; a detective; a window-trimmer; a life insurance executive. I finally decided that the only way I could capitalize on a lifetime's mistakes was to write about them, and have been writing about them ever since—a matter of some seven or eight years."

His first series characters, who appeared in several stories published in *Clues*, were also the most unusual: a pair of female private detectives operating out of Los Angeles. The dominant partner of the firm is Violet McDade, a 300-pound former circus fat lady who carries a sleeve gun on each arm and is not averse, in the words of Ron Goulart's *The Dime Detectives* (1988), to "scooping up any loose cash she might find lying around the scene of a crime . . ." Her cases are narrated in first person by her Chicana sidekick Nevada Alvarado. In what Goulart describes as "a sort of kidding racism," Violet likes to call her junior partner "Mex," but at least once the senorita flings back as good as she gets. "You—you lout! My family dates back beyond the conquistadors and the Spanish grants. Where did you come from? A circus tent!" Readers who want to sample this series will find a specimen in Bernard Drew's anthology *Hard-Boiled Dames* (1986). McDade and Alvarado debuted in 1935, a fact that gives Adams the dubious distinction of being the first writer to create his own variants on Rex Stout's immortal Nero Wolfe and Archie Goodwin, who had first seen the light of print a year earlier.

For the rest of his career Adams borrowed exclusively from Hammett and Chandler. All of his later series characters were men and most of them were private detectives. The Adams PI has many names—Rex McBride, Bill Rye, Jim Flagg—and sometimes, for example when he's called John J. Shannon or Steve McCloud, he has a cop's badge in some stories and civilian status in others. But regardless of official standing he's always the same figure, a sort of prose incarnation of Humphrey Bogart that predates the movies where Bogey played detectives. Both the Bogart persona and the Adams eye display an apparent hard shell that conceals a sentimental heart, but the Adams man's soft heart, unlike Bogey's, typically turns out to be yet another shell, one that conceals a brutal and cynical core. A few passages will help capture the flavor of the Adams hero.

> What a lovely world it would be if only everybody was as peacefully inclined as himself. He hoped he would not have to kill Mr. Walter Ambrose.

> "You wouldn't admit to any human emotion, would you?"
> "One," he said. "Avarice."

> "I'm a son of a bitch . . . But at least I'm not complicated. I don't have any aspirations beyond money."
> Quite suddenly his face became convulsed with rage and he shouted. "Listen, you kike bastard! I haven't got the rocks and I didn't knock anybody off." More quietly he added, "Not recently, anyway."

> He was inflexible. "What is Neil Buchanan to you?"
> Her eyes were a little scornful now. "Neil is my husband," she said steadily . . .
> He struck her across the face. "You tramp!"

Physically the Adams eye tends to be slim and dark, with sharply etched features like an Indian's. His eyes reflect a capacity for deep brooding silences, sudden ribald laughter, tremendous rages and aloof arrogance. He has come up from the gutter, the descendant of Black Irish railroad laborers who may have enjoyed some rolls in the hay with Sioux maidens. He has a wolfish, satanic look and a taste for gallows humor. He is perennially having an on-again-off-again affair with a tall cool intellectual woman who sees him as a wonderful caveman type until he starts slapping her around in one of his maniacal fits of rage. He is a supreme male chauvinist, demanding full freedom to chase other females but exploding like a cobalt bomb if "his woman" steps down for a split second from the pedestal to which he has nailed her. He's a fascist, a racist, a cynic and a hypocrite, but a sentimental ballad like "Sweet Leilani" can bring tears to his eyes. His capacity for liquor and physical punishment seems without limit. At bottom he's a pungent character but far from estimable.

About half the time Adams seems fully aware of his protagonist's shortcomings. Unlike Chandler, who said of his private eye that "He is the hero, he is everything," Adams often goes out of his way to make *his* PI look like a royal ass. In Chapter 14 of *Decoy*, for example, Rex McBride is in his girlfriend's apartment when a mad gunman breaks in. In true heroic manner McBride grabs a heavy crystal candlestick from the mantel and flings it with perfect accuracy at the gunman's wrist. The assassin drops the pistol and scurries out the door with McBride in hot pursuit—until our hero trips over the candlestick on the floor and falls flat on his face. Adams filled his novels with scenes of this sort, carefully designed to pull the rug out from under Chandler's knightly image of the private eye and reduce him to an oaf. In his final novel, *Shady Lady*, the female lead laughs in McBride's face and tells him: "For a man reputed to be shrewd you're the most transparent person I've met in years. And the biggest egotist, with your fatheaded assumption that everybody in the world except the great Rex McBride is either a halfwit or an idiot." In the tone of a man sorely put upon, McBride replies: "Well, aren't they?"

Around the Adams protagonist revolves a sort of repertory company of recurring characters, mannerisms, scenes, plot elements, even tag lines of description and dialogue. Pick up any of his novels at random and you'll find most if not all of the following: a good girl, a bad girl, a gambling czar, a good gray police captain, a sadistic toothpick-chewing Homicide cop, a corrupt politician, hired goons, a pompous businessman or government official, and a Runyonesque taxi driver who miraculously pops up every so often to pull the detective out of a hot spot. Every book contains a smoke ring blowing scene, a couple of drunk scenes, at least two beating scenes (with both the police and the gangsters getting a crack at the hero), and a confrontation between the detective and each of the women in the story, one of whom usually turns out to be the murderer. The same descriptions and lines of dialogue are recycled endlessly. If someone gave you a dollar for each time Adams wrote that one of his characters was "a very (supply your own adjective) man indeed," you'd be recession-proof forever; and likewise if you had a buck for each time a rich man or woman paradoxically tells the private eye that *he* is nothing but a snob. Lines like "The perfume of her hair was like incense [or alternatively like heady wine] in his nostrils" or "In the morning sun her hair was a blue-black casque" recur in book after book when the detective is smitten by female beauty.

Most of Adams' plots were combinations of the most familiar elements of hardboiled literature and he was an expert at lifting story structures from Dashiell Hammett, rewriting *Red Harvest* three times and *The Glass Key* twice. He loved to describe his characters so as to evoke the image of a movie actor, with a special fondness for creating people who looked like Edward Arnold, William Bendix or Sydney Greenstreet. Occasionally he converted these shticks into subtle insider jokes for film buffs. If you know that Edward Arnold played Paul Madvig in the first movie version (Paramount, 1935) of Hammett's *The Glass Key*, you'll understand why Adams in his two rewrites of the Hammett novel tells us that *his* political boss resembles Arnold. But even when he's relying on tried-and-true pulp formulas, Adams is a genius at juggling disparate groups of shady characters each with their own greedy objective, and at filling his stories with a raw readability that almost forces you to keep breathlessly turning pages.

When he reaches his last chapter and has to sort out what happened, Adams' books invariably collapse. In every one of his fifteen novels the detective enjoys a fantastic run of lucky guesswork, yet there are always sizable chunks of plot left unexplained. In his article "Motivation in Mystery Fiction" (*The Writer*, April 1942), Adams said: "In the generally accepted sense I myself do not plot." Instead, he allows plot elements to pile up around his protagonist until "the poor guy is in one terrific jam. Rarely do I bother with how I'm going to get him out—not at first. I'm too busy getting him in, and sweating with him, and getting kicked in the teeth. Then, along about the middle of the job . . . I go back and try to figure out why everybody did what he did. Sometimes," he observes in a gem of understatement, "this is pretty difficult."

~ ~ ~ ~ ~

The Adams touches weren't born full-grown in his first novel but appear in all their glory in the dozens of short stories and novelets he wrote for the pulps of the 1930s, a number of them later expanded to book length. A typical example of Adams' pulp output is "Private War" (*Detective Fiction Weekly*, October 2, 1937), in which Los Angeles detective lieutenant Steve McCloud, who's sweet on the wife of a convicted but escaped racket boss, mixes into the internal mob battle over the chief's hidden loot and comes out intact despite three bullet wounds, a sock in the jaw, a couple of tongue lashings plus the old reliable blow on the head. A fellow cop named Jake Kleinschmidt is treated like a hero because he joined the mob in order to "get 'em in a place they had no business to be, so I could smoke 'em and have a good legal excuse." Not only the police thuggery but countless other Adams hallmarks including sentimentality, gallows humor, lightning pace, raw readability and the ever-helpful Runyonesque cabbie crop up in this unmemorable but useful novelet. Fleshed out a bit more, they recur in all fifteen of Adams' novels.

For a lovely early specimen of Adams' ass-backward notions of plotting, one can hardly do worse than "Murder Goes Unshod" (*Detective Fiction Weekly*, December 17, 1938), a story in his series about Dewey and Englehardt, the cops who ride Car 97. On a rainy night, while the boys are parked on a suburban street, they witness what looks like a ghost gliding into a house. A man inside, the wealthy owner of a furniture store, screams and drops dead of fright. There are no footprints on the porch of the house through whose front door our heroes saw the "ghost" enter. Smitten by the charms of the dead man's young widow, whom the plainclothes dicks suspect of the murder, Dewey tries to prove that the "ghost" he saw was someone else, and succeeds with the help of Adams' shameless unfairness to the reader. How did the sheet-shrouded killer avoid leaving footprints on that porch? Why, by going barefoot! Such is logic in the world of Cleve F. Adams.

~ ~ ~ ~ ~

The best-known Adams protagonist is private eye Rex McBride, who stars in six novels and had been in pulp stories for at least two years before his hardcover debut. In *Sabotage* (Dutton, 1940), which had first appeared as a five part serial (*Detective Fiction Weekly*, March 11-April 8, 1939), Rex is hired by a cartel of insurance underwriters to investigate the too frequent "accidents" plaguing a huge Nevada dam site. He visits the dam exactly once, spending the rest of his time in the nearby boomtown of Palos Verde pitting each of the corrupt factions that run the town against each other in the classic *Red Harvest* manner. Whenever Adams tries to plot—as he does in the silly, cluttered, unfair and unnecessary last chapter—he makes a shambles out of whatever he touches. But in this first novel he proved to be a master of the hardboiled virtues of pace, action, violence and the evocation of credible evil.

And Sudden Death (Dutton, 1940), which first appeared as the six-part serial "Homicide: Honolulu Bound" (*Detective Fiction Weekly*, December 16, 1939-January 20, 1940), finds Rex trailing the wife of an escaped embezzler across the Pacific from Los Angeles to pre-war Hawaii in search of the two million dollars the husband took with him—a simple enough assignment except that also on board the *Honolulu Queen* with McBride and the woman are Rex's jealous girl friend, a murderous trio on their own quest for the two million, and an assortment of Japanese spies. After a welter of murders and double-crosses the tale climaxes in a blaze of action and pseudo-reasoning.

In *Decoy* (Dutton, 1941), which had also run as a *Detective Fiction Weekly* six-parter (January 25-March 1, 1941), the insurance company hires McBride to find out why so many of Continental Airways' passenger planes have vanished into thin air or been wrecked. The trail leads him to an old gangland enemy, a fraternity of grounded pilots, a nest of Fifth Columnists, and hidden madness in a respected family. In between making time with the case's several luscious females our hero is slugged, slapped, bombed, and in general treated impolitely by an equal number of irate males. His solution as usual is pure guesswork but Adams keeps the pace brisk and the plot complications under relatively tight control.

Despite their faults his first three novels had been quite good of their kind, but his fourth was less auspicious. The protagonist of *The Black Door* (Dutton, 1941) is Jim Flagg, a former Federal narcotics agent who's engaged to a millionaire's daughter and, like McBride, feels distinctly ill at ease among the elite. In every other respect too this fellow looks, talks and acts exactly like the great Rex, and Bogart could have played either man in his sleep. No sooner does Flagg recommend a private eye to shadow a U.S. Senator's hell-bent daughter than the eye is killed and Flagg finds himself neck-deep in the familiar farrago of gamblers, gunmen, tough cops, corrupt pols and eager wenches, plus an Edgar Wallace-model hidden mastermind called The Keeper who runs a criminal empire based on torture and blackmail. Adams makes not the slightest effort to tie together the strands of his chaotic plot, allows his hero the most colossal luck in getting out of tight corners and guessing guilty secrets, and lets the book culminate in an infantile and clumsily staged trap for the master villain. A poor performance any way you slice it.

His next novel wasn't much of an improvement. The shamus in *What Price Murder* (Dutton, 1942) is our old friend Steve McCloud from the pulps, only here he's an insurance detective indistinguishable from McBride except in name. Tracing down a lead on a $250,000 diamond hijacking, McCloud finds the lovely potential tipster dead and his own married sweetheart, with whose husband the dead girl had been playing around, standing with gun in hand over the corpse. A badger racket, a brutal cop, a lovestruck gambler, several attorneys and even more loose women swarm through the crackling-paced but ridiculous plot, throughout which everyone slugs, gets drunk with, shoots and makes love to just about everyone else. McCloud lacks McBride's cynical wit but shares Rex's ability to absorb physical abuse that would kill a buffalo. Most of Chapter Nine, for example, is devoted to a beating administered to McCloud at the stationhouse by Lieutenant Brannigan and his goon squad. By the end of Chapter Ten McCloud has recovered enough to decoy Brannigan into an alley and beat him to a pulp in return.

The hero of Adams' next book was ex-Lieutenant John J. Shannon, another pulp-story cop civilianized for hardcover. *The Private Eye* (Reynal & Hitchcock, 1942) is the Adams title most often reprinted in paperback and the only one specifically mentioned in Barzun & Taylor's *Catalogue of Crime*. It's also a return to Adams' best vein. Shannon is another carbon copy of McBride right down to his black Irish roots, taste for gallows humor, maudlin sentimentality, intermittent affair with an intellectual woman, manic rages, and complete inability to explain his "deductive" conclusions. The plot is the old *Red Harvest* standby about blowing the lid off the corrupt city, this time Las Cruces, Arizona, which is plagued by a feud between rival copper mine owners, a force of crooked cops, an illiterate mayor, a string of industrial "accidents," and a neat little racket involving a Polish Relief Society. When the Las Cruces police pass off the death of his old sweetheart's husband as suicide, Shannon storms into town, is nearly blown to bits on the night of his arrival, and proceeds to play each of the town's rotten factions against the others. If you ignore the senseless and arbitrary solution and concentrate on Adams' gifts of action and pace, his vivid depiction of the copper mining milieu in which he once worked, his control of intrigues within intrigues, his evocation of the private detective in all his seedy but effective loutishness, you can have a hell of an evening with this book.

The following year Adams stuck the McBride name back on his shamus and produced a novel that is neither his best nor his worst but certainly his most notorious. *Up Jumped the Devil* (Reynal & Hitchcock, 1943) is also the only Adams novel that recognizably takes place on the home front of a country fighting a world war, and the vivid details of time and place are the high spots of the book. When McBride scents something phony in the theft of a valuable necklace from a government bureaucrat, his suspicions lead him straight into a multiple murder mess involving Nazi spies, sadistic cops, nympho socialites, syndicate hoods and the like. Adams starts the book off with a whopping coincidence, allows McBride literally dozens of lucky guesses during the action, and leaves all sorts of gaping potholes along the road to the solution.

If a prize were offered for the heaviest doses of racism and fascism in a pre-Spillane hardboiled novel, *Up Jumped the Devil* would win in a walk. McBride throws around terms like kike, spic, nigger and wop with the same casual abandon that informs his gunplay, and Adams' third-person narration treats us to more of the same. "The door opened and the Negro maid Beulah, also with gun, looked at McBride with the insolence a Central Avenue nigger gives the hapless white who invades his territory." McBride solves the case by guessing at a suspect and having him tortured by friendly gangsters till he confesses. To the FBI agent who compares such tactics to the Gestapo's, McBride replies that "an American Gestapo is goddam well what we need . . . The only way you can lick these guys is to fight as dirty as they do . . . You think I liked doing what I did? You think it didn't make me sick at my stomach? . . . It was lousy, but by God it worked." No wonder the liberal Anthony Boucher was ambivalent about this novel. In his review (*San Francisco Chronicle*, June 6, 1943, reprinted in Volume I of *The Anthony Boucher Chronicles*, 2001) he described *Up Jumped the Devil* as "a grand piece of ultra-hardboiled action and dialogue in the toughest tradition, and at the same time a very nasty piece of work" that displays "a really vicious attitude."

Along with racism and fascism goes contempt for reason. In an uproarious little sequence at the beginning of Chapter Thirteen, McBride lies in bed with the covers up to his chin and gives himself over to the pure luxury of what good—or at least fictional—detectives are supposed to employ when in a quandary: ratiocination.

The hell with all this running around, he thought. The hell with wearing my shoes down to the last eyelet when I can just lie here and let the Induction-Deduction twins do my work for me. Let's see, now, what was it Rourke hired me to do? Oh yes, to get the Adelphi necklace back! Well, hell, that's simple enough. All you've got to do is find the guy that's got it and take it away from him. All right, then; so far, so good. Now who do we think has got it?

It was at this point that Deduction and Induction deserted McBride completely. He cursed them impartially . . .

The way to solve crimes Adams style is to kill the suspect first and prove he did it later. Here's one of McBride's tough-minded pals describing an experience in the trenches during World War I.

"Why, I remember once—this was in France in '18—some son of a bitch lifted my coat and I like to froze to death till I found it on a corpse."

McBride stared at him suspiciously. "How'd you know it was yours?"

"Because the guy was wearing two of 'em when I shot him," Butch said.

The Crooking Finger (Reynal & Hitchcock, 1944) was McBride's fifth book-length adventure, Adams' third rehash of *Red Harvest*, and the last novel to appear under his own name in his lifetime. The murder of a fellow operative who was investigating whether the reform district attorney of San Gorgonio, Nevada had sold out brings McBride and the dead man's widow to town—which he proceeds to blow apart by pitting the crooked factions against one another until the hidden mastermind controlling the vice rackets crawls out of the woodwork and into the open where our man can squash him. But by this time the whole Adams fireworks display had become deadeningly overfamiliar, and no amount of brisk telling and pacing could help.

~ ~ ~ ~ ~

During the years Adams was selling these novels under his own byline he sold others under pseudonyms. By all odds his worst book was *The Vice Czar Murders* (Wilfred Funk, 1941, as by Franklin Charles), a collaborative effort in which Adams and his friend and fellow pulpster Robert Leslie Bellem (1902-1968), the prolific creator of Dan Turner, Hollywood Detective ("Somewhere a roscoe sneezed: Ka-chow! Ka-chow!"), expanded Adams' novelet "Song of Hate" (*Double Detective*, August 1938) to book length, with some input from Adams' then agent August Lenniger. The protagonist is district attorney's investigator Bill Rock, who is framed for a stripper's murder, breaks jail, and stalks the city cracking skulls in his search for the hidden mastermind at the top of the vice rackets. He proves his right to the name Rock by being impervious to the bashings and other more exotic tortures inflicted on him by assorted cops and hoods. With clockwork regularity he suspects, manhandles and almost kills first his boss, then his girlfriend, then his sister and brother-in-law, until we begin to wonder whether he was named for the contents of his head. The climax is at once stupid, unconsciously hilarious, and at odds with most of the plot. Add to these gaffes plenty of racism, sadism, sniggering sex (the Bellem contribution?) and choppy writing and you have an unmitigated disaster.

If Adams as Adams had a tendency to rewrite *Red Harvest*, under the byline of John Spain his practice was to recycle *The Glass Key*. The first book in the Spain trilogy is *Dig Me a Grave* (Dutton, 1942), which recounts the tribulations of Bill Rye, amoral troubleshooter for California political boss Ed Callahan who is plagued by a nympho wife, a boozer son, a Mexican spitfire claiming to be his illegitimate daughter, various slimies who are harassing each of the Callahans, and a double murder someone wants to hang around Papa Ed's neck. Rye simultaneously mixes into all of these messes, demolishing male obstacles with guns and fists, female with kisses, and pulling off coups against his boss's enemies with the help of fantastic runs of lucky guesswork.

Death Is Like That (Dutton, 1943) continues Rye's adventures while protecting the Callahans from the consequences of their peccadilloes so that Big Ed's crooked candidate for governor can beat the crook who's supported by the other side. The fireworks begin when son Gerald is suspected of shooting his wife's ex-lover at the same time Gerald's mother disappears in the wake of two murders that might well be her handiwork. As usual the plot collapses under the gentlest scrutiny.

Protagonist of the final Spain novel, *The Evil Star* (Dutton, 1944) is Lt. Steve McCord of Homicide, an amoral lone wolf indistinguishable in character or ethos from Adams' private eyes. His headaches begin when the police find and then promptly lose again a young woman who had been beaten severely and was faking amnesia. It soon develops that she's one of triplets, and that someone with a spy in Headquarters is willing to commit multiple murder to keep her from being rediscovered. Jewel theft, intrigue over a $17,000,000 inheritance, political corruption and several more homicides are tumbled together in this fast-moving but ultimately chaotic package.

~ ~ ~ ~ ~

Adams published no books after 1944 but supported himself and his family on movie option money, uncredited screenplay-tinkering chores and an occasional radio sale. The only screen credit he ever received was for *The Fatal Witness* (Republic, 1945), a quickie thriller starring Evelyn Ankers and Richard Fraser and directed by action-film specialist Lesley Selander. The script was attributed to Jerry Sackheim but Adams was credited with adapting (which probably means Americanizing) the short story by English author Rupert Croft-Cooke on which the picture was based—the same story that was the basis of the *Alfred Hitchcock Presents* telefilm "Banquo's Chair" (1959), directed by Hitchcock himself.

At least one of the twelve novels Adams published in his lifetime made him movie option money even though no film based on the book was ever shot. Howard Hawks (1896-1977), the legendary director of macho action flicks and screwball comedies, bought screen rights to *The Black Door* soon after the novel came out and commissioned a script from Leigh Brackett which was completed in January 1945. The book was still under option to Hawks in April of 1951, and by then he had commissioned a second screenplay, entitled *Stiletto*. For whatever reasons, he chose not to go into production on the picture. The unused screenplays are archived with Hawks' papers in Provo, Utah, at the library of Brigham Young University.

Whatever money Adams made from Hollywood was supplemented at the end of the Forties by radio. Once CBS' *The Adventures of Sam Spade* proved a huge success, hardboiled PI series became a staple of the airwaves, and early in 1949 NBC proposed to bring Adams' Rex McBride to the listening audience in the person of actor Frank Lovejoy. The series was to be called *Here*

Comes McBride and the pilot episode, "The Missing Diamonds", aired on May 19. The script by Bob Wright was a 30-minute condensation of 1943's *Up Jumped the Devil*, with a huge amount of Adams' plot squeezed in but all the wartime ambience, Nazi spies and fascistic overtones squeezed out. If the pilot led to a McBride series, it was canceled almost as soon as it started.

~ ~ ~ ~ ~

On December 28, 1949, at age 54, Adams died in his Glendale home of pneumonia complicated by a heart ailment. "His son phoned me at four o'clock in the morning," W.T. Ballard recalled in his interview with Stephen Mertz, "to tell me Cleve had had a heart attack. He was dead before I could drive over." Adams' pulp compadre Robert Leslie Bellem helped the family through its financial crisis by doing what he'd done nine years before: taking one of the dead author's old novelets and expanding it without credit to book length. The Bellem contribution seems to have consisted mainly of the sort of nonstop sex teasing with which he filled his own Dan Turner stories. The posthumous collaboration was published, under Adams' byline alone, as *No Wings on a Cop* (Handi-Books pb #112, 1950). Protagonist John J. Shannon is once again a police lieutenant as he'd been in all his pulp adventures before *The Private Eye*, but like Steve McCloud and the rest of the Adams legion of lawmen, he's an aggressive and gun-happy lone wolf cut from the same cloth as the author's civilian sleuths. When the captain of his squad is both framed as a bribe-taker and murdered just before the city's mayoral election, Shannon's vow of vengeance against the skipper's killer quickly earns him a broken arm, which scarcely slows him down as he distributes and soaks up physical abuse over the rest of the book. The plot is fill of gamblers, loose ladies, corrupt cops, beatings, bullets, erotic innuendo and holes. But the pace is so headlong that anyone capable of stopping to examine the nonsensical infrastructure must be a strong-minded reader indeed.

Six months or so after his death, Adams' final novel was published by the same prestigious hardcover house that had been home to Hammett and Chandler. *Contraband* (Knopf, 1950) records the first and only case of Federal agent Reed Smith, another clone of the Adams eye. Assigned to shadow a millionaire's daughter suspected of smuggling narcotics in from Mexico, Smith winds up in a morass of gamblers, cops on the take, knife-throwing Latinos, and a beautiful young woman who runs a hideout for wanted criminals. Adams' pervasive cynicism is somewhat more muted and the plot's underpinnings a bit sturdier than the norm, with the exposure of the hidden racket-boss for once making some sense. Anthony Boucher in the *New York Times Book Review* (July 16, 1950) neatly summed up Adams' career when he said: "The stuff of [his] yarn is familiar enough . . . Few practitioners, however, know how to put these ingredients together with such biting, driving economy. You'll be hard put to it to stop reading for an instant."

The third and last of the posthumous Adams novels presents us with a bibliographic mystery, namely how much of it is by Adams. Apparently he completed all or most of a draft in 1948-49 and this was whipped into publishable shape after his death by Robert Leslie Bellem and W.T. Ballard. In his interview with Stephen Mertz, Ballard recalled that when Adams "had a grave illness while in the middle of a detective book manuscript Bob suggested that the two of us finish it for him." For some unfathomable reason Bellem and Ballard seem to have worked on the project independently of each other, the upshot being two sometimes radically different versions of the same Adams plot. One of these was published in an obscure pulp magazine as "Too Fair to Die" (*Two Complete Detective Books*, March 1951) and the other as the original paperback novel *Shady Lady* (Ace pb #D115, 1955). Mystery fan Brian KenKnight, who closely compared both versions, described the former as "a breathlessly fast-paced story which rarely pauses for scene setting or anything else" and the latter as "less lively but more carefully written" and with many scenes "much more extensively described . . ." His conclusion was that Bellem had more to do with the pulp version and Ballard with the softcover novel. How much of either rendition can be credited to Adams himself will probably never be known but, sweeping all questions of authorship under the rug, I would hazard the judgment that *Shady Lady* is the finest book of his career. Rex McBride trails a missing embezzler's girlfriend from Los Angeles to the mining metropolis of Copper Hill, Montana, and arrives just in time to become involved in a vicious gubernatorial primary, love affairs with two sisters, and a string of murders. Even in the book version the landscape is littered with loose ends of plot, but the overflowing abundance of strong character sketches and powerfully understated scenes suggests either that the principal author was W.T. Ballard or that Adams was evolving into a talent of almost Chandleresque proportions. The electoral contest provides a marvelous setting for Adams' gleefully ghoulish cynicism about American politics.

~ ~ ~ ~ ~

"We all grew up together, so to speak," Raymond Chandler wrote to Adams in September 1948, "and we all wrote the same idiom . . ." But, he went on, he and Adams neither wrote alike nor thought alike. "Your stuff could never have been mistaken for mine or mine for yours." W.T. Ballard made the same point about thirty years later when he told Stephen Mertz that Adams was "good, though hardly in a class with Ray Chandler."

In his seminal essay "The Simple Art of Murder" (*Atlantic Monthly*, December 1944), Chandler had commented: "It is not a very fragrant world, but . . . certain writers with tough minds and a cool spirit of detachment can make very interesting and even amusing patterns out of it." Was it Adams' world that he had in mind? Chandler went on to argue that this quality "is not quite enough," that there must also be a knightly hero to redeem and counterbalance the rotten milieu. But here is precisely where Chandler and Adams part company. For Adams there is no hero and the protagonist is as foul as everyone else, just tougher and luckier. The difference between Chandler and Adams is the difference between a disillusioned but still hopeful romantic on the one hand and a total cynic on the other. The world of Cleve F. Adams is surely not a fragrant world but he described it with incomparable raw readability and in his own way he captured as much of the feel of his time as his friend and contemporary Chandler, and created as powerful an image of the private eye.

> He stands in trenchcoat stony-eyed, surveys
> The bleak and gritty world of greed and gore,
> Then strides across the landscape of the night
> Where it is always 1944.

Francis M. Nevins

JOHN LAWRENCE

Among mystery writers he is king of the unremembered. In the Nineteen Thirties and early Forties, during the golden age of crime and detective pulps, John Lawrence appeared regularly in *Black Mask, Dime Detective* and all sorts of similar magazines, with his name often featured on their covers. Since then he's been almost completely forgotten, and not a word on him can be found in any of the major critical or reference books on the mystery genre, even those most partial to writers from the pulps. Search high and low and you'll find not an iota of proof that a crime author named John Lawrence ever existed. I tried for years without success to establish that he was a human being and not a house name. Then early in 1986 a friend who remembered my interest in Lawrence told me of an elderly acquaintance who had written for pulps of the Thirties and had mentioned casually that his best friend back then had been a fellow pulpster by the name of Jack Lawrence. That was the beginning of the end of my search.

I had discovered Lawrence years before while researching the pulp tales of his infinitely better known contemporary Cornell Woolrich. Unlike Woolrich, unlike Hammett and Chandler and Gardner and all the other pulp mystery writers who made it big, Lawrence never wrote a novel. But his best stories are as riveting as anything in those grand old magazines. Between 1931 and 1948 he sold close to a hundred pulp tales, most of them long and complex enough to be classified as novelets, a good many of them still compulsively readable after the passage of from 65 to 80 years. But in May 1986, when I visited a trim brownstone on Jane Street in Manhattan's West Village and taped an interview with the lively octogenarian who had been Lawrence's closest friend, I learned that the life of the man who had written those tales was just as fascinating as his fiction.

Charles Spain Verral was a native Canadian, born near Toronto in 1904. In the mid-1920s he emigrated to New York City with dreams of a career in commercial art, but he wound up editing various pulp magazines and eventually writing full time for the pulps himself. He was best known as the author of dozens of 1920s air adventure whizbangs starring Bill Barnes and his legion of fellow pilots who roamed about battling evildoers, For several years he turned out one of these 65,000-word epics every month, and they were so popular among young readers that the publisher had to hire a staffer just to answer the flood of fan mail that poured in. Later Verral met a number of World War II combat pilots who told him that their interest in the wild blue yonder had first been sparked by those pulp thrillers. In odd moments during the Thirties, Verral wrote scripts for the *Mandrake the Magician* radio series. After the decline of the pulps he went back to editing (for Reader's Digest Books) and to writing Golden Books, biographies of sports and science figures for teens, even the continuity for a comic strip. Still active and sprightly in his middle eighties, he was delighted to sit down with me and resurrect his memories of the old pulps and of his friend Jack Lawrence. Without his help and the leads he gave me, the story of Lawrence's life could never have been told.

John Frederick Brock Lawrence was another native Canadian, born at Windsor, Ontario on February 4, 1907. The most illustrious person in his family tree and the source of the Brock in his name was Major General Sir Isaac Brock (1769-1812), the Canadian military hero who was killed in the battle of Queenstown during the War of 1812. Apparently the marriage of Lawrence's parents broke up when Jack was a boy. "I never knew his father," Chuck Verral told me, "but Jack used to tell me stories about him. He must have been a very humorous guy. He left Gertie [his wife and Jack's mother but no relation to the actress Gertrude Lawrence] and married a younger woman. There was a lot of bitterness there." His mother was clearly the dominant parent in Jack's life.

After attending the Collegiate Institute in Windsor, Lawrence entered the Royal Military College at Kingston, Ontario, which is the Canadian equivalent of West Point. RMC records indicate that he enrolled there in September 1922, at the incredibly early age of fifteen years and seven months, and left prior to the graduation of his class, in January 1925, when he was not quite eighteen. His separation from the school was recorded as having been at his parents' request. According to what he told Chuck Verral ten to fifteen years later, he was expelled from the RMC for some escapade connected with drinking. But he seems not to have been shunned by his classmates and remained on good terms with a number of them.

After Lawrence completed his education elsewhere, he and his mother moved from Ontario to New York City. Jack quickly found work on Wall Street and, in those feverish late 1920s, made a great deal of money in a very short time. When the Crash came in 1929, he found himself out of a job almost overnight. Disgusted with the business world, he decided to write for a living.

At that time there was something of an Old Boy Network linking those Canadians who had migrated to Manhattan to seek their fortunes, and at the center of the web was Michigan-born Roy Mitchell (1884-1944), who had been educated in Toronto and spent much of his life there, first as a newspaper reporter and then, beginning in 1919, as director of the University of Toronto's newly opened Hart House theatre. By 1930 he was a professor in the drama department of New York University. He had earlier used his connections to help launch Chuck Verral's American career, and now, hearing of Jack Lawrence's desire and of Verral's success in the pulps, he brought the two young Canadians together.

"I was living then at 18 Christopher Street, in Greenwich Village," Verral recalled, "and Jack and his mother lived two blocks away, in a beautiful apartment on Waverly Place. They must still have had some money to be able to live in a nice place like that after the Crash. Gertie was a very attractive and handsome woman with jet black hair. She was very close to Jack, and I think he was scared of her. She was always most gracious to me, but I think it was mainly because she recognized that I could help Jack get started as a writer. He would come over to my place a lot and we would talk about writing. He knew little or nothing about story construction when we started."

Then as now, connections made careers. "Jack and I were both Canadians," Verral said, "went to the same kind of prep schools, played a lot of hockey and tennis. We became good friends. He kept quizzing me about all the aspects of writing—plotting, knowing your market, and so on. He was a fast learner and could absorb what you told him." Verral got married—and remained married to the same woman until his death in 1990—but, as he put it, "Jean got annoyed at Jack because he made a habit of hanging around in our place half the night. We were living in a one-room apartment in the Village and Jean had a job in publishing, she had to get up early and needed her sleep."

Mrs. Verral worked for Popular Publications, editing pulp magazines like *Gang World* and *Underworld Romances* under her maiden name Jean Mithoefer. "Jack heard through Jean," Chuck Verral said, "that they needed a story at Popular to fill out an issue.

Jack got busy and banged out a mystery, and through Jean he got it sold to Popular." Once his foot was in the door, Lawrence knew how to squeeze the rest of himself in. "Jack and I played tennis every morning except Sunday," Verral told me, "indoors, at the old Armory on 14th Street. We started to play doubles with Harry Steeger and Harold Goldsmith, the partners who owned Popular Publications. Jack began to sell regularly to Popular after he got in socially."

His first published stories seem to have been "Private Enemy Number One" and "The White Eye", which appeared respectively in the October and November 1931 issues of *Detective Action Stories*. In 1932 he sold two more tales to the same magazine, three to *Gang World*, and three private-eye novelets to *Dime Detective*. The following year he appeared six times in *Dime*, once in *Thrilling Detective*, and once in the crime genre's premier pulp ("Scarlet Stakes", as by Jack Lawrence, *Black Mask*, June 1933). His writing career had taken off like a barnstorming plane in a Bill Barnes adventure. "His early stories were sort of stiff and a little mechanical," Verral said, "but he began to smooth it out after a while. We used to sit side by side and spit olive pits into the fire, working on story ideas. If we were at my place, anything we said—ideas, terror traps, whatever—was my property. If we were at his place, anything we came up with belonged to him. We gave each other all sorts of ideas."

Eventually Lawrence worked out a fiction formula which he embodied in a two-page memorandum to himself, entitled "Construction of a Short Story". The memo begins with his definition of the form. "A short story is about a character faced with a problem and his reactions as he solves or fails to solve that problem. It is most desirable for the character to have one single outstanding characteristic (a short story has no room for more) and to have the problem solved through repeated operation of this characteristic." Then come six numbered paragraphs dealing with story construction and a single paragraph on unity of time, space and viewpoint. Finally Lawrence says: "What the writer is trying to say to the reader in a short story should be something like this: Here is a character. He was faced with so-and-so. He was this kind of person. He had a chance to solve so-and-so if he would do this-and-that. He tried to. Because he was the person he is, he did this. Then he had to do this, but again because he was the kind of person he was, he did that. Finally in desperation, as the crucial test came up, he hesitated. Ordinary logic told him to do A, but because he was who he was, he had to do B—and queerly enough, it came out fine. So you see, he really was the kind of person I told you in the first place."

Lawrence's practice was better than his theory. Whatever use of this rigid formula he thought he was making, I can find little if any trace of it in his stories. In any event, within a few years of his debut in print he was selling regularly and beginning to make a name for himself among the editors and readers of the crime pulps. But no matter how much he sold, he never seemed to have enough money and was always on the lookout for ways to make more. "During the Bank Holiday of 1933," Verral remembered, "he did something absolutely impossible. He went to a bank, told them some story, and got them to lend him money." Where the money went remained a mystery but a hefty chunk was needed to pay his bar bills. "Jack was a pretty heavy social drinker," Verral said, "although he never let it interfere with his writing. There was a speakeasy uptown where Legs Diamond used to hang out, and Jack would spend a lot of time up there. He knew a lot of gangsters. They fascinated him." Eventually, as we'll see, he wrote a long series of stories about them, calling them not gangsters but cops. Another hefty chunk was spent on impressing the men who bought from him. "He'd take Steeger or some other editor to dinner," Verral said, "and borrow the money from me to pay the bill. But in the end, when he got a check, he'd always pay me back. And if I ever came up short of cash, which was often, Jack would come to the rescue. He'd give you the ribbon off his typewriter."

When not drinking or writing, Lawrence continued to hang out with Verral. "Jack and I used to go down to the Hudson River very late at night and sit on the waterfront and yak away. You'd be mugged or killed if you did that now [in the 1980s when the area was dangerous indeed], but in the Thirties there was no danger at all." Much of their yakking had to do with stories, and because they didn't write in the same fields, each was able to help the other freely without cutting his own throat in the process. "We had a sort of unwritten rule," Verral said. "He didn't write sports or air stories and I almost never wrote a mystery." Outside of shoptalk Lawrence's favorite conversational subject seems to have been religion. "Jack was a Theosophist. He was brought in by Roy Mitchell, who used to be called the Pope of Theosophy. Roy gave lectures and Gertie, Jack's mother, was one of his group. Later Jack came in. He would talk theosophy by the hour."

The one thing he refused to talk about was his wife. "Her name was Muriel Bodkin," Verral recalled. "A beautiful, delightful woman, a few years older than Jack. She was exceptionally well read, she was a writer and a poet, she was an actress, she could do anything. But she wasn't very conventional. She had what they used to call a Bohemian lifestyle. Of course, so did Jack in a lot of ways. But that's not how his mother saw it. Gertie was dead set against her. I don't think anyone would have suited her as a mate for her son. She did her best to break them up." And Jack, remember, was afraid of his mother.

Although still living with Gertie, Lawrence secretly married Muriel in 1931 or thereabouts. From then on he paid her surreptitious visits whenever he could slip away from home, and also paid her a few literary compliments, such as giving the name Muriel to the female lead in his second story, "The White Eye." The only person he let in on the secret was Chuck Verral. Even Verral's wife found out only by accident. "One day Jean and her co-editors were having lunch in a tea room when who should walk in but Muriel. In some way the name John Lawrence came up and Muriel heard it and said: 'Do you know my husband?' And Jean said: 'Know him? He's *my* husband's best friend!' Well, Jean and Muriel got together and became good friends. But Jack was horrified that the thing had blown open, so we were both sworn to secrecy. Gertie never knew about the marriage until Muriel got pregnant, and then the fat was in the fire." Their daughter, Judith, was born in December 1934.

At the time I got to know Chuck Verral, Judy lived in Athens and, as J.A. Lawrence, had become known as a science-fiction writer. She remembered almost nothing of her father. "I didn't like him as a child," she wrote to me, "and later, when I was eighteen, tried to find out what anybody had seen in him, since I was told he was charming. I found him nuts myself." If Judy saw little of her father, she and Muriel saw even less of his money. "My mother says that she never saw any money from the sale of Jack's work. In fact she says that she didn't know he sold anything. *She* supported the house and me by writing romances, ad copy, anything she could. She believes that he started writing because he was going to show her that anyone could do it and she needn't be such a snob. We think he was probably giving the money to his mother."

In 1935 Jean Verral became very ill and underwent surgery. Afterwards, on her doctor's advice, she and Chuck moved to Fort Lauderdale, Florida. "We went for three months and stayed three years," Chuck said. "I didn't see much of Jack, although we did correspond." While the Verrals were in Florida and Chuck was banging out Bill Barnes adventures, Jack Lawrence left his mother and moved with Muriel and Judy to a house at Northport, Long Island. But by 1938, when the Verrals moved back to New York and into the brownstone which was their home for the rest of their lives, Jack and Muriel had split. Gertie Lawrence had finally broken up her son's marriage.

Jack did not go home to mother but moved into a midtown hotel and resumed his old friendship with Chuck Verral, which included borrowing money from him regularly. "He'd get so broke he couldn't pay his hotel bill," Verral recalled, "and they'd threaten to seize everything he owned. But he'd always manage to grind out a story and get in the clear, or else he'd find someone to give him a loan." Through it all he somehow managed to keep up appearances. "He was a man of impeccable manners, always well turned out in a very British kind of way. He was rarely seen needing a shave or a haircut. Women seemed to find him intriguing and charming. I'm told he was an excellent dancer. To men he was a good guy to be with, a topnotch athlete. He was a master of repartee and quips and appreciated the wit of others."

When Lawrence was in need, Verral would supply not only money but literary advice. "When he was working on a story and got stuck on a snag in the plot, he'd call me from his hotel and say: 'Come up for a drink. I want to talk to you.' And when I got there he'd say: 'Don't get drunk. I want your head.' And he'd ask me to help him around the snag." Once, Verral remembered, he and his wife invited Lawrence to their Jane Street house for dinner. "I can't come," Lawrence told them. "I don't have a nickel for the subway." Such was life for a struggling pulpster in the Thirties.

Some time during that decade, Lawrence's father died. One day in the middle of a week he said to Verral: "Well, I'll see you next Monday." Verral asked where he was off to. "I'm going to Detroit to plant my old man." Despite the flippancy, Lawrence seems to have thought a great deal of the father he had almost never seen, and his pose as a sort of Errol Flynn character, a hard-drinking hell-raising womanizing swashbuckler with a merry quip in the face of any adversity, can probably be credited to his wanting to be like the man he thought his father was. "When he went to his father's house," Verral said, "he found a huge bunch of pulps. It was obvious his father had been hunting around to find his stories. Jack was moved by this very much."

In 1939, when England and Nazi Germany went to war, one might have expected Lawrence to play the Errol Flynn role, throw down his typewriter and put on a uniform. In fact he kept writing as if nothing had happened. In August 1942 he did go back to Canada, where he applied for and was given a commission in the Royal Canadian Air Force. For the next two and a half years he was stationed in Canada, taking a number of training courses, serving as an administrative officer when he wasn't in school. "He was the adjutant of his unit," Verral remembered. "He used to tell me stories of when he'd be with the commanding officer at parades, when all the personnel of the unit were marching by, and the commander would whisper to Jack: 'What do I say next?' Jack always knew the answer. He was a very military guy." According to Verral he also took full advantage of the sexual freedom that the war brought in its wake. Eventually, Chuck said, "our relationship dwindled to just a few letters. He'd write and ask me if I could send him some item that was hard to come by in Canada, like golf balls for the officers' club."

The Verrals, who spent the war years in New York, couldn't see Lawrence any more but saw quite a bit of his ex-wife and the daughter she was raising. "One weekend when Jean and I happened to be going to Toronto, Jack got some leave time and came down here. He and Muriel and Judy all stayed here in our house. But they never got back together again as a family."

Early in 1945 Lawrence's outfit was shipped out to England, but by then the war was almost over in Europe and apparently he never saw combat. Discharged late that summer, he went back to Toronto and tried to start life over. "After the war he came to New York to see us a couple of times," Verral said, "and I always thought he was like a stranger then, not quite the same man he'd been. He was trying to get back as a writer and he was trying to get a job. Later we'd pick up news of him, usually from someone else in our group of New York Canadians who went back to Canada and saw him from time to time. Apparently he was having it rough and was always short of money. When he had an operation in Toronto, he had to borrow for it."

He did sell a few more stories which appeared in pulps between 1946 and 1948 but for all practical purposes his career as a magazine writer was over, and he had never wanted to graduate from the pulps into novels. He found a job with the Canadian Advertising Agency in Montreal and later became public relations man for a knitting company and a silk mill in Toronto. "He had an affair with a nurse up there," Verral recalled, "and she stayed with him all the way through."

On January 28, 1970, Lawrence died in Toronto Western Hospital at age 62. The autopsy listed the cause of death as cancer of the right lung coupled with pulmonary emphysema. "As I recall it," Verral said, "he'd descended to being the publicity man for a troupe of strippers." The Toronto newspapers never mentioned his death. After all, who had ever heard of the man?

While I was learning about Jack's life, Muriel Lawrence was in her eighties and living in a retirement home. She had no interest in helping reconstruct her ex-husband's life and was amazed that anyone could be interested in his writing. The scars of that broken marriage ran deep.

In 1963, when Judy Lawrence was in her late twenties, she met the science-fiction writer James Blish. They were married a year later. Blish introduced his bride to his literary agent, Ken White, who as editor of *Dime Detective* had bought dozens of stories from John Lawrence in the Thirties and early Forties. "Jim didn't give Ken my maiden name. Ken looked long and hard at me and said: 'You're Jack's daughter! The last time I saw you, you were chewing a gingham elephant!' Blish died in 1975. I am told that many of the *Star Trek* novelizations published in his last years under his byline were ghost-written by his then mother-in-law, Muriel Lawrence.

After he'd stopped writing, Lawrence apparently came to agree with his ex-wife about the quality of his work. He took drastic steps to keep his daughter from ever finding one of his stories, telling Judy that he wrote exclusively under pen names, making both Chuck Verral and his former agent promise never to show her any of his work. When I first wrote to her about her father, she had been trying off and on for years to crack his pseudonyms, never realizing that everything he'd published had been under his own byline. "For God's sake send me a story!" she pleaded.

So in one sense at least the tale of Lawrence's life ends happily: his child had a chance to read him. Perhaps others would like to join her?

~ ~ ~ ~ ~

Lawrence's success as a mystery writer hinged on his personal and professional rapport with Harry Steeger and Harold Goldsmith, who in 1930, defying the Depression and all conventional prudence, had given up editorial jobs with other firms and launched their own publishing venture which would soon grow into a pulp empire. Popular Publications hit America's newsstands in October 1930 with a line of four monthly magazines, one each devoted to air-war thrillers, gangster tales, Westerns and crime fiction. The feature attraction in the first issue of *Detective Action Stories* was "The Key to Room 537" by pulp king Erle Stanley Gardner, who appeared in every single issue of the magazine from its debut through the end of 1931. It was in this magazine that Lawrence broke into print late that year with "Private Enemy Number One" (October 1931) and "The White Eye" (November 1931).

Judging by the latter story, Chuck Verral's comments about the weaknesses in Lawrence's early efforts seem right on target. The setting is Greenwich Village and Barton Black, swashbuckling newshawk for the New York *Sentinel*, is on the trail of Jules de Rastignac, the French master criminal whose *nom de guerre* is Monsieur Blood. At four in the morning, homeward bound on the all but empty subway, Black encounters a wounded man and, at his request, takes him to the house of a doctor in the Village. Both the patient and the doctor turn out to be involved with Monsieur Blood. Walking from the doctor's house to his own apartment on Christopher Street, Black runs into a triple murder in Washington Square and the theft of the fabled diamond known as the White Eye. This too turns out to be Monsieur Blood's handiwork. Later that morning Black overhears a conversation between two petty hoodlums in a lunch wagon and the subject, as if you haven't guessed, is Monsieur Blood. In terms of plot, characterization, style and everything else, this story is a hunk of wildly overwrought melodrama.

> After what seemed years, Bart heard footsteps outside his door. The key turned. The two came in. The surface veneer was gone. Dirty, disheveled, panting—they looked like the human hyenas they were. Their eyes blazed with baffled greed, and from the corner of Monsieur Blood's thin lips drooled a thin trickle of saliva.

But the action scenes are slammed over with gusto, Greenwich Village is evoked vividly, and Lawrence betrays his origins with a string of British locutions like "he swung from his boot tops" and his taste for bizarre humor with the revelation that the ultimate hiding place of the White Eye is inside his hero's sinus cavity. It is not by chance that the heroine of the tale is named Muriel. Lawrence's pulpy hokum did not improve *Detective Action Stories'* low sales figures and the magazine was dropped in 1932 after nineteen issues.

In November 1931, the same month that "The White Eye" appeared, Popular launched one of the best known and most successful of all crime pulps, *Dime Detective*, and within six months of its debut Lawrence was in the lineup with "The Scarlet Coat" (April 1932), the first of his more than fifty sales to the magazine. In his second *Dime* tale, "The Torso Trap" (October 1932), he introduced two-gun New York PI Sam Beckett, with demon newshound Barton Black in a subsidiary role. The tough-guy dialogue in this one is overdone to the point of laughability, and Anglicisms still abound—even the same of Sam's business is Beckett Private Inquiry Agency—but the story is chock-full of action, climaxing in a motorized gunbattle through the West Village, and the plot with its bond theft from a brokerage house capitalizes neatly on Lawrence's Wall Street years.

Before long Lawrence was a *Dime* regular, appearing in six of the magazine's 1933 issues, seven in '34 and four in '35, almost all of them novelets featuring either Sam Beckett or another New York eye, Cass Blue. A typical specimen of the Blue series is "A Burial Is Arranged" (March 1, 1935). One black and wind-whipped night, Blue is hired by wealthy and terrified undertaker Mario Maresca to make a 1:30 A.M. visit to a little church off Times Square and pick up an affidavit swearing that Maresca several years ago inadvertently buried one of his customers alive. Maresca is shot and almost killed while explaining his predicament and Blue roars into action, shooting up a storm, threatening to frame or kill any innocent person in his way, blackjacking a cop and an old building watchman, breaking into his client's office, sitting on the face of a dead man, tearing about the Manhattan nightscape in a psychotic orgy of action that doesn't let up till morning. The story makes precious little sense and at least one major plot element, the matter of who shot Maresca and why, is dropped down the memory hole without a word of explanation. But Blue's first-person narrative is so wildly overwrought that you are caught up as in a whirlwind and tossed through events along with him.

In 1936 Lawrence created his first lone-wolf cop. Drago, a brown-faced and neatly dressed killer with a badge, appeared in four *Dime* short novels. The last of them, "Murder on Margin"

(June 1937), begins on another of those icy nights when the wind whips and howls through Manhattan's concrete canyons. A young cop on his beat along upper Broadway happens to encounter three men coming up out of a sidewalk freight elevator. One of the trio drops his keys. When the cop tries to return them, he's riddled with bullets. Ruthless Inspector McTigue, the young officer's mentor, sends out Drago with orders to find the murderers—and turn them over to him for "a taste of hell." The trail leads Drago into the world of stockbrokers and call options (the world in which Lawrence had lived before the Crash) and into the gunsights of rival groups of thugs searching for a slip of green paper worth half a million. The penultimate climax is set on the north shore of Long Island where Jack and Muriel Lawrence had lived before the breakup of their marriage. The story has its moments but it's too long, too unsubtly padded, sloppily written ("The store, if he recalled it, was a butcher store, in which nothing of value was stored overnight"), and fails to rhyme at the end. The brief Drago series isn't terribly important in its own right but did give Lawrence the chance to do some rough sketches for the kinds of stories and characters in his later, longer and far superior series about the Marquis of Broadway.

That series is Lawrence's chief claim to a place in crime fiction history. Lieutenant Martin Marquis and the men of his Broadway Squad are not only the most vicious group of cops in the literature but support a system in their own image, ruthless and tyrannical almost beyond imagining. With 22 legalized murderers under his control, Marquis's job is "to rule half the city's thieves" or, more precisely, the *other* half of the city's thieves. Marty is trimly built, dapper, deceptively slight, with a round and weathered face and small deep-set blue eyes. Like his creator, he prefers to be seen in fancy clothes. His habitual attire includes an imported derby, a tight black silk scarf, black kid gloves and shoes, a dark suit, an ankle-length black Chesterfield. Sound like a gangster? Marquis's behavior does nothing to change that perception. He thinks of himself as a polished and quiet man of culture but his immaculate appearance and good taste are a veneer, poorly concealing the brutal and insecure mugg from Avenue A who worships power with the intensity of a fanatic. He enjoys being mistaken for a vice-president, supports a widowed mother and two sisters in Brooklyn and visits them once a month, has had his Central Park West apartment redecorated "in proper old oak and leather" like an English gentleman's den, but he's just a gangster with a badge.

The men of the Broadway Squad resemble their leader: shrewd, discreet and amoral, a parade of thieves, blackmailers, sadists and killers. One robbed banks as a sideline while on the force. Another beat into near-insanity a victim who refused to pay graft. Marty's right-hand man on the Squad was a habitual taker of bribes. Now united under the Marquis, they rob and terrorize only at his orders, forming a tight-knit American S.S., not bound by the rules which tie the hands of the regular police, free to do virtually whatever they please as they perform their mission. Part of that mission is to maintain for the Squad a prestige so extravagant as to make them seem like gods beyond good and evil. I don't believe a more vivid picture of American fascism has ever appeared in fiction.

The jungle ethos of the Squad is perfectly captured in the first tale of the series, "Broadway Malady" (*Dime Detective*, February 1937). Marquis warns gambler Frankie May not to retaliate when young Jerry Lyle falls in love with Dorinne, a dancer in one of Frankie's joints, whom Frankie wants for himself. Frankie defies the Marquis and orders his goons to work Jerry over. Ordinarily Marquis would have had one of the Squad beat Frankie to a pulp in return, but Frankie's political pull is too strong. "He has his finger on the mayor." Frankie leans hard on Dorinne, sends hoods to shoot Jerry on the street and has an Inspector warn Marquis to lay off. Marty throws away his badge, then takes it back and, rather than quit, accepts a compulsory vacation. He goes to Chicago and locates Spender, a kidnaper who's notorious for killing his victims if ransom isn't paid to his precise orders. Marquis has Spender snatch Frankie May and hold him for ransom, knowing that Ginger, Frankie's ambitious second-in-command, will refuse to pay and thereby painlessly step into the boss's shoes. But Ginger proves loyal and agrees to pay, an act of decency that literally stuns Marquis. Recovering from shock, Marty rushes to the hideout where Spender is holding Frankie and gimmicks the phone so that Spender won't learn that the payoff is going through. Spender then wastes Frankie. End of story.

That is a model of moral probity compared with the second Marquis adventure, "Live Man's Shoes" (*Dime Detective*, August 1937), in which the Broadway Squad's prestige is on the line when Marty is skillfully framed for murder.

> It was the first time the Marquis had been framed. Rage had him speechless—rage and cold, instant perception of what he was up against. This was cool, devastating challenge to the

one thing that kept the Broadway Squad alive—prestige. Someone had dared thumb his nose at the Marquis of Broadway. He had to smash the killer mercilessly enough so that snickers would have no chance to start along the Stem.

Marty at once takes over the investigation of the murder, threatening to ruin the officials in charge both politically and physically if they interfere. "If you get in my hair in any way, shape or form," he tells an assistant district attorney, "I'll have you beaten up." His only clue to the person who framed him is a brass disk that formed part of a hotel-room key—the key, it turns out, to a room where another murder had taken place a few weeks before. As the hunt goes on, the Marquis reaches the conclusion that a member of the Broadway Squad is behind the frame. Having not a drop of evidence against his subordinate that would hold up in court, Marquis simply lures the suspect into a death trap in which other Squad members kill the man off.

Not all the Marquis stories are this brutal but the best of them are. When Lawrence toned down the nastiness, his technique seemed to suffer too, as in "Natural Killer" (*Dime Detective*, December 1937). One morning at dawn, an assailant perched on a rooftop above 52nd Street drops a sheet of plate glass on homeward-bound Eberhardt Hastings, a chubby, good-natured and free-spending Broadway character. Marquis determines to track down the perpetrator although Ebie insists that everyone loves him and that he hasn't an enemy in the world. It soon develops that he has three: tavernkeeper Leo Feinberg, who owes Ebie a lot of money he can't repay; Florence Hastings, Ebie's estranged puritanical wife; and Dan Morris, a struggling young actor who's in love with Mrs. Hastings. Eventually Marquis discovers Morris shot to death in Ebie's apartment, a sweepstakes ticket in his hand. The climax is both sloppy and absurd, with everything depending on Marty's having left his pistol in a spot where at the time he had no reason to leave it. It seems that Lawrence's cynicism and his storytelling savvy rose or fell together.

Between 1937 and the end of 1942 a total of 28 Lawrence short novels were published in *Dime Detective*. All but two dealt with the Broadway Squad but many of these were told in first person rather than in Lawrence's usual third-person narration, and Dirty Marty was often offstage or in a walk-on part while one or another of his subordinates such as Al Hackett, Ace McGuire or Big Johnny Berthold took over the case. One of the best later tales starring the Marquis himself is "Floater" (*Dime Detective*, June 1941), whose plotline owes more than a little to the classic Damon Runyon story and Frank Capra film *Lady for a Day*. Vicelord Nick Swaine asks Marty to run him out of town so that without alienating his gangster buddies he can leave the world of crime and become a respectable family man. What has inspired Nick's reform is his son, who has lived for years in South America in ignorance of Nick's underworld life and who's about to come back to the States and take up a career as a concert violinist. Marty agrees to cooperate. Then, at the last minute and due to a change in his son's travel plans, Nick begs for an extra day in New York but this time Marty turns him down. Early the next morning Nick and his girlfriend are machine-gunned on the street, the woman fatally. Blamed for the murder and forbidden by his superiors even to talk with Nick in his hospital room, Marquis tries desperately to persuade Nick's son that he's innocent. Eventually and quite neatly he exposes the real killer.

During the Marquis years Lawrence was also selling regularly to *Black Mask*. The most interesting of the characters he created for that magazine was special investigator Barron Hargraft, who debuted in "Club Fighter" (*Black Mask*, December 1937). On the surface Hargraft is a tough New York gambler but he's also an undercover agent for state betting commissioner Sam Hoyle, who uses Hargraft to discourage the fixing of sports events and to insure the success of Hoyle's private wagers. As the date approaches when upcoming middleweight champ Flash Laterno will defend his title against Nate Crowley, Hoyle sends Hargraft to Detroit to investigate a betting pattern which suggests that the champ may be about to take a dive. As soon as he arrives, Laterno's manager Pop Lingle is stabbed and dies in Hargraft's car. Hargraft dumps the body, conceals news of the murder even from Pop's daughter and son-in-law, and takes over as Laterno's manager himself. Returning to New York, Hargraft mixes into the gamblers' schemes for the big fight. In due course there's a second murder, this time with Hargraft himself as prime suspect. The climax during and after the big bout is both viscerally exciting and neatly clued. It's a shame Hargraft appeared only once more after his debut, in "Deed of Gift" (*Black Mask*, August 1938). Most of Lawrence's later sales to the magazine were Broadway Squad thrillers narrated in first person by various subordinates of Marty Marquis. Lawrence's last tale in the premier crime pulp was "Detour to Death" (*Black Mask*,

October 1942). By the time it came out he was back in Canada wearing a uniform.

As far as I and my pulpophile friends can determine, Lawrence sold only five short novels after the war. "Body in Waiting" (*New Detective*, July 1948) is a standard Forties PI yarn starring Joey Sapphire, a short, neatly dressed and ruthless shamus whose tactics might have been frowned on even by the Marquis. Sapphire invades the corrupt upstate New York community of Danvers City to avenge the murder of his friend and fellow eye Danny Dean. While stopping at a roadside diner for a bite to eat, Sapphire is attacked by two goons and his hand is cooked on an electric stove. (How the thugs knew who he was or where he'd choose to have a meal is one of many plot points Lawrence never bothers to explain.) Broiled and bandaged but unbowed, Sapphire hits town and quickly learns that its political boss, Frank Carllson, is the same man who had gotten away with the sadistic murder of Joey's girlfriend eight years before. Sapphire starts manipulating people and events so that Carllson, who is pathologically protective of his man-crazy 17-year-old sister, comes to believe she's having an affair with Jeff Larrabee, one of Danvers City's few honest cops. Then Joey knocks out both Larrabee and the kid sister with Mickey Finns, puts in an anonymous call to Carllson, sits back and watches the enraged brother riddle the innocent and unconscious cop with bullets. Since Larrabee was also well connected politically, we are assured that this is one murder Carllson will pay for. The next morning Sapphire plays master detective and exposes the murderer of his pal Danny Dean, and this perp too gets blown away by a well-placed slug. The tale is replete with out-of-place Anglicisms, sloppy writing ("I . . . looked up at the sturdy, gracious building, raising twenty stories from a square of emerald lawn"), and plotting gaffes, but offhand I can't think of a single PI in fiction who plays as dirty as this one. Perhaps that's what readers had come to expect from the creator of the Marquis of Broadway.

Marty's own swan song in print was "A Frame for the Marquis" (*Dime Detective*, June 1948), whose setting once again is New York during a bone-freezing cold wave. Doris Connelly, daughter of a wily old con man, now dead, for whom Marty had had a soft spot, begs the Marquis to find her brother Gerry, who vanished after having been framed (so Doris says) for the murder of a visiting Colorado cop. As usual Marty runs into interference from other public officials and threatens to punch out the assistant

D.A. in charge of the case. A few nights later Marquis finds Gerry's body, butchered in a warehouse on the Jersey waterfront, and soon learns that once again he himself has been neatly framed for the murder. Aside from a few minor peccadilloes like not reporting the finding of the body, Marty operates this time in an oddly restrained manner, and when he tracks down the mastermind behind the frame he becomes a veritable pussycat, shooting a gun out of the bad guy's hand Wild Bill Elliott style, then offering his adversary the services of his own lawyer! In the story's middle reaches Lawrence goes out of his way to suggest that the Broadway Squad isn't really a gang of cutthroats with badges but that they deliberately cultivate this image in order to cow the city's criminals. Believe that, as the fellow said, and I'll tell you another. The signals are clear all through this tale that the new watered-down Marquis will return for more adventures along the main stem, but as far as I can determine "A Frame for the Marquis" was the last story about him ever to appear in print. It's hard to disagree with Chuck Verral's verdict: "The war interrupted a promising writing career. It's a damned shame."

If he'd stuck with that career, he would probably have moved into paperback original crime novels in the early 1950s when the pulps faded away. Today he might be ranked alongside Day Keene and Harry Whittington and the rest of the pulp veterans who spent that decade cranking out swift-paced haste-flawed softcover suspensers by the score. As it is, his stories are buried in the far harder to access pulp magazines of the Thirties and Forties. But the best of them are worth the effort of tracking them down. If you're looking for a powerful tough-cop series and aren't too finicky about niceties of language and plot, you may find just what you want in the adventures of the Marquis of Broadway—and of mystery fiction's unremembered manhunters.

MILTON PROPPER

What kind of person wrote the classical detective story? After reading an assortment of Golden Age deductive puzzles one might guess that the typical author of such books would be a highly cultivated, even-tempered, psychologically and socially well-adjusted member of the upper middle class; a person whose voice is never raised, who never uses four-letter words, wears a silk dressing-gown when not in a suit, and smokes, if anything, a pipe. Milton Morris Propper wrote classical detective stories but his life was hardly serene. He was a poor drab haunted soul who, if he had been more flexible as a writer or luckier as a man, might have become another Ellery Queen, or at least another S.S. Van Dine. His legacy, for those with the persistence to hunt them out, consists of fourteen detective novels which are not consummate masterpieces of the genre but still hold enough interest to justify their rediscovery today.

Search in reference books for biographical data on Milton Propper and you'll find next to nothing. Perhaps the editors of those books never bothered to send him questionnaires, perhaps he thought silence wiser than putting down the truth. Thanks to the generous cooperation of his sister, Mrs. Madelyn Hymerling, a sketch of his life can now be offered.

He was born into a painfully middle-class Philadelphia family in 1906. From childhood he was a voracious reader and his favorites were standard for those who were growing up in this century's first decades: the "boys' books" published under the house name Burt L. Standish, the Tom Swift series, the historical novels of G.A. Henty. From the primary grades through high school he was a boarding student at Nazareth Hall Military Academy, about sixty miles north of Philadelphia and ten miles west of the Delaware River. The school closed its doors long ago but was deemed to have a quality curriculum. Propper amused himself in his student days by writing serials, skits and dramatizations. While an undergraduate at the University of Pennsylvania he earned pocket money by doing occasional book and theater reviews for Philadelphia newspapers like the *Public Ledger* and *Record*. After receiving his bachelor's degree in 1926 he entered the University of Pennsylvania Law School, where in senior year he was named an associate editor of the prestigious Law Review. He obtained his LL.B. and passed the Pennsylvania bar exam in 1929 but didn't bother to apply for formal admission because around that time his first detective novel had been accepted both for magazine and hardcover publication.

The world must have seemed a glorious place to the 23-year-old Propper, just as it must have appeared to the two young cousins from Brooklyn who only a few months earlier had unexpectedly won a $7500 prize contest with their first novel about Ellery Queen. But the beam had fallen on Frederic Dannay and Manfred Lee when the magazine sponsoring the contest went bankrupt and its successor awarded the prize to someone else, and a similar beam fell on Propper during the black year of 1929. A movie sale for his first novel was on the brink of consummation when the bottom fell out of the stock market and the studio broke off negotiations. Ellery Queen, author and detective, survived and prospered during the Depression years. Propper didn't. He wrote an average of a book a year throughout the Thirties and until 1943 but the market for his kind of mystery, the intensely complex plot told in a dull style and peopled by colorless nonentities, was dwindling year by year. Van Dine had earned several fortunes writing that kind of mystery but by the mid-1930s his heyday was over. Queen realized this and was flexible enough to adapt to a different kind of detective novel. Propper remained steadfastly on his original path until finally his publisher would no longer accept his books.

Like Cornell Woolrich, Propper had a very close attachment to his mother. During the early part of his literary career he lived at home with his parents, making little from his books but getting by because his needs were modest. Later when even this meager income began to taper off, he went to work for the Social Security Administration in a position that let him make use of his legal background. He continued to live with his parents until he was transferred to the Social Security office in Atlanta, where he was apparently still working when his last novel was published.

Little has been written about his fourteen books except for newspaper reviews at the time each first came out. From Howard Haycraft's *Murder for Pleasure* (1941) we learn only that Propper's detective protagonist is named Tommy Rankin. In Haycraft's mammoth anthology *The Art of the Mystery Story* (1946) and in Julian Symons' *Mortal Consequences* (1972) the name of Propper isn't even mentioned. Barzun & Taylor's *A Catalogue of Crime* (1971) contains one brief and insubstantial entry on one Propper title. The fullest discussions are in Sutherland Scott's little-known but valuable *Blood in their Ink* (1953) and Chris Steinbrunner & Otto Penzler's *Encyclopedia of Mystery and Detection* (1976) but even these are far from comprehensive. According to Scott, "Mr. Propper writes a thoroughly workmanlike story, omitting unnecessary frills, and tending to specialize in mysteries which depend on double identity or masquerade. His climaxes are always well arranged and nicely timed." Charles Shibuk, who wrote the entry on Propper for *Encyclopedia*, describes him as an American Freeman Wills Crofts, "in that he writes the type of police routine stories that were common in England in the 1920s and 1930s but were more rare on the opposite side of the Atlantic." Shibuk goes on to point out that "Propper was adept at devising puzzles and plots but not as good a prose stylist as Crofts was and could not create a fully three-dimensional character."

After reading all fourteen of Propper's novels I concur fully with that judgment. Indeed I would go a lot further in listing Propper's weaknesses. He writes hopelessly flatfooted narrative and dialogue, draws character in something less than one dimension, flaunts like a medal of honor his belief that the rich and powerful can do no wrong, casually justifies all sorts of criminal conduct when perpetrated by the police, and avoids deductive fairness to the reader as if it were a social disease. Yet he did know his craft well, and at their best his books hold something of the intellectual excitement of the early Ellery Queen novels. He likes to begin with the discovery of a body under bizarre circumstances, to scatter suspicion among several characters each of whom has a great deal to hide, to juggle clues and counterplots with dazzling dexterity. As a special attraction Propper arranges his stories so that as often as possible he can introduce either some form of mass transportation or some complex problem of succession to a large estate, and occasionally both in the same book. His delight in these subjects enlivens his flat and stately style.

Most of his books are marred by a recurring device which the reader can see coming 200 pages away. Invariably, about three-quarters of the way through the typical Propper novel, detective Rankin has established that all the suspects encountered so far are innocent. At this point he connects one or two as yet unexplained pieces of the puzzle and concludes that somewhere in the murder victim's past an incident occurred which led someone to want vengeance. What remains is a hunt for the avenger, who has infiltrated the victim's milieu under another identity, and a breakneck chase to collar the killer before he runs to ground again. Such is the standard pattern, although in his later books Propper labored mightily to ring changes on it. He was a meticulous planner who believed that the step-by-step logic of plot development was the alpha and omega of the genre, and despite a certain amount of predictability and a great deal of stylistic dullness, to the lover of detective fiction his work still holds a fair measure of interest.

In all but one of his novels the central character is Philadelphia police official Tommy Rankin, a young but highly competent homicide investigator whose character and methods are best described by Propper himself.

> It was characteristic of Tommy Rankin that, because he preferred to work alone whenever it was possible, he had not requested the aid of other Headquarters men. Unless the ramifications of the case in hand had become so widespread that it was not practicable for him to deal with each of them himself, he refused help except upon such routine investigation as anyone could capably perform. He was not unwilling to cooperate; rather, his attitude was the result of a desire to have all the clues within his own grasp. Barely thirty years of age, he had the self-confidence of youth, which . . . had more than once stood him in good stead. For he was no amateur at the game of detection, notwithstanding his years. Already he had earned a reputation for himself by his ability to tail fugitives from justice, and he possessed a widespread knowledge of the underworld. He was well acquainted with the criminal classes, and the chief haunts of those who combated authority. Among them, too, he had won a name of square dealing and a respect that was seldom granted even to older and more experienced men.
>
> Of medium size and weight, Rankin was good-looking, in a casual sort of way, with fair skin and dark brown curly hair. He had thin lips, close set. His dark, darting eyes were his most animated feature. He was quick of comprehension, and his mental alertness enabled him to reason logically from his premises and reach accurate conclusions, with, however, none of the phenomenal astuteness of fiction detectives. A common-sense method of proce-

dure, sheer perseverance, and constant enterprise caused him to succeed where others failed.

This passage from *The Boudoir Murder* is the source for most of what we ever learn about Tommy Rankin. He lives in a bachelor apartment off Rittenhouse Square but seems to have no home life, hobbies, family, or personal relationships off the job. Propper often tells us when Rankin takes a break from his investigation to grab a meal but rarely bothers to mention what kinds of food he likes. One can readily deduce, however, that Rankin enjoys traveling, for as many as four times in each of his cases he'll drop all other business and take a train or plane to some distant locale in order to run down a clue.

Rankin depends heavily on routine for his results but Propper has gifted his sleuth with two special investigative weapons, one unusual for any policeman in or out of fiction, the other all too common in both spheres. It's an axiom in Propper that the face is an index of the personality, even when that face is bandaged up like a mummy and even after death. Every character in the Propper canon in introduced to us with a facial description that is also a moral judgment. Here's a maid from *The Family Burial Murders*: "She was undeniably pretty in a commonplace way, with blonde, bobbed hair, and a bow mouth, which revealed fine teeth. Wide nostrils and high cheeks suggested a mid-European origin. In her the detective recognized the flirtatious type, while her tight-fitting dress revealed inviting curves. At the same time, her dark sharp eyes betrayed an unamiable disposition and a wicked temper, and her chin, an obstinacy of its own. When she spoke, her voice was shrill and grating." Clearly a member of the lower orders. For a portrait of one of the maid's betters we turn to this description of a prosperous realtor from *The Boudoir Murder*: "A tall and strongly built middle-aged man . . . he had the stern, resolute lineaments of one accustomed to command, and his fifty years rested light on his broad shoulders. Yet, it was in his very features and bearing that his age revealed itself. For his deep-set, expressive eyes, beneath silver hair, were weary and strangely careworn, with pouches under them. Deep lines creased his forehead, and, below the sensitive nostrils, a firm, steady mouth displayed furrows of care and strain. A chin that seldom relaxed drooped under the stress of some disquiet."

A person's face not only tells the reader whether its owner is likable or not, it also tells the police whether he's a crook. In *The

Student Fraternity Murder Rankin sends out his subordinate Sergeant Gilmore to sneak a quick look at a suspect they've never seen before. Reporting back, Gilmore describes the man as follows:

> "Well, he's a well-built, rather handsome chap . . . He has broad features and a decidedly strong nose. In fact, he'd be attractive, if it wasn't for his sullen, heavy lips and narrow, almost shifty eyes. That's what gives him away—that and his dissipated look. He has blond curly hair . . ."
> Rankin nodded. ". . . Given an adequate motive, would you suppose him capable of a serious crime?"
> The sergeant answered slowly and thoughtfully. "That's a difficult question, Tommy; but he has a decidedly vicious streak in him. I have studied human nature enough to recognize craftiness when I see it. There is cunning in his eyes and the way his mouth slants downward in a sneer that verges on malignance."

All this from a split-second glance at a face! Rankin of course is equally adept at the mystic science, and much of his reasoning in *The Divorce Court Murder* is based on the premise that the dead woman's face was inconsistent with the evidence that she'd been cheating on her husband. Silly as these episodes sound, after awhile they come to seem perversely enjoyable.

Far less enjoyable is the second of Rankin's special investigative weapons. Whenever a suspicion against someone crystallizes in Rankin's mind, he himself or a subordinate proceeds to burglarize the person's house for confirmatory evidence. "Breaking into a house without a warrant, and at night, was as illegal for him as for the ordinary citizen, and if apprehended, nothing could save him from being dismissed from the Detective Bureau. The authorities did not frown on this method of obtaining evidence if it succeeded; what was unpardonable, however, was the blunder of being caught." (*The Boudoir Murder*) Whenever someone on the force reminds Rankin that such capers are illegal, his reply is always: So what? Illegally seized evidence is admissible in Pennsylvania. Rankin's statement was correct, in the sense that no state court was constitutionally required to exclude evidence obtained by police wrongdoing until the Supreme Court's 1964 decision in *Mapp v. Ohio*, a decision that for better or worse has since been undercut by later Court rulings more sympathetic to the Rankin notion of police procedure.

As usual in Golden Age detective novels, Rankin is surrounded by a number of recurring police characters, the most important being Sergeant Gilmore—stout, gray-haired, balding, tough-minded, pipe-smoking—who gets a full-length case of his own in Propper's second novel. Also appearing throughout the series are Rankin's boss, Captain Thomas, and Thomas' boss, Commissioner Wainright, and the low-grade plainclothesman Jenks, and Johnson the fingerprint expert, and Dr. Sackett the police surgeon, and various minor evidence technicians and crime reporters for the city dailies. My favorite Propper newspaperman is Boyle of the *Record*, for his fascinating admission in *The Student Fraternity Murder*: "You know darned well that in these poison cases, we never print the name of the poison; we call it a 'deadly poison' and let it go at that. It's public policy to keep people in the dark, rather than take the chance of putting a bug in some reader's ear to try it out on himself or some other fellow." Propper does name the poison in this novel but for all I know he invented the toxicological details rather than give some shifty-eyed and weak-chinned reader a ready-made murder method.

We first meet Rankin and his colleagues in *The Strange Disappearance of Mary Young* (1929), which was serialized in *Pictorial Review* prior to book publication and almost made it to the movies. On a hot August night in Woodlawn Amusement Park, a young woman is stabbed to death during a pitch-black scenic railway ride known as Thrills in the Dark. Rankin is summoned to investigate and eventually discovers that Mary Young's lecherous employer, his girlfriend and two of his servants all happened to be at Woodlawn Park that night—a coincidence that Propper does nothing to make plausible as the story proceeds. Rankin takes charge of the investigation and the hunt for the killer leads him to a boardinghouse, a few stately mansions and some romantically imagined underworld haunts. But the best scenes are those where the detective juggles railroad timetables and races from Philadelphia to Gary, Indiana to New York City and back to Philadelphia, just in time to put the cuffs on a most improbably disguised murderer. Propper's flatly ponderous style, naïveté, racism, sexism, unfairness to the reader and overuse of coincidence add up to a less than awesome debut.

His much better second novel, *The Ticker Tape Murder* (1930), puts Rankin in a minor role and gives center stage to Sergeant

Gilmore, who is assigned to protect automotive tycoon Philip Nixon from anonymous death threats just hours before a South Jersey commuter train runs over Nixon's body on a lonely stretch of track. Suspicion is evenly balanced among the dead man's crooked chauffeur, his lovesick secretary, his desperate business rival, and the brothers of a farm girl he's seduced. The picture of the Jersey countryside and the railroading atmosphere are well handled and the intricacies of the Camden-Cape May timetable will delight the hearts of train and detective buffs alike. As usual there's a climactic auto chase before the murderer is arrested. Gilmore: "We have a hundred and fifty mile journey before us, between now and four o'clock today." Rankin [whistling in surprise]: "That's an average of thirty miles an hour for five hours continuously." But even without today's interstate highways they complete the trip just in time to catch the killer. Despite the book's full measure of transportation lore, Propper's writing remains dull, his Establishment bias blatant, his characters flat, his dialogue full of polysyllabic ponderosity even when it's a hillbilly speaking. The alert reader will spot the Least Likely Suspect about two hundred pages before Gilmore does.

Rankin is again the protagonist in *The Boudoir Murder* (1931), in which a designing woman is found strangled to death in a luxurious Philadelphia hotel during the party celebrating the engagement of the woman's former lover to a Main Line debutante. Propper reiterates *ad nauseam* his belief that the rich and powerful can do no wrong, and prefers to yank rabbits from hats rather than play fair with the reader. But by this third novel he had perfected his technique of interweaving the actions of all his suspects and had become an expert at fitting an array of counterplots into his master plan—a plan which in this case includes at least two whopping surprises. All in all a quite respectable performance.

Despite a promising opening, Propper's fourth novel turned out to be a disastrous backslide. *The Student Fraternity Murder* (1932) begins during an initiation rite at the University of Philadelphia, where one of the robed and hooded pledges is injected at some point in the ceremony with a fatal dose of the same kind of poison that killed Socrates. Rankin's investigation reveals many intriguing glimpses of undergraduate life during the 1930s, but Propper is so solemn in his assumption that college fraternities are the cornerstone of civilization, and so casual in his acceptance of any crimes the police deem expedient, that the book seems hopelessly primitive today. And the same primitive quality plagues the plot as well as the social attitudes: multiple implausibilities combine with multiple coincidence to pile up impossible complications, and the concealed identity of the killer is matched in absurdity only by the way Rankin tumbles to the truth.

Propper returned to form with *The Divorce Court Murder* (1934), although the title is a bit of a misnomer. The fatal chloroforming of an industrialist's wife just before her testimony at a heated divorce hearing takes place in a lawyer's office, not in court. Suspicion is scattered among four people present at the murder—the heiress who's suing for divorce, her attorney brother, her gangster lover, and the dead woman's jealous husband—but as usual the three-quarters mark finds Rankin turning up traces of an avenger out of the victim's past and using dogged routine to sniff out his present identity. The complex strands of plot are skillfully interwoven and the legal details well presented, especially that ancient absurdity of divorce law known as the doctrine of recrimination. (If husband and wife have both committed adultery prior to seeking a divorce, the court will punish them by keeping them stuck with each other forever.) There are one too many coincidences in the storyline but overall it's a fine effort.

And an even finer one, to my taste the best of Propper's first period, followed later that year with *The Family Burial Murders* (1934). Rankin is summoned to another of Philadelphia's stately mansions after one body too many turns up at the gravesite during the funeral of a wealthy dowager. The death of Isabel Hutton was clearly from natural causes but the bludgeoning of her nephew David is just as clearly murder, and Rankin's investigation turns up the usual variety of suspects with motive and opportunity. By this time Propper had become a master at juggling clues and counterplots, tossing legitimately prepared-for surprises like dust into the reader's eyes while presenting one of his favorite combinations of story ingredients: a problem in succession to a large estate coupled with an array of mass transportation elements including trains, trolleys, the Elevated, and interurban electric car lines. Despite the unfair solution, flat writing and incessant snobbism, this novel represents Propper at just about the peak of his form.

According to his sister, Propper was a staunch, politically aware Roosevelt Democrat who liked to prowl the all-night restaurants before elections, taking political soundings. But his only attempt at an overtly political mystery novel was *The Election Booth Murder* (1935), a transitional work in which for the first and last time he abandoned his usual uppercrust milieu and switched to a background of corrupt city politics and the numbers racket. The reform candidate for District Attorney is murdered on Election Day in the titular booth with Rankin only a few feet away, and Tommy instantly swings into a high-speed pursuit that apparently nets the wrong man. But the fastidiously elitist Propper can't make an underworld setting plausible for a microsecond and can't put a single breath of life into an action sequence, even though he fills the book with enough auto chases and gun duels for a Cagney gangster film. The result is an unexciting, unpuzzling misfire, with a solution at once unfair and easily guessable, and with Propper's contempt for everyone who lacks money or power saturating every page. If his sister is right that Propper's social views were more enlightened than his novels suggest, it's just one more indication of how damnably difficult it was for an author to express any but the most reactionary sentiments in the classic detective novel.

The novels Propper wrote between 1936 and 1943 can be seen as a series of attempts to break away from the strict pattern of his early books. Rankin is less blatant about violating suspects' rights, the snobbism is toned down considerably, the figure from the past becomes increasingly less crucial to the plots and is finally shelved, the transportation motifs are phased out and the succession-to-an-estate motifs multiply. The long-winded narrative and dialogue are condensed and the pace speeds up, although never to the point where one could confuse Propper with Chandler or Gardner. But the hallmarks of labyrinthine plot, dull style and nonexistent characterization remain intact, so that the later Proppers resemble his earlier work more closely than, say, the movie-influenced Ellery Queen novels of the late Thirties resemble first-period Queen.

One Murdered: Two Dead (1936) deals with the murder of a young socialite who is killed in her bed shortly before she's to have a baby. Rankin is called to the scene but refuses to accept the theory of lunkheaded detective Sanders that the burglar who was caught on the spot is also the murderer. In due course Rankin uncovers a number of equally likely suspects including the dead woman's husband, her doctor, her lover, and a young wastrel who stands to gain a fortune by the lady's death without issue. Eventually the Avenger from the Past is turned up and Rankin launches a wild chase to collar him, but this time the killer's identity is more surprising and the solution fairer to the reader than in most of the preceding Propper novels.

My personal choice for the best book of Propper's second period is *The Great Insurance Murders* (1937), which opens with a dissolute Philadelphia playboy being shot by ambush during a polo match at an exclusive country club. The initial clues point to the fiancé of a woman the playboy had aggressively sought for himself, but Rankin soon discovers that a mutual life insurance policy covering both the dead man and his business partner is connected with some chicanery over a trust fund and that both elements seem to be related to the murder. The estate-succession aspects are of minimal importance in this case and the transportation motif (an alibi based on a charming little trolley line through a city park) is likewise given short shrift, as though Propper were determined to do or die without his usual story ingredients. Some nicely involuted plotting combines with the faster pace and reduced snobbery to make the book a tight-knit, unpredictable, highly satisfying performance.

In *The Case of the Cheating Bride* (1938) Propper seems to become a momentary liberal, giving us not only a plot based on the tyranny a wealthy dead man can exercise on survivors through his will but also two minority characters who are not ethnic cartoons. The ship's stewardess, Miss Alvarez, is an intelligent and observant woman who speaks perfect English, and Inspector Julius Goldman of the New York Homicide Bureau, who had played a small part in *The Great Insurance Murders*, is given a role nearly as important as Rankin's. Goldman, a Jew without a single stereo-Jewish trait, is described as "a large, somewhat florid man of forty, with black curly hair and hebraic features, deceptively easy-going and good-natured" but "a shrewd, conscientious, dangerous officer, as many a complacent, too confident criminal learned to his cost." But as if to prove that he hadn't done a complete about-face, Propper also loads the book with a pair of black train employees whose dialect is ripest Stepin Fetchit. "Yassuh, sho Ah 'members dis lady and gent. He came in fust and picked de table Ah waited on. While dey ate, dey fo'get deyselves and talk excited lak; dey get so loud Ah know'd dey was fightin'." At the start of the story Rankin is in New York on business, and Goldman persuades him to take a hand when a young Philadelphia socialite returning from her shipboard honeymoon drops dead of poison on the pier. The trail leads to some credibly bizarre matrimonial restrictions in an old tyrant's will and a splitting of suspicion among the dead woman's husband (who was also her stepbrother), her lover, her greedy cousin, a professional smuggler, and the usual figure from the victim's past. Plausibility breaks down at one or two key points, and Propper strains madly to frustrate any routine police inquiry that might reveal the figure from the past's current identity. But otherwise this is vintage Propper, rich in train, ship and plane sequences and mind-boggling counterplots. The frequent British spellings in the American text suggest that the English edition came out first.

Hide the Body! (1939) provides one more demonstration of Propper's wizardry at precision dovetailing of counterplots. During an auction at the home of stockbroker Morton Logan, whose firm had recently gone bankrupt under suspicious circumstances, Logan is found shot to death—whether by himself or one of his firm's ruined clients or somebody else is unclear. Rankin carefully constructs the case for suicide and the arguments that each of various people murdered Logan, then finds that one of his chief suspects, the dead man's scapegrace son, has also been killed. Eventually the detectives pick up the trail of a crucial incident and a dedicated avenger in the victim's past, but despite the familiarity of this motif the solution is definitely a surprise even to the reader accustomed to Propper's gimmicks.

In *The Station Wagon Murder* (1940) the scene shifts to rural Pennsylvania and the summer homes of the super-rich. The police chief of the hamlet of Boyleton asks a vacationing Rankin for help when an adventuress with twin penchants for blackmail and stealing other women's men is found stabbed to death in the village's railroad depot late one night. Propper labors like a donkey engine on one of his own train lines to vary his usual pattern: this time the victim's secret past is uncovered early in the game and the avenger figure is not the killer but merely one suspect among many. The unhappy result is a far more routine performance than Propper usually turns in, although the case is enlivened by a few nice glimpses of Bucks County society and by a very clever alibi gimmick. Rankin violates suspects' Fourth Amendment rights with the carefree abandon of his earliest cases and Propper never hints that this procedure is wrong even when, as almost always happens, the illegally searched suspects turn out to be innocent.

The Handwriting on the Wall (1941) opens when a house-hunting young couple discover a decomposing corpse at the bottom of the laundry chute in a deserted mansion, and Rankin is drawn into a labyrinthine tangle involving a missing heir, a will studded with divesting conditions, multiple impostures, a five-year-old apparent suicide that might have been murder, and a parade of greedy relatives with designs on the fortune of a beer magnate. The plot is one of Propper's most complex, and for the first time he makes a real if feeble effort to play fair with the reader. But the storyline is seriously undercut by large and small implausibilities (not the least the near-photographic recall with which everyone remembers exactly what he or she was doing on specific occasions months in the past), and the solution will be no surprise to readers of early Ellery Queen.

The last of Propper's fourteen detective novels was written and published in the heat of World War II, but the ambience of *The Blood Transfusion Murders* (1943) is still that of the carefree Thirties, with the wartime situation barely hinted at in one brief reference apiece to draft cards, blacked-out headlights, defense industries and air-travel priority. The cousin of a young man seriously injured in a New Year's Eve auto smash-up is clubbed to death on the grounds of Universal Hospital shortly after agreeing to serve as blood donor for his relative. Lunkheaded Sanders from *One Murdered: Two Dead* is assigned to the case and arrests the obvious suspect, whose fiancée then begs Rankin to investigate on his own and prevent a miscarriage of justice. As usual in late Propper a complex pattern of succession to a large estate is at the bottom of the crime, but in this novel Propper follows up the initial killing with not one but several more actual and attempted deaths. The entire sequence of crimes is marred by several implausibilities and by enough imitation Mary Roberts Rinehart forebodings to choke a hippo, and the seasoned reader will have tumbled to the Least Likely Suspect long before the climax. At the end of his activity as a mystery writer Propper was still trying hard to put freshness into the classic pattern, but this time he failed badly.

In 1944, the year after *The Blood Transfusion Murders* was published, Propper's parents died within a few months of each other. The loss of his mother was as catastrophic to Propper as was the death of Claire Attalie Woolrich in 1957 to her tormented son Cornell. He inherited a few thousand dollars from his parents, arranged with the Social Security Administration to be reassigned to Philadelphia, and made up his mind to quit his job and live on his income as a writer. He was offered promotions many times during these years but always turned them down. Finally he resigned his position and moved in with his brother and sister-in-law, but his psychological problems grew worse and he eventually left them and moved into a one-room apartment in a run-down area of the city. He tried to compile an anthology of popular songs from the nineteenth century to the present. Publishers didn't want it. He tried to write more mystery novels in the old manner. Publishers didn't want them. He consoled himself collecting stamps and phonograph records and observing the political scene with the sardonic detachment we would expect from his portrait of Philadelphia politics in *The Election Booth Murder*. He had no relationships that might have helped carry him through: he was estranged from his family, women had never interested him and his sexual contacts with other men were casual and short. He tried to get his government job back but because the police had arrested him once during their periodic harassment of homosexuals he was not rehired. Like Woolrich, he became increasingly morbid and depressed. He both threatened and attempted suicide, was put under psychiatric treatment, tried to kill himself again and, in 1962, succeeded.

This was the man who celebrated the perquisites of being born with money and justified the illegal acts of anyone with a badge on his chest. Perhaps he needed to keep writing about that kind of world, to compensate for everything that had gone sour in his own. Be that as it may, his best books—*The Boudoir Murder, The Family Burial Murders, The Great Insurance Murders*—are worth the effort of tracking them down. He got little enough pleasure out of life but his ability to please the devotee of detection continues long after his death.

WILLIAM ARD

William Thomas Ard was born in Brooklyn on July 8, 1922. He took ROTC courses while a student at Dartmouth and, after graduating in 1944, went into the Marines. An accident that severed some tendons in his right hand kept him out of combat and he was discharged before the end of World War II. He returned to Brooklyn, moved in with his parents and worked briefly for a local detective agency. Then he got a copywriter's job with the Buchanan Advertising Agency, whose office was in Manhattan's Paramount Building. He fell in love with a young woman named Eileen Kovara who worked at the agency and married her in 1945. Ard's next job was as a publicity writer for the New York offices of Warner Brothers Pictures. He was eventually promoted to head of his department but quit around 1950 to become a free-lance writer. By that time the Ards had two small children, a daughter and a son, so that economic necessity reinforced Ard's natural bent to write swiftly and much. For the rest of the decade he produced an average of a book every four months, the vast majority in the private eye and hardboiled genres. The family lived first in Brooklyn, then in Scarsdale and New Rochelle, N.Y., before moving in 1953 to Clearwater, on the west coast of Florida which served as the setting for many of his later works. At age 37, and after turning out 32 books, all of them typed with two fingers, Ard died of cancer on March 12, 1960.

In the half century since his death he's been almost completely forgotten, and the leading reference works on crime fiction mention him not even in passing. Yet while he flourished he was considered one of the top private eye writers in the business. Anthony Boucher, mystery critic of the New York *Times* throughout Ard's creative life, praised him over and over for his "deft blend of hardness with human warmth and quiet humor," for the way he kept his novels "gratifyingly distinct from each other, and each one better than the last," for producing "masterpiece[s] of compressed narration . . . backed with action and vigor, written with style and individuality." Ard, Boucher wrote in 1955, "is just about unmatched for driving story-movement and acute economy."

In the early 1950s, when the dominant model for hardboiled writers was Mickey Spillane, Ard and a few others, most notably Ross Macdonald, resisted the pressure to imitate the surefire blend of sadism-snigger-and-sleaze in Spillane's Mike Hammer novels and carried on the tradition of Dashiell Hammett and Raymond Chandler, in which the private eye stands for personal and political decency, legitimate violence abounds but sadism is eschewed, sex is not a savage perversion but a restoration of oneself and a friendly caring for another. The writer most influential for Ard, however, was neither Hammett nor Chandler but John O'Hara, whom he mentions several times in his novels and from whom he apparently derived his simple yet vivid style, his habit of flashing back to explore various characters' social and economic origins, and his theme of dropping ethnicity (like stockbroker Louis Graziano/Gray in *.38*, gang boss Charlie Wilenski/Wilson in *Don't Come Crying to Me*, and vice cop Gordie Welliwicz/Wells in *Hell Is a City*) to achieve success.

What makes Ard unique is that despite his recurring use of dark alleys, gangsters, crooked cops and pols and sinister roadhouses and all the other standard mean-streets story ingredients, his heart was elsewhere, in the world of movies and stage musicals and Broadway nightspots and music, the world of popular entertainment. He loved that way of life and all who lived it and in novel after novel he bathed its every aspect in a soft romantic glow. The same romanticism permeates Ard's series characters, particularly private eye Timothy Dane, a shamus like no other in fiction: young, naïve, always tender with women, incompetent at machismo, incapable of extricating himself from tight spots single-handed, resorting to violence rarely and never in a sadistic way. There is about Dane a sweetness, a delicate simplicity whose very incongruity in a fictional PI somehow makes it work. In the Fifties, before Ross Macdonald replaced Spillane as the dominant influence and a sense of decency in a sour world became part of the eye's standard equipment, Ard's approach was a startling and sorely needed corrective.

Not that he was a paragon of all the literary virtues. He wrote rapidly and revised less than he should have if at all. His style is readable and efficient but his work lacks the hauntingly memorable, marvelously quotable lines that are common in Chandler and Macdonald. Despite his gifts of pace and economy and his unusual story premises, his plots have a tendency to fall apart, especially when he plays with the motifs of classic detective fiction. He seemed to have a mental block that made him forget the character names he had used in one book and recycle them unwittingly a few books later, so that Stix Larsen, a gangster killed in *.38* (1952), is revived in *The Root of His Evil* (1957) and again in *All I Can Get* (1959), and Wes Shell, a Florida orchestra leader in *Mr. Trouble* (1954), morphs into a Manhattan political columnist in *Hell Is a City* (1955). Sometimes a character's name changes halfway through the same book! But even Ard's worst efforts are infused with raw readability, and his best are among the finest hardboiled novels of the Fifties. We begin by concentrating on his strongest work, the ten hardcovers published under his own name and the six paperbacks under his byline that Ard actually wrote. Pseudonymous and ghosted novels get saved for later.

~ ~ ~ ~ ~

In Ard's first novel, *The Perfect Frame* (Mill, 1951), Dane is distinguishable from the standard Hammeresque Manhattan PI of the Fifties only marginally, although even here a few touches of Ard's naïve lyrical romanticism seep through the surface machismo. Narrated in first person à la Spillane, the book has Dane hired by a gorgeous blonde to visit a seedy Third Avenue bar, where he's quickly beaten to a pulp but recovers in jig time to mix into a rather neat marine-insurance swindle and a pair of murders. The usual tough-guy story elements pass in review on schedule, including filthy pictures, a sinister nightclub owner and an assortment of sadistic hoods. But despite the obeisances to convention and an extremely awkward climax it's a readable exercise, drenched in the feel of early-Fifties Manhattan.

Dane returned early the following year as narrator and protagonist of *The Diary* (Rinehart, 1952), in which a corporate tycoon about to launch a political career hires the young shamus to recover the missing secret journal of his tempestuous teen-age daughter. The trail leads Dane to a predictable mixture of sinister nightclubs, sleazy Latino hoods, corrupt cops and pols, sex teasing and shootouts. What makes this novel a huge improvement on its predecessor is not the ingredients but Dane's romantic naïveté, his complete inability to get out of a single tight spot without help (usually a woman's), his hopeless ineptitude at Hammerismo. Ard's blending of familiar mean-streets material with the elements of Hollywood sex comedy growing out of Dane's erotic mishaps with the women in the case makes this one of the more unusual private eye adventures of the Fifties.

At this point Ard seemed to become unhappy with the limitations of first-person narrative, for in the third Dane novel, unaccountably entitled *.38* (Rinehart, 1952), and in all of Dane's later cases, he switched to third person storytelling, kept his protagonist offstage for long stretches, devoted much time and skill to exploring the social and psychological roots of his characters, and displayed a wizardry at cinematic crosscutting between scenes. Even though *.38* takes place in Manhattan and a mob-run New Jersey vice town, the ambience is very close to that of a Western, and Dane's personality and actions are specifically likened to those of that hero of early-Fifties TV, Hopalong Cassidy. The story begins with a math error by a missing girl's distraught father which catapults Dane into the middle of a war among mob factions, but considering the premise there's remarkably little bloodletting in the book, and many developments in the later chapters are indebted not to Chandler or Spillane or the screen exploits of Hoppy but to the coincidence-packed traditions of Hollywood sex comedy. Contrived in spots, marked as usual by Ard's youthful romanticism, this is still one of Dane's best adventures, described by Anthony Boucher as "a singularly realistic study of the mechanics and intrigues of gang rule" but rising far above sociological reportage to become a sort of *locus classicus* of Ard's distinctive traits.

Nothing in the first three Dane novels could be mistaken for traditional detective fiction, but in *A Private Party* (Rinehart, 1953) Ard works along whodunit lines, with disastrous results. Released from custody after two potential witnesses against him turn up conveniently dead, corrupt dockworkers' union boss Al Stanzyck is himself shot to death at a roadhouse during his getting-out celebration. A not too plausible life insurance angle brings Dane into the case at the behest of Stanzyck's equally corrupt colleagues, who insist Al was killed by some policeman vigilante seeking justice outside the law. This theory becomes increasingly plausible to Dane as his own investigation is hampered by Detective Lieutenant Joe Bannerman and his squad. Our shamus follows a tortuous path, filled with innocent persons who were suspiciously prowling the scene just before the murder, awash with wacky behavior by both cops (a morally outraged plainclothesman sends hoodlums nonsensical threatening letters signed J. Lex) and crooks (the killer keeps the murder gun that can hang him and digs it out to use again when Dane baits him by publicly romancing his girlfriend). The solution is pure guesswork and comes about for no reason at all, but the telling is crisp and diverting and Ard does quite well at characterizing a variety of hangers-on without function in the story.

When a private eye becomes involved with an ancient tyrant and his two sexpot daughters, one of whom has a missing husband, the informed reader braces for another retread of Chandler's *The Big Sleep*. But in *Don't Come Crying to Me* (Rinehart, 1954) Ard plays some bizarre variations on those overworked themes: the unmarried daughter, the overt nympho, is about to give birth to an illegitimate child who is wanted very badly by its gangster grandpa and by three separate and distinct men claiming to be its father, and Dane is sucked into the Solomonic furor over rights to the baby. It's hard to believe that none of these street-wise characters ever thought of an abortion and even more incredible that so many gangsters could get so gooey over an infant. Add these problems to the chaotically constructed last chapters, splice in Dane's strange conviction that the baby is better off with its hoodlum grandfather than with any conceivable foster parents, and the result is a book whose flaws far outweigh the customary Ard virtues of pace, economy, and restraint with the sex and gore.

In *Mr. Trouble* (Rinehart, 1954), which is set not in Manhattan but on the west coast of Florida, Ard returns, with mixed results, to multiple viewpoint narration and comedy-of-errors plotting. While en route to the Sunshine State on commission from Fidelis Insurance to look into a suspicious stolen-jewelry claim, Dane is involved in a minor baggage accident at the airport that has twin consequences: two gamblers on the run from a gang boss mistake him for a hit man out to get them, while the real hit man, who happens to be on the same plane with Dane, mistakes the shamus for the gamblers' bodyguard. Despite a premise tailor-made for bloodletting, and two luscious women who become involved in the plot, the action and sex teasing remain minimal, and Dane's life is saved only through chance and a convenient police chief. One story element is simply beyond belief—after a murder attempt in a crowded hotel lounge no one bothers to call the cops—but otherwise this is a smooth if unchallenging novel, enriched by Ard's exploration of his characters' backgrounds and personalities and by his avoidance of Spillanean excess.

Hell Is a City (Rinehart, 1955) is by far the most powerful and exciting of Ard's PI novels, pitting Dane against the forces of law and order in a nightmare New York where the mayor, the police commissioner and most of the officials are in a corrupt alliance with the mobs and determined to hang onto their power in the forthcoming mayoral election. When a young Latino shoots a Brooklyn vice squad cop who was about to rape the boy's sister, the city bosses use their puppets in the media to portray the case as the coldblooded murder of a heroic officer and put out word to shoot on sight whoever might contradict the party line. Brought into the picture by a crusading newspaper editor, Dane at once finds himself in the position of the classic *noir* protagonist: knowing the truth, threatened by evildoers both with and without badges, hounded through city streets dark with something more than night. A gallery of sharply defined characterizations, breathless pace, an exceptionally strong premise and the evocation of Dane as a sleuth both more aggressive and brighter than before combine to turn this book into a masterpiece—until the climax, perhaps the first televised criminal trial in fiction, where all is set to rights in record time and impossibly ludicrous manner. With a sensible ending, what a movie Sam Fuller could have made out of this novel!

Until this point Ard had told us a great deal about the backgrounds of one-shot characters but nothing at all about Dane himself—a deficiency he corrected in *Cry Scandal* (Rinehart, 1956), which contains a vivid flashback to the detective's earlier years when he was in partnership with a man he knew to be corrupt but who had once saved Dane's life. When that ex-partner suddenly disappears, Dane is drawn into the affairs of a sleazy scandal magazine whose owners prey on Manhattan's theatrical and television celebrities. The adventure has much to commend it, including a succinctly convincing portrait of Broadway and its people, the usual fine character sketches right down to the walk-on parts, and even a modicum of reasoning in the search for the perpetrators. Dane's performance is rather passive, and only the chance intervention of a friendly ex-con saves him from being drowned in a marble quarry at the climax. Ard never bothers to give us an adequate explanation of why the scandal sheet was started, and treats us to one linguistic howler worthy of Michael Avallone: "There were audible gasps when Mike Carhart's rippling muscles strode from the wings." But in most respects, including the abundant sex teasing, this is pure Fifties nostalgia and good medium-grade Ard.

In Dane's ninth and last recorded adventure, *The Root of His Evil* (Rinehart, 1957), our hero sinks to stereotype, absorbing three brutal beatings and a serious knife wound within 48 hours yet still capable of derring-do in the bedroom and Tarzanesque rope-swinging in the chase after a mad killer. A nightclub singer hires Timothy to deliver the $100,000 he owes in gambling debts to a vicious Miami hoodlum. But unknown to Dane the money is intended to help finance a Latin American revolution, and the dictator in power is just as determined to sabotage the payoff as is the hoodlum to punish Dane for sleeping with a stripper he considers his property. It's a swift-paced book, full of interwoven diverse viewpoints, graced with the sexiest bedmate in the canon and climaxed by a grand race to save the lady from a Fate Worse Than Death. But otherwise the only notable feature of Dane's last case is the ease with which Ard mixes up the first names of his Latino characters.

~ ~ ~ ~ ~

During his peak years Ard wrote so prolifically that he needed five pseudonyms in addition to his own byline. Almost all of his work under other names, however, can be dismissed in a phrase coined by Anthony Boucher, who said that one of them "read like William Ard in an off moment." He used the byline of Ben Kerr for six mean-streets thrillers without series characters, ground out two more as Thomas Wills and a singleton as Mike Moran. All nine will be covered later.

As if that weren't enough work for one person, Ard also wrote a series of paperback Westerns for Gold Medal Books under the pseudonym of Jonas Ward. The protagonist is a gunfighter named Buchanan, after the advertising agency for which Ard had worked in the Forties. The first of the series, *The Name's Buchanan* (Gold Medal pb #604, 1956) is essentially a Westernized rewrite of *Hell Is a City*, with the hero once again trying to save the neck of a young Latino who's going to be legally murdered by corrupt officials for shooting the man who was raping his sister. This novel was the source for the only movie ever based on Ard and one of the last films to star Randolph Scott. *Buchanan Rides Alone* (1958) preserved the novel's structure but added full measure of those quirky human touches that were typical of its director, Budd Boetticher. Ard wrote a total of five Buchanan novels and died leaving unfinished a sixth adventure, which was completed by science-fiction specialist Robert Silverberg. Afterwards Gold Medal hired other writers to carry on the Jonas Ward byline as a house name. Just a few months before Ard's death he devised a final byline for what may have been his last Western (*Guns of Revenge*, Monarch pb #145, 1960, as by Ken Hamlin).

~ ~ ~ ~ ~

Under his own name Ard published not just the nine Dane novels but also four other books which are best discussed as a group. The earliest, *A Girl for Danny* (Popular Library pb #502, 1953), is only remotely a crime novel but demonstrates as well as Ard's mysteries his delicate blend of mean-streets atmosphere and gentle naïveté. The action takes place on a 5000-passenger excursion boat cruising from Manhattan to Poughkeepsie and back on a sweltering July 4, 1952. Among the passengers are a prostitute, a dead john, a heroin-crazed thief, a rape-traumatized young woman, a repulsive homosexual and a sadistic boat detective, each contributing to the education of virginal ship's cafeteria cashier Danny Shannon in this quickie *Bildungsroman*. Although by today's standards the sex scenes are strangely tender and unobtrusive, they must have seemed quite steamy in the early Fifties. And the McCarthyite hysteria of that time adds special flavor to the moment when Danny, trying to keep the boat detective from beating up the homosexual, is therefore accused of being "queer" himself. Paced as rapidly and told as economically as any Timothy Dane case, this is quintessential Ard in mood, tone and themes.

Which is more than can be said about *No Angels for Me* (Popular Library pb #591, 1954). As in the Dane series, the client here is irascible Joe Spencer of Fidelis Insurance, named of course after the motto of the Marine Corps in which Ard had briefly served. But this time Spencer takes his business to Manhattan's All-States agency, whose chief operative Luke MacLane is one of those Mike Hammer clones to whom women bare their breasts five minutes after the first hello. When fellow sleuth George Epply is found shot to death in the New Jersey meadowlands, MacLane inherits his colleague's current case, a diamond heist from a Jersey pier, and is soon eyebrows-deep in gunmen, sinister roadhouses, bosomy babes and the rest of the standard equipment of the Fifties tough-guy story. Ard tries to freshen the mixture with a traditional whodunit element but handles it so ineptly that the exposure of the "surprise" killer (mostly by guesswork) simply adds one more coincidence to a plot already riddled with implausibilities and contradictions.

Five years later, and two years after abandoning Timothy Dane, Ard launched a new character and series which were abruptly terminated by his early death. The protagonist of these novels is Mike Fontaine, who is 30 years old, big and dark and handsome, half French, half Irish, and such a compulsive romantic that he must help any and every troubled woman who crosses his path. Although he aspires to Broadway stardom, and once appeared in the male chorus of *South Pacific*, his penchant for rescuing ladies has caused most of his adult life to be spent behind bars. At the start of Ard's final hardcover novel, *As Bad As I Am* (Rinehart, 1959), Fontaine is released on parole after serving five years for a fistfight in which he killed a man who was beating a woman, but the wacko terms of that parole require him to avoid all social contact with women for the next eighteen months. Fontaine however is one of those sexually magnetic men at first sight of whom women tear off their clothes and offer themselves, and to make matters worse his parole officer is a sadistic creep who aches to catch the young man off base and send him back to the slammer. Fontaine returns to the family home on East 97th Street which his younger sister shares with her husband, plainclothes cop Harry Taggart, but finds that during his imprisonment the block has been absorbed into the slums of Spanish Harlem and that the upper floors of the house are being rented to Puerto Ricans. While hunting for an acting gig, Fontaine happens to meet and instantly propels into an erotic tizzy the gorgeous redheaded TV starlet Gloria Allen. Then, about a hundred pages into the book, he discovers that his brother-in-law is on the take, collecting a commission on each patron of the Puerto Rican prostitutes to whom he's rented rooms in the 97th Street house. Taggart breaks in on Fontaine's enraged attempt to throw the whores out, tries to kill Danny on the spot but is himself shot to death in the struggle. The prostitutes and their current customer flee and, just as in Ard's *Hell Is a City*, the dead cop's equally corrupt superiors form a politically motivated conspiracy to whitewash the officer, brand the innocent young man who shot him as a mad-dog copkiller, and put out orders that he be shot on sight. This version lacks the power and nightmarish intensity of the 1955 Timothy Dane novel but is rather better constructed, with the burden of saving the young victim of municipal corruption placed on the shoulders of the starlet Gloria, a high-powered talent agent, a tax lawyer with romantic yearnings of his own, and a shrewd Broadway private eye named Barney Glines. (This is clearly not the Glines who was protagonist of Ard's 1952 paperback *You'll Get Yours*, published as by Thomas Wills, nor is he the Glines who used to be Timothy Dane's partner and was killed in *Cry Scandal*. Ard seems to have been almost pathologically careless about recycling that name.) The climax is set at a criminal trial turned media event just as in *Hell Is a City* but this time—except for Ard's illusion that the Supreme Court is New York State's highest court rather than, as in fact it is, its lowest— the judicial proceedings are considerably more believable. Anthony Boucher, who always had a kind word even for Ard's lesser efforts, summed up this one best when in a review for *EQMM* he called it a "happy, exciting romance-melodrama of rogue cops, the theatre, and young love—Ard's longest and probably his most entertaining."

In his second and final adventure, which occurs three weeks later, Fontaine's first name has magically changed from Mike to Danny: whether because a real Michael Fontaine threatened to sue, or Ard simply forgot, or because the author changed too, history does not record. He has just married Gloria Allen and is about to begin a new career as partner in Barney Glines' detective agency. This premise comes from *Cry Scandal*, at the end of which Timothy Dane had offered a job in *his* agency to the likable ex-convict Johnny Packerd who had saved Dane's life at the Tuckahoe quarry, although Packi was never mentioned in the single subsequent Dane novel. But the resurrection of this story thread in *When She Was Bad* (Dell pb #B145, 1960) proves a disaster. A titled, recently widowed and astonishingly sexy young Englishwoman comes to Manhattan and hires the Glines agency to find her stepdaughter, who's threatening to sell some of the lady's passionate love letters to a London scandal sheet. Glines assigns the case to Danny, whose bride has just flown to Hollywood to appear in a Frank Sinatra-Dean Martin-Tony Curtis sex comedy. The real sex comedy unfolds in Manhattan and Bermuda as the stepdaughter's trail brings the hapless Fontaine into the eager clutches of uncountable nubile lovelies lusting for his manly body. Sex titillation consumes most of the pages of this adventure, and what crime plot there is turns out to be as skimpy and flimsy as the bikini panties discarded by every female in the case at first sight of Fontaine. Ard's last novel published by a major house is so long, slow, clumsily paced, lackadaisically told and non-urgent that one could easily believe it was ghosted from an Ard outline or rough draft (or maybe *ex nihilo*) by someone infinitely less talented.

~ ~ ~ ~ ~

The last publisher to issue an Ard series was Monarch Books, a short-lived paperback house based in Connecticut and specializing in titillation. Between 1959 and 1962 Monarch issued seven sleazy-covered novels under the Ard byline, six of them starring private eye Lou Largo. Despite the lurid jacket copy and artwork, the three genuine Ard books in the group bear all the hallmarks of his world.

Except for a Marine background paralleling his creator's, Largo is simply Timothy Dane under an alias, a Manhattan PI with a curiously gentle personal style, a Times Square office, a rented apartment in a converted brownstone, a host of acquaintances in the entertainment world and a penchant for cases that take him to the Florida west coast after one of whose towns he was named. The two authentic Largos are marked by motifs from Hollywood's screwball sex comedies, an interest in characters' social and psychological roots, insightful glances at underworld politics and the corrupt politics of the upperworld, cinematic crosscutting between scenes, and an occasional incident or bit of dialogue that reminds us irresistibly of Ard's sideline as a writer of Westerns. Although not in the same league with the Timothy Dane series, they are unmistakably from the same pen.

In the first and better of the pair, *All I Can Get* (Monarch pb #124, 1959), Largo's client is Milt Weston, the crusading, incurably romantic New York newspaper editor who had been a major figure in *Hell Is a City*, and the detective's assignment is to check the background of a sex goddess whom Weston has just met and now wants as his eighth (or perhaps, depending on certain legal technicalities, his ninth) wife. As Largo contrives to meet, rapidly becomes enchanted by and starts bedding this lusty wench, we are treated to one-third of a book's worth of Hollywood sex comedy unadulterated by the slightest criminous interest. Then Weston takes his fiancée to Gulfside, Florida and instantly becomes embroiled in a newspaper circulation war, the murder of a local sheriff, and rivalry between the Cuban gangsters and the Mafiosi across the Bay Bridge in the corrupt city of Tampa. Largo is hired to come down and take a hand and the book's final hundred-odd pages turn into a fast-paced, action-crammed cornucopia of customary Ard motifs, graced with a neat detective subplot, spiced by the continuing sex-comedy scenes with which the ongoing crime story is ludicrously incompatible, climaxed by a shootout between an honest and a crooked deputy sheriff that might have come straight out of a Jonas Ward Western. This may not be great literature but it's a splendid piece of storytelling that still holds up well today.

In *Like Ice She Was* (Monarch pb #147, 1960) Largo is to some extent Hammerized, being portrayed as a compulsive gambler, a raging bull in brawls and bed, a macho immune to torture and bullets, but underneath these trappings he retains much of the gentleness of the Ard hero. Hired by a professional gambler to recover a million dollars in dirty Canadian money which he claims was stolen from him two years before by a Quebec prostitute and her pilot boyfriend, Largo follows the trail to Saratoga and an excess of sadistic encounters with various creeps who also want the money. The thin storyline is held together by guesswork and wild coincidence but the main emphasis is on Ard's unique brand of sex comedy, albeit with more explicit bedplay than usual, stemming from the juxtaposition of Largo and the Quebec hooker and his own temporary assistant, a wealthy young criminology student beneath whose prim exterior lurks an erotic tigress aching for release. An exciting race-against-time at the climax, plus some wonderful bit parts like the Jewish beatnik cabdriver and the ex-Marine deputy sheriff with a sideline as applejack bootlegger, are enough to remind readers of this quickie how good Ard at his best could be.

His third and final Monarch paperback under his own name was not a Largo but a long, vividly written and minimally criminous novel that he hoped would be his breakthrough into the mainstream. *The Sins of Billy Serene* (Monarch pb #152, 1960) follows the transformation of Gino Serini, a young Brooklyn street tough who happens to have a magnificent voice, into a Sinatraesque superstar with the de-ethnicized titular name. Along the way he encounters pals and punks galore: a baseball-nut priest, a sadistic cop, orchestra musicians and press agents and film-makers and, at every stop on his road to the top, legions of models and showgirls and starlets who yearn to share his bed. It's a rich book, full of Ard's soaring romanticism, his O'Hara-derived interest in characters' socioeconomic roots, his love of movies and stage shows and night clubs and most of all his fascination with the making of music, with the art of the great songwriters like Cole Porter and Jerome Kern and that of the singers and musicians who make the lyrics and melodies come alive. Despite the misleading title, Gino/Billy like almost all Ard protagonists is an overwhelmingly decent person, his worst sin having been a youthful stint as numbers runner for his Mafia cousin. He is loyal to his men friends, particularly the pianist Mike Dushane who superintends his rise to fortune, and once he learns in the bed of a kindly older woman that his partners are supposed to enjoy it too, he treats all his ladies, up to and including the octoroon actress passing for white whom he briefly and tragically marries, with exemplary care and gentleness. Ard must have dreamed about how *Billy Serene* might be made into a movie, maybe even a stage musical like the O'Hara-inspired *Pal Joey*. He died a month before the novel was published and never saw a copy. It was reviewed nowhere and vanished almost at once into the Bermuda Triangle of forgotten books.

After Ard's death Monarch editor Charles Heckelmann made a deal with the Scott Meredith literary agency for ghost writers who'd continue the Lou Largo series under the Ard byline, with the ghost taking three-quarters of the proceeds and Ard's widow 25%, minus of course Meredith's commission. This arrangement quickly transformed Largo into a superstud caricature of no interest to us here. Of the four posthumous Largos, the first was penned by the eventually-to-become-famous crime novelist Lawrence Block and the final three by John Jakes, whose later Bicentennial series netted him more fame and money than Ard saw in his life.

~ ~ ~ ~ ~

In the ten years between his debut as a writer and his death, Ard completed a prodigious amount of fiction: sixteen crime novels under his own byline, six Westerns as Jonas Ward and one as Ken Hamlin, plus nine crime novels under pseudonyms. Those nine are fully consistent with the portrait of Ard that emerges from the books published under his own name. What he wrote as Thomas Wills, Mike Moran or Ben Kerr reflects just as much as the orthonymous books his struggle to balance the ambience of 1950s hardboiled fiction with his own tendency to soaring romanticism, his desire to write in the tradition Mickey Spillane then dominated without losing his individuality. In the pseudonymous nonet one finds Manhattan and Florida settings, gambling casinos, boxing, crap games, political corruption, the sudden birth of sweet love in the back alleys of the big city, action and sex that never descend to sadism or smut. With one early exception they are marvels of storytelling economy, compressing a multitude of events into approximately the number of pages in a Simenon. Swift-paced, uncluttered in style, filled with casual references to the Marines and to the movies and other embodiments of Fifties pop culture, these books are well worth the attention of the Ard fan and of anyone who admires pure unputdownable readability.

His most frequently used crime-novel alias was Ben Kerr, which appeared on six books beginning with *Shakedown* (Henry Holt, 1952). Manhattan PI Johnny Stevens boards the train for Miami on assignment to protect the vicious son-in-law of a food tycoon from a blackmailing doctor. On the streamliner he meets and quickly beds a bosomy blonde exotic dancer who happens to know the son-in-law. The next morning in Florida he happens to meet an office receptionist who turns out to be the son-in-law's estranged wife. The apartment that is rented for him chances to be in the same building where his blonde trainmate lives. Ard keeps piling up coincidences like a hardboiled Harry Stephen Keeler but takes pains to sabotage his hero's credibility as a Mike Hammer type by surrounding his pub-crawling, crap-shooting, lovemaking and liquor-guzzling with a halo of sweet romanticism. This Johnny Stevens is a lame excuse for a detective: he can't identify dried blood smears when he sees them and he catches his man by resorting to the old bait-a-trap-and-see-who-falls-into-it gambit of the worst Charlie Chan movies. The paper-thin plot is needlessly unfair to the reader, the style is far more verbose than Ard's spare best, the Florida background is only barely sketched in. What makes it all acceptable is that at bottom it's not a mystery but a Hollywood sex comedy, marked by swift pace, light tone, and a gallery of likable oddballs such as the gangster-fixated old jail guard and the honest nightclub proprietor with a private army of ex-Marine buddies. Even under an alias Ard shows remarkable skill at avoiding the worst Spillanery of the early Fifties and at remaining true to his romantic nature. No other writer would have had his detective blurt out for no reason at all that his favorite name is Elaine—which happens to have been the name of Ard's wife.

His next pseudonymous novel and his first paperback original under any name was *You'll Get Yours* (Lion pb #87, 1952), published as by Thomas Wills. This one is narrated in first person by Manhattan PI Barney Glines, who really does come across as something of a Mike Hammer stand-in. The storyline is nothing if not conventional: Glines is named go-between by the thieves who stole budding movie star Kyle Shannon's jewelry, falls hard for the lady and quickly finds himself awash in pornographic pix, heroin, lechery and murder. As a reasoner Glines belongs in the subcellar with Mike Hammer and Ed Noon, as when he concludes that if two female names in a certain Little Black Book have the same initials they must be the same woman. Ard telegraphs the king toad's guilt in the first chapter, never explains why the leading lady didn't burn the nude photos long before Page One, and reaches his climax only by having Glines let the badguy go free in an earlier confrontation. (The genuine Hammer would have pumped six slugs into the louse's gut and ended the book twenty pages sooner.) But it's fascinating to watch the tightrope walk as Ard tries to recreate the Spillane milieu without ridiculing his hero's romantic side. He must have loved the name Barney Glines with a passion: as we've seen, he used it again for Timothy Dane's murdered ex-partner in *Cry Scandal* (1956) and a third time for the shrewd little Broadway sleuth of *As Bad As I Am* (1959) and *When She Was Bad* (1960).

His next Manhattan PI was Tom Doran, who in *Double Cross* (Popular Library pb #494, 1953, as by Mike Moran) is hired to visit an upstate New York farm turned training camp and protect a sadistic young heavyweight from the mobsters who are out to take over his management. A bomb is planted under the hood of Doran's car in Chapter One, and from then on he encounters sabotage, seduction, murder, mayhem and love in a setting more reminiscent of Woody Allen's *A Midsummer Night's Sex Comedy* than of hardboiled fiction. Doran seems to have an infinite capacity both for taking and dishing out physical punishment, being beaten to a pulp by four gangsters one evening and serving as sparring partner in a fight ring the next afternoon. But in most other respects—naïveté, romanticism, tendency to act like a Boy Scout—he's a spiritual brother of Ard's better known PI with the same monogram, Timothy Dane. (The final sequence where Doran is taken to a flooded Tuckahoe marble quarry to be killed is reprised with Dane the intended victim in 1956's *Cry Scandal*.) It's hard to accept a protagonist who's Mike Hammer redux in one scene and a dewy-eyed innocent in the next. But on the plus side there's plenty of sweet sex, a convincingly evoked 1950s boxing milieu, at least one memorable character (the cocky and pathetic little fight manager Blinky Miller), and a pace so swift that the pages seem to be turning themselves.

The first of Ard's paper originals to appear under the Ben Kerr byline was *Down I Go* (Popular Library pb #653, 1955), which was published a few months before *Hell Is a City* and shares an initial premise with that finest of Timothy Dane novels. The metropolis—not New York this time but Bay City, three hours by plane from Miami—has been taken over by crooked politicians and crooked cops. Lou Bantle, a former officer who had been framed by corrupt colleagues and sent to prison, is out on parole, working as bouncer in a sleazy night spot and thirsting for payback. Then he discovers that the club's lovely new hat check girl is none other than Rita Largo, sister of a reporter who had been railroaded to the pen in the same way, and the coincidence helps him find not only vengeance but lawful justice and even love. Eventually, just as in *Hell Is a City*, the police hierarchy get worried that the protagonist knows too much and put out word that he's a mad-dog killer to be shot on sight. This rough sketch lacks *Hell*'s raw power, and the nightclub sequences are only minimally related to the rest of the book. But it's a swift and action-crammed little number, authentically tough without sliding over into Spillanery, and Ard keeps the romance element carefully muted as befits the situation. A few years later he joined the first name of his male lead and the last of his female to create the signature of his final PI character.

If you were an adolescent during the golden age of B Western films as Ard was, you could hardly avoid seeing, not just at one Saturday matinee shoot-em-up but again and again, the old chestnut about the Texas Ranger or deputy marshal who pretends to go bad so he can join the outlaws and break them up from within. In *Mine to Avenge* (Gold Medal pb #490, 1955, as by Thomas Wills) Ard updated this storyline, with Big Joe Derek, vice squad sergeant in the city of Bayside, playing the part of cop-on-the-take so he'll be invited into the mob, based in the evil city of Kingston across the bay, that murdered the squad's commander. Complications arise when the commander's daughter comes to Bayside for the funeral and falls in love with Derek, making it harder than ever for him to maintain his corrupt pose. It's a competent and fast-moving but undistinguished thriller in which all the usual bases are touched: sinister nightclubs, dope, prostitution and, as Anthony Boucher put it, "almost every cliché and corny improbability you choose to name." The porno photography gimmick is the same one Ard had used in *Down I Go* just a few months before. His cinemania resurfaces when he gratuitously tells us that Big Joe's father is named John Derek.

The next Ben Kerr paperback, *I Fear You Not* (Popular Library pb #763, 1956), is at bottom a rewrite of Hammett's *The Glass Key* by a man who was in process of creating a huge indestructible Western hero named Buchanan and wanted to transplant the same sort of character into the mean streets of the Fifties. Ard's version of Ned Beaumont is ex-Marine pilot and Korea combat vet Paul Crystal, who is "built along the generous lines of a John Wayne" and currently runs an illegal gambling casino in a nameless city and state. Paul Madvig and Senator Henry from *The Glass Key* are combined into Crystal's mentor Frank Marsh, the city's patrician political boss, who is cursed with a nymphomaniac wife and a morphine-addicted daughter by an earlier marriage. As in *The Glass Key*, the leitmotif here is the war for control over the city between the viewpoint faction and a rival group. But unlike Hammett, who with cynical honesty portrayed each side as no better than the other, Ard struggles to make Marsh and Crystal and their allies look like angels next to the opposition, a gaggle of black-hearted scoundrels including a mulatto hit man with a penchant for raping blonde white women. The storyline is conventional but moves like a tornado, with Ard jumping backward and forward in time from scene to scene but keeping the plot under control every step of the way. The last third of the book offers one action sequence after another: Crystal begins the night getting beaten to a pulp with blackjacks, has sex in the wee hours with a lovely undercover IRS agent, spends the next day shooting up underworld dives, takes a slug in the ribs himself, escapes from the hospital, dodges bullets all the way across town, fights a duel to the death with the sadistic mulatto and ends the night in bed with the Fed gal again. Accept all that and you'll enjoy not only this book but also the adventures of the equally invulnerable gunfighter Buchanan, which began appearing in mid-1956 under Ard's Jonas Ward byline. *I Fear You Not* was the third Ard novel in two years with a corrupt cop named Bull Hinman and the second with an honest cop named Ben Driver (both names were used in *Mine to Avenge*, as by Thomas Wills, and there's also a Hinman in *Hell Is a City*), but from the context it's clear that these are five different characters.

The name Driver surfaces yet again in the next Ben Kerr paperback, *Damned If He Does* (Popular Library pb #785, 1956), but this time its owner's first name is Frank and he stars in a minimally credible quickie about a racketeer's reformation. Driver has come to Spring City, Florida as undercover advance man for a gambling czar. But his assignment to soften up the town for mob takeover is blown to smithereens when he meets and falls for lovely Ann MacLean, daughter of the retired Marine general who's the community's leading citizen. Instantly this ten-year veteran of the underworld starts dreaming of orange blossoms, starting his own little business, the paradise of middle-class respectability. Among the obstacles on his path to Fifties-style salvation are his boss Al Stanton's refusal to let him leave the rackets, Stanton's sister's refusal to let him leave her bed, a vicious rival mob, a local cop with his own designs on Ann, and the weight of Driver's past. This is one of Ard's least convincing and least socially critical novels, asking us to believe not only in an instant reformation and a morally perfect Establishment but in a hero who can enjoy sex after a brutal beating, keep a woman successfully hidden in his hotel suite all through the police investigation of a murder in his living room, and escape from the city jail virtually by snapping his fingers. As if to confirm that Ard dashed off this one without much thought, the first name of one character shifts from James to John in midcareer, and there's a reference to yet another in the small army of Ard gangsters named Stix Larsen. But it's fast and momentarily diverting, and the flashback to the origins of de-ethnicized hit man Joey Constant is as skillful as the similar vignettes in the Timothy Dane novels.

The next Ben Kerr, *Club 17* (Popular Library pb #803, 1957), was Ard's best book under any pseudonym and one of his finest ever. Undercover New York cop Mike Riordan, on assignment to pose as a rich john and crack a top-bracket call girl ring operating out of the titular night spot, falls in love with starving actress Joan Knight, who's just been recruited into the stable. Meanwhile his police superiors are frantically trying to protect the department from attacks in the media by a hypocritical anti-vice crusader, whose wife turns out to be both a hooker for and a full partner in the vice ring. Riordan unlike many Ben Kerr protagonists is convincing as both romantic and roughneck, and the amounts of physical punishment he's called on to administer and consume remain within the bounds of credibility. Even his one truly dumb move—hiding out the novice call girl in the apartment where he keeps photos of himself in uniform—somehow seems in character. For a single moment Ard slips, committing a priceless Brooklyn-accented malapropism when he describes "the cluster of buildings that adjourned" a highrise. But that's the only weak spot in a furiously readable novel where fast action, characterization, Manhattan-after-dark atmosphere and eroticism remain in perfect balance. Ard achieves marvels of cinematic cross-cutting between scenes and makes room for two more of those John O'Hara-inspired flashbacks to the social origins of a louse. With its events compressed into well under 24 hours and less than 130 pages, *Club 17* is a superb blend of seaminess and romanticism in the uniquely Ard manner and a book that's impossible to lay aside until the last breathless page.

The final Ben Kerr, *The Blonde and Johnny Malloy* (Popular Library pb #EB104, 1958), begins with rare promise as Ard introduces Malloy and his fellow convicts on a rural Florida road gang and their brutal overseers. Johnny has served five years for a hit-run killing actually committed by his gangster brother-in-law Frank Trask, who is about to divorce his wife, Johnny's sister, so he can marry Nelli Rivera, a hostess at his gambling casino. Trask arranges parole for Johnny, welcomes him back to Gulfside, lavishes money and gifts on him as thanks for taking the prison rap, and sets him up for another fall, but things come unstuck when Johnny and Nelli fall for each other. The long-memoried reader will notice a cornucopia of borrowings from earlier pseudonymous Ard novels—several character names from *I Fear You Not* and *Damned If He Does*, the unfixing-the-championship-bout routine from *Double Cross*—and, about three-quarters of the way through the book, will catch Ard repeating his gaffe in *You'll Get Yours* when Johnny has Trask at his mercy but, with countless reasons to kill him, lets him go so the novel can continue for another 25 or 30 pages. But it's a swift and readable piece of storytelling as usual, and one who reads it today may feel a special sadness on reaching the last line: "'That's the end of it,' he said." For this was Ard's last crime novel under any byline besides his own, and two years after its publication he was dead.

It was a sad and sudden end for a writer who in his brief prime added a distinctive voice to the popular literature of the Fifties. Since his death Ard has been all but forgotten, his books unreprinted, his career unmentioned even in fairly comprehensive reference works on mystery fiction. The republication of his best books for the benefit of readers who have never experienced his unique blend of mean streets and singular tenderness would be a sweet romantic touch he would have appreciated.

PROFILES

MICHAEL AVALLONE

Some mystery writers turn out superbly crafted books so different from one another that each might have had a separate author. Others write mysteries whose characters, scenery, viewpoint, concerns and style are so similar from book to book that together they form a world of their own, personal to the author and recognizable to the reader as one recognizes the El Greco look or the Bartok sound. Those authors are the universe makers, and Michael Avallone was one of them. What set him apart from his colleagues is that he built his world in the way that the British once claimed to have built their empire: by inadvertence.

The son of a stonecutter, Avallone was born on October 27, 1924 and raised in a Bronx tenement among sixteen siblings. As a teen growing up in the Depression he wrote incessantly—in subways, buses, cafeterias and the family bathroom—and just as compulsively went to the movies, seeing anything and everything that was shown and forgetting nothing. He went from high school into World War II, serving as a line sergeant with a mechanized cavalry unit in Europe, and after his discharge returned to New York, broke but intent on becoming the postwar Thomas Wolfe. For five years he lived with his first wife and their infant son in a furnished room on Manhattan's West 82nd Street just off Central Park, selling stationery and candy and pots and pans by day, writing his arm off night after night without cracking a single market. Late in 1951 he turned his back on critically respectable literature and decided that if the public wanted girls-and-gore sagas in the manner of the then best-selling Mickey Spillane, then Avallone would pump them out. The result was a cycle of close to forty novels about Manhattan PI Ed Noon.

One of Noonland's many hallmarks is an outlandishly arranged list of *dramatis personae* capped with an atrocious pun. In *The Tall Dolores* (1953) the arrangement is by height, from 6'6" Harry Hunter, through Noon himself who is six feet even, down to a 5'2" runt "and several horizontal people." Dolores—"a Glamazon, a regular Empire State Building of female feminine dame"— barges into Noon's office and hires him to locate a rodeo rider who's taken off with five thousand of her dollars. When he gets a tip that a man answering the lost rider's description has just been stabbed to death on the steps of the Museum of Natural History, Noon visits the scene, wisecracks the cops into the ground, messes into the case on his own and soon becomes a fugitive from justice. Whenever he gets bogged down, Avallone conjures up a huge coincidence to assist him. It all turns out to be a messy replay of the quest for the Maltese Falcon, with a cache of diamonds concealed by a limerick-loving thief filling in for the black bird. With its endless allusions to baseball and old movies, its venom against intellectuals and homosexuals, the awful Noon wisecracks which drive all the other characters into gales of mirth, this debut novel threw the Nooniverse into the genre like a beanball. For the rest of his life Avallone considered it a supreme classic. "There isn't a faster-moving, more economically written Eye novel, accomplishing so much with a minimum of wordage. It is also the most human of all Eye epics anywhere. Ask the people who really know about writing and books." Of course, he described just about everything he'd ever written with the same superlatives.

After *Dolores*, the deluge. Besides the Nooners Avallone wrote Gothics under five female bylines, juveniles, espionage thrillers, sex novels, movie and TV tie-in books—more than 150 paperbacks, each written in anywhere from four days to three weeks with never a word revised or reconsidered. In the Sixties he reconfigured his alter ego for the era of Cold War espionage fiction, putting on Noon's office desk a red-white-and-blue phone whose ringing would signal a new job for him in his role as personal investigator for the president of the United States.

Unlike most purveyors of drugstore fiction, Avallone was a true *auteur*, with a unique personality discernible throughout most of his books and especially throughout the Nooniverse. For despite his original intention, Ed Noon is no more than a distant literary cousin of Mike Hammer. Avallone's Manhattan gumshoe is a cockeyed optimist, a motormouthed clown, a movie and baseball nut, a lover of lush ladies and lousy jokes ("Hi, Noon!" his friends greet him), an emotional pushover, and in many respects a child in an adult's body. Avallone himself, of course, was an even more fanatical old-movie buff than his fantasy alter ego. He wasn't just in love with the products of Hollywood's golden age but immersed in those flicks, drunk on them, obsessed by them, so that when he sat down at the typewriter the unrelated fragments of dozens of vintage films leapt from his cine-satiated mind to the pages and filled them with chaotic, jumbled, raucous and frenetic life. Pick up a Nooner and you're likely to find on one page a character modeled on Boris Karloff or Sydney

Greenstreet, on the next an incident or a line of dialogue from *Foreign Correspondent* or *Casablanca*, then an allusion to an ancient Gary Cooper vehicle followed by three successive scenes from Hitchcock or Orson Welles or John Huston films, and on and on till the fadeout. Part of the fun of reading Avallone lies in meeting the most film-intoxicated man of his time.

By conventional standards his output is a mess. His anarchic plots, all of them dealing with various groups of nasties competing for some outlandish McGuffin or other, were simply improvised as he went along, and his style is an ungrammatical brain-jangling approximation of normal English, rife with misspellings and malapropisms and an aura of great pother and thunderation.

> The U.N. Building . . . a towering beautiful slab of crystal pie standing tall and proud on New York's very dirty feet. (*The Living Bomb*, 1963)

> A gilt-framed reproduction looked down on we poor mortals. (*The Fat Death*, 1966)

> His thin mustache was neatly placed between a peaked nose and two eyes like black marbles. (*Assassins Don't Die in Bed*, 1968)

> She had tremendous hips and breasts encased in a silly short black fur jacket and calf-high boots.

> The cube flashbulbs which could shoot a set of four pictures without bothering to make adjustments was all set.

> Mady Lopez was stark naked, on her knees, still wearing the calf-high boots.

> She . . . unearthed one of her fantastic breasts from the folds of her sheath skirt.

> My stunned intellect, the one that found death in his own backyard with him standing only feet away, hard to swallow in a hurry, found the answer. (All from *The Horrible Man*, 1968.)

> Serena tried to wither me with a ton of scorn unloadingfrom her green glims. (*Death Dives Deep*, 1970.)

His freshest laurel wreath was his recent interpretation of such tough aces like Stravinsky and Shostakovich; rendering their works on violin strings was like pushing peanuts up Mount Everest with your nose. (*Killer on the Keys*, 1973)

Among the typical inhabitants of the Nooniverse are a 440-pound mattress tester, a set of homicidal triplets, an evil college professor complete with pet assassin, a deadly female cosmetics tycoon, and an evangelist crusading against fat. Martinis are described as "amber and delicious," a doctor takes a patient's temperature by feeling his pulse, two lovers in bed are compared to a tossed salad, the traditional Jewish toast is rendered *lach heim* and the traditional Italian farewell is twisted into *Caio, piasano*. When the plot screeches to a halt, a tongueless black dwarf is likely to invade the mouse auditorium walking on his hands and carrying a .45 in each foot. (The mouse auditorium is Noon's name for his one-room office and like every other phrase in Avallone it comes from a movie, in this case Howard Hawks's 1939 flyboy flick *Only Angels Have Wings*.) Make the language do flipflops, mangle the metaphors like a trash compactor, slap down as many allusions to characters and incidents and lines and settings from old movies as the page can hold, spice with an occasional dash of liberal sentiment from the social consciousness flicks of the Thirties and Forties, bring the formula into the Vietnam era by tossing in gobs of revulsion at hippies, perverts, Commies, pacifists, longhairs, pointyheads, dissidents, militant blacks, liberated women and all other traitors to the John Wayne ethos. Add a barrel of *chutzpah* and you have the recipe for the Nooniverse. "I was all tangled and brangled in a mystery and fantasy that made absolutely no sense," Noon remarks in *Death Dives Deep*, and so is every reader who ever dived into an Avallone novel. But somehow the whole impossible slumgullion lingers on the palate. Those who keep coming back for more servings are known as Noonatics.

In the Sixties the royalties from his smoking typewriter enabled Avallone and his family to migrate to Middlesex County in suburban New Jersey. I had barely heard of him before the spring of 1970 when I moved to East Brunswick, within walking distance of the house where he was living with his second wife and their son and daughter, batting out the words as speedily as ever: articles, rambunctious letters to editors, a torrent of correspondence, diatribes and self-advertisements beyond counting, plus between fifteen and twenty paperbacks a year that were making him pots of money. I was a nobody just beginning to get my feet wet in the sea of mystery but we soon discovered many shared enthusiasms—Ellery Queen, Cornell Woolrich and old movies, just to name three—and a special bond developed between us. I began reading and collecting his books and stalking the wild eyeball-popping locutions with which they were peppered. I moved to St. Louis less than two years after meeting him but we stayed in touch. In my first novel, *Publish and Perish* (1975), there was a character named James Foxworth who was an anorexically disguised Avallone. He later told me that not long before my novel came out he was trying (without success) to sell a paperback historical adventure series about an Errol Flynnesque pirate by the name of, you guessed it, James Foxworth. Strange are the ways of fate! I continued to read and collect him and correspond with him. He never agreed with me that his special place in literature rested on the art of the Avalloneism but somehow he didn't seem to mind what I said about him in print, or if he did he kept it well concealed, although he tended to go ballistic when anyone else even hinted that he wasn't necessarily the peer of Hammett and Chandler. Sometimes we'd put on a panel together at a convention, just the two of us, and we made a wonderful Odd Couple. Asked to list the ten best PI novels, he included *The Tall Dolores* and was widely criticized for it. Not by me: I applauded his superhuman restraint in listing *only* one of his own titles.

Twice in the years after I left the east coast, Avallone banged out a book that could stand as his testament. *Shoot It Again, Sam* (1972) opens with the President ordering Noon to escort a dead Hollywood star's body on a transcontinental train ride. While the "corpse" sits up in its coffin, Chinese agents raid the train, kidnap Noon and use brainwashers made up to look like Gable, Cagney and Peter Lorre until Noon is convinced that he is none other than Sam Spade (as portrayed, of course, by Bogart). It's all part of the screwiest assassination plot ever concocted by a movie maniac. But that Nooner is a paradigm of sweet reason next to *High Noon at Midnight* (1988), in which our hero either dies or goes bonkers (it's not clear which) and is visited in the twilight world by the ghost of his idol Gary Cooper, who enlists him in a crusade to save the dear old USofA, not to mention the rest of the planet, from Zevada the Noseless One and his horde of extraterrestrial nogoodniks. In the last scene, Noon's role models from adventure fiction and movieland convene in his hallucinations and vie with each other to do him homage, climaxing with an ode by Rafael Sabatini's swashbuckling Scaramouche:

> In love and battle he ever fought off ruin
> This man the angels named Ed Noon . . .

You may love this off-the-wall stuff or fall on the floor howling at it, or both, but only Avallone could have imagined or written it. It was Noon's last appearance in print and one of the last Avallone books to be published. He had lost most of his markets by then, and for a while was forced to deliver pizzas to make ends meet, but he never stopped writing and hoping. He had at least thirty unpublished novel manuscripts in his luggage in the mid-1990s when he and his wife moved from New Jersey to southern California to be closer to their now adult children. He died in Los Angeles on February 26, 1999, at age 74.

There's a word I've seen often in crossword puzzles but never anywhere else. The usual clues given for it are "lollapalooza" or "sockdolager" or "nonesuch." As all cruciverbalists know, the word is "oner." Mike Avallone deserves that tag more than anyone else I've known. Of course, he saw himself differently. "Strong, tough, Manhattan cynical but underneath still a small boy. Cried when dogs got run over, helped little old ladies across the street, works for principle and integrity. Not an anti-hero. He believes the home team will win the old ball game in the ninth, that nice guys will not finish last and when the climax comes, the Good Guys will always beat the Bad Guys. He grew up that way, through the Depression years, a second World War and all the time he dreamed in a million darkened movie houses. He embraced the word Hero; he believed there was no other way for a man to be." Thus his fantasy image, developed in book after book. He could be called many things: fascist klutz, bastion of sanity and tradition, born storyteller, the Ed Wood of the written word, *enfant terrible*, patriot, pig, idealist, fool, some kind of a nut, a hell of a nice guy. But whatever else might be said about Michael Avallone, one must say what Casper Gutman said to Sam Spade in *The Maltese Falcon*: "By Gad, sir, you're a character, that you are!"

EDWARD D. HOCH

If ever there was a member of an endangered species it was Ed Hoch, the last person alive who made his living writing mystery short stories. Between 1955 and his death in January 2008 he sold around 950 tales. As if turning out two to three dozen stories a year were not enough, he also published five novels and filled his odd moments with chores like writing a monthly column for *Ellery Queen's Mystery Magazine* (1980-85), editing the annual *Year's Best Mystery and Suspense Stories* anthologies (1976-1995), and serving tirelessly on various committees of Mystery Writers of America (MWA). Yet he never seemed harried or overcommitted and impressed all who knew him as an amazingly placid and easy-going fellow. His secret? If you are doing precisely what you want to do with your life, and making it pay besides, the distinction between work and play vanishes and every hour is a pleasure.

Edward Dentinger Hoch was a Washington's Birthday boy, born in Rochester, New York on February 22, 1930. His father, Earl G. Hoch, was a banker, but despite the precarious nature of that line of work during the Depression the family weathered the Thirties without serious problems.

From a very early age he was fascinated by mystery fiction. "When I was a young child," he said, "I used to draw cartoon strips and have masked villains running around. They were terrible, just stick figures, because I wasn't much of an artist, but I'd try to draw in cloaks and masks to identify the villains so that I could have a final unmasking to surprise the reader. Of course, I was the only reader. No one else saw those strips."

In June 1939, when the 60-minute *Adventures of Ellery Queen* series debuted on the CBS radio network, nine-year-old Ed Hoch quickly became one of its staunchest fans. Later that year, when Pocket Books, Inc. launched its first 25-cent paperback reprint titles, the boy discovered that his hero Ellery Queen was not only a radio sleuth but the protagonist of novels and short stories dating back to shortly before he was born. The first adult book he ever read was the Pocket Books edition of Queen's *The Chinese Orange Mystery* (1934). "It was among the first group of paperbacks published, and I recall going down to the corner drugstore and seeing them all lined up with their laminated covers. I debated for some time between James Hilton's *Lost Horizon* and an Agatha Christie title [probably *The Murder of Roger Ackroyd*], and finally settled on Ellery Queen because I had heard the Ellery Queen radio program which was so popular in those days. I bought *The Chinese Orange Mystery* and was completely fascinated by it, sought out all the other Ellery Queen novels I could find in paperback, as Pocket Books published them over the next few years, and from there went on to read other things. I discovered Sherlock Holmes at about that time too."

It was during the Forties that, one by one, Ed Hoch discovered the masters of fair-play detection: Conan Doyle, Chesterton, Christie, John Dickson Carr, Clayton Rawson and countless others besides of course the cousins Frederic Dannay and Manfred B. Lee who wrote as Ellery Queen. In 1947, after completing high school, he entered the University of Rochester but left two years later to take a researcher's job at the local public library. He enlisted in 1950, during the Korean conflict, and once out of basic training was assigned as a military policeman at Fort Jay, on Governor's Island just off Manhattan. He took advantage of being stationed near the headquarters of Mystery Writers of America, which was then only five or six years old, to attend the organization's monthly meetings (in uniform) and to mingle with the giants of deductive puzzlement on whose books he'd been hooked since age nine. Discharged from the service in 1952, he went to work in the adjustments department of Pocket Books, the house that had started him reading detective fiction, and continued to write short stories as he had since high school. In 1954, back in Rochester, he took a copywriter's job with the Hutchins advertising agency, and late the following year he knew the special pleasure of seeing his first published story on the newsstands. That was the start of his real career, one that lasted for more than half a century and well over 900 stories.

For more than a dozen years after that first sale he kept his day job and saved fiction writing for evenings, weekends and vacations. But he was so fertile with story ideas and such a swift writer that editors and readers could easily have mistaken him for a full-timer even in those early years. In 1957 he married Patricia McMahon, with whom until his death he shared a small neat house in suburban Rochester. Two of its three bedrooms were soon converted into his office space and the basement into a library filled with thousands of mystery novels, short story collections and magazine issues, few of them without at least one Hoch story. The field's top publications, the

Ellery Queen and *Alfred Hitchcock* mystery magazines, began printing his tales in 1962. Six years later, having won the coveted Mystery Writers of America Edgar award for one of his stories ("The Oblong Room," *The Saint Magazine*, July 1967), he decided that he could support himself and his wife on his writing income and left the advertising agency. He continued to write full-time (many would say more than full-time) until the day he died. During 1982-83 he served as president of the organization to whose annual dinners he had first come in military khaki more than thirty years earlier, and in 2001 he was named an MWA Grand Master. He never showed signs of slowing down, and readers around the world hoped he'd stay active well beyond his thousandth story.

Why only five novels and so many short stories? It boils down to Hoch's special affinity for the short form. "Writing a novel has always been, to me, a task to be finished as quickly as possible. Writing a short story is a pleasure one can linger over, with delight in the concept and surprise at the finished product." Or, as he put it elsewhere, "I guess ideas just come easily to me. That's why I've always been more attracted to the short story form than the novel. I am more interested in the basic plotting than in the development of various sub-plots. And I think the basic plot, or gimmick—the type of twist you have in detective stories—is the thing I can do best, which explains why so many of my stories tend to be formal detective stories rather than the crime-suspense tales that so many writers are switching to today."

Those words are misleading in one sense: more than two hundred of his published stories were non-series tales of crime and suspense, and a few of the finest will be considered here later. But most of his energies went into the creation of short-story series characters and the chronicling of their exploits. He created a total of 28 series, dealing with all sorts of protagonists from an occult detective who claims to be more than two thousand years old to a Western drifter who may be a reincarnation of Billy the Kid to a science-fictional Computer Investigation Bureau. Whatever the concept of a series, whatever its roots, Hoch's tendency was to turn it into a cycle of miniature detective novels, complete with bizarre crimes, subtle clues, brilliant deductions and of course the ethos of playing fair with the reader that distinguishes the work of Carr, Christie and Queen. The best introduction to the world of Ed Hoch is a quick tour through each of his series in the order of their creation.

SIMON ARK, the two-millennia-old Satan-hunter, was the central character in Hoch's first published story, "Village of the Dead" (*Fa-*

mous Detective Stories, December 1955), and appeared in many tales which editor Robert A.W. Lowndes bought for the Columbia chain of pulp magazines during the late Fifties. The ideas in these apprentice stories are occasionally quite original (e.g. the murder of one of a sect of Penitentes while the cult members are hanging on crucifixes in a dark cellar), but the execution tends at times to be crude and naïve and the Roman Catholic viewpoint somewhat obtrusive. Eight of the early Arks were collected in two rare paperback volumes, *The Judges of Hades* and *City of Brass*, both published by Leisure Books in 1971, but the most readily accessible book about this character is *The Quests of Simon Ark* (Mysterious Press, 1984). In the late 1970s Simon was resurrected for new cases in the *Alfred Hitchcock* and *Ellery Queen* magazines, but these tales pare down the occult aspects to a bare minimum and present Ark simply as an eccentric old mastersleuth specializing in impossible crimes. The sixtieth and last of his cases was "The Christmas Egg" (2006), published as a holiday-gift pamphlet by the small firm of Crippen & Landru, which issued six collections of Hoch stories during his lifetime.

PROFESSOR DARK, apparently an alter ego of Simon Ark, popped up in two obscure pulp magazines of the mid-1950s under Hoch's pseudonym of Stephen Dentinger, but they have never been reprinted and are of interest only to completists.

Private eye AL DIAMOND began life in "Jealous Lover" (*Crime and Justice*, March 1957), which featured a walk-on part by a certain Captain Leopold, later to become Hoch's most frequently recurring series detective. After two appearances Diamond's name was changed to AL DARLAN so as to avoid confusion with Blake Edwards' radio and TV private eye Richard Diamond. Although little known and rarely reprinted, the best Darlan tales, like "Where There's Smoke" (*Manhunt*, March 1964), are beautiful examples of fair-play detection within the PI framework. "A Wandering-Daughter Job" (*Ellery Queen's Mystery Magazine*, June 2008), nineteenth and last story in the series, was published soon after Hoch's death.

BEN SNOW, the Westerner who may be Billy the Kid redux, was created by Hoch for editor Hans Stefan Santesson, who ran Ben's adventures in *The Saint Mystery Magazine* beginning in 1961. Perhaps the finest of the early Snows is "The Ripper of Storyville" (*The Saint Mystery Magazine,* December 1963), a first-rate Western whodunit which became the title story in the only collection of the character's exploits published in Hoch's lifetime (*The Ripper of Storyville and Other Ben Snow Tales*, Crippen & Landru 1997). With "The Vanished Steamboat" (*EQMM*, May 1984), Hoch launched a new series of frontier puzzles for Ben to solve. There are a total of 44 Snow stories, and as with the Al Darlan series the last of them ("Madam Sing's Gold" *EQMM*, July 2008) appeared posthumously.

CAPTAIN LEOPOLD, that most unprocedural of policemen, was perhaps the most vividly drawn Hoch protagonist and certainly the most long-lived, racking up an astonishing 107 cases between early 1962 and less than a year before the author's death. Why so many stories about him? Probably because this series was Hoch's most flexible and least restrictive. A Leopold tale required no new worthless object to be stolen, no innovative piece of espionage-detection, but just a fresh detective plot, and these seemed to come to him as naturally as breathing. Perhaps more important is that, unlike any other Hoch series, this one frequently offers more than clever plots and gimmicks. In the finest Leopolds the detective gamesmanship stuff of the Ellery Queen tradition is fused with elements derived from Graham Greene (Hoch's favorite author) and Georges Simenon, with unexpected nuances of character and emotion buried beneath the surface of deceptively simple prose. And beyond their individual strengths, when these stories are read in chronological order, as nineteen of the finest are arranged in *Leopold's Way* (Southern Illinois University Press, 1985), they take on something of the nature of an episodic novel, with characters who appear, vanish and return, grow and suffer and die. Up to a point, Leopold ages more or less in real time, being around 40 when we first meet him in "Circus" (*The Saint Mystery Magazine*, January 1962, as by Stephen Dentinger) and near 60 in "The Most Dangerous Man Alive" (*Ellery Queen's Mystery Magazine*, May 5, 1980), the last story in *Leopold's Way*, and these nineteen tales reflect not only his own development during those turbulent years but also that of the large northeastern city he serves. That city is almost never named, but in the uncollected "The Killer and the Clown" (*Alfred Hitchcock's Mystery Magazine*, October 14, 1981) it's called Monroe, which is the New York county whose seat is Hoch's native Rochester. As he visualized the fictitious city, he has said, it "bears some slight resemblance to Rochester turned upside-down, with the Sound substituting for Lake Ontario." Leopold's name came "from Jules Leopold, a frequent contributor to a puzzle magazine I read as a youth." But it's only in the uncollected "Suddenly in September" (*EQMM*, September 1983) that Leopold admits that his first name is Jules, which of course is also the first name of Simenon's immortal Maigret. What superb serendipity! For the Simenonian feel in many of the finest Leopold tales is palpable, and

Leopold himself is a sort of Maigret who works by rational deduction rather than immersion in a milieu and intuition.

The main events of the character's life are described at various points in the stories and form a biography as complete as the sketches Simenon habitually prepared for the protagonists of his non-series novels. Jules Leopold was born in Chicago in 1921. His parents died in an accident when he was eight and he spent the next six years in the midwest community of Riger Falls, being raised by relatives whom we meet in "Captain Leopold Goes Home" (Ellery Queen's Mystery Magazine, January 1975). At age 14 he came to Monroe, apparently to stay with other relatives, and graduated from George Washington High in 1939. Even then he was considered the class brain. He entered Columbia University, was awarded his degree during World War II and joined Army Intelligence, serving first in Washington and later in North Africa where he interrogated Italian prisoners. After the war he opted for a police career and spent a short time with a force out west, then a stint in Monroe, then a period with the NYPD. In the late 1950s he returned to Monroe to head the city's Homicide Squad. He had married several years earlier but the ten-year relationship shattered a few years after he accepted the Monroe position and he never saw his wife again until their tragic reunion in "The Leopold Locked Room" (EQMM, October 1971). After the divorce he lived an exceptionally lonely life, drowning his solitude in work. His one serious affair of the Sixties ended when he had to arrest the woman for murder in the uncollected "The Rusty Rose" (Alfred Hitchcock's Mystery Magazine, May 1966). Thereafter his only pleasures in life were the solitary satisfactions of drinking, smoking and reading. By the late Sixties he was fighting to kick the tobacco habit and apparently licked it at last, but he remained an avid reader, referring at various times to Chesterton, Stevenson, James Fenimore Cooper, Oscar Wilde, Hemingway and John Le Carré among others. By the Seventies he's become "middle-aged and stocky" but feminism and the sexual revolution begin to enrich his emotional life as he encounters a number of younger professional women. With policewoman Connie Trent, who entered the saga in the uncollected "Captain Leopold Gets Angry" (EQMM, March 1973), he was clearly tempted to have more than a working relationship, but resisted for the same reason that he wouldn't bring his personal auto to be washed at the police garage and forced himself to think of her as the daughter he never had. His relationship with pathologist Dr. Lawn Gaylord, who first appeared in the uncollected "Captain Leopold Looks for the Cause" (EQMM, November 1977), was less inhibited but led nowhere. His luck improved with defense attorney Molly Calendar, who first encountered him in "Captain Leopold Beats the Machine" (EQMM, June 1983) and became his second wife at the close of "Finding Joe Finch" (EQMM, February 1984). They were still together several years after Leopold's retirement when he made his 107th and final appearance in "Leopold Undercover" (EQMM, May 2007).

In many respects the Leopold saga mirrors the development of American social concerns since the Kennedy years. There's a clear line of evolution, for example, from the primitive brutalizing tactics of detective Mat Slater in the pre-*Miranda* days of "Circus" to the quiet professional interrogations of suspects in the later tales, and another evolution in Leopold's attitude towards women from the early years when he said flat out that their function is to stay home and have babies to the decade when he came to accept them both in his personal life and in the police department. But not every detail in the lives of Leopold and his colleagues was worked out in advance. Even though he and his first wife are clearly together in the uncollected "The Tattooed Priest" (*The Saint Mystery Magazine*, British edition, November 1962, as by Stephen Dentinger), he tells several people in later stories that they'd broken up before his move back to Monroe. Of course, many divorced men misremember or lie about the circumstances surrounding the collapse of their marriage, and Leopold in "Circus" and other early tales seems exceptionally sensitive to questions about his marital status and whether he has children. But what are we to make of the remarkable ocular transformations of Connie Trent, who enters the police department with brown eyes which turn green a few months later in "Captain Leopold Plays a Hunch" (*EQMM*, July 1973) and then go back to brown? And how do we account for the miraculous move of the entire city of Monroe from upstate New York, where it's firmly situated in the early stories, to Connecticut where it stayed since the uncollected "Bag of Tricks" (*Alfred Hitchcock's Mystery Magazine*, November 1970)? Here's a puzzle by which even Hoch's maven of the impossible Dr. Sam Hawthorne might be stumped!

FATHER DAVID NOONE, parish priest and occasional detective, began life in 1964 as Hoch's version of a clerical sleuth in the manner of G.K. Chesterton's Father Brown. He was dropped after two rather feeble cases but made a few reappearances in the last years of Hoch's life. His favorite among the seven Noone stories was "The Sweating Statue" (in *Detectives A to Z*, ed. Frank D. McSherry,

Jr., Martin H. Greenberg & Charles G. Waugh, Bonanza Books 1985).

RAND, of Britain's Department of Concealed Communications, was created in 1964 for *EQMM* and appeared in a total of 84 episodes of espionage laced with cryptography and detection. Originally called Randolph, he was renamed because *EQMM* editor Fred Dannay wanted a name subliminally evoking James Bond even though there was nothing Bond-like about the stories. The series began with "The Spy Who Did Nothing" (*EQMM*, May 1965) and, until a few years after Dannay's death in 1982, most of the Rands retained "The Spy Who" in their titles, reminding us that the greatest espionage novel of the era in which the character came to life was John LeCarré's *The Spy Who Came In from the Cold*. Seven of his early cases were collected in the paperback volume *The Spy and the Thief* (Davis Publications, 1971) and fifteen from later decades in *The Old Spies Club* (Crippen & Landru, 2001). Rand retired in due course but continued to be brought back for assignments on a regular basis. His final exploit, "The Alexandrian Solution" (*EQMM*, December 2008), was one of the last stories Hoch completed.

Perhaps the best-known Hoch character is NICK VELVET, a thief who steals only objects of no value and who is usually forced to play detective in the course of his thieving. He debuted in "The Theft of the Clouded Tiger" (*EQMM*, September 1966) and quickly became an international hit, racking up a total of 87 adventures. Seven of Nick's early capers were included in *The Spy and the Thief* and a total of fourteen (of which two come from the earlier volume) are collected in *The Thefts of Nick Velvet* (Mysterious Press, 1978), with another fourteen brought together in *The Velvet Touch* (Crippen & Landru, 2000). Several books of Velvet stories have been published in Japan and, rechristened Nick Verlaine, our contemporary Raffles has been the star of a French TV mini-series. The character was under option by 20th Century-Fox for several years but never made it to prime time over here. The 87th and last of his adventures was "The Theft of the Ostracized Ostrich" (*EQMM*, September-October 2007).

HARRY PONDER, a short-lived spy-cum-sleuth whose name suggests the Len Deighton-Michael Caine movie spy Harry Palmer, first appeared in "The Magic Bullet" (*Argosy*, January 1969), an excellent mix of espionage and impossible-crime detection, but was dropped after one more case.

BARNEY HAMET, a New York mystery writer, turned amateur sleuth in Hoch's first novel, *The Shattered Raven* (Lancer, 1969), in which he helped untangle a murder at the MWA annual dinner. In two later short stories he also probed killings among his colleagues.

CARL CRADER and EARL JAZINE, who solve crimes for the federal Computer Investigation Bureau in the early 21st century, first appeared in "Computer Cops", a story Hoch wrote for Hans Stefan Santesson's science fiction-mystery anthology *Crime Prevention in the 30th Century* (Walker, 1969). Later they starred in Hoch's trilogy of futuristic detective novels *The Transvection Machine* (Walker, 1971), *The Fellowship of the Hand* (Walker, 1972) and *The Frankenstein Factory* (Walker, 1975).

DAVID PIPER, director of the Department of Apprehension and also known as The Manhunter, shows that even when Hoch created a character with a superficial resemblance to the Executioner, The Butcher and similar macho action heroes, he would reconfigure the man as a mainstream detective. Piper starred in a six-installment serial, "The Will-o'-the-Wisp Mystery", published in *EQMM* between April and September 1971 under the byline of Mr. X. The entire serial was reprinted under Hoch's own name in *Ellery Queen's Anthology*, Spring-Summer 1982.

ULYSSES S. BIRD was Hoch's attempt to create a criminal who would not turn into a detective-in-spite-of-himself. The first of this con artist's four published exploits was "The Million-Dollar Jewel Caper" (*EQMM*, January 1973), but all of them were negligible except the third, "The Credit Card Caper" (*EQMM*, October 1974), which is a gem.

SEBASTIAN BLUE and LAURA CHARME, investigators for Interpol, vaguely resemble the stars of the classic British TV series *The Avengers*, but as usual when Hoch spun off a series from a pre-existing source, he moved it into the realm of fair-play detection. From "The Case of the Third Apostle" (February 1973) to "The Case of the Drowned Coroner" (January 1984) the duo appeared in fourteen issues of *EQMM*.

PAUL TOWER, who becomes involved in crime problems while visiting local schools as part of the police department's public relations program, was suggested to Hoch as a character by Fred Dannay. "The Lollipop Cop" (*EQMM*, March 1974) and Tower's two subsequent cases were excellent, and it's a shame the character was retired so quickly.

DR. SAM HAWTHORNE, by far the most successful of Hoch's later series characters, narrates his own reminiscences of impossible crime puzzles which he unofficially investigated between the early 1920s and the World War II years while serving as a physician in the

New England village of Northmont. Beginning with "The Problem of the Covered Bridge" (*EQMM*, December 1974), Dr. Sam spun yarns and offered listeners a "small libation" on a total of 72 occasions which collectively leave no doubt that Northmont is small-town America's Mecca for bizarre crimes. *Diagnosis: Impossible* (Crippen & Landru, 1996) brings together a dozen of the early Hawthornes, and fourteen more are collected in *More Things Impossible* (Crippen & Landru, 2006), the last volume of Hoch stories published in his lifetime.

BARNABUS REX, a humorous sleuth of the future, debuted in "The Homesick Chicken" (*Isaac Asimov's Science Fiction Magazine*, Spring 1977) and appeared in only one other story. But two cases make a series character even in the world of tomorrow.

TOMMY PRESTON, the young son of a zookeeper, was created by Hoch for the juvenile market. In *The Monkey's Clue & The Stolen Sapphire* (Grosset & Dunlap, 1978) he solves a pair of mysteries involving animals.

NANCY TRENTINO, an attractive policewoman with a deductive flair, could almost be Connie Trent from the Captain Leopold series under a different name. This is precisely what she was until the editors of *Hers* (later *Woman's World*) who bought her first solo case asked Hoch to ethnicize her. Beginning with "The Dog That Barked All Day" (*Hers*, 1 October 1979) she solved four mini-mysteries.

CHARLES SPACER, electronics executive and undercover U.S. agent, figures in five espionage-detective tales beginning with "Assignment: Enigma" (*EQMM*, 10 September 1980), which was published as by Anthony Circus although the four later Spacers appeared under Hoch's own name. The ambience of all these tales and the pseudonym on the first may vaguely suggest John Le Carré, but the leitmotif as usual in Hoch is the game of wits.

SIR GIDEON PARROT, whose name evokes two of John Dickson Carr's mastersleuths and one of Agatha Christie's, appeared in five gently nostalgic parodies of the Golden Age deductive puzzles on which Hoch was weaned. His first appearance was in "Lady of the Impossible" (*EQMM*, May 20, 1981).

LIBBY KNOWLES, ex-cop and professional bodyguard, debuted in "Five-Day Forecast", a Hoch story first published in *Ellery Queen's Prime Crimes* (Davis, 1984), an anthology edited by Eleanor Sullivan who took over at *EQMM* after Fred Dannay's death. Three later cases, two of them published in *EQMM*, established her as the second female recruit in Hoch's small army of series characters.

MATTHEW PRIZE, criminology professor and ex-private eye, was the detective in a pair of paperback mystery puzzles inspired by Thomas Chastain's best-selling *Who Killed the Robins Family?* (1983). Hoch created the plot outlines for these books, just as Fred Dannay had done for the Ellery Queen novels, and Ron Goulart did the writing. *Prize Meets Murder* (Pocket Books, 1984) and *This Prize is Dangerous* (Pocket Books, 1975) were published as by R.T. Edwards.

MICHAEL VLADO, farmer, horse trainer and leader of a gypsy community in Romania, is perhaps the most unlikely amateur sleuth in the Hoch gallery. His first appearance was in "The Luck of a Gypsy" (in *The Ethnic Detectives*, ed. Bill Pronzini & Martin H. Greenberg, Dodd Mead 1985). Within a few days after the publication of that anthology he became a series character with "Odds on a Gypsy" (*EQMM*, July 1985). Fifteen of his exploits were collected in *The Iron Angel and Other Tales of the Gypsy Sleuth* (Crippen & Landru, 2003). The thirtieth and last was "Gypsy Gold" (*EQMM*, December 2007).

All eleven of the cases of SUSAN HOLT, department-store buyer and solver of enigmas, were published in *EQMM* and, from "A Traffic in Webs" (Mid-December 1993) to "A Gateway to Heaven" (January 2008), all had the same title pattern. More enigmas would surely have been tossed at her if Hoch hadn't died in the month of the last story's publication.

ALEXANDER SWIFT, who takes on special assignments for George Washington during the Revolutionary War, is Hoch's only protagonist of a historical detective series other than Westerner Ben Snow. He debuted in "The Hudson Chain" (*EQMM*, September 1995) and appeared in a total of thirteen stories—just enough for a posthumous collection. His last outing was in "Swift Among the Pirates" (*EQMM*, May 2007).

The arrival of the 21st century failed to stop Hoch from creating new series. His first of the new millennium dealt with STANTON & IVES, a pair of professional couriers whose work takes them into the sideline of unraveling riddles. Their first adventure was the aptly named "Courier and Ives" (*EQMM*, November 2002), and their twelfth was the story Hoch was working on when he died of a sudden heart attack. Since his tendency was to plot in his head, he left no written notes of how the tale was to end, but fellow mystery writer Jon L. Breen followed the clues in the early pages and their collaboration appeared as "Handel and Gretel" (*EQMM*, November 2008).

The last Hoch series character and his fourth female sleuth was San Diego policewoman ANNIE SEARS, all three of whose cases appeared in *Alfred Hitchcock's Mystery Magazine* from "The Cactus Killer" (October 2005) to the posthumous "Baja" (September 2008).

There in 28 nutshells is the Hoch every mystery enthusiast knows, the Will Shortz of detective fiction, the puzzlemaster par excellence. But he also wrote well over 200 non-series stories linked by no common character or thread. Some of them abound in fair-play detection, like that supreme impossible-crime puzzle "The Long Way Down" (*Alfred Hitchcock's Mystery Magazine*, February 1965), while others have none. A non-series story by Hoch might have a protagonist who could easily have become a series character, like songwriter Johnny Nocturne of "The Night My Friend" (*The Saint Mystery Magazine*, British edition, July 1962, as by Stephen Dentinger), or one who could never return, or no central figure at all. *The Night My Friend* (Ohio University Press, 1991) brings together 22 of Hoch's finest non-series tales, including a boxing story, a juvenile delinquency story, a prep-school reunion story and a fable about a wandering minstrel and his harmonica. The collection also includes more than one tale about the aftermath of World War II—including "To Slay an Eagle" (*The Award Espionage Reader*, ed. Hans Stefan Santesson, Award Books 1965, as by Stephen Dentinger) which is as bleak as any spy novel by Graham Greene or John Le Carré—and several thrillers with a *noir* ambience reminiscent of one of the classic TV series of the Sixties, *The Fugitive*. With their unusually vivid and visual prose, off-trail settings, complex characterizations and emotions that run deep, these stories reflect a side of Hoch's literary personality that sometimes got short shrift in his series tales other than those about Captain Leopold. A second collection of twenty non-series tales was published as *The Night People and Other Stories* (Five Star, 2001).

In the last year of his life he was turning out a new story every three weeks, and at that rate he would have completed his thousandth tale sometime after turning 81. He died of a sudden heart attack a month before his 78th birthday and about fifty stories short of that goal. He was the last of his kind. In terms of both quality and quantity, detective fiction at shorter than novel length will never see his like. Not all of his stories will survive, but an awesome number of them will probably continue to be read and admired and enjoyed well into the 21st century.

HARRY STEPHEN KEELER

You may have seen the T-shirt. A skinny nerdy-looking man with a spitcurl over his forehead sits at a typewriter from whose carriage streams an endless roll of paper at whose far end sits a cat. His name was Harry Stephen Keeler, and when he was born the mold found voice and said "Never again!" For more than half a century he stomped through the staid precincts of mystery fiction like King Kong crossing a country churchyard. His more than 90 novels form a self-contained world of brain-boggling intrigues, a world at once farcical and dead serious, a firestorm of radical social criticism and a labyrinth in which he hid himself. He invented the webwork novel, in which the bizarre events that explode like cigars in the white-knight hero's face turn out to be mathematically interrelated, with every absurd incident making blissfully perfect sense within the cockeyed frame of reference. His favorite devices for tying story elements together were the loony law, the nutty religious tenet, the wacky will, the crackpot contract and, commonest of all, the network of backbreaking coincidences. He loved to make up outrageous ethnic dialects for characters, and to attack the social evils he saw: racism, brutal cops, the military, corrupt pols, capital punishment, the maltreatment of the mentally ill, all the dark underside of an America where "Money was Emperor, and Might was Right." Most of all he loved cats, even dedicating novels to them at times.

Born in Chicago on November 3, 1890, Keeler grew up among Victorian thespians in the theatrical boarding-house his mother was forced to run after her first husband died in Harry's infancy and her second gambled away the family funds and killed himself. He once said that on the day his school taught grammar and rhetoric he played hooky and caught perch at the foot of Superior Street. In 1912, after spending about a year in a mental hospital to which his mother for vague reasons had him committed, he obtained an electrical engineering degree from Armour (later Illinois) Institute of Technology. During the next two years he worked as an electrician in a South Chicago steel mill and wrote short stories, most of them heavily influenced by O. Henry, on the side. Typical of these early tales is "Victim No. 5" (Young's Magazine, September 1914), for which he was paid a lordly ten dollars. The protagonist is a professional burglar who always strangles the people he robs and ends his days locked in a vaudeville performer's theatrical trunk and squeezed to death by the pet boa constrictor that lives inside. This and most of Keeler's other early stories are collected in Strands of the Web (2009).

Between 1914 and 1924 Harry sold dozens of novelettes—which he liked to call novellos, most likely with the accent on the first syllable!—and magazine serials with titles like "The Trepanned Skull", "The Stolen Finger" and "The Giant Moth", perfecting his webwork technique in the process. In 1919 he married short-story writer Hazel Goodwin and took a part-time job as editor of the magazine *10-Story Book*, a position he held for the next 21 years.

His first novel, *The Voice of the Seven Sparrows* (1924), is a wild comic intrigue about rival Chicago newsmen searching for a publisher's vanished daughter and encountering along the way characters like Ng Chuen Li Yat, the Chinese millionaire who bet a fortune that he could walk across South America in a year and a half, and Peter Zeller, the shipwreck survivor who mailed out 14,257 identical deuce-of-spades cards in order to trap one man. In *The Spectacles of Mr. Cagliostro* (1926) Jerry Middleton, heir to a Chicago patent-medicine fortune, is replaced by an impostor and railroaded into the state mental hospital, where he's befriended by the genuine madpersons, hilariously analyzed by that world-renowned shrink Herr Doctor Meister-Professor von Zero, and nearly killed by an assassin who's been hired to get admitted to the asylum and slice up our hero. In *Sing Sing Nights* (1927) three authors are about to be electrocuted for the same murder (I refuse to explain how this came about) when the governor offers one man a blank pardon and the writers agree that each will tell an impromptu story to the uneducated death-house guard, the pardon to go to the teller of the tale the guard likes best. The three stories (which had first seen life years before as unrelated magazine novellos) are intercut with mind-blowing discussions of the nature of storytelling. Thanks to a typical Keeler Koincidence all three penmen go free in the last chapter. *Thieves' Nights* (1929) concerns penniless Chicago drifter Ward Sharlow, who is hired to impersonate a look-alike missing heir and runs into a slew of oddball dilemmas trying to keep up the deception. One problem is a disfigured butler, the author of a long novelette about characters telling each other stories about characters telling each other stories. (What a way to recycle Keeler's old magazine tales!) Late in the novel the leftist thief who figures in the innermost layer of stories turns out to be "real," hopping into the book's outer circle just in time to extricate Sharlow from a fine filet of pickle, then going off to help build socialism in the Soviet Union.

These are typical early Keeler novels—generally set in Chicago, creatively varying the Arabian Nights framework, full of grotesque characters and events, packed with coincidence and bitter social comment and Victorian dialogue so as almost to suggest an American Dickens. Many Keelerganzas of these years are of truly elephantine proportions, such as *The Amazing Web* (1930) with its 532 pages; the 741-page *The Matilda Hunter Murder* (1931), starring Tuddleton T. Trotter, that aged bedraggled universal genius and patron of homeless cats; and *The Box from Japan* (1932), whose 765 closely printed pages make it the heavyweight champ of all time. Others, like *The Washington Square Enigma* and *The Face of the Man from Saturn* (both 1933), are extremely short and tight and move at jumbojet speed. Embedded within *The Face* is Keeler's best-known short story, "John Jones' Dollar" (*Black Cat*, August 1915), which describes, in the form of a history professor's lecture in 3255 AD, how one morning back in AD 2961 the investment by John Jones of a single dollar bill more than a millennium earlier suddenly brought the entire solar system to "the true socialistic and democratic condition for which man had futilely hoped throughout the ages."

By the mid-1930s Keeler's books had become longer, wilder, wackier and less constrained by conventional discipline than ever. The first of his two-volume meganovels was published as *The Marceau Case* and *X. Jones of Scotland Yard* (both 1936) and consists of hundreds of documents—letters, telegrams, newspaper columns, photos (one of a bare-breasted lady and another of Keeler himself), cartoons, ads, courtroom transcripts and booklets of Chinese dialect jokes—all combining to tell the story of the Aeronautic Strangler-Baby case. Who garroted midget-hating tycoon André Marceau in the center of his croquet lawn without leaving a single mark in the freshly rolled earth or any other clue except the victim's dying words: "The Babe from Hell!"? Keeler comes up with a gaggle of outlandish alternate solutions, some of them indeed spilling over into a later novel, *The Wonderful Scheme of Mr. Christopher Thorne* (1937), where they crop up amid disquisitions on Asian philosophy and savage indictments of America delivered by half-black half-Indian Ebenezer Sitting-Down-Bear.

Keeler all but anticipated *Catch-22* in the two-volume novel published as *The Defrauded Yeggman* and *10 Hours* (both 1937), another Arabian Nights offshoot which consists largely of the tales told by three hobos at their court-martial. The trio had happened to alight in a Texas bordertown where martial law has been declared because a demented Mexican general, equipped with an air force and strong views on reincarnation, has threatened to bomb the town after the local authorities sold his dead brother's skull. The tramps' trial is a model of procedural outrage, with a sadistic prosecutor, inept defense counsel, a secret agreement among the officer judges to finish the case in a couple of hours, and a war order (printed, with fine care for due process, in both English and Spanish) forbidding any civilian court to interfere. Harry can be called many things but never a fan of the military.

The most personal of Keeler's meganovels, *The Mysterious Mr. I* (1938) and *The Chameleon* (1939), deals with the nameless narrator's attempts to collect $100,000 by returning an escaped millionaire to the lunatic asylum before midnight. On his quest he trips blithely through close to a hundred separate identities, posing in turn as a tycoon, a safecracker, a locomotive engineer, a gambler, several different detectives, several writers, a couple of actors, a philosophy professor and God knows what else, until we finally realize that the seeker is hunting no one but himself. After 500 pages of lies within lies our fictional forerunner of The Great Impostor seduces a nun, arranges to make her a rich woman, and returns freely to the asylum where he will spend his days reading British magazines and sipping Chateau d'Yquem with his keeper. In these novels Keeler painted his clearest self-portrait: metaphysician and storyteller and gleeful madman, torn by the real world's rot and horror, creating alternate universes of his own with the ease and delight of a child blowing bubbles.

During the '40s and '50s Keeler abandoned meganovels and alternated between single titles, of standard length and brain-boggling contents, and several series of novels dealing respectively with the adventures of a book, a circus, a house, an industrial plant, and a skull. Most of these are set not in Chicago but in unnamed corners of middle America and many include Hazel Goodwin Keeler's whiskered old magazine stories, which Harry spliced into the text just as he had used to throw his own short stories into his novels and attribute them to writer characters.

The so-called Skull in the Box series consists of four novels: *The Man with the Magic Eardrums* (1939), *The Man with the Crimson Box* (1940), *The Man with the Wooden Spectacles* (1940), and *The Case of the Lavender Gripsack* (1944). The final novel not only brings the tetralogy to a climax but thrusts onto center stage one of the first female lawyers in American fiction. Elsa Colby, recent graduate of Chicago's Northwestern Law School, has signed a typical Keeler Kontract that will divest her of title to a valuable piece of real estate known as Colby's Nugget, and vest title in her rascally uncle Silas Moffit, if she should be disbarred or lose a criminal case within a certain number of months. For obvious reasons Elsa is accepting no cases and spends her time making a quilt. Moffit pressures Judge Hilford Penworth, also known as Ultra Legal Penworth, to compel her to defend a capital case she can't possibly win and to disbar her on the spot—which is within the judge's power as Chief Commissioner of the Ethical Practices Subdivision!—if she refuses. The trial—for a murder that took place less than 24 hours earlier!—is to be held in the drawing room of Judge Penworth, who is suffering from a bad case of gout. A redheaded young man who has insisted on this instant trial but refuses to tell his lawyer anything, not even his name, is charged with the murder of night watchman Adolph Reibach and the theft from the private safe of District Attorney Louis Vann of a crimson box containing a skull. The skull in question appears to be that of Wah Lee, son of a Chinese restaurant tycoon and victim of a kidnap-murder-decapitation plot 13 years earlier by the notorious Parson gang, whose members wear clergymen's costumes to avoid suspicion. The gang's leader, Gus McGurk, is about to be released from prison on another charge and can be tried for the Wah Lee murder only if the skull's pedigree can be established in court; and, as we learned earlier in the tetralogy, McGurk has sent word through the prison grapevine to the last Parson at large that the skull has to be stolen from Vann's safe or, to use Keeler's version of underworld lingo, his pete. The evidence that Elsa's involuntary client did the dirty work seems beyond refutation: just a few hours after the crime, which Vann has kept secret, no less a dignitary than the Archbishop of Chicago encountered the redhead on the steps of the old Post Office and, on asking what was in the box, was told: "Wah Lee's skull; I cracked Vann's pete." The courtroom action in *Gripsack* is light on Q-and-A but overflows with Keeler's inspired daffiness, and the crossword-puzzle exegesis in Chapter 13 is guaranteed to pop every cruciverbalist's eyeballs. The courtroom speeches are deliberately longwinded—for roughly the same reason that they were in *The Defrauded Yeggman/10 Hours*—and the surprise ending will knock the socks off any reader with the patience to keep going till the end. Law in Keeler's world has no more connection with real-world jurisprudence than a toad has wings, but the Skull series is so wildly inventive no one cares.

In *The Peacock Fan* (1941), first of Keeler's novels with a book as protagonist, author and Sinophile Gordon Highsmith, about to be hanged for his wife's murder, frantically tries to prove his innocence from his deathhouse cell, with the help of an old friend and spiritual adviser from a religious brotherhood originally known as The Order of the Holy Nail. (Toilet-bowl tycoon Gregory Phemaster endowed the order with a fortune on condition that it change its name to the Gregory Phemaster Order of the Holy Nail and appoint his nephew the abbot.) Meanwhile Keeler introduces us to Highsmith's publishers, the diabolical Vinnedge brothers. Simon is a greedy-eyed swine given to rewriting his authors' wills and sneaking trick clauses into their contracts, while his brother Dolliver is a pervert with a compulsion to marry hunchbacked black women. These publishing paragons are determined to make sure Highsmith is hanged on schedule: slipping into the prison, impersonating first the warden and then Highsmith's new lawyer, sending whoever may help the condemned man off on wild goose chases. As in later entries in the series, that rare volume of Chinese aphorisms *The Way Out* provides the protagonist with just that at the crucial moment. Having signed a multibook contract with Keeler, the E.P. Dutton firm was obligated to publish this bitter satire on the publishing racket but dropped Harry as soon as it legally could. This explains the three years' delay between the release of the first three volumes of the Skull in the Box series and the fourth, which was issued by the bottom-of-the barrel Phoenix Press.

In the circus novels we follow that benevolent loon Angus MacWhorter, proprietor of MacWhorter's Mammoth Motorized Shows, and his wild escapades guiding the troupe through the serpenttine coils of a road from nowhere to nowhere called Old Twistibus. In *The Vanishing Gold Truck* (1941) the circus is camped at the west end of the road, outside a town where the telephone, the telegraph and all other modern communication devices are illegal. Meanwhile one lone circus truck, containing driver Jim Craney and a lioness, is at the east end of Old Twistibus, trying desperately to rejoin the circus. Learning that MacWhorter's elephant has knocked down the bridge across Bear Creek, Jim persuades Sheriff Bucyrus Duckhouse to let the truck use a completed but not yet officially opened superhighway on pillars that tunnels through the mountains and cuts hours off the trip. Little does he know that Al "Three-Gun" Mulhearn and his gang are about to steal a load of gold bars from the Cedarville bank and make their getaway via the same highway. Eventually both the Craney circus truck and the truck containing the robbers are reliably reported to be on the Straightaway while Duckhouse sits with his shotgun at the west end of the tunnel, waiting to nail the thieves. The Craney truck comes through the tunnel and its driver tells Duckhouse that another truck is indeed on the road behind him. But the robbers' truck never comes through, and it's physically impossible for it to have left the road! This miracle problem worthy of John Dickson Carr is capped with an outrageous solution that no one but Keeler could have conjured up.

In *The Case of the Barking Clock* (1947), social outcast Joe Czeszcziczki (whom everyone mercifully agrees to call Zicky after a few pages) is about to be executed for the murder of State's Attorney Umphrey Ibstone and appeals for help to Tuddleton T. Trotter, the cat-loving universal genius who fifteen years earlier had solved *The Matilda Hunter Murder*. Although the ancient gentleman takes two-thirds of the book just to contact Zicky in the death house, he proves his client's innocence in jig time and earns a comfortable retirement for himself and his beloved cat Sebastian Sixsmith.

Sadly, the wilder grew Keeler's flights of fancy, the fewer readers flew with him. After *The Case of the Transposed Legs* (1948) he lost his American publishers, and his British firm gave up on him after the MacWhorter novel *Stand By—London Calling* (1953). Harry didn't stop writing but from then on his books appeared only in Spanish and Portuguese translations if at all. Among these late works are gems of insanity like *The Case of the Transparent Nude, The Man Who Changed His Skin, The Affair of the Bottled Deuce, The Riddle of the Wooden Parakeet.* One of the maddest of all the late Keelers is *The Six from Nowhere*, in which MacWhorter and the circus folk counter the efforts of Gonwyck Schwaaa and his gang to steal a pulp detective magazine from Angus's safe, with the quest for the magazine intertwined with the affairs of a British woman mathematician, an educated hobo, the ashes of a corrupt politician in a Chicago crypt, and a pair of circus cats who have left 2,000,000 progeny across the United States.

In 1960 Hazel Keeler died of cancer and Harry became desolate. He gave away carloads of his books to Chicago secondhand dealers and lived alone, starting many novels but finishing none. His only regular writing during the early '60s was a mimeographed newsletter he turned out for friends, filling the multicolored pages with theosophical and literary and cat lore and paeans to the fascist dictator Franco, whose Spain was the only place in the world where he was still in print. In 1963 he married Thelma Rinaldo, who had been his secretary briefly in the late 1920s, and with her love and care he was, like Dickens's Dr. Manette, recalled to life. The last novels he completed, *Strange Journey* and *The Scarlet Mummy*, were never published even in Madrid.

Keeler died in his sleep on January 22, 1967, leaving a dozen books unfinished, confident that one day he'd be read again. And he was right! Today there are elaborate websites and a bi-monthly newsletter devoted to him, a small publishing house systematically issuing his complete works (including those never published in his lifetime), a book-length "Companion" to his wild and woolly world, a much longer collection of his multicolored newsletters, and an assortment of Keelerbilia including that T-shirt. One can almost see him sitting on a cloud saying: "Told you so!"

Whatever fame he reaps in the third millennium he richly deserves. He spun an alternate universe all his own from its metaphysical underpinnings to the speech and costumes of its inhabitants. Committed humanist-radical and exuberant zany, he was the true original of Kesey's R. P. MacMurphy and Vonnegut's Kilgore Trout, the sublime nutty genius of the age, a man so far ahead of his time we still haven't caught up to him. "A wonderful man, that old Socialist John Jones the first . . . considering that he lived in such a dark era as the twentieth century."

Profiles

JOHN LUTZ

He's a native Texan, born in Dallas on September 11, 1939. When he was four years old his photographer father moved the family to St. Louis. Soon after the end of World War II the elder Lutz opened a tavern which he continued to own and operate for more than twenty years. John graduated from Southwest High School in 1957 and, having not the foggiest notion what he wanted to do with his life, found a job as a movie theater usher. The following year, at age 19, he married Barbara Jean Bradley, who worked at the same theater as (if I am permitted to recycle that now archaic word) an usherette. More than half a century later they're still together.

A young man who becomes a husband and father before he's old enough to vote, and who has to support the family putting in long hours at low-level jobs, will rarely have the energy to read for enjoyment, let alone to write, during what little free time he has. John Lutz did.

In the early 1960s he was working on various night shifts as a civilian switchboard operator for the St. Louis Police Department, a forklift operator, and a warehouseman for a grocery chain. By daylight he was reading voraciously—among his favorites at the time were John D. MacDonald, Ross Macdonald, John Collier, Gerald Kersh and Roald Dahl—and pounding out dozens of his own short stories at warp speed, sometimes not even bothering to make a carbon. When or if he slept remains a mystery. "It looked easy," he said, "so I tried it and found out it wasn't." None of his stories sold but that, he said after making the grade, was "part of the learning process." Dozens of rejection slips in a row have aborted countless potential writing careers but Lutz refused to get discouraged. "I saw I could improve, so I kept at it." After a while the editors who turned down his material began to write supportive comments in their sorry-we-can't-use-this letters. "That's a good sign. I'd know I was close to a sale then." Most of his stories were mysteries because he liked to read them and thought they were relatively easy to sell. One frabjous day in early 1966 he opened his mail and out popped a contract. He was still working the night shift at a grocery warehouse when his first story came out. "Thieves' Honor" (*Alfred Hitchcock's Mystery*

Magazine, December 1966) opened the door for him, and acceptances soon began pouring in. Six of his tales appeared in 1967, ten in '68, five more in '69. Within a few years of his unheralded entry into the genre he was being published in *Ellery Queen's Mystery Magazine*, *Mike Shayne Mystery Magazine*, the science-fictional periodical *Galaxy*, the Diners Club magazine *Signature*, men's mags like *Knight* and *Swank* and *Cavalier*. But the majority of his stories sold to *Alfred Hitchcock's Mystery Magazine* and many of those are among his finest. In 1975, his tenth year in the field, eighteen new Lutz tales were published including five (under his own name and four pseudonyms) in a single issue of a single magazine. Now that's productivity!

Even after 1971 when his first novel was published, John prudently held onto his job as night warehouseman. Eventually he found a better-paying position as a truck driver. In 1973, after being laid off from that job, he decided to take a crack at full-time writing. Two years later he and Barbara and their three children and their dog moved across St. Louis County to a stucco house on a wooded corner lot in suburban Webster Groves, where they lived for the next thirty-odd years.

~ ~ ~ ~ ~

There are no series characters in most of his short stories but there are what one might call series elements. The two that are identified with him are husbands seeking a method of wife-disposal and off-the-wall business organizations. Occasionally, like the creator of two different series detectives who has his sleuths work together on a particular case, he uses both signature elements in a single story, for example "Fractions" (*Alfred Hitchcock's Mystery Magazine*, June 1972), which is about a company that manipulates unwanted spouses into cheating.

Lutz can create a new business as easily as a rabbit can create another rabbit, but most of his imaginary entities share a common factor. Beneath the impressive facade and the smiles and the handshakes they're out to take us. He was never all that fond of the self-congratulatory social Darwinism known as the free enterprise system, and even when dealing with businesses that exist in reality he combined a healthy cynicism with imaginative bizarrerie and came up with dandy items like "Mail Order" (*Alfred Hitchcock's Mystery Magazine*, April 1975) and "Understanding Electricity" (*Alfred Hitchcock's Mystery Magazine*, August 1975), which read as if

Kafka had come back from the grave to collaborate with Ralph Nader. Not all his stories are of this sort, but the best do tend to stem from wildly distinctive premises, like "The Real Shape of the Coast" (*Ellery Queen's Mystery Magazine*, June 1971) with its lunatic detective trying to solve a murder in the asylum, or "Dead Man" (*Alfred Hitchcock's Mystery Magazine*, March 1974) where we share the last hours of a tycoon locked inside a walk-in vault with a few hours' air supply as he gropes desperately for a clue to the identity of his own murderer.

His first decade as a writer also saw the publication of his first two novels. *The Truth of the Matter* (1971) is a paperback thriller about a fugitive couple being stalked across the Midwest by the police but mainly by their own lies and self-deceptions and fears. *Buyer Beware* (1976) introduced St. Louis PI Alo Nudger, whose trademark is a nervous stomach and whose specialty is the legal counter-kidnaping of children kidnaped by non-custodial parents. Then came four breakthrough books that established him as a writer to contend with. *Bonegrinder* (1977) is a bit like *Jaws* out of water, pitting a rural sheriff against a Bigfoot-like monster terrorizing a small town in the Ozarks. *Lazarus Man* (1979) is a Watergate-era political thriller in which the G. Gordon Liddy figure gets out of prison determined to kill the Nixon figure and his cronies one by one, only to find that they're just as bent on killing him. *Jericho Man* (1980) is the first but far from the last novel in which Lutz mined the Lawrence Sanders vein of urban violence, with a tough NYPD captain and a young architect battling the madman who planted dynamite in the foundations of several high-rises when they were under construction. In *The Shadow Man* (1981) a U.S. Senator is stalked through the Manhattan nightscape by what seems to be a psychotic political assassin with the power to be in several places at once.

Lutz never stopped writing short stories even when he was turning out a novel a year, but his magazine appearances became rarer. A few of his tales from this period featured series characters like Nudger or *Bonegrinder*'s Sheriff Billy Wintone, and an occasional non-series story furnished raw material for a later novel, like "The Other Runner" (*Ellery Queen's Mystery Magazine*, October 1978), the source for one of the scariest of the murders in *Lazarus Man* a year later. But stories like "Pure Rotten" (*Mike Shayne Mystery Magazine*, August 1977) and "Dear Dorie" (*Alfred Hitchcock's Mystery Magazine*, September 16, 1981) are as crazy as any Lutz dreamed up in his early days, and "High Stakes" (*The Saint Mystery Magazine*, June 1984) is one of the most terrifying short stories of suspense since the death of Cornell Woolrich. The Edgar that Mystery Writers of America awarded him for the Nudger story "Ride the Lightning" (*Alfred Hitchcock's Mystery Magazine*, January 1985) was an honor well deserved and long overdue.

In *The Eye* (1984) Lutz and co-author Bill Pronzini revisited Lawrence Sanders country and came up with a powerful *noir* thriller. A wealthy madman living in a Jersey Palisades highrise keeps his balcony telescope trained on the residents of a single block of Manhattan's West 98th Street. His name is God, and those who violate his commandments he kills. Assigned to the series of West 98th Street murders is plainclothesman E.L. Oxman, a diligent plodder trapped in a cancerous marriage and desperate for affection on almost any terms. When he takes up with the promiscuous young artist who lives on the murder-plagued block, they both unwittingly nominate themselves as God's next targets.

Next Lutz revived Alo Nudger but in a somewhat reconfigured version. The character's ill-advised first name is almost never mentioned, he no longer specializes in the legal kidnaping of children (or anything else), the narration has shifted from first to third person, and the protagonist's symbiotic relationship with his city has become almost as strong as Spenser's with Boston or Philip Marlowe's with L.A. The new Nudger comes close to being a total loser, plagued by overdue bills and deadbeat clients and a bloodsucking ex-wife and shoddy consumer goods and that old nervous stomach and most of all by his near-paralyzing unaggressiveness and compassion. His office is above a doughnut shop in a dreary suburb of north St. Louis County. He drives a dented old Volkswagen Beetle that he has trouble finding whenever he parks in a shopping center lot ands which tends to die on him for lack of maintenance when he uses it to chase or shadow someone. He shares the world of Charlie Chaplin's tramp: whatever can go wrong for him, will. In *Nightlines* (1984) Nudger encounters a suicidal woman whose life is even more messed up than his own while hunting the slasher who's been using the phone company's private equipment-testing lines to make blind dates with his female victims. *Ride the Lightning* (1987), expanded from his Edgar-winning short story, puts Nudger in a hopeless race against the clock to save a petty criminal from being electrocuted for one crime he may not have committed. The tenth and apparently final novel in the series was *Oops!* (1998).

One Nudger book a year left Lutz ample time to launch a second private eye series, this one set in central Florida and featuring a character for whom the perfect movie incarnation would have been

Robert Duvall. Fred Carver is a balding fortyish ex-cop whose police career ended when he was kneecapped by a Latino street punk. Vegetating in the beachfront bungalow he bought with his disability pay, Carver is pushed into PI work by friends on the force who want him to stop pitying himself and get on with his life. In *Tropical Heat* (1986) Carver is hired by a lovely realtor to find her lover, who in the middle of a solitary continental breakfast on her terrace either walked out on her for no reason, or jumped off a cliff into the ocean, or was pushed off. The search leads to a condominium time-sharing scam, a drug deal (in Florida what else?), an underwater duel with a knife-wielding Marielito, an airboat chase through the Everglades, and an emotional entanglement which neither Carver nor his client is equipped to handle. The plot is of the bare-bones variety but the meat on those bones is prime *noir*, saturated with vivid descriptions of the Florida heat. All the subsequent Carver novels had one-word titles: *Scorcher, Kiss, Flame, Bloodfire, Hot, Spark, Torch, Burn*, and finally *Lightning* (1996). For me the finest of the lot is *Kiss* (1988), one of the most disturbing and downbeat of all PI novels.

Interspersed among his PI books are about sixty short stories published in anthologies of original fiction plus several stand-alone thrillers. *SWF Seeks Same* (1990) is a prime specimen of *noir contemporaine* in which a young woman in New York advertises for someone to share an apartment with and winds up with the roommate from hell. This became by far the best known Lutz novel when it was filmed by director Barbet Schroeder as *Single White Female* (1992), starring Bridget Fonda and Jennifer Jason Leigh.

His novels of the 21st century are about twice as long as any of his previous books and, like *Jericho Man* and *The Eye*, concentrate on protracted urban duels between a cop and a serial killer. *Night* was in the titles of the first half-dozen, beginning with *The Night Caller* (2001), but more recently the pattern has been dropped. As of this writing his latest mega-thriller is *Urge to Kill* (2009).

Today John is seventy, living with Barbara in a lovely house in the affluent suburb of Des Peres that is large enough to accommodate frequent visits from children and grandkids. Their winters are spent in Sarasota and they love to visit New York for a concentrated week or two of theatergoing. Alone among the authors covered in depth here, he is alive and well and still writing up a storm, filling his monitor screen with the doings of lovers and losers, butchers and victims, fools and clowns, hunters and prey. May that situation continue for years to come.

JOHN D. MacDONALD

In his time he was *the* consummate storyteller, who with his energetic prose, vivid sense of character, near-miraculous skill at describing every sort of person and setting and event with economy, elegance and total credibility, made millions of readers from the Truman era to that of Reagan turn and turn his pages with minds in awe and hearts hovering around the Adam's apple. John Dann MacDonald was born in Sharon, Pennsylvania on July 24, 1916. His father was a strong-willed workaholic who rose Horatio Alger-like from humble origins to become a top executive at a firearms company in Utica, New York. A near-fatal attack of mastoiditis and scarlet fever at age 12 confined young MacDonald to bed for a year, and lack of anything else to do in those days before radio and TV virtually forced him to read or have his mother read to him huge quantities of books. As soon as he was back on his feet he began haunting the public library, compulsively devouring every book on the shelves.

After graduating from the Utica Free Academy in 1933 he took some courses at the University of Pennsylvania's Wharton School of Finance, then transferred to Syracuse University where in 1938 he received a B.S. in Business Administration. He married fellow Syracuse graduate Dorothy Prentiss the same year and was awarded an M.B.A. from Harvard Business School in June 1939. After an assortment of jobs that he hated, he accepted a lieutenant's commission in the Army in June 1940 and was assigned to procurement work in Rochester until June 1943 when he was sent overseas to Staff Headquarters, New Delhi, India. A year later he was recruited by the Office of Strategic Services, the forerunner of the CIA, and served in Colombo, Ceylon (now Sri Lanka) as branch commander of an Intelligence detachment, rising to the rank of Lieutenant Colonel.

During the idle times, instead of sending his wife letters that he knew would be heavily censored, MacDonald began writing and sending her short stories. One of these Dorothy sold for $25 to Whit and Hallie Burnett's prestigious *Story Magazine*, where it appeared as "Interlude in India" (July-August 1946). "I can't describe what it was like," MacDonald said decades later, "when I found out that my words had actually sold . . . I felt as if I were a fraud, . . . as if I were trying to be something that I wasn't. Then I thought, my goodness, maybe I could actually be one."

At the end of the war MacDonald was entitled to four months of stateside terminal leave with pay before his official discharge. He spent the time behind the typewriter, working harder than ever before in his life, putting in 80 hours a week, cranking out 800,000 words worth of short stories, keeping 30 to 35 yarns in the mail at all times—and selling not a word. Finally, early in 1946, a few of the mid-grade pulps like *Detective Tales* and *Mammoth Mystery* began buying from him, and by the end of the year he had earned about $6,000, enough to support himself and Dorothy and their seven-year-old son in modest style. For the next half-dozen years most of MacDonald's income came from magazines, primarily the great pulps like *Black Mask, Dime Detective, Doc Savage, The Shadow* and *Mystery Book* whose gaudy and lurid covers could still be seen on every newsstand in those immediate postwar years. Once in a while he'd sell to a slick periodical like *Esquire, Liberty* or *Cosmopolitan* that paid top dollar, but the vast majority of his tales of the late Forties and early Fifties went to the pulps and his name became a fixture on those garish covers. He made so many pulp sales so quickly that some magazines would run two, three or even four of his stories in a single issue, one under his own byline and the rest under so-called house names.

MacDonald was the last great American mystery writer to hone his storytelling skills in the action-detective pulps as Hammett and Chandler and Gardner and Woolrich had done before him. During the half-dozen years after the war he wrote more than 200 pulp tales whose variety in length and content is astonishing. There were two Westerns, at least 21 sports stories, well over forty ventures into science-fiction, but most of MacDonald's energies during these formative years were concentrated in the crime-suspense genre, to which he contributed more than 160 stories between 1946 and the early 1950s.

Several of MacDonald's earliest pulp crime stories were set in the China-Burma-India locales where he'd spent the war. A better than average specimen is "The Startled Face of Death" (*Doc Savage*, November 1946, under the house byline of Scott O'Hara). Insurance detective Stan Carvell is sent to New Delhi to find a necklace that had vanished before the outbreak of war and to learn why two earlier investigators died on the same quest. A pair of scorpions slipped into his luggage in the night convince him that he's close to the answers.

The solution is mostly guesswork but there is detection of sorts and the atmosphere is authentically steamy.

It was magazine editor Babette Rosmond who persuaded him to take off the pith helmet and start writing about the United States, and from then on most of his stories dealt with the postwar American scene. Indeed MacDonald portrayed more vividly and knowledgeably than any other crime writer the readjustment of American society in general and American business in particular from a war footing to a consumer-oriented peacetime economy which would soon be spewing out megatons of self-destructing plastic junk and incurring the wrath of the later MacDonald and his beach bum-philosopher-adventurer hero Travis McGee.

One can see this theme at work in MacDonald's "When You Got a Pigeon" (*Shadow Mystery Magazine*, December 1947-January 1948), which is set in the thriving postwar manufacturing community of Acton, New Jersey and deals with a power struggle among the top executives of Haydon Motors. Baker Hay, plant engineer and son of one of the founders, joins forces with the Old Guard in an attempt to keep the general manager's position out of the hands of the coldly brilliant but ruthless Randolph Post. Hoping to discredit Post, Hay investigates the apparent suicide of Julia, his adversary's wife, to whom Hay himself had been engaged before the war. With the help of the switchboard girl in the Posts' apartment building, Hay learns some facts which suggest the possibility that Julia was murdered by one of those Rube Goldberg killing devices which the young MacDonald loved to dream up. Luckily for everyone but himself, the exposed murderer elects to jump out of a high window despite the absence of any legal evidence against him. All flaws aside, this is a taut, well-told tale with a realistic industrial setting.

The theme most often employed in these pulp stories is psychological: the redemption and return to the real world of a man on the verge of self-ruination with drink and detachment. "You've Got To Be Cold" (*Shadow Mystery Magazine*, April-May 1947) opens in a bar where we meet Walker Post. He lives hand-to-mouth: drinking, sleeping in cheap sour furnished rooms, walking the streets and not giving a damn. Reason: his wife and mother had been killed in an auto smashup while he was fighting in the South Pacific and he's come home to an empty future. He's rescued from a barroom brawl by Drake, a smooth efficient immoralist who runs a "rest camp" deep in the woods and is looking for a tough young man to keep the place up. Post couldn't care less but accepts the job and accompanies Drake to the lakeside camp, where he discovers that half the handful of residents are vicious and the others frightened senseless. Eventually he forms an uneasy alliance with a young woman who along with her wealthy father is a reluctant guest at the camp, and they attempt to escape and bring back help for the other prisoners. All the snarls are perhaps a bit too neatly disentangled at the end of this smoothly written, sharply paced and impossible-to-leave-unfinished story.

We find the same theme in "The Tin Suitcase" (*Doc Savage*, May-June 1948, under the house byline of Peter Reed). Judson Brock is a recovering alcoholic and ex-cop working as a laborer in a scrap metal yard. The murder of his wife by a lover she had taken while Brock was at war had driven him to the bottle. Now he's on the wagon but the near-fatal shooting of an office girl with whom he was beginning to fall in love comes close to destroying the fragile foundations of his new life. In a tense alliance with former friends on the force who now despise him as a drunk, Brock tries to find out who shot the woman and why, planning to exact his own vengeance when he learns the answers. This first-rate story combines cerebral, emotional and fast-action elements into a plot organically related to its postwar industrial setting.

The postwar business theme returns in "A Corpse in His Dreams" (*Mystery Book Magazine*, February 1949), in which the mystery-suspense interest is held back till near the end while MacDonald absorbs us in tangled emotional relationships. The protagonist is a figure who appears in a huge number of 1940s crime stories, the mentally disturbed combat veteran with fears of past or future blood on his hands. (Today we call them victims of PTSD.) Before the war young Matthew Otis had been responsible for his fiancée's death in a drunk-driving accident. For the next nine years Alicia haunts his dreams, and after surviving World War II and the subsequent Chinese civil war he returns to his New England home town, hoping to exorcise her memory. As soon as he hits town he becomes involved in a struggle for control of a pneumatic tool manufacturing company and is forced, not totally against his will, to postpone his self-imposed confrontation with a ghost. It's only in the sixth of the story's seven chapters that we encounter an overt mystery element and once again it's a Rube Goldberg killing machine. The final pages are all fast action and violence in the best pulp tradition.

Not all of MacDonald's redemption stories stand up so well, and one of the silliest is "A Coffin a Day" (*FBI Detective*, February 1949). There's little action and less interest in this farrago in which ex-FBI agent Mitch Lang turns into an instant drunk after being dumped by Bonny, a Bad Woman with whom he's fallen hopelessly in love. The "web" of subversives to which Bonny belonged kills her off for Knowing Too Much and pins the crime on Lang. Celia Amert, a rich girl who joined the "web" for kicks, pretends to befriend Lang and hide him from the police, but it's all part of a plan to have him Shot While Resisting Arrest. Whether MacDonald intended readers to identify the Websters as Communists is unclear—they have names like Karl, Stefan and Georges, each seems to come from a different country and their ideological sympathies are never mentioned—but 1949 readers almost certainly would have done just that.

Also common in Macdonald's early work are stories told from the viewpoint of professional criminals. One of his finest in this vein is "Three's a Shroud" (*New Detective*, January 1949). Syndicate torpedo Wally Gerrit is sent to an upstate New York city to get rid of its incorruptible police chief, poses as a journalist to set the chief up for the kill but goes soft for his target's secretary, who is herself in love with her boss. After shaking up some local vice lords Gerrit runs afoul of his ambitious supervisor in the Syndicate and ends up in prison, a self-made loser.

"Heritage of Hate" (*Black Mask*, July 1949) chronicles the rise of young Harry Hask through Syndicate ranks. His secret: playing his boss and the next higher-up against each other until the latent violence explodes into a dispassionately described but bloody gun battle that leaves few survivors. The multiple double-crosses are so neatly handled that we always know exactly what's happening and why but have no idea just which side Hask is on until the end.

In a general sense MacDonald was influenced by Hammett and Chandler but a more pervasive echo sounding through his early work is that of Cornell Woolrich, who wrote of loneliness and despair like no one else. In "Come Die with Me!" (*New Detective*, January 1948) a vengeance-driven young widow assumes a new identity to track down and execute the murderers of her husband—precisely the premise of Woolrich's *The Bride Wore Black* (1940). Carol Ann Morten travels 1400 miles to the small corrupt Florida community of Crown Palms, where she maneuvers herself into a job as B-girl at the plush Tarana Club, the last place her Johnny was known to have visited before his gruesome "accidental" death. The repulsive Tarana and his hoods on one side of society's fence are matched on what is nominally the other side by Shane Kander, a venal and sadistic cop and one of the first in MacDonald's long line of evil Florida enforcers. Only with help from a convenient undercover G-man does

Carol evade a messy death in this hard, fast, vivid novelet of legitimate violence and credible villainy.

Carol is a reasonably convincing female protagonist but even MacDonald's staunchest fan couldn't pin that description on Laura Lynn, songstress and narrator of "Bedside Murder" (*Mystery Book Magazine*, Summer 1949). After several near-fatal "accidents" she seeks protection not from the cops as might be expected but from a young lawyer whose bodyguard qualifications are nil. Suspects are introduced and mishaps continue until the least likely perp, who sticks out like a two-foot thumb, gives himself away.

The protagonist of "You Remember Jeanie" (*Crack Detective Stories*, May 1949) is even more reminiscent of Woolrich's love-haunted losers than Carol Ann Morten, but only up to a point. Policeman Frank Bard hits the skids after his girlfriend is killed by a drunk in Allison's, a seedy waterfront bar. He becomes a sodden dockside bum, lurching into Allison's regularly and ordering cheap booze for himself and Jeanie, who he says is standing beside him and to whom he speaks as if she were. He keeps a tube of her lipstick and some strands of her hair in his pocket and fondles them each night before curling up to sleep in a packing case at the foot of an alley. Woolrich would have made this the last scene but for MacDonald it's only the beginning: in reality Bard is putting on an elaborate act to make Jeanie's killer betray himself. Then at the last moment of the story we hear the soft echo of Woolrich again as Bard thinks he feels a ghostly touch on his arm.

MacDonald's ultimate claim to fame, of course, was Travis McGee. Reading through his pulp stories, one can find occasional prototypes of that perpetually disillusioned boat bum and modern knight. Such a figure appears but does not star in "Loot for the Unlucky Lady" (*FBI Detective*, April 1949). A single phone call from the criminal she loves is enough to make the rather masochistic female protagonist abandon her job and all trace of her normal life and spend 16 hours a day walking up and down Times Square, waiting for him to stroll by and slip her a package. When he finally shows up, the package turns out to contain the loot from a casino holdup which both the gamblers and the cops are on the lookout for. The woman flies off for a Florida rendezvous with her lover, shadowed by the slightly McGee-like PI Steve Harris whom the gamblers have hired to retrieve the loot. Vivid writing, sharp cross-cutting between viewpoints and a constant edge of excitement add up to a superior piece of pulp storytelling.

Somewhat closer to McGee is Max Raffidy in the atrociously titled "A Corpse-Maker Goes Courting" (*Dime Detective*, July 1949). He's a reporter whose paper has just gone bankrupt and we first see him in a bar, drinking himself into detachment from the reality of being jobless in a jobless city. A beautiful bruised young woman blunders into the tavern, calls Max "Jerry" and sits down with him, followed by two large unpleasant-looking men. In pure McGeean manner Max comments to himself: "Sir Lancelot Raffidy roars in on his white horse." The woman turns out to have both amnesia and a vanished fiancé. After the usual shadowing and slugging episodes the gangland double-cross that motivated the plot is revealed and the Syndicate's power in the city is broken.

Gingerly turning the now brown-edged pages of dozens of old pulps and tracing MacDonald's apprenticeship, we can watch him trying out every conceivable kind of story all but simultaneously, growing stronger in countless ways in record time. I nominate the following as among his best of various types and lengths.

The caper story: "The Little People" (*Doc Savage*, November 1946). A gangster organizes a fleet of trucks and a large group of ex-GIs for a carefully planned military assault on an upstate New York town. A number of short and bloody vignettes show the "little people" of the community—cops, laborers, farmers, businessmen, an old coot who claims to be a Civil War veteran—killing off the invaders one by one.

The espionage tale: "Private War" and "Eight Dozen Agents" (*Doc Savage*, December 1946 and January 1947). Two interconnected stories in which footloose veteran Benton Walters is recruited as a secret agent and gets into various shadowy skirmishes with a neo-Fascist group.

The psychological suspenser: "Miranda" (*15 Mystery Stories*, October 1950). From the first word to the last we are confined within the consciousness of George Corliss, who was physically ruined in an auto accident he knows was caused by his sexpot wife and her grease-monkey lover, and we witness his plan for revenge, abetted by his hospital nurse, a psychotic who at whim whispers messages either of death or of life into the ears of the dying.

The mini-mini: "Murder in Mind" (*Mystery Book Magazine*, Winter 1947-48). A lethargic and laconic country cop investigates the murder of a wealthy woman in the woods during deer hunting season. Honorable mention: "You'll Never Escape" (*Dime Detective*, May 1949). A vicious escaped convict pistolwhips an itinerant laborer to death and tries to use the man's wife, children and ancient auto to get past a police roadblock. Unimpressive surprise ending but fantastic descriptive skill.

Are all of MacDonald's pulp stories as good as the ones I've singled out? Far from it. At times his protagonists are just silly, as witness the narrator of "Dead to the World" (*Dime Detective*, February 1947). Bud Morse gets a job as pianist at his war buddy Howler Browne's nightclub and takes a hand when protection racketeers lean on the Howler for tribute money. He makes a royal ass of himself at every step, and only some arbitrary assists by MacDonald save the day. At times MacDonald's plots are equally silly, as witness "Crime of Omission" (*Detective Tales*, August 1951). On a skiing vacation with his young wife and young partner, an aging lawyer becomes convinced that he's seen the two kissing. Instantly he concludes that they've been doing much more behind his back and decides to kill his partner. But when the younger man falls into a hole in a frozen lake, the older attorney acts on instinct and saves the other's life. Then he learns that his partner had not been kissing his wife but pulling a ski off her mouth!

I was offered a chance to read every one of MacDonald's pulp crime tales in the early 1980s when plans were afoot to collect the best of them for his millions of contemporary readers. Photocopies of those old stories circulated among myself and three other readers who made notes on all those old tales and shared them with each other. Some, as we've seen, were masterful, others marginal. We finally settled on thirty stories. MacDonald axed three of them but the other 27 were published in the collections *The Good Old Stuff* (1982) and *More Good Old Stuff* (1984). Unfortunately MacDonald also insisted, over howls of protests from all four editors, on rewriting most of the stories—and often eliminating precisely the immediate postwar ambience that made the stories so attractive. The feeble updating efforts didn't seem to slow down sales of the collections. But I still hope that someday they'll be reprinted, using the texts as MacDonald originally wrote them.

JACK RITCHIE

His colleagues in crime described him best. Donald E. Westlake called him "a brilliant man in the wrong pew, a miniaturist in an age of elephantiasis." Anthony Boucher said: "What I like best about [his] work is its exemplary neatness. No word is wasted, and many words serve more than one purpose. Exposition disappears; all needed facts are deftly inserted as the narrative flows forward. [He] can write a long short story that is virtually the equivalent of a full suspense novel; and his very short stories sparkle as lapidary art." He was that rarest of literary birds, a professional writer of short fiction, turning out close to 350 tales in his thirty years of creative life. He attempted only one novel but *Tiger Island* (1987) remained unpublished until after his death and was forgotten as soon as it appeared. "I've always felt," he said, "that there hasn't been a novel published that couldn't be reduced to a better short story . . . Victor Hugo put about 30,000 words into *Les Miserables* delineating the history, structure and whatnot of the Paris sewers. Now if I'd been in his shoes I could have described the sewers in two paragraphs. Maybe one. *Les Miserables* itself would have become a novelet. Possibly even a pamphlet."

Welcome to the micro-world of Jack Ritchie.

~ ~ ~ ~ ~

He was born John George Reitci in Milwaukee, Wisconsin on February 26,1922. His father was a tailor, his mother a housewife with modest literary ambitions. After finishing high school in the late Thirties he decided not to let himself be pushed into the work force right away and, while still living at home with his parents, entered what was then the only four-year public institution of learning in the area, Milwaukee State Teachers' College. "I had no intention of ever, *ever* becoming a teacher," he said. World War II saved him from classroom routine and introduced him to what turned out to be his career.

"I spent three and a half years in the army," he recalled, "two in the Central Pacific, mostly on small islands, counting the days. I'd rather forget than remember. However, it was on the island of Kwajalein that I read my first detective novel. Kwajalein, at that time, was a no-beer, no-women, no-nothing kind of place and I was stuck there for eleven months. There wasn't much to do but read and pray to get shipped out. Anywhere. Our company received a shipment of Armed Forces Library books, about two hundred of them. I read about 160 of the books and then there was nothing left but the mysteries. At that time I was sort of an Edmund Wilson snob about the mystery novel, but worse. I hadn't read one of them in my entire life. So there I was, desperate, and I finally succumbed and opened one of the mysteries. I was hooked. Addicted. So much so that to this day I very seldom read 'straight' novels any more."

Hooked he might have been, but he had no desire to write whodunits of his own, or war stories, or anything else. "After the war," he said, "I tried going back to college under the GI Bill, but it didn't work out. I was also in no particular hurry to go anywhere and I figured that after three years, three months and twenty-one days—but who counts?—in the army, I was due for a long vacation. So I settled for working in my father's tailor shop for room and board."

It was a congenial life for a young man who could never be mistaken for a fireball but eventually, as he put it, "I was forced to face the fact that the tailor shop wouldn't go on forever and neither would my father. And I wasn't all that keen to take over the shop anyway. My father would say . . . 'I've been a tailor for forty years, and I *still* don't like it.'"

Around 1952 Ritchie's mother joined a Milwaukee writers' club and attracted the attention of Larry Sternig, a local literary agent. One can almost see the light bulb going on in Jack's head: If Mom can write stories, why can't Sonny? "I sat down and wrote a sports story about an ambidextrous pitcher," he said, "and when Larry showed up one day to talk to my mother I handed him the story. He had that 'Oh, God, *everybody* thinks he can write' expression on his face. But he showed up the next day with a smile, and that started the whole thing."

Ritchie made up his mind to give himself an acid test. "I decided I'd write fifty short stories, one a week, while still working in the tailor shop, and if none of them sold during that year, then the hell with it. The eighth story sold and that settled the question. So did most of the other seven eventually, including the sports story." Larry Sternig's records indicate that Ritchie's first published tale was a lighthearted short-short, "Always the Season" (*New York Daily News*, December 29, 1953), for which he was paid a then-generous

$50. Many of Ritchie's earliest stories were sports or romance quickies for daily newspapers, but by 1954 he'd also begun selling to the new hardboiled mystery magazine *Manhunt*, and most of his crime stories of the Fifties are in the grim, no-frills style which *Manhunt*'s editors fostered. The best of those tales are fine examples of Fifties Noir which deserve to be collected someday.

At a New Year's Eve party just after the publication of Ritchie's first story, Larry Sternig introduced him to another of the Milwaukee writers he represented, a young woman named Rita Krohne. Within a year they were married and had moved from the city to tiny Washington Island, on the thumbtip of the Wisconsin mitten. "We spent the first two and a half years in a log cabin," Ritchie recalled. "A *genuine* log cabin. None of your fancy inside paneling or running water, but plain old peeled Lincoln logs between us and Mother Nature. We used most of our free time to pound the chinking back into the spaces between the logs and discovered that trying to heat a log cabin with just a fireplace when the temperature drops below freezing is impossible. We had to get an oil stove and spent our Januarys and Februarys within six feet of the thing, praying it wouldn't go out. Once we were snowed in for ten days." For anyone else it would have been chilly hell but for the solitude-loving Ritchie it was paradise. "I like country, and the farther out the better . . . It was my kind of place and I loved it."

Rita's first pregnancy put an end to their roughing-it lifestyle. They bought a two-story frame house set in four densely wooded acres for $7,400—were those the days or what?—and raised two daughters and two sons on the income from Jack's short stories and Rita's historical novels for young adults. Unhappiness with the local school system led them to move in time from Washington Island to a rented farmhouse near Jefferson. By that point in his career Jack Ritchie had found his distinctive criminous voice.

Near the end of 1956 readers and writers of short suspense fiction found on their newsstands a new periodical called *Alfred Hitchcock's Mystery Magazine*, a spin-off from the fabulously successful *Alfred Hitchcock Presents* TV series which had debuted in the fall of 1955. Larry Sternig wasted no time exposing the *AHMM* editors to Ritchie's work. Included in its second issue (January 1957) was "Bullet-Proof", a *Manhunt*-style tale and the first of a mind-boggling 123 Ritchie stories that the magazine bought over the next quarter-century. Most of his *AHMM* tales of the Fifties were in the *Manhunt* mold, but the sales he continued to make in other markets—sports stories, frothy romances, spicy tidbits for the men's magazines, even an occasional Western—prove that even then he was one of the most versatile writers in the game. By 1960 the uniquely Ritchiean hallmarks were firmly in place, as witness "Politics Is Simply Murder" and "9 from 12 Leaves 3," both of which appeared in the same issue of the same periodical (*Alfred Hitchcock's Mystery Magazine*, November 1960), the latter under a pseudonym. Throughout the Sixties he continued to write his share of straightforward crime-thrillers—like that marvelous novelet "The Operator" (*Alfred Hitchcock's Mystery Magazine*, June 1963) which in anyone else's hands would have bloated into a 100,000-word gargantua—but more and more often he'd cook up one of his corkscrew plots, add black humor and an unmistakably personal narrative voice, get it down on paper with a bare minimum of words, and end up with a story inimitably his own. The tales of this sort, the ones nobody else on earth could have written, are what made Ritchie famous. Eighteen of these were collected in his lifetime in *A New Leaf and Other Stories* (1971) and 31 after his death in *Little Boxes of Bewilderment* (1989).

A Victorian writer he isn't. Ritchie never wastes a word describing landscape, architecture, clothing or the way people look. Usually he doesn't even bother to tell us where a story is taking place, although more often than not it's Wisconsin. There are no series characters in these stories but their first-person protagonists seem remarkably alike in personality and narrative voice, which for me is the voice of that most Ritchiean of actors, Tony Randall. "All I've ever wanted," Ritchie once said of himself, "was a quiet day, no fuss, and time to myself." The same could be said of most of his first-person characters, a small army of cool fastidious bookish unemotional Midwesterners who want only to be sheltered from the mess of the everyday world. To live in a womb with four walls, surrounded by good music and books and wine. Alone. Unentangled.

It was from this mold that, relatively late in his career, Ritchie cast his first and most striking series character, Detective Sergeant Henry S. Turnbuckle, that muddle-headed Milwaukee Maigret whose deductions are always wrong but make up in Beauty for what they lack in Truth.

At the kickoff Ritchie clearly had no idea where this series was headed. In his first two cases the protagonist's name is Henry H. Buckle, and thanks to a political *faux pas* (arresting the mayor's son for speeding) he's been condemned to internal exile and ordered to spend all his time reading unsolved-crime files. "Take Another Look" (*Alfred Hitchcock's Mystery Magazine*, August 1971) and "The Griggsby Papers" (*Mike Shayne Mystery Magazine*, October

1971) show us a Henry who finds in those ancient documents the clue everyone else has missed and eventually unravels the puzzle. These are perfectly straightforward detective tales of the sort Ritchie had grown to love while on that Pacific island during the war. The only problem was that a long series with such a thin premise would soon become dull and repetitive. Solution: Change the premise.

The result was Henry II, the *true* Henry, the naïve whiz kid with the full Turnbuckle name and the inimitably crusty sidekick Ralph and the penchant for solving cases not wisely but too well. From "Bedlam at the Budgie" (*Alfred Hitchcock's Mystery Magazine*, May 1975) till the series' untimely end, Ritchie set out to make each Turnbuckle adventure (a) a genuine if farfetched whodunit complete with fair-play clueing in the manner of Carr, Christie and Queen, and at the same time (b) a spoof of the stereotyped characters and plot gimmicks so common in traditional detective fiction.

If this sounds like an easy task for a writer to take on, keep in mind that one (or, depending on how you count, two) of the masters of traditional detective fiction had been trying without success throughout the Sixties to do it. Ellery Queen, meaning the cousins Frederic Dannay and Manfred B. Lee who wrote as Ellery Queen, had flubbed the job over and over in novels like *The House of Brass* (1968) and most of the stories collected in *Q.E.D.: Queen's Experiments in Detection* (1968). In the Seventies and early Eighties Ritchie figured out how to do it right, how to have endless fun tweaking the noses of the hoary old whodunit clichés while staying squarely within the great tradition's confines. It's a classic case of the author having his cake and eating it too, with results delicious for readers as well. The complete 30-story canon was collected as *The Adventures of Henry Turnbuckle* (1987).

By his sixtieth birthday Ritchie was acclaimed as one of the finest short story writers the mystery field had ever seen. Hundreds of his tales had been published in magazines, dozens reprinted in anthologies. His "The Green Heart" (*Alfred Hitchcock's Mystery Magazine*, March 1963) had been the basis of the big-budget movie *A New Leaf* (1971), starring Walter Matthau and Elaine May and directed by May. Several other Ritchie stories had been adapted for episodes of TV series like *The Alfred Hitchcock Hour* and *Tales of the Unexpected*. A few years after creating Henry Turnbuckle he had launched a second series, this one starring Cardula, a private eye who is also a—well, if the name doesn't clue you in, you're unclueable. (With the public's appetite for stories about you-know-what being apparently insatiable, why haven't the Cardulas been collected in one volume?) His recent non-series tale "The Absence of Emily" (*Ellery Queen's Mystery Magazine*, January 28, 1981) had received the Mystery Writers of America Edgar award as best crime short story of the year. As a writer Ritchie was at the top of his game. Otherwise, just the opposite. In the late Seventies, soon after the marriage of their oldest child, Jack and Rita divorced. Jack moved to a small apartment in the town of Fort Atkinson where he lived, let us hope, surrounded by good music and books and wine. But his health rapidly went downhill, his stories fell off to a trickle. In April 1983, after checking into the local VA hospital, he died of a heart attack. His finest tales (and there are dozens) will last a lot longer than 62 years.

His colleagues in crime described him best but his own effort isn't bad either. Interviewed near the end of his life, Ritchie quoted the shortest story he'd ever written. It went:

When it was all over, only two people remained on the face of the earth. After twenty years, the older man died.

Then he said: "I think I can still cut it a little."

BROTHER AGENTS

JAMES ATLEE PHILLIPS

When I met Jim Phillips he was a few months short of seventy and looked like a Hemingway code hero who had somehow made it to the golden years. He was built like a bear, had a Texas-scratchy voice (thanks to Scotch and cigarettes as well as a Fort Worth upbringing) and projected an aura of having lived much and hard. In reality, of course, the best known part of his professional life had been spent behind typewriters, and he was familiar to devotees of espionage fiction as Philip Atlee, the author of the Joe Gall spy novels.

If those books are well known, the man who wrote them was just the opposite. He was one of the most private persons in the crime-suspense field, avoiding almost all contact with the media, refusing to fill out the questionnaires of *Who's Who* and other reference works. He never joined the Mystery Writers of America organization, which would love to have signed him up. It was more than five years after his move from Arkansas to St. Louis County, Missouri that I learned—purely through coincidence—that he'd become more or less a neighbor. We taped the following conversation in August 1984 in his townhouse apartment.

The writer with whom Phillips seemed to me to have the most in common is Raymond Chandler. The surface differences between the Philip Marlowe private eye novels and the Joe Gall spy thrillers are obvious, but their authors shared an extremely vivid language sense (although Phillips avoided the profusions of metaphor and simile which make Chandler so easy to parody) and a preference for strong individual scenes and memorable moments over careful plotting. All too many Phillips books suffer as do Chandler's from near-chaotic structure, but his finest scenes are so fresh and alive on the page that, as Chandler said of Dashiell Hammett's, they seem never to have been written before.

As if that were not reason enough to admire Phillips' books, he gave us another in the way he portrayed his main character. On one level, of course, Joe Gall is the stoic code hero of the Hemingway tradition, and on another he stems from Ian Fleming's James Bond, the professional assassin on behalf of his government, the larger-than-life secret agent forever besting villains of the mythological monster variety. In the conventional patriotic thrillers of this sort, we are never allowed to doubt that whatever our side does is right because it's our side that does it. At his best, as in *The Green Wound* (1963), Phillips subverts this nonsense and brings us to realize, as does John Le Carré, that perhaps at bottom We and They are mirror images of one another, beasts of a feather. Not all of Phillips' books reflect this perception, but those that do are the ones most likely to last.

Enough of me. It's time for Jim Phillips to speak for (and of) himself.

~ ~ ~ ~ ~

N: I guess the best place to begin is where you began. You know, the most complete reference book there is on mystery writers is *Twentieth Century Crime and Mystery Writers* (1980), edited by John Reilly. It has a thousand-word essay on you, which is the longest they give anybody, but the biographical entry on you is two words long: "Born 1915." So could you start by saying a little about your background?

P: I was born on January 8, 1915 in Fort Worth, Texas, the second son of a lawyer who later had two more sons. I attended high school in Fort Worth and was enrolled at the University of Texas when I was fifteen years old. It was at midterm, and I just turned 16 when the term began. I went to Texas for a year, then to Texas Christian University for two years, then to the University of Missouri at Columbia for two years. At the end of that time, in 1939, I went to work in New York for Billy Rose, the showman. He had run a show down in Fort Worth that was called the Frontier Centennial and it was an enormous success, one of the first of the great water shows. I went to work for him in New York at the World's Fair, where his Aquacade played to about 14,000,000 people in two years.

N: What kind of work did you do for Billy Rose?

P: I was a second-string publicity man. Michael Mok was the chief publicity man, a very fine writer who's still working, you see stuff by him every now and then. It was our job to get the Rose name and the Rose activities in as many New York newspaper columns every day as we could, and in the news columns as legitimate news whenever possible. We also handled a great deal of national publicity on Rose and his operations all across the country.

N: Then you were working for Rose in 1940 when your first novel, *The Inheritors*, came out?

P: I was. It had been mostly written before I went to New York. It came out in early 1940, published by Dial Press. I had been working for Rose since the World's Fair opened in 1939. In an article in the *Texas Monthly* in 1981, A.C. Green, who is a noted critic, picked it as one of the best books written about Texas.

N: So from that mainstream novel you moved on to your first mystery novel, *The Case of the Shivering Chorus Girls* (1942)?

P: That was written in about ten days. I had a job with Billy Rose but I was going up to Harlem most nights after our supper show. My office was in the Paramount Hotel on the mezzanine floor, and we had the whole basement of the hotel for the Diamond Horseshoe nightclub, and then he had his operation at the World's Fair too. But I traveled extensively in Harlem late at night, something that you could never do now, and in order to get some quick money I wrote *The Shivering Chorus Girls* in ten days. I wrote it simply—it was a culling job. I did a lot of submissions to Dorothy Kilgallen, Winchell, Leonard Lyons. We would send five or six items to these columnists, and one of them, preferably the most interesting, would have Billy Rose's name in it, so if we were lucky we got to plug him. I also used to ream out acres of background stuff about newspapers blowing through Times Square around the statue of Father Duffy at midnight. So I just pulled all that stuff out and used it as background in *The Shivering Chorus Girls*. I really didn't have a whole lot of new writing to do on it.

N: What writers had you been reading before you started writing mysteries?

P: I had admired Thomas Wolfe very much, although I didn't admire his prolixity. I liked Faulkner. I liked Hemingway, who was still writing a more pure narrative then. When I was at Texas Christian my English professor, Lorraine Shirley, sent in a collection of my poems called *The Metal Forest* to be entered in the Yale competition for younger poets. Well, I didn't win it, I won second place, but what

I treasured was that I got a letter from Stephen Vincent Benet, who said that he'd thought mine had been the best but that he'd been overruled. That was highly important to me because I thought he was a great narrative storyteller.

N: Had you read many mystery writers before you became one yourself?

P: Not a great many. Even back then I was reading Simenon. And of course Poe, the originator of the form.

N: *The Case of the Shivering Chorus Girls* is a sort of imitation Nero Wolfe book. Had you been reading Rex Stout?

P: Oh, all of Stout. I liked his approach very much. And, well, I've always been an omnivorous reader, I read everything, so I'm sure I covered everybody working in the field. Even now I read an average of ten to twelve books a week. I read very swiftly and I can retain it pretty well too.

N: After *The Shivering Chorus Girls* you didn't write any books for several years. How did you spend World War II?

P: I went back to Fort Worth in 1940. I was the operations manager of Hicks Field, which was a primary training contractor for the U.S. Army Air Force Services. We trained four thousand pilots a month. I was there at Hicks when Pearl Harbor happened. Then a bit later on I met Owen Johnson, a vice-president of Pan American Airways, who was passing through Fort Worth. He was picking up people for the China National Aviation Corporation, CNAC, which was preparing or had just begun to fly from India over the mountains to China—Kunming, Chungking—because there was no other access to China. The seas were blocked, and it was the only way China could be supplied. I signed on with them and was in China for two years.

N: I guess the two best known people from the entertainment world who served over there during the war were Gene Autry and John D. MacDonald. Did you get to meet either of them?

P: Never did, but that's not surprising because I was not in Calcutta, which was the great hub and the maintenance and office base in India, and then on the China side it was Kunming and Chungking.

I was based in Dinjan, in upper India, which was the jump-off point. I scheduled all the cargo flights in the war zone. I chose the crews, the planes, the radio operators, the flight mechanics and so forth.

N: You came back to the States after two years over there?

P: Came back and joined the Marine Corps. When I went through Parris Island I joined the staff of *The Leatherneck*, the Marine Corps official magazine, and was an associate editor there for nearly two years, until the war in Europe was over. In that capacity I traveled with a photographer all over the United States and the Canal Zone, even Alaska. I was directed to go to Okinawa but Marine headquarters would not let me go out of the country because I had just come out of two years in a war zone over in CBI. Although we were a civilian air line, we'd been flying through a combat area in the China-Burma-India theatre of war.

N: But even while you were in the service you were selling stories to *Collier's* and the *Saturday Evening Post* and other magazines?

P: I was. I sold quite a lot to *Argosy* and *Blue Book*. I was selling stories to *Collier's* when I went to CBI, and when I entered the Marine Corps camp I had a story in *Collier's* ["Lend-Lease Christmas Tree", *Collier's*, January 1, 1944].

N: How did you break into the top magazines?

P: I sat down and analyzed the stories in the *Saturday Evening Post* and *Collier's*, and I decided that my best approach would be through sports, because I was a participating athlete in a good many sports. So I wrote mostly sports stories and Westerns. I did some rodeo stories like "Trick and Fancy" [*Collier's*, January 13, 1951] which is about a rodeo event, trick and fancy riding, and "First Blood" [*Collier's*, July 7, 1945] which is about a boy who rides a bull in a rodeo competition.

N: Nice supplement to your Marine pay. What did you do after the war?

P: I moved to Mexico, to San Miguel de Allende in the state of Guanajuato in north central Mexico. 1 kept making a couple of sales a year to *Collier's* and the others and that was all I needed. For $60 a month I had a house with about fourteen rooms, three baths, a *sala* (living room), a *comedor* (kitchen), two patios, tile all around everything.

N: Did you have a family then?

P: Yes. In 1940, when I was at Hicks Field, I married the daughter of a doctor in Fort Worth. Our son Shawn was born in '43. I was still living in Mexico when I wrote my next book, *Suitable for Framing*, which is an adventure novel with a Mexican setting. It was published in 1949. We were divorced that year and I returned to Burma.

N: What did you do over there?

P: A fellow I knew from the war, named Roy Farrell, had been given a contract by the government of the Union of Burma to bring in his own airplanes and fly military charter and transport for the government. He had a fleet of amphibians based in the Philippines, and he called it Amphibian Airways. I was managing director and operations manager for him in Burma. We were paid at the rate of $330 per flying hour, which is the highest price that had ever been paid for that kind of work. Now those damned planes wouldn't hold many soldiers or a hell of a lot of cargo, so at those prices it was a steal. When the Burmese civil war was over, we flew out the Burmese treasury, which was in U.S. dollars and Swiss francs, and left there and sold the airplanes, which were pretty well worn out, and got out free. It was a perfect operation. Got the planes shot at a lot, but nobody got hurt.

N: Then your experiences in Burma gave you the background for your next book, *Pagoda* (1951), which was the first Joe Gall novel?

P: Yes, I wrote that when I came back from handling the Burmese airway, and it was the first appearance for Joe Gall. But when I did that book I had no thought of creating a series character. I simply wanted to use the material I had absorbed in the government of the Union of Burma when it was fighting for its independence.

N: Where did you go after Burma?

P: In 1951 I moved to the Canary Islands and leased a very beautiful villa on the main island of Tenerife, on the Atlantic Ocean side.

There was a beautiful black sand beach below the house. I lived there for three years and married a Swedish baroness in 1952. Baroness Hermelin her name was. We were divorced in '58.

N: Wasn't it around the early Fifties that you started getting involved with the movies?

P: Right after I came back from Burma, I guess it was, and before I moved to the Canaries. I had had a two-part golf story in *Collier's* ["Just Like I Hate Money", *Collier's*, July 23 and 30, 1949], and this make-up man named Layne Britton called me from Hollywood at midnight one night. He was drunk. A lot of drunk people call me at night. And he said: "I thought that was a wonderful story. I'm a movie producer." And I said to him: "Mr. Britton, I'm delighted to hear that you're interested. Do you always do business at this hour?" And he said: "Yes. I'm going to sell that story for you. If I do, will you piece me out, will you give me something?" And I said: "Certainly I will. I'm not going to sell it. My agent in New York might but I'm not." And a few days later somebody from RKO called and asked me if I'd take $10,000 for a movie option on the story. I said I certainly would, and they sent me a check, and I sent a check for $2500 to this make-up man Layne Britton that I'd never seen. They never made a movie out of the story as far as I know.

N: What was your next movie deal?

P: Well, again nothing ever came of it, but John Wayne got in touch with me after *Pagoda* came out, that was in 1951, and he wanted to make a movie out of it, and he asked me to do a treatment on it so I sent him a 60-page treatment. And while that deal was up in the air, Robert Mitchum called me and asked if I wouldn't come out and talk to him about doing a moonshiner picture with him. I think that Layne Britton character had done make-up on a Mitchum picture and told him about me. Anyway, I was in Mitchum's dressing room batting around this moonshiner thing when John Wayne called me from Hawaii and said he had a hell of a problem and could I help. That's how I got involved with *Big Jim McLain*.

N: That's one of the Red Menace espionage pictures of the McCarthy era, isn't it? What did you do on that one?

P: Wayne was in Honolulu doing *Big Jim McLain*, which was the first independent picture of Batjac, his own production company. And he said to me: "My writer's in the bar, I've got a payroll over here of about $22,000 a day, he doesn't have anything written and he's in the bar downstairs, and any time I speak to him all he'll say is that he hopes I get cancer." And I said: "Well, Duke, you can't shoot much of that, can you?" And he said: "No. Will you fly over here?" And I said yeah. I didn't have any idea what was going on, but I flew over there and they gave me a suite in the Edgewater Hotel and told me what had happened. It was simple anti-Communist baloney, so I sat down, and he got me two stenographers, and I'd dictate for four or five hours at a clip. All it was was cars coming in and out of drives and furtive-looking heavies trying to bash the United States' dream of freedom. Want to know what sold Wayne on it?

N: Keep talking, keep talking!

P: He said: "Now I understand that we're doing this so fast it can't be much good, but how are we going to open it?" And I said: "Well, you're going to show a launch leaving the shore and going out to a platform, and then the camera's going to go over the platform and pan down slightly until you can see the battleship that was sunk at Pearl Harbor, the Arizona. The camera picks up the name of the ship and an offscreen voice is going to say, 'This is the battleship Arizona. She is still a ship of the U.S. Navy, and the 1240 men of her crew are still between her decks.' Then we're going to pan away from there and into a stormy forest and we're going to come to the grave of Daniel Webster. And a voice will say from the gravestone, 'How stands the republic, neighbor?' And unless you can say that the republic stands copper-bottomed and solid, why that old man will come up out of the ground." And oh, shit, John thought that was great. And I said: "And then we pan into your cops-and-robbers story." We went out to the University of Hawaii together and we got the story "The Devil and Daniel Webster" from the library, and he's got that stuff in the first part of the picture. At least it took the kiss of death off the beginning, but it was so bad that nothing could help the rest of it.

After I had worked over there for nearly three weeks, trying to salvage *Big Jim McLain*, Wayne said: "What do I owe you?" And I said: "You don't owe me anything, because I didn't do much for you, all I did was to give you something to shoot." When I landed in Los Angeles, two of Wayne's lawyers met me and said: "Now, man, take something, take a thousand dollars, five thousand dollars." I said: "No, I don't want to." I don't know why I said that. I didn't need the money at the time and I just didn't want to do it so I didn't take anything. Then I moved to the Canary Islands.

The day I got off the ship in the Canaries, there was a letter waiting for me that had been smuggled out of the prison in Taipei, on Formosa, from Millard K. Nash, who was one of the best pilots on the Hump route during the war. He was serving a nine-year sentence at hard labor for being caught smuggling wall hangings into Taipei with narcotics inside. He said that he had lost 42 pounds, and he said: "Please see if you can help me get out of this son of a bitch, it's pretty hard." So I got to thinking about it, and after I had rented this villa I wrote Wayne a letter. Now this was soon after Dwight Eisenhower had been elected President. I wrote Wayne a letter and I said: "Yes, there's something you can do if you feel you owe me something because of the work I did in Honolulu. I've got a pilot friend that Chiang Kai-Shek has got in jail on Taiwan. Go see if the bald-headed general in Washington can't get him sprung. That's no place for a good pilot to have to spend years." And damned if Wayne didn't get him out of there in about six months. Now where are we?

N: I guess we're at your one and only Dell paperback original, *The Deadly Mermaid* (1954). How did that come about?

P: I was traveling in the Caribbean. A fellow I knew named Allen Connell was in the area and asked me to come along on an underwater filming expedition off Carcol Reef in Haiti. They had a crew of six or seven men and a Fenjohn underwater camera, something that had just been invented. The water was beautiful, the camera worked perfectly, we got about ten hours of gorgeous underwater footage. Then Connell said: "For God's sake, come with us and try to write some kind of story we can use with this film." So I wrote him a treatment, and we went to New York, and we needed to find someone who could sort of organize all that underwater footage. A young fellow by the name of Stanley Kubrick was recommended to us, and we ran some quickie picture he did on a shoestring [probably *Fear and Desire*, 1953] and hired him. The whole project turned into a drunken brawl and fell apart. As far as I know the footage was never used. Maybe it was sold to a library for stock footage, I don't know. Anyway, *The Deadly Mermaid* came out of my living in Port au Prince and Cap Haitien and everything that happened to us there.

N: What happened next in your life?

P: I signed a contract with RKO for a year, year and a half. Jane Russell was responsible for that. I had a story called "The Wife Who Lived Twice" [*Collier's*, February 19, 1954]. As far as I know it was the first story about corneal transplants. This man's wife died in Mexico, and the corneas of her eyes, which were blue, were transplanted into a Mexican peasant girl. It was a real weeper. Jane Russell read it in *Collier's* and made RKO put me under contract because she said no one was writing for women any more. [The story was not filmed at RKO but became the basis of a 30-minute film drama aired on NBC's *Fireside Theatre*, October 26, 1954.]

N: Did you get any screen credits during that time?

P: Not a one. They had me working on an oilfield story I'd done, "The Big Rig" [*The Nation's Business*, February 1953]. I'd worked in those oilfields and I tried to write an authentic story. All Howard Hughes cared about was designing new brassieres for the women. Nothing came of that project either. The only other picture I've done is *Thunder Road* with Mitchum, the moonshiner picture, but that came later.

N: You made some sales to TV in the Fifties too, didn't you?

P: Yes. *Pagoda* was done on *Studio One* [February 11, 1952] with John Forsythe playing the lead, and a Portuguese dancer named Sono Osato played the girl dancer in the book. John Frankenheimer directed it and it was lousy, and I can't understand why. And Jackie Cooper was in a basketball story, "Fast Break" [*Schlitz Playhouse of Stars*, February 25, 1955], which was based on something of mine in *Argosy* [May 1952].

N: Then later in the Fifties you worked on the *Thunder Road* project with Mitchum?

P: Right. We made that in Asheville, North Carolina, shot all of it outside there. That was my last picture. I could see what would happen if I stayed in Hollywood. I'd buy a quarter million dollar or half million dollar house and then I'd have to pay for it, I'd be there awhile. And I had no intention of dealing with those types for that length of time.

N: So finally in the Sixties you got into the paperback original field and made Joe Gall a series character. How did that begin?

P: I moved to Eureka Springs, Arkansas, because I had been so far outside the United States for so long, and I decided to go as near the center of the country as I could. I started doing Fawcett Gold Medal paperbacks because of Knox Burger. He'd been the fiction editor at *Collier's*. He bought a lot of stuff from me, and I doctored a number of stories for him too. He used to give me a thousand dollars for stories in his inventory that he couldn't use, and I'd revise them and he'd publish them in the magazine under the names of the original writers after I'd salvaged them. Then in 1960 or '61 I wrote *The Green Wound*. I liked the way it felt and I wrote Knox, who was then at Gold Medal, and said that I wanted to make a series out of it. He said: "You can't do it. You won't be able to sustain it, because you won't stick at it long enough. You'll go haring off to Timbuktu or someplace." And I said: "Well, that may be the idea. Maybe I'm trying to get to Timbuktu." But then I followed it up, and I wrote the first three or four Joe Galls here in the States, and then I took off to—you'll never guess where—Grenada. [The island was very much in the news in 1984, mainly because the U.S. had invaded it.] For about eight months I lived down there, in the clubhouse on the golf course. Then I started moving all around the world, Canada, New Zealand, Australia, back through Asia, Hong Kong, Korea, Japan, the whole works.

N: Did Gold Medal have a format for a spy series that you had to follow?

P: Gold Medal didn't even know where I was. They not only didn't give me any suggestions, they never knew anything except that I kept sending the manuscripts in from Addis Ababa or Perth, Australia or someplace, and they just kept publishing them. I would stay at least three or four months in every location I used in a Joe Gall book. If nothing else, I at least made it a good travel guide, so you'd know the real estate and the customs and so forth. I could usually find some kind of story hook to hang the local color on.

N: Did Gold Medal give you a travel budget to get all this local color?

P: They never gave me a nickel. Toward the end, if I told them I was going to write a new one, they'd give me a $10,000 advance. I paid for my travel out of the profits from the books. I made about half a million dollars out of them.

N: What spy books had you read before you started the Joe Galls?

P: I guess most that had been written, because as I said, I was always an omnivorous reader. I don't know that I patterned after anybody. Graham Greene is my idea of a very good writer. Not a good mystery writer, not a good puzzle writer, but just a good writer. But other than that I can't really remember. The only thing I was afraid of in this whole caper was that my younger brother, David Atlee Phillips, might get into trouble because of me. He resigned a couple of years ago from the CIA after getting high enough to be, toward the end of his tenure, chief of all covert operations from Mexico on down to Antarctica. I could see the built-in danger there, so he and I didn't correspond, we didn't see each other for years and years. Of course, he was all over the world. He was shot down over Germany in World War II, he was taken prisoner and got out, and went down to Santiago, Chile and bought an English-language paper and was enlisted by the CIA. From there he worked for them in Cuba and Mexico, he was in Lebanon when the Marines went in in 1958, he worked all over the place.

N: He didn't give you any material or ideas?

P: I made it impossible for that charge ever to be made. Because, you see, our names were so similar. We never had any kind of contact. I asked him to please make it clear to his superiors that we weren't in touch with each other.

N: What did he think of your books? Did he read them?

P: He read them, and said that as far as spycraft went there wasn't much in them. He said: "They're very imaginative, and we might even have used some of it in real life, but I don't know how you'd do as a field agent day in and day out."

N: You put Joe Gall in more or less the same part of Arkansas you were living in. Was his Ozark castle a real place or did you make that up?

P: All of that was imaginary. It was a place I was looking for. Oh, bits and pieces of it are out there. There's a beautiful place called Blue Springs which is a subterranean glacier, and it's magnificent, it's freezing cold the year round. And there are houses without a nail in them that have been standing for a hundred years. So Gall's castle is a combination of all those things, a kind of remote little Shangri-La that a man would like to have.

N: You used a lot of your own experiences in those books. In *The Silken Baroness* (1963) you even had him marry a Swedish baroness the way you did yourself.

P: That was the only time that anybody ever changed a title on me without my permission. We were divorced in 1958, as I said, and I married my present wife in '61, but I am not so flagrant that I would have stuck an ex-wife of mine on a book as the title of something. Knox Burger stuck it on there, and I didn't know it until I saw the book. I wasn't real pleased. He thought it was very funny.

N: You stayed with Gold Medal and the Joe Gall series for more than a dozen years, right?

P: Man, how could you beat it? I could get the *Journal of Commerce*, which is the national journal of shipping and tells you what ships leave and where they're going, and I could pick the ship that had the best food and the best accommodations for one passenger and that was going where I wanted to go. A ship that isn't designed for passenger travel but has a single cabin for one person is the best place to work ever invented by man. Nineteen times I've gone down the Mississippi and down that big crescent turn from New Orleans on freighters headed every place in the world. Just about the only trip I haven't taken is that train trip across Russia. In Istanbul I went to the Soviet Embassy—it was there then and not in Ankara—and tried to make reservations, but they said that in order to get a stateroom on that train to Vladivostok I would have to buy four tickets. That made it a little too rich.

N: So that was your lifestyle when you were writing Joe Gall. It's amazing how many of your own experiences pop up in the series. Not just Gall's Marine background, and the Ozarks setting and the Baroness, but all sorts of other things. In *The Star Ruby Contract* (1967) he's put in charge of civil aviation in Burma. In *The Underground Cities Contract* (1974) he tries to get a young American out of a Turkish jail on a drug sentence. In some other books he poses as a Texan.

P: You're doing the talking.

N: Okay, it's your turn again. Maybe now's a good time to clear up a literary mystery of sorts. Several of the early Galls had an endorsement on their covers from Raymond Chandler, who was quoted as saying "I admire Philip Atlee tremendously" or words to that effect. How could he have said that when he'd died in 1959, four years before your first Gold Medal paperback was published? Had you known Chandler?

P: I had read and admired his work for years. He was always vivid and always had the gift for felicitous phrases. He could describe the seamy side of the West Coast better than anybody who ever lived. Then one night—this was sometime in the middle or late Fifties, I guess—he called me up. It was around midnight California time and a couple of hours later where I was, I guess. He was in his cups. He said he just wanted to tell me how much he'd admired some story of mine that he'd read in *Collier's*. I really couldn't take it very seriously because I knew that anybody who wrote as well as he did wasn't going to admire anything of mine he'd read in *Collier's*. Those stories had to be workmanlike, and I'm sure that he thought I wrote a fairly clean line, but you weren't going to find anything in the *Saturday Evening Post* or *Collier's* that would compare with Chandler's. They wouldn't have published anything that good, because their stories were written to a formula. Anyway, he called me three or four times. I remember now. I had a big house in Fort Worth then, and it was always around 3:00 A.M. Texas time when he called, and he was always loaded to the gills. He was just as garrulous as a country farmer.

N: And he also wrote you a lot of letters?

P: No, only the one letter. I mentioned it several years later to Knox Burger and he took it from me and ran that quote. I never got the letter back and I don't know what ever happened to it.

N: The impression I got from the Joe Gall books is something like the impression I got from reading Chandler, that the setting and the strong individual scenes and moments came first in your mind and that the plot was never very important to you.

P: Absolutely, absolutely. Because otherwise it wouldn't have been worth doing. I just did the books to get in those things.

N: And to justify your traveling all over too?

P: Right. One of the most memorable trips I ever took was on the—What is that railroad that runs all the way across Canada? I got on the train at Montreal and rode to Vancouver. I had a beautiful stateroom with a big plate glass wall, and I could see Medicine Hat and Calgary and the Great Plains and Banff and all of those beautiful Canadian scenes all the way across. I worked in Victoria on the island of Vancouver for over a year. I did two Joe Gall books on Canada [*The Canadian Bomber Contract* and *The White Wolverine Contract*, both 1971].

N: One of the most interesting things about *The Green Wound* and some of the other Galls is that they're sort of schizophrenic. On one level they're cut from the same cloth as *Big Jim McLain*. But on another level, Joe Gall knows, and tells us he knows, that he's on the wrong side, that he's a professional killer for money and that some of the people he kills and some of the causes he fights are in the right. At least this is true some of the time. Others read more or less like the James Bond books, where you never feel that our side is just as bad as theirs, but I think that the Gall books that work the best are the ones that are divided against themselves, like *The Green Wound*.

P: That's because there was a bifurcation in my own temperament. As a writer I know that if you don't have the bullshit to keep it moving from page to page, you're going to lose the readers. At the same time I wasn't willing to admit to being such an absolute dunce that I didn't know it was bullshit in the first place. The personality was split, there's no question about that. Gall knew what he had to do but he knew that it was a lot of bullshit too, and that he was on the wrong side.

N: You write on one level like Ian Fleming and on a deeper level like John Le Carré.

P: Well, that's a great compliment. I appreciate that. That shows at least that you have seen what I wanted to do.

N: What made you stop writing the books?

P: I thought after the Korea book [*The Last Domino Contract*, 1976] that I'd just got Gall at the end of his tether. One thing I have always done is follow very closely the factual reports, and if you've read some of the reports about these burned-out characters in the CIA, you know that contract agents tend to come to grief. Often they come to grief in some seedy little motel, just completely strung out and lost. It is the end of the line.

N: But why did you stop writing the series?

P: Because I had proved that I could do 22 of the things and that was enough. All I was doing anyway was exploiting real estate. I had done Australia, New Zealand, everything but Tibet and inside the Soviet Union. I was just selling real estate, and I ran out of it.

N: What has your writing life been like since then?

P: Oh, I've got a couple of projects. One of them is biographical, it's the story of this Roy Farrell I told you about, the pilot who worked for us on the Hump. He had never flown anything bigger than Piper Cubs when he went over there, and he got to be one of the best pilots we had, and founded three airlines. All three of them were successful. One of them was Cathay Pacific, which is the great airline of Asia today, although the British made him sell out. The manuscript is 309 pages long right now, but I just got another box of material and I want to add another hundred pages. I want this to be very good and I'm not going to turn it loose till it is. Couple of publishers want to see it when I'm finished.

N: Any other projects?

P: I would like to do a study of the Himalayan captains generally, because I'm a primary source and it's part of history. It's an empty frame that should be filled in and nobody's done it.

N: Do you ever plan to write any more novels?

P: I would like to do one that is autobiographical, a book about how the world looked to me. That would have to be a long one, it would cover a lot of territory.

N: But you don't see any more espionage novels in your future?

P: No. Because I was saleable but I was never the best at them.

N: Then who are the best of the current crop?

P: John Le Carré and that other Englishman, Len Deighton. I was faking a lot of it, but they're good.

N: And do you have any thoughts about where the spy novel is going?

P: Only that as long as the United States maintains a hidden and secret government like the CIA, which in effect many times determines foreign policy, then I think there will be great scope for this kind of fiction.

~ ~ ~ ~ ~

It's amazing how much dialogue two people can produce in roughly an hour's time. Jim Phillips enjoyed posing as an old curmudgeon—"I wouldn't join any group that would let me in," he says, "and I remain a member of the human race under duress"—but I couldn't help wondering how much of that wasn't a Joe Gall-like cover identity. If he was such a relentlessly anti-social person, where did he learn to talk so well?

Late in his career Jim apparently came to dislike his own novels intensely, calling them "nothing but cops and robbers, international background" and "a pretty good swindle to pay for" his compulsion to travel. "Do it fast enough so you get them out of the theater before they realize they've been defrauded." Certainly his work is not to be compared with Le Carré. But in the critical essay on Phillips in

Twentieth Century Crime and Mystery Writers, spy-fiction specialist R. Jeff Banks predicted that the Joe Gall books "may well be regarded by future generations as the best American espionage series of the latter half of the twentieth century."

The books Jim spoke of as works in progress were either never completed or never published. He moved back to Texas and on June 2, 1991, at age 76, he died in his sleep at his Corpus Christi home. Who could have guessed how soon after our conversation the Berlin Wall would fall and the Soviet Union crumble? One might almost belive that Jim could no more survive without the Cold War environment than a fish can live out of water. By the end of the 20th century, the espionage fiction and other cultural artifacts of that era had become museum pieces. But I still have a hunch that R. Jeff Banks was right.

DAVID ATLEE PHILLIPS

My interview with Jim Phillips went so well that arrangements were made for me to follow up by interviewing his younger brother David the next time I was on the East Coast. We had never met. He knew that I was coming down from New York on the Amtrak Metroliner that particular day and that I'd be schlepping two suitcases and wearing a beat-up Indiana Jones hat. I knew that he'd be waiting for me at Washington's Union Station in a beat-up red Toyota. Once I was out of the station and in the parking area it took us just a few seconds to spot each other. Very much like an agent meeting his case officer. We slung my bags into the Toyota's trunk and got acquainted over an excellent lunch at La Mirabelle, a restaurant in McLean, Virginia favored by many in the CIA. In fact a retirement party for an Agency secretary was going on, he told me, a few tables from ours. Afterwards we drove to his cheerfully disordered split-level in suburban Bethesda, Maryland and went to work. Off and on during the taping we were spied on by Bos, short for Bosun's Mate, a 90-pound black lab, as friendly as a puppy and quiet as a guppy. Who thinks of spooks as the owners of pets?

David Atlee Phillips was born in Fort Worth, Texas, on October 31, 1922, almost eight years after his brother Jim. His early career as a touring actor was aborted by World War II and the draft. Bailing out over Austria from a disabled B-24, he was captured by the Germans and put in a prison camp from which he escaped a year later. After the war he dabbled in various media jobs—actor, radio announcer, hopeful playwright—and in the late 1940s, he and his first wife moved to Latin America where they could live cheaply. His writing aspirations fizzled but he wound up owning the *South Pacific Mail*, an English-language newspaper published in Chile, and moonlighting with a little-theater group. That was his situation in 1950 when he was invited to become a part-time operative for the CIA. He joined the Agency as a career employee five years later.

For a quarter of a century Phillips alternated between Washington assignments and tours of duty in Latin America—Guatemala, Cuba, Mexico, the Dominican Republic, Brazil, Venezuela—and was involved in several of the most hotly debated and widely condemned covert operations of the Cold War era. In 1975, in the wake of Watergate and Congressional probes into CIA "dirty tricks," he took early retirement and became a sort of unofficial public relations man for the Agency, writing and lecturing and debating on college campuses and in the media about the CIA's role in a free society. His autobiography, *The Night Watch*, was published in 1977.

He was in his early sixties when I taped the following conversation with him but could easily have passed for under fifty. Decades in Latin America had eroded the rich Texas accent still detectable in his brother Jim. Tall, genial, relaxed, he came across as a friendly professor, not at all as one of the foremost practitioners of covert action. After retiring from the CIA he wrote a number of nonfiction books and one novel, *The Carlos Contract* (1978).

N: How were you recruited into the CIA?

P: I received a telephone call from a man I had known previously only as a diplomat in the American Embassy, and I wondered why he was inviting me to such a remote restaurant on the outskirts of town.

N: What town?

P: Santiago, Chile, in the year 1950. Josef Stalin was still alive. The Cold War was a very serious thing. And so this diplomat explained over coffee that he was the local chief of the CIA. And I said: "The CIA? What's that?" Because at that time the CIA was the least known of American agencies, not the best known the way it is today. He explained that his job was secret operations, and he wanted to know whether I would help him out on a part-time basis. He said he could pay me $50 a month plus $12.50 a month expenses. And I said: "Why me?" And he said: "Because you have three of the four qualifications an intelligence officer needs to work undercover overseas. First, you have language. Then, you have cover, you have a business to explain your presence in the country. And then, you have access, you have a reason to get around and ask questions. The only thing you don't have is experience, but we'll see that you get that." That was the beginning of my 25-year experience with the CIA.

N: Much of that experience was concentrated in Latin America?

P: It was. I was a specialist in the area. My only foreign tour outside of Latin America was in the Middle East, in Lebanon, in the late 1950s. They were searching for someone in the Agency who knew something about the media business, who spoke French, and who knew the Arabs. I knew something about the media business, and I spoke French, but I didn't know the Arabs. They said: "You know Latin Americans, that's close enough." And the next thing I knew, I found myself in Lebanon.

N: While you were in Latin America, you got involved in a number of rather controversial episodes in recent history, including helping to overthrow the elected government of Jacobo Arbenz in Guatemala, helping to plan the Bay of Pigs invasion of Cuba, supporting the Marine invasion of the Dominican Republic, and later working on the plan to overthrow the elected government of Salvador Allende in Chile. In *The Night Watch* you say that in your entire career with the Agency you were never asked to do anything that you considered unethical. Or am I misremembering what you said?

P: I don't recall writing that. What I did say was that espionage is illegal in every country in the world, and consequently it's unethical in every country in the world. I then went on to say that sometimes we were asked to do things that might give one pause from the standpoint of personal morality or ethics. But you do not make your decision on the basis of a single incident. Instead you decide whether you're in a business which over a period of time, in the long run, is working for the good of your country, for the public good. If we had an intelligence agency where men and women of conscience resigned in protest every time they had an assignment they felt was questionable, we would soon have an agency filled with people who were willing to accept *any* assignment, and they would be walking around in storm trooper boots. That's the way real trouble has started in a number of countries, because a secret organization in any society is a threat. In our society we must have one, because on balance the net gain is more than the net loss would be if we didn't have such organizations. It's a demanding occupation, a challenging one, and it calls on its practitioners to confront and survive situations that are not found in the Boy Scouts.

The simplest matters of everyday life raise ethical problems for an intelligence officer. Leading a double life, it's necessary that you protect your cover if you're going to be effective overseas, indeed if you're going to survive in some countries of the world. And that means that even when you come back to the United States for a periodic tour, which is obligatory, during that period you must keep your cover intact. You must lie to your lawyers, lie to your bankers, lie to your neighbors. In your personal life you must decide whether you're going to have a dinner party just for professionals from your office, or perhaps a few people from the Department of State or the military whom you've worked with overseas, or whether you're going to have your neighbors. Because if you have your neighbors, they're going to think that you and your wife are absolutely the dullest people they've ever met, because you won't be able to talk about what you really do. I remember the night I was at a dinner party near here, in Chevy Chase, and a woman turned to me—at that time my cover was as an officer in the Department of State—and she said: "What do you people do down at the State Department all day?" And I said: "Well, mostly we shuffle papers." And she looked at me as if to say *What a dull fellow!* and turned away and wouldn't talk to me for the rest of the evening. In fact I had spent that day with Henry Kissinger and Richard Helms, and it would have made very engaging dinner conversation had I been able to talk about it.

N: What kinds of things would you have resigned from the Agency rather than do if you had been asked to do them?

P: I've asked myself that question many, many times. What obviously comes to your mind first is if you were given the order to assassinate someone. In wartime that's almost par for a rough course. In peacetime I like to think that if someone had ever come to me and said: "We're going to ask you to go assassinate someone," I would have said: "Thanks a lot, but no thanks." I can't say for sure, though, because it never happened. No one ever asked me. I am, however, aware of several instances—not several, but a couple of instances—where someone was asked to participate in that kind of plan. We are now aware, from the investigation of the intelligence community by the Senate, that on two occasions the murders of foreign leaders were planned: Lumumba in Africa and Castro in Cuba. And I am aware of situations where two CIA officers were asked to participate. One of them simply replied: "I can't, I'm Catholic." And the other one said: "I don't believe in that; no way I'm going to do that. Get somebody else." And he turned around and walked out. Both of those officers survived and remained in the service, and someone else did take on the assignments. So the answer to your question is, I don't know. I'd like to think that I would have said: "Thanks a lot but no thanks, get someone else to do that."

N: But you're talking about a personal ethical code of your own, not one that is necessarily shared by all CIA agents or by the Agency as an institution?

P: That's correct.

N: This is hypothetical, of course, but do you think that the identity of the target would make a difference in most agents' ethical judgments? I'd imagine, for example, that some agents might respond differently if they were asked to help assassinate Khadafy or if, let's say, they were asked to help kill Martin Luther King.

P: I think it would make a difference. In my own judgment I think that a line has to be drawn very quickly when you consider such things. It's been my experience, in a situation where a person has been in power, like Idi Amin, who is so totally unacceptable, that when they're replaced, they are so often replaced by someone just as bad if not worse. In the case of Fidel Castro in Cuba, that's a situation I know quite well. If Fidel Castro were to die of a heart attack or be assassinated today, the leadership would remain intact, and one of two men—either his brother Raul or Carlos Rafael Rodriquez, one of the founders of the Cuban Communist Party —would take over, and both of them are more anti-American than Fidel Castro is! In peacetime it's probably a very good rule of thumb to rule out assassination as a useless and impractical tactic without even approaching it from a moral standpoint.

N: You mention ethics now and again in your book but in almost every instance you talk about moral problems purely in pragmatic terms. For example, when you discuss the overthrow of Arbenz in Guatemala, you say it was more or less justified by hindsight because afterwards you discovered in his papers that he had a lot of connections with Moscow. Then you talk about how you tricked a Chilean Marxist bookstore owner named Juan into spying for you, and how you resolved that moral problem on the ground that the end justified the means.

P: However, I must interject that it took me over twenty years to realize that, because after I recruited Juan I moved out of that sphere of operations. I had no need to know what had happened to Juan afterwards, and so I wasn't told. Then about twenty years later, I became the chief of all Latin American operations, so I once again knew what was going on in Chile. I then realized, after more than two decades, that Juan was a very valuable agent for our side, and that's when I decided that, yes, the end justified the means.

N: But suppose Juan had been caught, tortured and killed? Might you have reacted differently?

P: (after some hesitation): Possibly. Possibly.

N: And it's just dumb luck that didn't happen, that it worked out well from the Agency's point of view?

P: Yes, but—Remember baseball manager Branch Rickey's definition of luck: "Luck is the residue of design." A little bit of luck will topple towers in most businesses and professions, and it's that way in the intelligence business. But when you talk about something over a period of years, it's more than luck.

N: You also talk about the moral aspects of the Bay of Pigs. You said you had no moral qualms at all about the operation but only pragmatic objections, because it was stupidly planned. And when the Marines invaded the Dominican Republic, that didn't raise any moral issue for you. The only thing that did, you said, was the Track II operation to overthrow Allende in Chile.

P: That's correct.

N: I gather the reason that gave you moral qualms was because, as far as you could tell, Allende was not a puppet of the Soviet Union but, if I may coin a phrase, a Protestant Marxist?

P: Yeah, I think that's a good description. He was a very honest man. I knew a lot about him because he was around when I was living in Chile years before. He had been running for the presidency for thirty-two years and he was totally honest, saying all the time: "If I'm elected president, I intend to create a Marxist state after the democratic election." So he was perfectly honest. And thus, when I first arrived back in the United States from an overseas post during the days of Track II, that was the nearest I ever came to resigning in protest. This was for two reasons. One was ethical: it didn't seem to me to be the right thing to do. The other, as you said, was pragmatic. It was obvious to me, and to some of my colleagues who knew Chile and Chileans, that it was a loser from the beginning, that it wasn't going to work.

However, when it comes to resigning in protest, consider a book by Edward Weisband called *Resignation in Protest,* which came out in 1975. It was a study of American political figures who had resigned in protest and of the effects their resignations had on our system. One man was totally successful. In 1933, Harold Ickes resigned as Secretary of Interior because he didn't like U.S. petroleum policy, and a couple of days later they said: "Harold, come on back, we'll do it your way." He went back and he won. During Watergate, on the night of the Saturday Night Massacre Elliot Richardson resigned in protest, and that resignation worked. Weisband defies the reader to come up with any other examples of people who resigned in protest and effectively created change. I decided to stay within the system and try to correct things that I thought wrong. But yes, that single incident was the one that most bothered me during my career.

N: Let me ask you a more general question. Why do you think the CIA is necessary?

P: If all men were angels, we wouldn't need the CIA. Indeed, if all men were angels we wouldn't need much of an army. But I've found, after twenty-five years of working in the CIA and more years studying international relations, that the affairs of most of the countries of the world are not governed by angels. That's why we need the CIA.

N: Your book gives the impression that the CIA's only function is to respond to hostile initiatives from other nations, mainly of course from the Soviet bloc, and that we have no positive designs of our own. On the other hand, most books about the CIA see the Agency's function as supporting all sorts of corrupt right-wing dictatorships in the Third World. Near the end of his *CIA Diary,* for example, Philip Agee says: "The CIA, after all, is nothing more than the secret police of American capitalism, plugging up leaks in the political dam night and day so that shareholders of U.S. companies operating in poor countries can continue enjoying the rip-off." How do you account for the fact that intelligence officers like yourself and Agee had more or less similar experiences in the same part of the world in the same decade yet write about them from such radically different perspectives?

P: Well, I'm not sure, but I invite you to look at it as I do now. It's true that my book was the first which, on balance, defended the intelligence establishment in the wake of books like Agee's *CIA Diary*, and *The CIA and the Cult of Intelligence* by Victor Marchetti and John Marks, and several others. What has happened to those people since they wrote those books? Right now, I feel I'm playing a responsible role in American society. I play a role in education by participating in an honest way in the controversy about intelligence. Now let's look at those other gentlemen. Mr. Agee has been out of this country for a dozen years. Why? He doesn't have an American passport. The Supreme Court took it away from him. Mr. Marchetti is now a journalist. He works for a magazine called *Spotlight,* the publication of an organization called the Liberty Lobby, which is far to the right of Lyndon LaRouche. I defend my position over the past twelve years, since the time I took early retirement, by honestly believing that I have been a responsible citizen and remain a responsible spokesman. And I've watched the others grow shriller and shriller, and some of them get to the point where there's simply no way you can talk to them. I've participated in a lot of college campus debates, and I've had to give up debating except with Frank Snepp. At least you can carry on a dialogue with him. These other people—Marchetti, Agee, John Stockwell, who wrote a book about the CIA called *In Search of Enemies*—I've given up debating with them, because they just start yelling out nonsensical things. I believe it's a simple fact that the debate is over in this society today. The controversy is over about intelligence and espionage. The great majority of Americans know that we must have espionage activity, that we must gather and process intelligence for our military and political leaders. The controversy that remains is a separate subject.

N: You mean support of right-wing dictatorships?

P: I mean covert action in any of its forms. That's what the current debate is about. People don't object to the idea that the CIA is abroad gathering secrets. The controversy that remains is covert action, supporting another government, supporting this movement against that movement, meddling around in other people's affairs. That subject is certainly worthy of debate, and many intelligence professionals would like to see the CIA get out of the business of covert action. This is for two reasons. One, these days there is no such thing as covert action, there is only what's called overt covert action, when the President of the United States makes a statement saying: "We have decided that in Angola our best course is covert action." The second reason intelligence professionals at times kind of wish covert action would go away is that it's created a tremendous brouhaha which jeopardizes the integrity of the basic mission of the intelligence services, which is espionage and counter-espionage and liaison with our other services. I say this realizing that I was one of the principal practitioners of covert action, and that my book is one long compendium of covert action activities, some of them quite controversial.

N: Do you think the CIA could operate without covert action? Could it divorce itself from all covert action and still function in today's world?

P: I think so, but apparently I'm the only intelligence officer in America who does. In 1975 I testified several times under oath before the Church committee—that was Frank Church's Senate committee to investigate the FBI and the CIA—because they wanted to know what had happened in Chile and other places. Then they held their first public session, and they invited four people to talk about the future of covert action. One of the witnesses they called at that public session was Clark Clifford, advisor to presidents. He said: "Don't be silly, of course we have to have covert action." The next witness was Cyrus Vance, soon to be Secretary of State for Jimmy Carter. And in anguished tones he said: "I suppose we should have some capability but not too much. It's really not the right thing to do." The next witness was a man named Morton Halperin, who was an anti-establishment figure. He said: "Abolish it." I was the fourth witness, invited because I had been a practitioner of covert action. My recommendation was that covert action be taken away from the CIA, that it be given to a small new office reporting directly to the White House and to the Congress, and that it should be composed by statute of only 100 employees, including the people who answer the phones, clean the johns and watch the building at night, and that they should be allowed to engage in only two forms of covert action for the U.S. government. One, it should be able to give advice to friends, and two, it should be able to give them what British intelligence officers call King George's Cavalry: money. At the time I made that suggestion, it horrified all my colleagues in the intelligence business. I explained that I felt the CIA was really the place to keep covert action but that, given the society we have in our country after Viet Nam and after Watergate, the chances of covert action remaining covert were minimal. And if we can't do it secretly, we shouldn't do it. If we're going to do something abroad and we can't do it secretly, then we should let the military do it if we decide it's that important. I'm the only person in the United States who has ever come up with that idea, and not one person has ever said to me: "What a good idea that is!" So in answer to your question, yes, I think covert action could be separated from the CIA. Will it be? Absolutely not.

N: But you're not against covert action as such, you're just against the CIA doing it?

P: That's right. I believe in covert action in selective situations. There are times when it's absolutely necessary that we have what one writer has called "the tool of middle resort," between sending in the Marines on the one hand and making an ineffective diplomatic protest on the other.

N: Of course, with only 100 employees including janitors, the covert action unit that you visualize wouldn't be able to support too many right-wing dictatorships. In fact, they probably couldn't support one!

P: They couldn't support secret armies. It's been my experience that covert action has been successful on those occasions when we've helped people to do things they wanted to do very badly themselves. And we've gotten in trouble when we've tried to help people to do things that would benefit us rather than them. Consequently I think my idea would be a very good way to keep us from getting out of bounds, so that we don't leave people hanging. I remember only too vividly the broadcast from the beach at the end of the Bay of Pigs, when the military leader cursed us—those of us in Washington who were listening to him on the radio—because we had left him without any air cover. We should never be in that position again. Right now in Central America, with the Contras, we should reach a national consensus. Are we going to support the Contras? Then let's support them. Are we not? Then let's cut the ties. But let's not leave them in a situation like the Bay of Pigs where the only alternative they're going to have is to disappear into the swamps. I just feel strongly that if our country believes there are certain things that have to be done, that require military force, then we'd better have the guts to make the decision to do it and do it openly.

N: You certainly don't believe in that kind of decision being made by a President and a small inner circle of advisors, the way so many recent decisions have been made?

P: I think it's great as long as that President's decision is reflecting a national consensus. In the past, in the Chile case for instance, it was Richard Nixon and Richard Helms who said: "This fellow Allende has just been elected in Chile. We don't want him to be inaugurated." That was not a national consensus.

N: I suppose of all the recent incidents, the one where there's the clearest national consensus was the air raid on Libya.

P: Absolutely. It's too bad, however, because it was the perfect opportunity to conduct covert action, which would have been more effective. This is a particular instance where the people have supported the President and his military strike, and from the military standpoint it was very effective. But what a marvelous example of one of those few highly selective situations I was talking about! If we had had the capability of moving covertly, and of seeing to it that twenty of Khadafy's officers moved against him and assumed control of that government, the way he assumed control of it when he overthrew King Idris nineteen years ago, that would have been a much better solution, especially when you consider the way our allies in Europe reacted to the air raid. But the capability doesn't exist at this time.

N: What do you think the next act is going to be in the terrorism drama?

P: Well, I share the concern of many people that we might see some major terrorist action in this country. Terrorism is here. The first terrorist was an ancient Greek named Herostratus, who burned down the Temple of Diana. And the authorities caught him and asked him: "Why did you do that?" And he said: "I did it for the publicity." So I can see groups who are angered by what we did in Libya trying to pull a major terrorist act in the United States, which to date they have not been able to do. I'm convinced they're going to try. I don't know whether they will succeed. In fact I doubt if they will, because to have successful terrorism you have to have a support base. To pull off a successful series of terrorist acts, things that will make the headlines over weeks and months, you have to have bankers, you have to have underground hospitals, you have to have couriers, safe houses, places to launder your money. And that support apparatus doesn't exist in this country.

N: It apparently exists in Europe, which I suppose is why terrorism is so successful over there.

P: That's why the Red Brigades in Italy and Germany are so successful, and why Carlos, the famous terrorist, time and time again has pulled off those audacious coups, because Carlos always has a safe house to go to, he always has some place to go to get a change of clothing or a new suitcase full of money, a place to look for safe haven. And so I think they're going to try, but I don't think they're going to be successful.

N: Does the CIA have a role to play in combating terrorism either domestically or abroad?

P: Sure. It certainly does abroad; a very definite role which it's had for years and which it's performed reasonably well, and that is protecting the people and property of the United States abroad. Domestically, our role is limited to being able to say to the FBI: "Yes, that man who just came in from such and such a country has this background and this experience." But protecting us against domestic terrorism is the FBI's responsibility, and they've proved their capabilities. Acts of terrorism have declined drastically in the United States in the last few years.

N: From my outsider's point of view, it seems the CIA is quite poor at infiltrating Islamic organizations, much more inept than it is in infiltrating most other organizations it has to contend with. Am I correct in this view?

P: Well, you're surely correct, and one reason is that the CIA, with its own people, would really be ridiculous to try and penetrate those organizations on a large basis, because a bright young man from Harvard or Yale, or even an American of ethnic background, but obviously an American, who goes around the Middle East walking into bars and trying to make friends. It's not a very effective way to do it. What you do is, you have countries in that part of the world that are friendly, and you get the countries to help you, and their people do have the ability to go in and get that information. But you must keep in mind that a terrorist target is the most difficult in the world.

N: Because they're organized into such small cells?

P: An agent will go to a meeting—someone who works for you, in a terrorist unit—and the leader tells him: "We're going to kidnap the American ambassador. There are only nine of us that are going to do this, and we're going to do it right now. Nobody goes to the telephone to talk to their wife. Nobody goes to the john. If I see anybody writing anything on a piece of paper and dropping it on the floor, I'll shoot you in the back of the head." They go kidnap the American ambassador, and for six weeks you have a situation where the American ambassador is guarded by a CIA agent but he can't get the word back. It's the toughest, toughest target in the world.

N: You describe that situation as if it actually happened.

P: It has actually happened in my experience.

N: Can you say where?

P: In Latin America.

N: But you can't give more detail than that?

P: (Silence)

N: There's an incident in your book which I think crystallizes beautifully the difference between the way you think back on your career and the way, say, Philip Agee thinks back on his. You were on an inspection trip to Peru and the Chief of Station took you on a tour of Lima, first through the slums where the very poor lived and then through the neighborhoods of the very rich, and then he told you that the answer to the Third World lies somewhere between these extremes. For Philip Agee, the answer to the Third World lies in proletarian revolution and the end of capitalism. Do you think that incident in your book crystallizes the difference between your view and his?

P: Absolutely. It's an expression of philosophy with which I agree one hundred percent. That Chief of Station, Dick Welch, he and I talked about it many, many times. In dealing with problems overseas, I think our country must realize that we're never going to find a solution with the extreme right or with the extreme left. We're going to find it somewhere in the middle, with leaders who care about their people.

N: You seem to suggest that the answer for Third World countries is to become bourgeois liberal democracies, more or less like the United States.

P: You've got it right. For the last thirty years I've been saying that what we really want in every country in Latin America is for a time to arrive when the great majority of families can buy a refrigerator that works, and can afford to keep some beer in it. And we will never have any problems because they will then have their middle class on which they can build their own destinies, and we will no longer be tempted to send in Marines or interfere in business that's not ours. And the symbol of reaching the middle class in Latin America is to have electricity and a refrigerator.

N: Of course, there first has to be a middle class to reach.

P: The middle class does everything in Latin America. It decides whether or not there will be a change in government. But the problem is that in some countries there simply is no middle class, there are just the haves and the have-nots, and the great majority of people simply sit there over the centuries, watching events take place around them in which they do not participate. That's changing, slowly, but in many places, Haiti for instance—The middle class in Haiti consists of about four people, and nobody can find them!

N: One word I didn't notice anywhere in your book is overpopulation. Do you see that as one of the permanent reasons for the problems in the Third World?

P: People talk so much about terrorism and Communism, the threat they pose to the United States. A lot of people talk about the threat from a Communist Mexico. The chances of Mexico going Communist are very small. The Mexican government is a rather well-run operation. So I have no concern whatsoever about Mexico on our southern border going Communist. I do have concern about this: In the year 2000, the largest city in the world won't be New York or London or Tokyo or Los Angeles, it will be Mexico City. There are going to be 25,000,000 people living in Mexico City. The second largest city in the world is going to be São Paulo, Brazil. And the danger to the United States comes from what could happen in Mexico if a situation already bad now is exacerbated by the continuing growth of population. If it goes unchecked, what is going to happen when Mexico City, which is now a mess from the standpoint of traffic and pollution, is ringed by people who arrive five thousand a day to live in shantytowns around the city? What is going to happen in the year 2000 when there are 25,000,000 people there? Then Harlingen, Texas might really be in danger.

N: Do you think they will learn to control their numbers, as the Chinese are trying to learn?

P: I think they have to, and I trust they will.

N: I don't think you mention any incident in your book where your life was at risk. I got the impression that your career was a physically safe one, without James Bond incidents. Is the book lacking such incidents because they didn't happen or because you're not allowed to describe them?

P: They happened on a couple of occasions. For instance, when I was living in Rio de Janeiro with my first wife and seven children, and I had to explain to them that the great big black car parked around the corner, filled with goons, was there because a terrorist group had found out where I lived and was planning to try to do some harm to me or my family.

N: When did that happen?

P: When we were in Brazil, in 1970-71. That was very difficult, but probably the most dangerous part of my career was surviving the Rio de Janeiro traffic. You have to realize it was only recently intelligence officers overseas—not spies but the people who openly work for their government—it's only recently that our occupation has become terribly hazardous. Before, the people who were kidnaped and assassinated were American ambassadors and military attachés, people who were highly visible. In the last twenty years, which is a period that includes the Viet Nam war, more ambassadors have been killed overseas than admirals or generals. There was a period when CIA people, usually operating sub rosa and certainly with a low profile, were not tempting targets. The problem now is that for anyone working for the U.S., not only in the foreign service but even as a professor at a foreign university, in many countries of the world the situation is essentially quite dangerous. And intelligence officers share that danger. Otherwise they're pretty much protected by the unwritten code. The easiest way in the world to gather information about what the Russians are up to in a country abroad is to find their diplomatic courier, hit him over the head with a brick, and steal his diplomatic pouch. There's only one problem. You do that, and they're going to do the same thing to you next week. You don't do it. It's not reasonable. Underground warfare between services can't happen. And so you reach sort of an understanding with your Russian counterparts. At a cocktail party you know who they are, they know who you are. "Igor, how are you?" "Fine, and you?" So the danger for intelligence agents is a recent one, and it's shared by all Americans abroad.

N: What's the funniest thing that happened to you as an agent?

P: The one I remember as most humorous has been published. I was a young agent stationed in Washington, and a man jumped into my office doorway and said to me: "We're going to have the greatest psychological operation of all time! We're going to manufacture condoms, rubbers, and we're going to drop them all over the Soviet Union. They're going to be four feet long, and each one is going to be stamped MADE IN U.S.A. MEDIUM SIZE." That was called "Operation Penis Envy." I didn't know it at the time, but it was an old story out of the OSS, and all neophytes get hit with it when they go in. The incident that I remember in the most bemused way was in the Dominican Republic, when a sneak thief came into my home and stole my gun. And that was terrible, it was like a cowboy having his horse stolen. So I asked my deputy: "What are the folks in the office saying about the fact that my gun was stolen?" He said: "You don't want to know." I said: "Just tell me." He said: "You have a new nickname. Zero Zero Thirty Eight."

N: What was the saddest incident that happened to you as an agent? Or is that something you can't describe?

P: Well, the saddest incident might be described generically as seeing people who had worked for you as spies—not intelligence agents but spies, local people who betrayed their own government, not always for money but because they believed that your system was better than theirs, that it was a form of protest against their government, maybe they thought their government was a lousy right-wing dictatorship or they thought like Colonel Oleg Penkovsky who was the most valuable spy the West ever had in Moscow—seeing those people become the victims of their perilous trade. It wasn't all that dangerous being an intelligence officer. Being a spy is a very dangerous occupation.

N: Now you're talking about the kinds of things that happen in John Le Carré novels.

P: And when you see those people, and you have to leave them in the cold, because they're caught in something and you can't help them, you can't send a protest note through the American embassy because that would only confirm the fact that they had been helping Uncle Sam—those certainly were the saddest things. The saddest event I felt was after my retirement from the CIA, when my good friend Richard Welch was assassinated in Greece. But in general it's the Le Carré thing, the person who's left out in the cold, the inevitable loneliness of people who do things for a variety of motives, sometimes for money, at other times for loftier motives. That's the saddest thing, to see them come up croppers.

N: In your book you portray your 25 years in the CIA as something of a game of wits, almost on the level of the kinds of jokes rival college fraternities pull on each other, rather than in the Le Carré vein we've just been talking about. Near the end of your book, you say that your job with the CIA gave you the most satisfaction that a person could get from work. No Le Carré spy would say that!

P: You have to realize that Le Carré writes these books because people enjoy them. He's writing about people who do exist, but they constitute perhaps one-half of one percent of the intelligence community. He's writing about the people who do the kind of counterespionage work that means going deep, deep down underground, burrowing like a mole. But they're only the smallest percentage of the people who really work in the trade. Most of them are people who, because they must be introverts in their job, in fact are extroverts as persons. And it can be dull, but also it can be very persons. And it can be dull, but also it can be very challenging and rewarding and a fun kind of occupation. I don't want to make light of it and claim that it doesn't involve certain responsibilities and moral considerations, but if the insurance salesmen of America will forgive me, it's more interesting than selling insurance.

N: After you left the CIA you started a new career as a writer. Your first book was *The Night Watch,* but you've also written novels. How many?

P: Only one, *The Carlos Contract,* which came out in 1978.

N: Carlos, the terrorist, is never mentioned in *The Night Watch.* What got you interested in writing a book about him?

P: Well, you have to realize that *Night Watch* is a book which I, as a loyal member of the establishment, had to submit to the Agency for clearance before it was published. When I went to work for the CIA, I signed a contract that I had to submit all my writings before I could publish them. I believe it's reasonable that that contract be honored.

N: So you had reason to be interested in Carlos while you were an agent. You can say that much but you can't say more?

P: That's right. I couldn't write about him in a nonfiction book without compromising my sources.

N: Was it a coincidence that the title, *The Carlos Contract,* is in the same pattern as the titles in your brother's Joe Gall series?

P: It's not a coincidence at all. That's what the publishers told me the title was going to be. I wanted to call the book *The Eye of Violence.* The reason was that one of the most famous victims of terrorism was Ambassador Jackson, a British ambassador captured by the Tupamaros. He was held for nine months, and later he wrote of that experience. He said it had this lasting effect on him, that after he got out, he could see—on the streets, in the parks, on television screens—he could look at the faces and see the eye of violence. I wanted to use that. The publishers said: "Ahhhh, that's too literary. The name of the book is *The Carlos Contract,* because it's about somebody who takes a contract to kill Carlos." So that was the name.

N: You also collaborated with your brother Jim on a novel. What was that book about and what was its fate?

P: Well, my brother Jim has written 22 novels in the Joe Gall series. Now, the protagonist in *The Carlos Contract* was named Mac McLendon. It occurred to me that it would be fun for Jim and me to write a novel together, in which we would have our two protagonists work as a team; a team that didn't get along too well but managed to get the job done. This caused a Constitutional problem. At the end of the thing, I said to Jim: "By the way, you know of course that we're going to have to submit this novel to the CIA for clearance." He said: "The hell we do." I said: "Well, *I* have to." We had each written alternating chapters, so he said: "The only time I worked for the government was when I was in the Marines. They're not going to look at my writing." So I submitted one-half of that book to the CIA. That half of the book was cleared. Later, at a cocktail party, I met the lawyer who had that clearance job, and he was furious. I thought it was kind of funny. He said: "Goddamn it, how do we know which half of the book had the secrets in it?"

N: What was the name of that book?

P: That book was called *Double Blind*. It was never published. It's still on the shelf.

N: One final subject: would you mind explaining why you took early retirement from the Agency in 1975?

P: I did it because a series of things were happening in early 1975 that bothered me a lot. The first one was that our best agents overseas were saying: "Thanks, but no thanks." There was so much controversy—the investigation of the intelligence services, the sensational stories in the *New York Times* by Seymour Hersh. There was so much publicity that our best agents overseas were saying: "If we're going to work for an intelligence service, we'll work for the British or the French or the Israelis. We don't want to work for you." I was bothered at that time because of an official lunch I had in downtown Washington with the Washington chief of one of the world's major intelligence services. He said he was going to pay for the lunch because he had a favor to ask, and the favor was would I please hand back to him all the papers his service had loaned the CIA over the years. He was afraid to have those papers in the light of publicity. I was concerned because a man who had worked in the same area that I did in Latin America, Philip Agee, had left the CIA and had gone into the business of revealing the identities of American men and women abroad he said were CIA. Since Mr. Agee had worked only in Latin America, he had three tours, at the time he started doing that, I was the chief of Latin American affairs, so whenever he correctly identified someone—and he was in a position to know pretty well, he wasn't 100% correct but largely accurate—every time he revealed one of those persons, it was part of my responsibility to see that they were taken care of. So you can see that I didn't like that very much at all.

Finally, I went through a personal experience which bothered me a great deal. There's a myth that intelligence officers don't tell their families what they do. That is a myth, at least as far as Americans are concerned. Maybe the Russians can get away with something else, but if you're an American, you tell your spouse and even your teen-age children what you do. You don't have to go into great detail, but at least you let them know what you do. My first four experiences of this kind with teen-agers were very positive ones. Their reaction was: "Gee, my old man's in the same league with James Bond and *Mission Impossible*!" When I went through my fifth such experience, with a 15-year-old, her reaction when I told her I worked for the CIA was: "But that's dirty!" Now, I realized that in 1975 that represented a feeling in our country, a perception that anyone who worked for the FBI or the CIA was going around impervious to good judgment, and was some kind of zealot up to no good. But it did bother me an awful lot. And these basically were the reasons I retired from the CIA to form an association of former intelligence officers. There are maybe five hundred of us and we're in the business of trying to play a constructive role in the discussion of intelligence, acting as a clearing-house for the media, testifying in Congress, and having annual conventions where we put on name tags and pretty much act like Rotarians do when they get together.

N: Would it be fair to say that your organization is a sort of unofficial public relations arm for the CIA?

P: Yes, except that it defends the *concept* of intelligence and explains the *need* for intelligence, but it doesn't defend mistakes.

N: So you don't feel obliged to defend everything the CIA does?

P: No, I don't accept the label of apologist. I'm quite sure that the people in the CIA are glad such an organization exists. All of the directors who have left the CIA since the organization started have joined the organization. But times have changed. Things are different. I began to notice the difference in the case of my 15-year-old daughter who said it was dirty to work for the CIA. A couple of years past, she came to me and said: "Hey, I understand that they have summer interns over at CIA. Is that true?" I said: "That's right." She said: "I've also heard that they always use the children of CIA people. Is that true?" I said: "Yes, and the reason is very simple. If you're going to work there, even for a few weeks in the summer, you have to have a very expensive security clearance. So they use the children—the family is already cleared—to avoid that expense." She said: "I see. Could you get me a job over there?" That was only a couple of years ago. Now the change is almost total in our society, and I refer especially to the difference on college campuses from the way it was back in '76 and '77. There were several occasions when I spoke on college campuses, and certainly it was more dangerous than anything I ever did in the CIA. There are still serious questions today, and tough questions, but it's in the form of a dialogue, and that's a huge change.

N: Do you think it will change back again if the political situation changes? For example, if we invade Nicaragua?

P: One of the reasons it was so bad before, and the intelligence services were in such ill repute for a while, was because of a general lack of faith in our government following two events, Viet Nam and Watergate. Consequently, if something happens in the future, of the dimensions of either of those things, then that could change things again.

N: Do you think an invasion of Nicaragua would be another Viet Nam?

P: I personally think so. I think it would be a very bad mistake indeed. A terrible mistake.

My conversation that afternoon in Bethesda was roughly twice as long as the published version. In much of the omitted material David Phillips discussed some of the then current espionage novelists—among his favorites were Charles McCarry and W.T. Tyler—and various books he was working on or hoped to write. By far the most significant passage that was left on the publisher's cutting room floor had to do with an incident on the streets of Havana in the late Fifties when the young Phillips was shadowing Graham Greene. I did not want to see that incident lost to posterity. I shared David's account of it with Greene scholar Norman Sherry, who printed it in the third and final volume of his magisterial Greene biography. In David's words:

"Well, I was stationed in Havana at the time, in deep cover, so I kind of wandered around, finding out what was going on. These were the days right after Castro had taken over. Graham Greene went over to Havana to watch the making of the movie [*Our Man in Havana*, based on his novel], which starred Alec Guinness. And at one point Greene said to the director [Carol Reed]: "All right, we should change this line and have him say the following." And Alec Guinness said: "Fine." But then a *comandante*, a man with a star on his shoulder, a military censor, walked up and said: "No, you can't change that line." I'll never forget the look on Graham Greene's face when he realized for the first time that there might be some flaws in the new Cuban society. And so they went ahead and cut it out, but I'm sure that later, when the film was pieced together, they put it back in. But I'll never forget the look on Graham Greene's face when his work was suddenly subject to censorship."

David Atlee Phillips died of lung cancer on July 7, 1988, at age 65. His second and final novel, *The Terror Brigade* (1989), came out about six months later. In the last years of his life and perhaps even more since his death he's become a hugely controversial figure. He's suspected by some of having been deeply involved in the Kennedy assassination and by a few of having been the mastermind behind it. That topic never came up in our conversation and I am no expert on it, but anyone interested in discovering and connecting the dots will find ample raw material on the Web, of varying degrees of reliability.

His original career ambition was to be an actor. Could he have been a consummate actor, an Olivier of espionage, playing the part of reflective moderate for me? I will never know how much of what he said to me was true. All I can attest to is that this is what he said.

PLEASE READ BEFORE THE LIGHTS DIM

Of all the people I've known who consider themselves movie buffs, the one with by far the most encyclopedic knowledge of film was William K. Everson (1929-1996), a professor at NYU and other schools, the author of several major books on film history, and the proud owner of several thousand film prints. He was like the clever men of Oxford in Mr. Toad's song, knowing "all that was to be knowed" about movies. I had attended some of his film series when I was a student in New York and we stayed in touch after I moved to St. Louis and became a law professor. Eventually he gave some lectures at Webster University, a small liberal arts college in St. Louis County, and we organized a film series to be presented there, running two features a week which collectively, we hoped, would constitute a cross-section of the detective-crime-suspense film from the early 1930s to 1950. Some of the titles were well-known, others were obscure gems which Bill in New York would loan us for a particular program. I prepared notes for each film, making use of and often completely reworking the long chatty notes Bill had written for the hundreds of film series he had run in New York. The series worked well, and later we put together another one that carried the story of the genre forward to the late Fifties. For this book I've expanded the credits for each picture and tightened the notes here and there.

THE NIGHT CLUB LADY (Columbia, 1932)

Producer	none credited
Cinematographer	Ted Tetzlaff
Film Editor	Maurice Wright
Music Score	none credited
Screenplay	Robert Riskin
Source Novel	Anthony Abbot (Fulton Oursler), *About the Murder of the Night Club Lady* (1931)
Director	Irving Cummings
Thatcher Colt	Adolphe Menjou
Lola Carewe	Mayo Methot
Tony Abbot	Skeets Gallagher
Kelly	Ruthelma Stevens
Mrs. Carewe	Blanche Frederici
Mike	Nat Pendleton
Vincent	Albert Conti
Eunice	Greta Granstedt
Unbilled Bit Parts	Ed Brady, William von Brincken, George Humbert, Lee Phelps, Tetsu Shimada, Niles Welch

Copyright Date: 3 Aug 1932 Running Time: 66-70 min.

Anthony Abbot was the mystery-writing pseudonym of Fulton Oursler (1893-1952), editor of *Liberty* and *Reader's Digest* and the author of religioso blockbusters like *The Greatest Story Ever Told* (1949). In his younger days Oursler used the Abbot byline for eight detective novels starring New York City Police Commissioner Thatcher Colt, who despite his official position falls squarely into the Intellectual Mastersleuth tradition of his best-selling forerunners Philo Vance and Ellery Queen. Colt's cases, like those of Vance and Queen, tend to begin with a body found under bizarre circumstances, to feature strange clues pointing at a host of suspects, to be punctuated by conferences where each detective offers a different theory of the crime. The Colt series began with *About the Murder of Geraldine Foster* (1930).

Columbia Pictures brought Colt to the screen two years later in *The Night Club Lady*, based on the third Abbot novel, in which the dapper Commissioner tries to save a cabaret owner from an anonymous prophecy that she'll die at one minute after midnight. Colt was played by debonair Adolphe Menjou and the terrified Lola Carewe by Mayo Methot, best known to film buffs as the first wife of Humphrey Bogart. It's a neat fast-paced mystery with unusually mobile camerawork by Ted Tetzlaff, who directed some fine thrillers himself in the Forties. The murderer is not hard to guess but director Irving Cummings (1888-1959) and his cohorts scatter suspicion evenly around the characters and keep the clues more or less in plain sight. The only other Columbia Colt picture was *The Circus Queen Murder* (1933), also starring Menjou and based on an Abbot novel, and directed by Roy William Neill, who is famous for his Sherlock Holmes series with Basil Rathbone and Nigel Bruce.

PENGUIN POOL MURDER (RKO, 1932)

Executive Producer	David O. Selznick
Associate Producer	Kenneth MacGowan
Cinematographer	Henry Gerrard
Film Editor	Jack Kitchin
Music Director	Max Steiner
Screenplay	Willis Goldbeck
Source Novel	Stuart Palmer, *The Penguin Pool Murder* (1931)
Director	George Archainbaud
Hildegarde Withers	Edna May Oliver
Inspector Oscar Piper	James Gleason
Barry Costello	Robert Armstrong
Gwen Parker	Mae Clarke
Philip Seymour	Donald Cook
Donovan	Edgar Kennedy
Bertrand B. Hemingway	Clarence Wilson
Fink	James Donlan
Dr. Max Bloom	Gustav von Seyffertitz
Unbilled Bit Parts	Joe Hermano, Rochelle Hudson, William LeMaire, Mary Mason, Spec O'Donnell, Guy Usher

Copyright Date: 19 Dec 1932 Running Time: 69-75 min.

Wisconsin-born Stuart Palmer (1905-1968) changed his life forever in his mid-twenties when he launched a series of detective novels featuring Hildegarde Withers, umbrella-wielding spinster schoolteacher and amateur sleuth, and Inspector Oscar Piper of the NYPD, the cigar-chomping vulgarian who can't abide Hildy, with her awful hats and her insistence on correcting his grammar and meddling in his cases, but can't do without her either. Voila! The genre's first Odd Couple. RKO bought movie rights to the series soon after the first Withers novel was published, and the first of its six Miss Withers films, *The Penguin Pool Murder*, was based on that debut book in which Hildy discovers a dead body in the penguin pool of the municipal aquarium while taking her students on a class trip.

Director George Archainbaud (1890-1959) handles the opening scene beautifully, and the casting of Edna May Oliver and James Gleason as Miss Withers and Inspector Piper is perfect. The rest of the picture is not as visually imaginative as the first reel but it keeps nicely on the move, with plenty of plot surprises (emphatically not including the identity of the murderer) and lots of caustic repartee between Oliver and Gleason and also between Oliver and the children in her class. The first three pictures of the sextet were the best: Oliver was replaced in the fourth by Helen Broderick and in the fifth and sixth by ZaSu Pitts, and these three are best forgotten. By the time the series ended, in 1937, Stuart Palmer had come to Hollywood and begun a prolific screenwriting career which was to include scripts for cinematic adventures of Bulldog Drummond, The Falcon and The Lone Wolf. He also continued to write Miss Withers novels off-and-on until his death.

Please Read Before the Lights Dim

THE KENNEL MURDER CASE (Warner Bros., 1933)

Producer	none credited
Cinematographer	William Reese
Film Editor	Harold McLernon
Music Score	none credited
Screenplay	Robert N. Lee & Peter Milne
Source Novel	S.S. Van Dine (Willard Huntington Wright), *The Kennel Murder Case* (1933)
Director	Michael Curtiz
Philo Vance	William Powell
Hilda Lake	Mary Astor
Sgt. Ernest Heath	Eugene Pallette
Raymond Wrede	Ralph Morgan
Archer Coe	Robert Barrat
Brisbane Coe	Frank Conroy
Dr. Doremus	Etienne Girardot
Liang	James Lee
Sir Thomas MacDonald	Paul Cavanagh
Gamble	Arthur Hohl
Doris Delafield	Helen Vinson
Eduardo Grassi	Jack LaRue
Unbilled Bit Parts	Wade Boteler, Don Brody, George Chandler, Spencer Charters, Robert McWade, Henry O'Neill, Charles Wilson

Copyright Date: 22 Nov 1933   Running Time: 73 min.

Convalescing after a bout of overwork and emotional strain, art critic Willard Huntington Wright (1888-1939) began reading detective fiction for amusement. After devouring several hundred he decided he could write better whodunits than what he'd read, and proved it by creating Philo Vance, an insufferable mandarin and amateur sleuth who is the first important character in the history of novel-length American detective fiction. Published under the pseudonym of S.S. Van Dine, the Vance novels beginning with *The Benson Murder Case* (1926) became instant best-sellers, and by 1929 Paramount had begun releasing movies based on the books, with suave William Powell in the starring role. When Powell moved to Warner Bros. a few years later, one of the first properties the studio purchased as a vehicle for him was the then latest Philo Vance novel, which Warners' director-for-all-seasons, Hungarian-born Michael Curtiz (1888-1962), transformed into one of the most dazzling detective films ever made.

Powell had always been an ideal choice to play Vance since his charm converted the literary character's detached coldness into a sort of smug amiability, but in *Kennel* he was assisted by a formidable supporting cast, a classic locked-room puzzle plot, and Curtiz' visual flair. The director breaks up potentially static scenes with camera movement, lighting effects, swish pans and low-angle shots. When Vance has to deliver a long explanation, Curtiz avoids the Talking Heads syndrome by using illustrative flashbacks complete with marvelous miniatures of the crime scene. Foreground dialogue is always witty and informative while the all-but-thrown-away background dialogue is cracklingly naturalistic. There's one fascinating glitch in the ultimate reconstruction which you probably won't spot, but even if you do, *The Kennel Murder Case* is a delightful specimen of the American detective film at its finest.

THE MYSTERY OF MR. X (MGM, 1934)

Producer	Lawrence Weingarten
Cinematographer	Oliver Marsh
Film Editor	Hugh Wynn
Music Score	none credited
Screenplay	Howard Emmett Rogers
Adaptation	Philip MacDonald
Source Novel	Martin Porlock (Philip MacDonald), *X v. Rex* (1933; U.S. title *Mystery of the Dead Police*, as by Philip MacDonald, 1934)
Director	Edgar Selwyn
Nick Revel	Robert Montgomery
Jane Frensham	Elizabeth Allan
Inspector Connor	Lewis Stone
Sir Christopher Marche	Ralph Forbes
Sir Herbert Frensham	Henry Stephenson
Joseph Horatio Palmer	Forrester Harvey
Hutchinson	Ivan Simpson
Mr. X	Leonard Mudie
Judge Maplas	Alec B. Francis
Willis	Charles Irwin

Unbilled Bit Parts Robert Adair, Norman Ainsley, Barlowe Borland, Alfred Cross, Captain Francis, Victor Gammon, Douglas Gordon, Olaf Hytten, Colin Kenny, Richard Lancaster, Claude King, Raymond Lawrence, Raymond (Ray) Milland, Clive Morgan, Pat Moriarity, Henry Mowbray, John Power, Harrington Reynolds, C. Montague Shaw, Milton Royce, Pat Somerset, Terry Spencer, William Stack, Pearl Varvell, Eric Wilton

Copyright Date: 2 Mar 1934 Running Time: 85-91 min.

British-born Philip MacDonald (1899-1981), grandson of the Scottish poet and juvenile novelist George MacDonald, served in a cavalry regiment in Mesopotamia during World War I and afterwards trained horses for military service. His career as a mystery writer began with *The Rasp* (1924), and he had written several memorable whodunits and thrillers before he and his wife moved to Hollywood in 1931. During the Thirties he alternated between mystery novels and screenplays, including two cinematic adventures of Charlie Chan and three of Mr. Moto; and when MGM bought the movie rights to his 1933 thriller *X v. Rex* (U.S. title *Mystery of the Dead Police*), he got to work on the script himself. The best known of the films he was associated with are John Ford's *The Lost Patrol* (1934), set in the Arabian desert of MacDonald's war service, and Hitchcock's *Rebecca* (1940).

The Mystery of Mr. X stars Robert Montgomery as the suave and mysterious Nicholas Revel, who becomes involved in the hunt for a psychotic murderer of policemen. It's a satisfying if somewhat genteel picture in the English style, with early moments of near horror and many elements—such as the protagonist on the murderer's trail while being chased himself by the police—that are usually connected with Hitchcock. The picture offers as much banter and romantic byplay as melodrama, but the climax is packed with thrills in the cliffhanger serial tradition. Although set in England the film was shot in Hollywood, and even though the moviemakers Americanize some of the police procedure, for example by issuing guns to the constables and allowing break-ins without a warrant, most of the atmosphere is reasonably convincing, especially the pub scenes. *The Mystery of Mr. X* is a rarely seen little picture that should delight any fan of the genre.

THE THIN MAN (MGM, 1934)

Producer	Hunt Stromberg
Cinematographer	James Wong Howe
Film Editor	Robert J. Kern
Music Score	Dr. William Axt
Screenplay	Albert Hackett & Frances Goodrich
Source Novel	Dashiell Hammett, *The Thin Man* (1934)
Director	W.S. Van Dyke II
Nick Charles	William Powell
Nora Charles	Myrna Loy
Dorothy Wynant	Maureen O'Sullivan
Guild	Nat Pendleton
Mimi Wynant Jorgenson	Minna Gombell
McCaulay	Porter Hall
Tommy	Henry Wadsworth
Gilbert Wynant	William Henry
Arthur Nunheim	Harold Huber
Chris Jorgenson	Cesar Romero
Julia Wolf	Natalie Moorhead
Morelli	Edward Brophy
Clyde Wynant	Edward Ellis
Tanner	Cyril Thornton

Unbilled Bit Parts — Polly Bailey, Arthur Belasco, Raymond Brown, Ruth Channing, Clay Clement, Nick Copeland, Kenneth Gibson, Creighton Hale, Sherry Hall, Edward Hearn, Robert Homans, Thomas Jackson, John Larkin, Dixie Laughton, Walter Long, Tui Lorraine, Fred Malatesta, Garry Owen, Bert Roach, Rolfe Sedan, Gertrude Short, Ben Taggart, Phil Tead, Dink Templeton, Douglas Walton, Huey White, Leo White, Charles Williams

Copyright Date: 24 May 1934 Running Time: 91 min.

The Thin Man was the last novel of Dashiell Hammett (1894-1961), written in New York after his private-eye and *noir* classics *The Maltese Falcon* and *The Glass Key* had introduced him to big money and after his new lover, Lillian Hellman, had introduced him to the Algonquin Hotel world of verbal glitter and bitchy wit. The book was dedicated to Hellman and clearly owes its cocktails-and-wisecracks ambience to the nature of Hammett's life with her. MGM paid him another pile of money for movie rights and the film came out within months of the novel.

Director W.S. Van Dyke II (1889-1943) was known as One-Take Woody for his lightning shooting speed. His habit was to have technicians set up Scene B behind the camera while he was making Scene A, then to have everyone make a 180-degree turn and do Scene B while the technicians prepared what had been the A area for Scene C. It was Van Dyke's idea to cast Myrna Loy, who had usually played exotic temptresses, as Nora Charles opposite William Powell as the sardonic and sophisticated Nick. As every trivia buff knows, *The Thin Man* does not refer to Nick but to the vanished inventor he's trying to restore to the bosom of his wacky family in the odd moments when the film bothers with plot at all.

Van Dyke shot the picture in 18 days and no one expected it to be a huge success. But the Powell-Loy chemistry, the jolly alcoholic buzz and witty one-liners, the presentation of murder as a diversion in the lives of wealthy and blasé socialites, proved to be just what Depression-weary audiences were hungering for. *The Thin Man* inspired not only five Powell-Loy sequels but dozens of imitations of its formula by other Hollywood studios and even in England. An entire subgenre of cinematic whodunits stems from this still hugely enjoyable detective comedy of manners.

BULLDOG DRUMMOND STRIKES BACK
(20th Century/United Artists, 1934)

Producer	Darryl F. Zanuck
Cinematographer	Peverell Marley
Film Editor	Allen McNeill
Music Score	Alfred Newman
Screenplay	Nunnally Johnson
Adaptation	Henry Lehrman
Source Novel	Sapper (H.C. McNeile), *Bulldog Drummond Strikes Back* (1933)
Director	Roy Del Ruth
Capt. Hugh Drummond	Ronald Colman
Lola Field	Loretta Young
Algy	Charles Butterworth
Prince Achmed	Warner Oland
Gwen	Una Merkel
Inspector Neilsen	C. Aubrey Smith
Dr. Owen Sothern	Arthur Hohl
Singh	George Regas
Mrs. Field	Ethel Griffies
Hassan	Mischa Auer
Parker	Douglas Gerrard
Constable	Halliwell Hobbes
Constable	E.E. Clive
Unbilled Bit Parts	Wilson Benge, Billy Bevan, Kathleen Burke, H.N. Clugston, Gunnis Davis, Creighton Hale, Olaf Hytten, Charles Irwin, Charles McNaughton, Paul Somerset, Doreen Monroe, Yorke Sherwood, William O'Brien, Vernon Steele

Copyright Date: 18 Jun 1934 Running Time: 80-83 min.

Captain Hugh "Bulldog" Drummond, one of the most popular British thriller heroes of the Twenties and Thirties, was created by former Royal Engineers officer Herman Cyril McNeile (1888-1937), who wrote under the name of Sapper. A demobilized World War I hero, Drummond found peacetime life tedious, advertised in the newspapers for adventure and, in a series of novels beginning with *Bull-Dog Drummond* (1920), wound up saving dear old England from one conspiracy of filthy foreigners after another. The character appeared in

British movies as early as 1922 but it wasn't until Ronald Colman portrayed him in *Bulldog Drummond* (1929) that he became an American screen success. The makers both of that film and *Bulldog Drummond Strikes Back* trashed the Fascistic right-wing xenophobia of McNeile's novels and reworked Drummond into a dashing, romantic, essentially comic character, all his adventures played tongue in cheek.

The lady-vanishes plot of *Strikes Back*, predating Alfred Hitchcock's use of the same storyline by four years, enables director Roy Del Ruth (1895-1961) to balance the comedy and mystery elements in perfect equipoise, and the acting, set design, camerawork and art direction all exude tremendous polish and expertise. For anyone who knows Captain Hugh only from the novels or the routine Bulldog movies of the later Thirties, *Strikes Back* should come as a special treat.

Please Read Before the Lights Dim

THE CASE OF THE HOWLING DOG (Warner Bros., 1934)

Producer	none credited
Cinematographer	William Rees
Film Editor	James Gibbon
Music Score	none credited
Screenplay	Ben Markson
Source Novel	Erle Stanley Gardner, *The Case of the Howling Dog* (1934)
Director	Alan Crosland
Perry Mason	Warren William
Bessie Foley	Mary Astor
Sgt. Holcomb	Allen Jenkins
Claude Drumm	Grant Mitchell
Della Street	Helen Trenholme
Elizabeth Walker	Helen Lowell
Lucy Benton	Dorothy Tree
Arthur Cartwright	Gordon Westcott
Sam Martin	Harry Tyler
Clinton Foley	Russell Hicks
Dr. Cooper	Frank Reicher
Judge Markham	Addison Richards
George Dobbs	James Burtis
Ed Wheeler	Eddie Shubert
David Clark	Harry Seymour
Bill Pemberton	Arthur Aylesworth

Copyright Date: 22 Sep 1934 Running Time: 75 min.

A unique blend of lawyer, writer and fighter, Erle Stanley Gardner (1889-1970) loved a good scrap either with bare fists or in court, and created his world-famous Perry Mason character in his own image. The early Mason novels are steeped in the tough-guy tradition and read like Dashiell Hammett with legal trimmings. This may help explain why Warner Bros. bought film rights to the books soon after the first Mason novel came out in 1933. Before long Gardner was to wish he hadn't made that sale.

When the studio assigned the Mason role to Warren William, that William Powell clone of the early Thirties, it was clear that the movie Mason would not be a tough guy but rather a sort of Philo Vance with a law degree. None of the six pictures in the Warners series (1934-37) comes close to capturing the courtroom fireworks and the thrust and parry of cross-examination that were Gardner's hallmarks, but the four with William in the lead were at least neatly written and full of plot twists.

Silent-film veteran Alan Crosland (1894-1936) directed Mason's screen debut in *The Case of the Howling Dog*, which was based on Gardner's fourth Mason novel, and pepped up the rather talky script with mobile camerawork and atmospheric trappings. Helen Trenholme makes a charming and resourceful Della Street and Mary Astor is nicely ambivalent as Mason's client. Crosland and his colleagues eliminated the Paul Drake character and gifted Mason with a huge office full of secretaries and junior attorneys, but despite all these liberties Gardner liked the picture. Later entries tended to make Perry and Della into another Nick and Nora Charles, and those Gardner hated so vehemently that for the rest of his life he refused all further movie offers.

MISTER DYNAMITE (Universal, 1935)

Associate Producer	E.M. Asher
Cinematographer	George Robinson
Film Editor	Murray Seldeen
Music Score	none credited
Screenplay	Doris Malloy & Harry Clork
Original Story	Dashiell Hammett
Director	Alan Crosland

T.N. Thompson	Edmund Lowe
Lynn Marlo	Jean Dixon
Jarl Dvorjak	Victor Varconi
Charmian Dvorjak	Esther Ralston
Mona Lewis	Verna Hillie
Clark Lewis	Minor Watson
Chief of Detectives King	Robert Gleckler
Carey Williams	Jameson Thomas
Jans	Greta Myers
D.H. Matthews	Frank Lyman

Unbilled Bit Parts   Augusta Andrews, Chet Bartosch, Ed Berger, James Burtis, Jack Cheatham, G. Pat Collins, Joyce Compton, Ann Darcy, Anne Darling, Curley Dresden, Idolyn Dupre, Earl Eby, Richard Elliott, Knute Erickson, Sam Flint, Grace Goodall, Huntley Gordon, Jack Hatfield, Al Hill, Grace Hoyle, Olaf Hytten, Hans Joby, Nanette Lafayette, Connie Lamont, Matt McHugh, Monte Montague, Ferdinand Munier, Bradley Page, Lee Phelps, Joseph Remington, Don Roberts, Matty Roubert, Gay Seabrook, Harry Semels, Lee Shumway, Lillian Smith, Billy Sullivan, Richard Tucker, Harry Tyler, Mary Wallace, Eric Walton, Billy West

Copyright Date: 10 Apr 1935   Running Time: 69-75 min.

In 1931, at the peak of his powers and commercial success, Dashiell Hammett (1894-1961) wrote an original screen story called "On the Make" as a vehicle for William Powell. Powell's studio, Warner Bros., paid Hammett $10,000 for the story and then rejected it. In September 1934 Hammett sold the same story to Universal, which turned it over to director Alan Crosland (1894-1936) and two contract screenwriters.

Several months and countless alterations later, *Mister Dynamite* rolled off the studio's assembly line.

The screen story as Hammett wrote it is synopsized at length in Richard Layman's excellent biography *Shadow Man: The Life of Dashiell Hammett* (1981). Its protagonist, corrupt private eye Gene Richmond, says frankly: "I'm in the game for money. Sure, I'm always on the make." Hired by a wealthy socialite to clean up the mess when a Federal agent is killed by the bootleggers the socialite was financing, Richmond sees that his client has a beautiful daughter and decides to string out the case and, if possible, wind up marrying money. Crosland and the scriptwriters changed Richmond's name to T.N. Thompson (T.N.T., Mr. Dynamite, get it?), reconfigured him into a maverick version of Nick Charles, changed the wealthy socialite to a gambling casino owner, added four new murders to spice up the action, and permeated the picture with all the cocktails-and-wisecracks routine that audiences had associated with Hammett since the huge screen success of *The Thin Man* (1934). There may not be much of the authentic Hammett left in this movie but it's still a slick, fast-paced and complex little number, packing an an immense amount of material into a scant 69 minutes.

CHARLIE CHAN IN EGYPT (Fox, 1935)

Producer	Edward T. Lowe
Cinematographer	Daniel B. Clark
Film Editor	Al de Gaetano
Music Director	Samuel Kaylin
Screenplay	Robert Ellis & Helen Logan
Director	Louis King

Charlie Chan	Warner Oland
Carol Arnold	Pat Paterson
Tom Evans	Thomas Beck
Nayda	Rita Cansino [Rita Hayworth]
Snowshoes	Stepin Fetchit
Unbilled Bit Parts	Anita Brown, Frank Conroy, John Davidson, Nigel de Brulier, James Eagles, George Irving, Paul Porcasi, Gloria Roy, Arthur Stone, Jameson Thomas

Copyright Date: 21 Jun 1935 Running Time: 72 min.

Earl Derr Biggers (1884-1933) lived to write only six Charlie Chan books, but those hugely popular novels displaced the Fu Manchu Yellow Peril stereotype of Asians in crime fiction and created a vogue for polite, philosophical, dignified Oriental detectives. Chan's first movie appearance was in 1926 but the character didn't catch on among filmgoers until 1931, when the Fox studio launched a series starring Swedish-born Warner Oland. The earliest Fox Chans were based on Biggers novels, but by the time of *Charlie Chan in Egypt*, eighth in the series and one of the best ever, the films were being shot from original scripts.

Chan flies to the land of the pyramids to investigate the theft of artifacts from the recently opened tomb of Pharaoh Ameti. The professor who led the Ameti expedition has vanished. When Chan examines the ancient pharaoh's mummy, it turns out to be the body of the professor—with a bullet in its heart. And so the sleuthing starts, intercut by director Louis King (1898-1962) with sequences of action, suspense and near horror that are enhanced by creepy background music, effective set design and superb camerawork. King and his collaborators chose to give Charlie's traditional Number One Son a vacation in this picture and substitute in the Dumb Sidekick role none other than Stepin Fetchit, dean of black stereotype comics, but that unwise decision at least gives us a chance to see a Fetchit performance for ourselves and judge whether blacks' distaste for him in recent generations is justified. Those uninterested in racial issues may feast their eyes on a very young and stunning Rita Hayworth (still billed as Rita Cansino at the time) as an exotic Egyptian beauty.

REMEMBER LAST NIGHT? (Universal, 1935)

Producer	Carl Laemmle, Jr.
Cinematographer	Joseph Valentine
Film Editor	Ted Kent
Music Score	Franz Waxman
Screenplay	Harry Clork, Doris Malloy, Dan Totheroh
Source Novel	Adam Hobhouse, *The Hangover Murders* (1935)
Director	James Whale
Danny Harrison	Edward Arnold
Tony Milburn	Robert Young
Carlotta Milburn	Constance Cummings
Vic Huling	George Meeker
Bette Huling	Sally Eilers
Jake Whitridge	Reginald Denny
Penny Whitridge	Louise Henry
Faronea	Gregory Ratoff
Fred Flannagan	Robert Armstrong
Billy Arliss	Monroe Owsley
Baptiste Bouclier	Jack LaRue
Maxie	Edward Brophy
Prof. K.H.E. Jones	Gustav von Seyffertitz
Mme. Bouclier	Rafaele Ottiano
Phelps	Arthur Treacher
Florabelle	Alice Ardell
Unbilled Bit Parts	Wade Boteler, James Burke, Alex Chivra, E.E. Clive, Charles de la Motte, James Flavin, Monte Montague, Corbett Morris, Joe North, William Pawley, Kate Price, Frank Reicher, Warner Richmond, Dewey Robinson, Frank Terry, Harry Woods

Copyright Date: 1 Nov 1935 Running Time: 76-81 min.

No movie of the Thirties was more imitated than *The Thin Man*, whose huge success led to a wave of detective films featuring marital spats, nonstop tippling and amateur detection by a husband-wife team. Perhaps the most original of all these spinoffs is *Remember Last Night?*, directed by James Whale (1896-1957) of *Frankenstein* and

Bride of Frankenstein fame, and based on a long-forgotten novel by a long-forgotten author who apparently never wrote another book. Edward Arnold as an overweight NYPD detective, and Robert Young and Constance Cummings as the Nick-and-Nora pair, confront a genuinely baffling plot and almost too many suspects and motives. What Whale contributed to this *Thin Man* spinoff was his flair for macabre humor, a photographic and lighting style much like that of his Frankenstein films, and a zany near-surrealistic sense of pace. Arnold's characterization of the plainclothesman—tough, irked by the superficial playboys and playgirls among whom he's investigating a murder, liking them as friends but knowing that one of them is the killer he must arrest—stands out amid the razzle-dazzle and almost constant noise and movement. It takes at least three viewings to sort out all the ramifications of the plot, and one tends to share Arnold's discomfort among so many self-centered adult brats who treat murder as less important than the consumption of cocktails. But Whale also makes us feel that the lives of the idle rich are redeemed at least a little by their stylishness, and his own style—huge glossy sets, smooth glistening camerawork, recognizable signature images—turns *Remember Last Night?* into one of the most purely enjoyable of all Thirties detective films.

Please Read Before the Lights Dim

THE PREVIEW MURDER MYSTERY (Paramount, 1936)

Producer	Harold Hurley
Cinematographer	Karl Struss
Film Editor	James Smith
Music Score	None Credited
Screenplay	Robert Yost & Brian Marlowe
Original Story	Garnett Weston
Director	Robert Florey
Peggy Madison	Frances Drake
Johnny Morgan	Reginald Denny
Claire Woodward	Gail Patrick
Jerome Hewitt	George Barbier
E. Gordon Smith	Ian Keith
Neil Du Beck	Rod La Rocque
Edwin Strange	Conway Tearle
Detective McKane	Thomas Jackson
George Tyson	Jack Raymond
Studio Manager	Colin Tapley
Jack Rawlins	Jack Mulhall
Carl Jennings	Bryant Washburn
James Daley	Franklyn Farnum
Chief of Police	Lee Shumway
Watchman	Spencer Charters

Unbilled Bit Parts   William R. Arnold, George Barton, Sidney Bracey, Fritz Collings, Chester Conklin, Nell Craig, Eddie Dunn, Estelle Etterre, Hyman Fink, John George, Charles Hamilton, Edward Hearn, Henry Kleinbach [Henry Brandon], Isabelle La Mal, Frank Losee, Jr., Wilfred Lucas, Hank Mann, Carl McBride, Philo McCullough, Torben Meyer, Frances Morris, Jack Norton, Paddy O'Flynn, Franklin Parker, Jack Paul, Earl M. Pingree, Ed Schaefer, Ferdinand Schumann-Heink, Clarence Sherwood, Phillips Smalley, Claude Stroud, Hatto Tappenbeck, Monte Vandergrift, Luz Vasquez, Lawrence Wheat, Neil Wheeler

Copyright Date: 28 Feb 1936   Running Time: 60-65 min.

Robert Florey (1900-1979) was one of the finest craftsmen among Hollywood's "B" movie directors, with a genius for marshaling all a studio's resources under the old contract system and making a $50,000 picture that looked as if it had cost ten times as much. *The Preview Murder Mystery*, about a series of killings in a movie studio itself, is not only imaginative and good to look at but shows Florey's genuine love of movies and respect for Hollywood's past. He doesn't play fair with the audience, using low-key lighting and editorial tricks to cast suspicion on all the characters, but makes abundant and creative use of every aspect of work at Paramount as a backdrop to the story, providing a much more accurate account of how films were made under the studio system than many a glossy "A" production. In addition to a lively story, Florey tips his hat to silent movie days by casting a number of veterans in major parts, and also tosses in a few private jokes at the expense of certain movies he doesn't care for, including Paramount's own Marlene Dietrich vehicle *The Devil Is a Woman* (1935). The cast is first-rate, the technicians top-notch (film editor James Smith had worked in the same capacity for D.W. Griffith, and cinematographer Karl Struss had photographed F.W. Murnau's 1927 classic *Sunrise*), and all in all *The Preview Murder Mystery* is a grand tribute to the solid craftsmanship that a director like Florey could bring to a lowly 60-minute programmer.

THE EX-MRS. BRADFORD (RKO, 1936)

Associate Producer	Edward Kaufman
Cinematographer	J. Roy Hunt
Film Editor	Arthur Roberts
Music Director	Roy Webb
Screenplay	Anthony Veiller
Original Story	James Edward Grant
Director	Stephen Roberts

Dr. Lawrence Bradford	William Powell
Paula Bradford	Jean Arthur
Inspector Corrigan	James Gleason
Stokes	Eric Blore
Nick Martel	Robert Armstrong
Miss Prentiss	Lila Lee
John Summers	Grant Mitchell
Mrs. Summers	Erin O'Brien-Moore
Leroy Hutchins	Ralph Morgan
Mrs. Hutchins	Lucille Gleason

Unbilled Bit Parts   James Adamson, Johnny Arthur, Willie Best, Stanley Blystone, Tom Bower, Spencer Charters, Chuck Collins, John Collins, Frankie Darro, Doe Dearborn, John Dilson, Jim Donlan, Jerry Dundee, Paul Fix, Evelyn Fontaine, Dorothy Grainger, Duke Green, Jockey Haefeli, Sam Hayes, Herb Imes, Rollo Lloyd, Edward McWade, Bruce Mitchell, Frank Reicher, Charles Richman, Al St. John, John Sheehan, Henry Stone, Jack Storey, J. Tanzel, Frank M. Thomas

Copyright Date: 15 May 1936   Running Time: 80-81 min.

After making film history in his four Philo Vance pictures at Paramount and Warners and in MGM's *The Thin Man*, debonair William Powell was loaned out to RKO for a pair of urbane mystery-comedies in the *Thin Man* vein, both directed by the versatile Stephen Roberts (1895-1936), whose promising career was cut short by early death. In *Star of Midnight* (1935) the Nora stand-in had been played by Ginger Rogers, while in *The Ex-Mrs. Bradford* the part went to Jean Arthur, whose husky aggressive voice and scatterbrained vivacity are perfect foils for Powell's dulcet tones and unflappable suavity. As a society doctor formerly married to a daffy mystery writer, Powell becomes entangled in a race-track murder which soon leads to other killings, and when he finds himself the prime suspect, Arthur as his ex-wife sets out to clear him by helping him expose the real murderer. With its complex plot and witty vivacity, this is one of the best of the many 1930s detective films that are indebted to *The Thin Man*, and makes us wish that Powell and Arthur with their unique chemistry had made more than this single picture together.

SEVEN SINNERS (Gaumont-British, 1936)

Producer	None credited
Cinematographer	Mutz Greenbaum
Film Editor	Michael Gordon
Music Director	Louis Levy
Screenplay	L. DuGarde Peach, Sidney Gilliat, Frank Launder
Source Stage Play	Arnold Ridley & Bernard Merivale, *The Wrecker* (1927)
Director	Albert de Courville
Harwood	Edmund Lowe
Caryl Fenton	Constance Cummings
Paul Turbe	Thomy Bourdelle
Axel Hoyte	Henry Oscar
Sir Charles Webber	Felix Aylmer
Elizabeth Wentworth	Joyce Kennedy
Registrar	O.B. Clarence
Chief Constable	Mark Lester
Wagner	Allan Jeayes
Reception Clerk	Antony Holles

Copyright Date: 2 Aug 1936 Running Time: 69-70 min.

The Wrecker (1929), released by Britain's Gainsborough Pictures in both silent and sound versions at the dawn of the talkie era, was a rousing old-fashioned thriller about a hidden master criminal's campaign to bankrupt England's railroads by staging a series of train disasters. The film was directed by Geza von Bolvary with a great deal of Germanic lighting and camera angles in the Fritz Lang style. The footage of train wrecks and derailings was genuine, and so impressive that it was recycled intact seven years later when the picture was remade under the totally meaningless title *Seven Sinners*.

In the mid-1930s the Gaumont-British studio released many cinematic thrillers that attempted to duplicate the mood of fun and menace associated with Alfred Hitchcock. *Seven Sinners* clearly belongs in this category: director Albert de Courville and chief screenwriters Frank Launder and Sidney Gilliat junked the Fritz Lang overtones of the earlier version and substituted a lighter Hitchcockian tone as well as some elements from the climax of Hitchcock's 1935 classic *The Thirty-Nine*

Steps. But far from being a lazy imitation, the lively and funny script in many ways anticipates the Launder-Gilliat screenplay for another Hitchcock classic, 1938's *The Lady Vanishes*. Another influence on *Seven Sinners* is *The Thin Man*, with Edmund Lowe and Constance Cummings agreeable Nick-and-Nora types. It's a well constructed and handsomely mounted film, combining civilized wit and wild action in a tight 70 minutes of running time.

THIS MAN IS NEWS (Paramount-British, 1938)

Producer	Anthony Havelock-Allan
Cinematographer	Henry Harris
Film Editor	Reginald Beck
Music Director	Percival Mackey
Screenplay	Roger MacDougal, Basil Dearden, Allan MacKinnon
Original Story	Roger MacDougal & Allan MacKinnon
Director	David MacDonald
Simon Drake	Barry K. Barnes
Pat Drake	Valerie Hobson
MacGregor	Alastair Sim
Inspector Holly	Edward Lexy
Johnnie Clayton	John Warwick
Sgt. Bright	Gary Marsh
Harelip Murphy	Philip Lever
Ken Marquis	Kenneth Buckley
?	Bobby Gall
Unbilled Bit Parts	James Birrie, Tom Gill, James Harcourt, David Horne, David Keir, Edwin Laurence, Jack Vyvyan

Copyright Date: N/A   Running Time: 74-77 min.

During the 1930s, American studios were required by English law to make a certain number of films in Great Britain or its dominions if they wished British release for their U.S.-made pictures. This policy led to dozens of ghastly "quota quickies" and a handful of unpretentious gems like *This Man Is News*, which delighted both critics and audiences with its unforced laughs and fast lighthearted style. Barry K. Barnes and Valerie Hobson make a delightfully polished, witty and mature Nick-and-Nora team and the supporting comedy is equally good even if Alastair Sim's rendition of the Scottish scenarists' dialogue in a Scottish burr strikes non-Scots ears as a foreign language. The plot is unusual and director David MacDonald makes a stylish attempt to build up the at first unseen criminal as a mastermind in the tradition of Fritz Lang's Dr. Mabuse. The Barnes-Hobson-Sim combo immediately followed this picture with a sequel, *This Man in Paris* (1939), which MacDonald also directed. The outbreak of World War II brought what might have been a long-running "This Man" series to a sudden and premature end.

Please Read Before the Lights Dim

IT'S A WONDERFUL WORLD (MGM, 1939)

Producer	Frank Davis
Cinematographer	Oliver T. Marsh
Film Editor	Harold F. Kress
Music Score	Edward Ward
Screenplay	Ben Hecht
Original Story	Ben Hecht & Herman J. Mankiewicz
Director	W.S. Van Dyke II
Edwina Corday	Claudette Colbert
Guy Johnson	James Stewart
Cap Streeter	Guy Kibbee
Sgt. Koretz	Nat Pendleton
Vivian Tarbell	Frances Drake
Lt. Miller	Edgar Kennedy
Willie Heyward	Ernest Truex
Major Willoughby	Richard Carle
Dolores Gonzales	Cecilia Callejo
Al Mallon	Sidney Blackmer
Gimpy	Andy Clyde
Capt. Haggerty	Cliff Clark
Madame Chambers	Cecil Cunningham
Herman Plotka	Leonard Kibrick
Stage Manager	Hans Conried
Lupton Peabody	Grady Sutton
Unbilled Bit Parts	Eddie Acuff, Murray Alper, Monya Andre, Dorothy Ates, Lulu Mae Bohrman, Harry Burns, George Chandler, Frank Coghlan, Jr., Hal Cooke, Maurice Costello, Nell Craig, Rae Daggett, Edgar Dearing, John Dilson, Lester Dorr, Peter Du Rey, Rex Evans, Frank Faylen, Bess Flowers, Tom Hanlon, Harold Hoff, William E. Lawrence, Wally Maher, Fay McKenzie, Bud McTaggart, George Meeker, Harold Miller, Albert Morin, Philip Morris, Louis Natheaux, David Newell, Jack Norton, Jack Raymond, Mary Louise Smith, Carl Stockdale, William Tannen, Phillip Terry, Monte Vandergrift, Ray Walker

Copyright Date: 4 May 1939   Running Time: 84-86 min.

This film has nothing in common with Frank Capra's *It's a Wonderful Life* except three words of its title and Jimmy Stewart, but perhaps the classic status of the Capra picture has contributed to the obscurity of this one, a breathless screwball comedy-thriller indebted equally to *The Thin Man*, Capra's *It Happened One Night* and Hitchcock's *The Thirty-Nine Steps*. "One-Take Woody" Van Dyke, who had helmed *The Thin Man* five years earlier, turned out this jet-paced funfest in less than twelve working days, with the result that it lacks the traditional MGM polish but is full of sharp edges that give the picture an engaging vitality and spontaneity, a freewheeling looseness and comic zest. Stewart plays a private eye trying to clear his eccentric playboy client (Ernest Truex), who's been framed for murder and sentenced to death. On the way to prison himself for withholding evidence, Stewart jumps off a train, kidnaps a giddy poetess (Claudette Colbert), commandeers her car, eventually enlists her help—which has a habit of backfiring on him—and ultimately wins her love. If the film's plot framework is that of a suspense thriller not all that different from Cornell Woolrich's *Phantom Lady*, the stress throughout is on comedy, although Van Dyke still invests the genuine suspense sequences, like the ones in the summer stock theater where the real killer is on the loose, with a Hitchcockian sense of menace. Few if any Hollywood movies have so perfectly mixed comedy and thrills as this one.

Please Read Before the Lights Dim

TELL NO TALES (MGM, 1939)

Producer	Edward Chodorov
Cinematographer	Joseph Ruttenberg
Film Editor	W. Donn Hayes
Music Score	Dr. William Axt
Screenplay	Lionel Houser
Original Story	Pauline London & Alfred Taylor
Director	Leslie Fenton
Michael Cassidy	Melvyn Douglas
Ellen Frazier	Louise Platt
Arno	Gene Lockhart
Matt Cooper	Douglass Dumbrille
Lorna Travers	Florence George
Dr. Lovelake	Halliwell Hobbes
Mary Anderson	Zeffie Tilbury
Charlie Daggett	Harlan Briggs
Miss Brendon	Sara Haden
Alley	Hobart Cavanaugh
Lydia Lovelake	Jean Fenwick
Mrs. Haskins	Esther Dale
Chalmers	Joseph Crehan
Phil Arno	Tom Collins

Unbilled Bit Parts   Joseph Bernard, James Blaine, Gladys Blake, Charles Brown, Everett Brown, Ben Carter, Chester Clute, Heinie Conklin, Nick Copeland, Jack Daley, Harry Depp, John Dilson, Claire DuBrey, Billy Engle, Pat Flaherty, James Flavin, Bess Flowers, Mary Gordon, Hilda Haywood, Brandon Hurst, Roger Imhof, Gladden James, Thaddeus Jones, Fred Kelsey, Rosalie Lincoln, George Magrill, John Marlowe, Mantan Moreland, James C. Morton, George Noisom, Frank Orth, Lee Phelps, Renie Riano, Addison Richards, Claire Rochelle, Mme. Sul-te-wan, Gertrude Sutton, Ben Taggart, Phil Tead, Harry Tyler, Monte Vandergrift, Ray Walker, Anthony Warde, Alyn Warren, Ernest Whitman, Norman Willis, Ward Wing, Ian Wolfe

Copyright Date: 8 May 1939   Running Time: 68-69 min.

If the mystery movies of the early 1930s were dominated by gentlemen detectives like Philo Vance and Charlie Chan, the same sorts of movies in the late Thirties and early Forties tended to feature cynical, disillusioned sleuths like Sam Spade and Philip Marlowe. The fantasy world where courtliness and good manners and taste and consideration for others seemed to have meaning was one of the many cultural casualties of World War II.

One can discern both the past and the future of detective films in *Tell No Tales*, a 68-minute MGM gem from 1939, starring Melvyn Douglas as a newspaper editor who ventures into high society and low, and runs into all sorts of unrelated scandals and crimes, as he personally investigates a kidnaping. The film marked the directorial debut of former actor Leslie Fenton (1902-1978), who invests the usually debonair Douglas character and the tangled plot with the labyrinthine quality one associates with private-eye novels and movies like *The Big Sleep*. In one of the finest scenes in *Tell No Tales*, Douglas's search for the kidnap victim thrusts him into the middle of a black wake, which Fenton portrays without any of the gross racial stereotyping common at the time. This may not be the most logical mystery film ever made, but it's one of the most satisfying and least known.

Please Read Before the Lights Dim

THE MALTESE FALCON (Warner Bros., 1941)

Producer	Hal B. Wallis
Cinematographer	Arthur Edeson
Film Editor	Thomas Richards
Music Score	Adolph Deutsch
Screenplay	John Huston
Source Novel	Dashiell Hammett, *The Maltese Falcon* (1930)
Director	John Huston
Sam Spade	Humphrey Bogart
Brigid O'Shaughnessy	Mary Astor
Iva Archer	Gladys George
Joel Cairo	Peter Lorre
Lt. Dundy	Barton MacLane
Effie Perine	Lee Patrick
Casper Gutman	Sydney Greenstreet
Detective Tom Polhaus	Ward Bond
Miles Archer	Jerome Cowan
Wilmer Cook	Elisha Cook, Jr.
Luke	James Burke
Frank Richman	Murray Alper
Bryan	John Hamilton
Unbilled Bit Parts	Charles Drake, Creighton Hale, William Hopper, Walter Huston, Hank Mann, Jack Mower, Emory Parnell

Copyright Date: 18 Oct 1941 Running Time: 100 min.

It has been said that traditional detective fiction takes place in the Garden of Eden, i.e. in a just society where people are good, love and friendship are real, reason works, problems are solved and truth is found. By standing these axioms on their heads, Dashiell Hammett (1894-1961) revolutionized mystery fiction, nowhere more radically than in *The Maltese Falcon* (1930), the definitive private-eye novel and a seminal work of *noir* literature.

Warners had filmed the book twice previously—casting Ricardo Cortez as Sam Spade in the first (1931) and hopelessly miscasting Warren William in the second (1936)—but the third and last version, which was also the first picture directed by John Huston (1906-1987), best captured Hammett's spare style and bleak vision, creating a nightworld of treacherous and deadly people, making momentary alliances of convenience with each other but each betraying everyone else in the quest for the fabled black bird, "the stuff of dreams," which of course turns out to be junk. Huston's casting is so perfect that one can't imagine others in any of the key parts even though Mary Astor looks far too old for the role of Brigid, the definitive Film Noir Woman, and even though Humphrey Bogart as Spade was a late replacement for George Raft.

In the world of Hammett no one can know or trust anyone else. Huston does tone down the novel's pessimism a bit, making Bogart's Spade more honorable and less psychotic than Hammett's "blond Satan," and also making him capable of love so that when he sends Brigid over during the unforgettable climax one senses that his self-imposed code of ethics is real and tearing him apart. But in most respects the film tracks the book closely and the result is that Hollywood rarity, a truly great movie based on a truly great novel.

THE FALCON TAKES OVER (RKO, 1942)

Producer	Howard Benedict
Cinematographer	George Robinson
Film Editor	Harry Marker
Music Director	C. Bakaleinikoff
Screenplay	Lynn Root & Frank Fenton
Source Novel	Raymond Chandler, *Farewell, My Lovely* (1940)
Director	Irving Reis

Gay Lawrence (The Falcon)	George Sanders
Ann Reardon	Lynn Bari
Inspector Michael O'Hara	James Gleason
Jonathan "Goldy" Locke	Allen Jenkins
Diana Kenyon	Helen Gilbert
Unbilled Bit Parts	William Alland, Roxanne Barkley, Turhan Bey, Ward Bond, Fred Carpenter, George Cleveland, Hans Conried, Kernan Cripps, Edward Dew, Frank Fanning, Edward Gargan, Charles Hall, Selmer Jackson, Warren Jackson, Lew Kelly, Gayle Mellott, Amarilla Morris, Paul Norby, Frank O'Connor, Anne Revere, Louise Richie, Harry Shannon, Mickey Simpson, Robert Smith, Chester Tallman, Ken Terrell, Elinor Troy, Juan Varro

Copyright Date: 13 May 1942 Running Time: 62-67 min.

The Saint, that devil-may-care thriller hero created by Leslie Charteris (1907-1993) at age 21, came to the screen in 1938 when RKO bought movie rights to the series. George Sanders starred in five of RKO's seven Saints, bringing to the role his unique suavely sardonic unflappability. When RKO grew tried of Charteris' financial demands, its executives unearthed a character vaguely similar to The Saint in an obscure short story by Michael Arlen (1895-1956), bought movie rights to that character for a relatively modest sum, and instantly transformed the Saint films into cinematic exploits of The Falcon.

The new films had not the slightest connection with Dashiell Hammett's *The Maltese Falcon* nor with John Huston's film. But *The Falcon Takes Over*, third in the series, was connected quite closely with the other superstar private eye writer of the time, Raymond Chandler (1888-1959). RKO had already bought movie rights to Chandler's second novel, the classic *Farewell, My Lovely*, and some front-office genius decided that the book should be the basis of Sanders' third outing as the Falcon. This time it's not Philip Marlowe who's propelled into hulking ex-con Moose Malloy's bloody search for his beloved Velma, but the plot of the film will surprise no one who has read Chandler's novel or seen one of the later versions (with Dick Powell, 1944, or Robert Mitchum, 1975). *The Falcon Takes Over* isn't on a par with those pictures but in its own terms it's one of the better Falcons, and historically fascinating thanks to the Chandler connection. After one more appearance in the role, George Sanders was replaced by his brother Tom Conway, who carried on as RKO's Falcon until 1947.

Please Read Before the Lights Dim

PHANTOM LADY (Universal, 1944)

Associate Producer	Joan Harrison
Cinematographer	Elwood Bredell
Film Editor	Arthur Hilton
Music Director	Hans J. Salter
Screenplay	Bernard Schoenfeld
Source Novel	William Irish (Cornell Woolrich), *Phantom Lady* (1942)
Director	Robert Siodmak
Jack Marlow	Franchot Tone
Carol "Kansas" Richman	Ella Raines
Scott Henderson	Alan Curtis
Estela Monteiro	Aurora
Inspector Burgess	Thomas Gomez
Ann Terry	Fay Helm
Cliff March	Elisha Cook, Jr.
Bartender	Andrew Tombes
Detective	Regis Toomey
Detective	Joseph Crehan
Kettisha	Doris Lloyd
Dr. Chase	Virginia Brissac
District Attorney	Milburn Stone
Unbilled Bit Parts	Bob Bain, Barney Bigard, Dave Coleman, Roger Hanson, Dole Nicholls, Howard Ramsey, Freddie Slack

Copyright Date: 7 Feb 1944 Running Time: 85 min.

Cornell Woolrich (1903-1968) was the Poe of the 20th century and the Hitchcock of the written word, the greatest of all suspense writers, a doom-haunted recluse whose bleak, stunningly vivid novels and stories created much of the literary basis for what we know as *film noir*. Low and medium budget movies had been adapted from his mystery tales since 1938, but it was his classic novel *Phantom Lady* (1942) that made studios recognize the potential of his fiction for top-of-the-line features. The book takes off from one of those waking-nightmare situations at which Woolrich excelled. A man charged with his estranged wife's murder insists he'd spent the evening with a woman he'd picked up in a bar, but the lady seems to have vanished into thin air, and everyone in a position to know swears no such woman ever existed. The man is sentenced to die and his secretary, who loves him, races the clock on a hunt for the phantom through the night catacombs of the city.

Universal Pictures bought movie rights to the novel and assigned the project to associate producer Joan Harrison, a protégée of Hitchcock, and to German émigré director Robert Siodmak (1900-1973). The film-makers followed Woolrich's plot for about half the picture's 87 minutes, then wandered off on their own paths. But throughout the movie Siodmak and his brilliant cinematographer "Woody" Bredell employ a visual style in perfect harmony with the Woolrich spirit, and the film's most powerful sequences—the cat-and-mouse on the elevated railway platform between Ella Raines and Andrew Tombes, the orgiastic jam session among the jazzmen—are taken straight from the novel. Siodmak spent the rest of the decade directing a cycle of masterful *films noir* including *The Killers* (1946), *Cry of the City* (1948) and *Criss Cross* (1949).

LADY ON A TRAIN (Universal, 1945)

Producer	Felix Jackson
Cinematographer	Elwood Bredell
Film Editor	Ted Kent
Music Score	Miklos Rosza
Screenplay	Edmund Beloin
Original Story	Leslie Charteris
Director	Charles David

Nicki Collins	Deanna Durbin
Jonathan Waring	Ralph Bellamy
Wayne Morgan	David Bruce
Mr. Saunders	George Coulouris
Danny	Allen Jenkins
Arnold Waring	Dan Duryea
Haskell	Edward Everett Horton
Miss Fletcher	Jacqueline DeWit
Joyce Williams	Patricia Morison
Aunt Charlotte	Elizabeth Patterson
Margo Martin	Maria Palmer
Mr. Wiggam	Samuel S. Hinds
Sgt. Christie	William Frawley

Unbilled Bit Parts   Eddie Acuff, Poni Adams, Ernest Anderson, Eddie Bartell, Barbara Bates, Eddie Bruce, Charles Cane, Ben Carter, Hobart Cavanaugh, Nora Cecil, George Chandler, Andre Charlot, Joseph Crehan, Charles Clute, Charles Deschamps, Robert Dudley, Tom Dugan, Eddie Dunn, Sarah Edwards, Al Ferguson, Clyde Fillmore, Alice Fleming, Mary Forbes, Mabel Forrest, Thurston Hall, Ethel May Halls, Dick Hirbe, Alfred [Lash] LaRue, Perc Launders, George Lewis, George Lloyd, Lockard Martin, Sam McDaniel, Matt McHugh, Bert Moorhouse, Jack Norton, Kathleen O'Malley, Ralph Peters, Karen Randle, Addison Richards, Bert Roach, Charles Sherlock, Jean Trent, Eddy Waller

Copyright Date: 27 Aug 1945   Running Time: 94-105 min.

How many movies could comfortably assimilate as many layers of material as *Lady on a Train*? On the simplest level it's a vehicle for Deanna Durbin, designed to give her an adult and rather sexy image while still calling on her to sing and project ebullient charm as she had in the pictures that had made her a pre-adolescent star. Roughly half of the film's story content comes from the cocktails-and-banter whodunits of the Thirties; the other half, plus all the visual style, is pure Forties *film noir*. Although attributed to a story by Leslie Charteris, creator of The Saint, the premise of Durbin glimpsing a murder through an open window from a passing elevated train and then being stalked by the killer goes back to Cornell Woolrich's 1936 thriller "Death in the Air," and was recycled by him (without trains) in 1942's "Rear Window," the literary source for Hitchcock's classic film. With cinematography by Woody Bredell and music by Miklos Rosza and a key role for Dan Duryea, and with its intricate lighting effects and gliding dolly shots, the film stands squarely in the *noir* tradition. It's full of brisk physical action, lavish sets and Hitchcock-like suspense, with even piles of white grain taking on a nightmarish quality as a background for an attempted murder. French émigré Charles David (1906-1999) directed only two Hollywood films before marrying Deanna Durbin and taking her back with him to France, where they lived for decades in comfortable retirement.

Please Read Before the Lights Dim

THE WALLS CAME TUMBLING DOWN (Columbia, 1946)

Producer	Albert J. Cohen
Cinematographer	Charles Lawton, Jr.
Film Editor	Gene Havlick
Music Score	Marlin Skiles
Screenplay	Wilfrid H. Pettet
Source Novel	Jo Eisinger, *The Walls Came Tumbling Down* (1943)
Director	Lothar Mendes
Gilbert Archer	Lee Bowman
Patricia Foster	Marguerite Chapman
George Bradford	Edgar Buchanan
Matthew Stoker	George Macready
Susan	Lee Patrick
Capt. Griffin	Jonathan Hale
Ernst Helms	J. Edward Bromberg
Catherine Walsh	Elisabeth Risdon
Dr. Marke	Miles Mander
Bishop Martin	Moroni Olsen

Unbilled Bit Parts   Julio Abadia, Alfred Allegro, Steve Benton, Charles Cane, Noel Cravat, Gary Del Mar, Forrest Dickson, Franklin Dix, Ralph Dunn, Jack Ellis, Katherine Emery, Mary Field, Bess Flowers, Fred Godoy, Richard Gordon, Buddy Gorman, Ray Hughes, William Kahn, Milton Kibbee, Charles LaTorre, Arthur Loft, Charles March, Harold Miller, Pat O'Malley, Wanda Perry, Jack Raymond, Bob Ryan, Reginald Sampson, Larry Steers, Dan Stowell, John Tyrrell

Copyright Date: 7 Jun 1946 Running Time: 81 min.

John Huston's *The Maltese Falcon* was imitated again and again, in whole or in part, for decades after it came out. One of the most interesting *Falcon* clones is this little-known thriller from 1946, directed by the curious and erratic émigré Lothar Mendes (1894-1974) and based on a novel by a writer who never wrote another whodunit. Lee Bowman is the Bogart stand-in, playing a newspaper gossip columnist named Archer, which was also the name of Sam Spade's murdered partner. Lee Patrick, who portrays Bowman's efficient secretary, had played Spade's secretary in *Falcon*. J. Edward Bromberg and George

Macready fill in nicely for Peter Lorre and Sydney Greenstreet. Whether Marguerite Chapman turns out as deceitful as Mary Astor's Brigid O'Shaughnessy it would be churlish to reveal here. The black bird in this version is trifurcated: a priceless Leonardo and two ancient Bibles with clues to the lost painting's whereabouts. But if the inspiration for this movie is obvious, its innovative details make it quite watchable in its own right. The initial premise is unusual—Bowman investigating the apparent suicide of a friend who was a priest—and much of the dialogue is extremely sharp. Mendes' visual style, even in this his last film, could never be mistaken for John Huston's. *The Walls Came Tumbling Down* is a crisp little picture that doesn't deserve the obscurity in which it has long languished.

BLACK ANGEL (Universal, 1946)

Producers	Roy William Neill & Tom McKnight
Cinematographer	Paul Ivano
Film Editor	Saul A. Goodkind
Music Score	Frank Skinner
Screenplay	Roy Chanslor
Source Novel	Cornell Woolrich, *The Black Angel* (1943)
Director	Roy William Neill
Martin Blair	Dan Duryea
Cathy Bennett	June Vincent
Marko	Peter Lorre
Capt. Flood	Broderick Crawford
Mavis Marlowe	Constance Dowling
Joe	Wallace Ford
Bartender	Hobart Cavanaugh
Lucky	Freddie Steele
Kirk Bennett	John Phillips
Bartender	Ben Bard
Dr. Courtney	Junius Matthews
Flo	Marion Martin
Mitchell	Michael Branden
Dance Team	St. Clair & Vilova
Detective	Robert Williams
Unbilled Bit Parts	Florence Auer, Ralph Brooks, Eddy Chandler, Bob Crosby, Gary Delmar, Mary Fields, Dorothy Granger, Eula Guy, Chuck Hamilton, Shepard Houghton, Mauritz Hugo, Clark Kuney, Bud Lawler, Ann Lawrence, Steve Olsen, Pat Starling, Wally Webb, Dick Wessel

Copyright Date: 14 Aug 1946 Running Time: 80 min.

Cornell Woolrich (1903-1968), whose haunting novels and stories of suspense are the prose counterparts of Hitchcock's darkest films, shared with Hitchcock the compulsion to rework and recycle motifs again and again. His classic 1943 novel *The Black Angel*—in which a terrified young wife races against time to prove that her husband, convicted and sentenced to die for the murder of his mistress, is innocent and that one of the other men in the dead woman's life is guilty—bears a certain family resemblance to his 1942 novel *Phantom Lady*. Universal bought film rights to both books but the two resulting movies had little in common besides being first-rate specimens of *film noir*.

The director of *Black Angel*, British-born Roy William Neill (1886-1946), had made most of Universal's Sherlock Holmes pictures with Basil Rathbone and Nigel Bruce, and a number of these, notably *The Scarlet Claw* (1944), had added *noir* coloration to the clues and deductions. Neill and screenwriter Roy Chanslor radically altered Woolrich's novel but the finished film is permeated by the bleak Woolrich spirit. From the opening sequence with its complex boom shot from the street to the interior of the soon-to-be-murdered woman's penthouse, Neill and cinematographer Paul Ivano invest every shot with a visual style that translates Woolrich into film with total fidelity to mood and almost none to literal text. It was Roy William Neill's finest film, and his last. In December 1946, while on a visit back to England, he died of a sudden heart attack.

SO DARK THE NIGHT (Columbia, 1946)

Producer	Ted Richmond
Cinematographer	Burnett Guffey
Film Editor	Jerome Thoms
Music Score	Hugo Friedhofer
Screenplay	Martin Berkeley & Dwight Babcock
Original Story	Aubrey Wisberg
Director	Joseph H. Lewis
Henri Cassin	Steven Geray
Nanette Michaud	Micheline Cheirel
Pierre Michaud	Eugene Borden
Mama Michaud	Ann Codee
Dr. Boncourt	Egon Brecher
Widow Bridelle	Helen Freeman

Unbilled Bit Parts   Frank Arnold, Francine Bordeaux, Marcelle Corday, Adrienne d'Ambricourt, Gregory Gay, Cynthia Gaylord, Theodore Gottlieb, Paul Marion, Andre Marsaudon, Alphonse Martel, Louis Mercier, Emil Rameau, Billy Snyder, Esther Zeitlin

Copyright Date: 10 Oct 1946 Running Time: 71 min.

In 1945-46 *film noir* came into its own as a stylistically distinct type of American movie, and suddenly a small army of directors and cinematographers seemed to become obsessed with offbeat camera angles, expressionistic shadows, warped and haunted characters in an ambience of the dark city. Joseph H. Lewis (1907-2000) joined the *noir* movement at this time after several years of directing visually dazzling "B" Westerns. Perhaps his roots in outdoor action pictures led him to set *So Dark the Night* in rural locations, with the pastoral tranquillity counterpointing the unsettling chiaroscuro and depth staging and abundant mirror and window shots. So vividly did he recreate the French countryside in southern California that at least one trade journal blasted him for making the picture outside the United States!

The story, in which a famous Paris detective on the verge of breakdown comes to a peaceful village for a rest and gets involved in the hunt for a psychotic serial killer who just may be himself, owes equal debts to Sophocles' ancient tragedy *Oedipus Tyrannus*, the novels of Georges Simenon and the bleak spirit of Cornell Woolrich. Lewis invests the plot with a hypnotic visual style of the sort that was making the Thirties type of Talking Heads whodunit film more unattractive and obsolete each year. One can't help but wonder what cinematic fireworks he might have set off if he'd been tapped to make a Philo Vance or Charlie Chan!

GREEN FOR DANGER (Individual/Rank, 1946)

Producers	Frank Launder & Sidney Gilliat
Cinematographer	Wilkie Cooper
Film Editor	Thelma Myers
Music Score	William Alwyn
Screenplay	Sidney Gilliat & Claud Gurney
Source Novel	Christianna Brand, *Green for Danger* (1944)
Director	Sidney Gilliat
Nurse Frederica Linley	Sally Gray
Dr. Barney Barnes	Trevor Howard
Nurse Esther Sanson	Rosamund John
Inspector Cockrill	Alastair Sim
Mr. Eden	Leo Genn
Sister Marion Bates	Judy Campbell
Nurse Woods	Megs Jenkins
Joseph Higgins	Moore Marriott
Mr. Purdy	Henry Edwards
Dr. White	Ronald Adam
Detective Sgt. Hendricks	George Woodbridge
Rescue Worker	Frank Ling
Sister Carter	Wendy Thompson
Porter	John Rae
Unbilled Bit Parts	Hattie Jacques, Elizabeth Sidney, Ronald Ward

UK Release Date: 5 Dec 1946 Running Time: 91 min.

In the immediate postwar years when the American mystery film was dominated by *noir*, Britain produced a genuine detective movie of classic status. *Green for Danger* was based on the famous whodunit by Christianna Brand (1907-1988), last survivor of the Agatha Christie generation of women crime novelists, and was directed and co-produced by Sidney Gilliat (1908-1994), who had worked with his fellow producer Frank Launder on the script of Hitchcock's *The Lady Vanishes* (1938). Brand, who was married to a surgeon, based her novel on experience during Hitler's air raids. A postman injured during the blitz is taken to the nearby military hospital for a simple operation but dies on the surgical table from other than natural causes. The murderer must be one of the six medical people who were operating on him. Which of them had motive to kill a perfect stranger? Enter Brand's best-known series detective, Inspector Cockrill.

Gilliat follows not only Brand's plot but her scrupulous sense of fair play with the reader, eschewing the silly red herrings and all-too-obvious least Likely Suspects with which conventional whodunits abounded. Each member of the superb cast is not a stick figure but a quirky, fallible human being faced with life-and-death decisions under the air raids' ceaseless pressure. The ambience of the hospital and the interplay of its personnel are as fascinating as the plot. Gilliat switches effortlessly from deductive reasoning to wry wit to desperate wartime passion to sheer terror—as when the doors of the deserted dispensary swing open and shut to reveal split-second glimpses of the surgically gowned and masked killer preparing to strike again—and the solution is both logical and packed with suspense. Alastair Sim, shrewd and dotty by turns, tossing off one-liners as skillfully as he questions suspects, is a perfect Inspector Cockrill, and *Green for Danger* is a perfect English detective film.

KISS THE BLOOD OFF MY HANDS (Norma/Universal, 1948)

Producer	Richard Vernon
Cinematographer	Russell Metty
Film Editor	Milton Carruth
Music Score	Miklos Rozsa
Screenplay	Leonardo Bercovici
Adaptation	Ben Maddow & Walter Bernstein
Source Novel	Gerald Butler, *Kiss the Blood Off My Hands* (1940)
Director	Norman Foster
Jane Wharton	Joan Fontaine
Bill Saunders	Burt Lancaster
Harry Carter	Robert Newton
Tom Widgery	Lewis L. Russell
Landlady	Aminta Dyne
Mrs. Paton	Grizelda Hervey
Sea Captain	Jay Novello
Judge	Colin Keith-Johnston
Superintendent	Reginald Sheffield
Publican	Campbell Copelin
Tipster	Leland Hodgson
Young Father	Peter Hobbes
Unbilled Bit Parts	Harry Allen, Jimmy Aubrey, Timothy Bruce, George Bunny, Valerie Cardew, Jack Carol, Harry Cording, Leslie Denison, Thomas P. Dillon, David Dunbar, Al Ferguson, Art Foster, James Fowler, Fred Fox, Richard Glynn, Harold Goodwin, Arthur Gould-Porter, Joseph Granby, Duke Green, Frank Hagney, Mildred Hale, Robert Hale, Alec Harford, Kenneth Harvey, Keith Hitchcock, Wesley Hopper, Robin Hughes, Tommy Hughes, Suzanne Kerr, Patty King, James Logan, Ola Lorraine, Don McCracken, David McMahon, Charles McNaughton, Lora Lee Michel, Tom Pilkington, Felippa Rock, Wally Scott, Jack Stoney, Anne Whitfield, Marilyn Williams, Harry Wilson, Ben H. Wright

Copyright Date: 16 Nov 1948 Running Time: 79 min.

Critics of the late Forties hailed crime novelist Gerald Butler (1907-1988) as the British counterpart of James M. Cain and Cornell Woolrich. No one reads or remembers Butler today, but during his brief vogue his books did remotely inspire two fine *films noir*: Nicholas Ray's *On Dangerous Ground* (1951) and this one, with Burt Lancaster as a violence-prone concentration camp survivor who's accused of a murder and runs for his life through a nightmare vision of postwar London, and Joan Fontaine as a lonely woman who falls in love with the fugitive and risks her own life to help him start over. *Kiss the Blood Off My Hands* owes only its title and a few miscellaneous plot elements to Butler's near-unreadable novel. What makes it so fascinating is the bleak visual pyrotechnics of its director.

Norman Foster (1900-1976) began as an undistinguished star of "B" pictures and broke into directing in the late Thirties with entries in the Charlie Chan and Mr. Moto series. In the Fifties and Sixties he made Disney features and similar family fare for television. By all odds his best films were *noir* thrillers. Much of the credit for directing Foster's *Journey into Fear* (1942) is often given to its star, Orson Welles, and *auteur* theorists would probably be listing *Kiss the Blood Off My Hands* too among Welles' unofficial credits if Welles had been signed to play Robert Newton's part, a sleazy penicillin racketeer quite similar to Welles' own Harry Lime role in *The Third Man* a year later. Certainly Foster's finest work is in the Welles vein, and except for a deplorable compromise ending at literally the last minute, this film is as visually and thematically powerful as any of Welles' own *noir* classics.

D.O.A. (Cardinal/United Artists, 1950)

Producer	Leo C. Popkin
Cinematographer	Ernest Laszlo
Film Editor	Arthur H. Nadel
Music Score	Dmitri Tiomkin
Screenplay	Russell Rouse & Clarence Green
Director	Rudolph Maté
Frank Bigelow	Edmond O'Brien
Paula Gibson	Pamela Britton
Majak	Luther Adler
Miss Foster	Beverly Campbell
Mrs. Philips	Lynn Baggett
Halliday	William Ching
Stanley Philips	Henry Hart
Chester	Neville Brand
Marla Rakubian	Laurette Luez
Sam Haskell	Jess Kirkpatrick
Sue Haskell	Cay Forrester
Dr. Mason	Frank Jaquet
Dr. Schaefer	Lawrence Dobkin
Dr. MacDonald	Frank Gerstle
Kitty	Carol Hughes
Dave	Michael Ross
Nurse	Donna Sanborn
Unbilled Bit Parts	Bill Baldwin, Teddy Buckner, Frank Cady, Jadie Carson, Edwin Chandler, Frank Conlan, Roy Engel, Douglas Evans, William Forrest, George Guhl, Shifty Henry, Ray Larue, Virginia Lee, Peter Leeds, George Lynn, Harold Miller, Hugh O'Brian, Jerry Paris, Phillip Pine, Lynne Roberts, Von Streeter, Ivan Triesault, Cake Wotchard

Copyright Date: 21 Apr 1950 Running Time: 83 min.

Frank Bigelow (Edmond O'Brien), an insignificant accountant leading a life of suffocating routine, discovers that he's been poisoned and has only a few days to live. In a frenzy of desperation he flails through the menacing cityscape, struggling till his last breath to learn why he must die. What more perfect premise for *film noir* than a man trying to solve his own murder?

Director Rudolph Maté (1898-1964), who had been one of Hollywood's top cinematographers before changing careers, shaped *D.O.A.* into an intense nightmarish thriller, full of images and elements characteristic of *noir* at the end of its first decade. Like so many postwar crime films, it was shot not in the studio but on location, much of it in the streets of San Francisco. Neville Brand turns in the performance of a lifetime as a sadistic and psychotic hit man of the sort that abounded in *film noir* ever since Richard Widmark gleefully threw that crippled old lady down the stairs in 1947's *Kiss of Death*. The waterfront nightclub scene with its passionate jazz score and close-ups of black musicians' sweat-soaked faces, the impenetrable labyrinth of plot in the Raymond Chandler manner, the Cornell Woolrich signature theme of the race against time and death, the pure *noir* revelation at the climax that the reason Bigelow must die is no reason at all but an absurdity, all these aspects and countless others saturate the picture with the ambience of a lost world, a place where (as Chandler put it) the streets are dark with something more than night. The detective film of the early Thirties, where Philo Vance and Charlie Chan reigned supreme, and reason combined with civilized wit and charm were the order of the day, that sort of film ends here.

STRANGERS ON A TRAIN (Warner Bros., 1951)

Producer	Alfred Hitchcock
Cinematographer	Robert Burks
Film Editor	William H. Ziegler
Music Score	Dmitri Tiomkin
Screenplay	Raymond Chandler & Czenzi Ormonde
Adaptation	Whitfield Cook
Source Novel	Patricia Highsmith, *Strangers on a Train* (1949)
Director	Alfred Hitchcock
Guy Haines	Farley Granger
Anne Morton	Ruth Roman
Bruno Antony	Robert Walker
Senator Morton	Leo G. Carroll
Barbara Morton	Patricia Hitchcock
Miriam	Laura Elliott
Mrs. Antony	Marion Lorne
Mr. Antony	Jonathan Hale
Capt. Turley	Howard St. John
Prof. Collins	John Brown
Mrs. Cunningham	Norma Varden
Hennessey	Robert Gist
Unbilled Bit Parts	Joel Allen, Murray Alper, Monya Andre, John Butler, Leonard Carey, Edward Clark, John Doucette, Roy Engle, Tommy Farrell, Sam Flint, Edward Hearn, Harry Hines, Mary Alan Hokanson, Edna Holland, J. Louis Johnson, Louis Lettieri, Charles Meredith, Ralph Moody, Rolland Morris, Odette Myrtil, Minna Phillips, Georges Renavent, Janet Stewart, Shirley Tegge, Laura Treadwell, Howard Washington, Dick Wessel

Copyright Date: 2 Jun 1951 Running Time: 100 min.

Strangers on a Train is the definitive treatment of that compulsively recurring Hitchcock theme, the exchange of guilt. On a train from New York to Washington, politically ambitious tennis champ Guy Haines (Farley Granger) is approached by indolent psychopath Bruno Antony (Robert Walker). Guy hates his estranged wife (Laura Elliott), who refuses to divorce him so he can marry a senator's daughter (Ruth Roman); Bruno hates his wealthy father (Jonathan Hale). "All right," Bruno playfully suggests, "let's swap. You kill my father, I kill your wife." Guy laughs the proposal off as a sick joke. (Or does he?) Bruno fulfills his end of the bargain, then pressures Guy to reciprocate, and as so often in *film noir* and in Hitchcock, the noose tightens around a guilt-marked protagonist desperately clawing for a way out of the trap. It's a suspense classic, full of stunning visuals and black humor, with the best climactic action sequence of any Hitchcock film. The Fifties proved to be Hitchcock's richest decade in terms of *film noir* as *Strangers on a Train* was followed by *I Confess* (1952), *Rear Window* (1954), *The Wrong Man* (1957), *Vertigo* (1958) and *Psycho* (1960).

ON DANGEROUS GROUND (RKO, 1951)

Producer	John Houseman
Cinematographer	George A. Diskant
Film Editor	Roland Gross
Music Score	Bernard Herrmann
Screenplay	A.I. Bezzerides
Adaptation	A.I. Bezzerides & Nicholas Ray
Source Novel	Gerald Butler, *Mad with Much Heart* (1945)
Director	Nicholas Ray
Mary Malden	Ida Lupino
Jim Wilson	Robert Ryan
Walter Brent	Ward Bond
Bill Daly	Charles Kemper
Pete Santos	Anthony Ross
Capt. Brawley	Ed Begley
Carrey	Ian Wolfe
Danny Malden	Sumner Williams
Lucky	Gus Schilling
Willows	Frank Ferguson
Myrna	Cleo Moore
Mrs. Brent	Olive Carey
Bernie	Richard Irving
Julie	Pat Prest

Unbilled Bit Parts Frank Arnold, Leslie Bennett, A.I. Bezzerides, Eddie Borden, William Challee, Jimmy Conlin, Joe Devlin, Homer Dickinson, Don Dillaway, Jim Drum, Art Dupuis, Budd Fine, Dee Garner, Ronald Garner, Tommy Gosser, Bill Hammond, Mike Lally, Kate Lawson, Ruth Lee, Al Murphy, W.J. O'Brien, Nestor Paiva, Gene Persson, Steve Roberts, Tracy Roberts, Vera Stokes, Nita Talbot, John Taylor, Ken Terrell, Harry Joel Weiss, Esther Zeitlin

Copyright Date: 12 Dec 1951 Running Time: 82 min.

Most of Nicholas Ray's early films—*They Live by Night* (1948), *Knock on Any Door* (1949), *In a Lonely Place* (1950)—are firmly in the *noir* tradition, and so is *On Dangerous Ground*, which stars Robert Ryan as that paradigm figure of *noir* fiction and film, the brutal bitter lone-wolf cop, hunting a psychopath who in more than one respect is the mirror image of himself. But Ray had a strong romantic streak contending with his dark side, so his Noir Cop is offered a way out of the psychological trap in the person of a young blind woman (Ida Lupino) who falls in love with him, despite the fact that the killer he's hunting is her brother (Sumner Williams). A nice balance between urban nightscapes and snow-covered mountain scenery, virtuoso lighting effects by George Diskant (who also photographed Ray's *They Live by Night*), a superb Bernard Herrmann music score, and fine performances by the principal players more than make up for the untypically upbeat fade-out.

COUNT THE HOURS (RKO, 1953)

Producer	Benedict Bogeaus
Cinematographer	John Alton
Film Editor	James Leicester
Music Score	Louis Forbes
Screenplay	Doane R. Hoag & Karen DeWolf
Original Story	Doane R. Hoag
Director	Don Siegel
Ellen Braden	Teresa Wright
Doug Madison	Macdonald Carey
Paula Mitchener	Dolores Moran
Gracie Sager	Adele Mara
D.A. Jim Gillespie	Edgar Barrier
George Braden	John Craven
Max Verne	Jack Elam
Alvin Taylor	Ralph Sanford

Unbilled Bit Parts   Marshall Bradford, Ralph Brooks, Benny Burt, Jack Carr, Robert Carson, Ralph Dumke, Richard Emory, Roy Engel, Sam Flint, Dolores Fuller, William E. Green, John Harmon, Edward Hearnj, Al Hill, Paul Hoffamn, Harlan Howe, I. Stanford Jolley, Gayle Kellogg, Richard Kipling, Jess Kirkpatrick, Herbert Lytton, Michael McHale, Lee Morgan, Richard Norris, Kathleen O'Malley, George Pembroke, Lee Phelps, Lorin Raker, Alvin Ray, Lanny Rees, Norman Rice, Vernon Rich, Kay Riehl, Gene Roth, Dick Scott, Carl Sklover, Brick Sullivan, Michael Vallon, Charles Victor

Copyright Date: 26 Mar 1953   Running Time: 74 min.

The strongest outside influence on *film noir* of the early 1950s was McCarthyism, which inspired Red Menace films like *I Was a Communist for the FBI* and *Pickup on South Street* and also, in a backhanded way, inspired several anti-McCarthy pictures like *Count the Hours*. A migrant farmworker and his wife (Teresa Wright) are accused of the brutal murder of their employer. A local lawyer (Macdonald Carey), assigned to defend the man, is ostracized by friends and clients and dumped by his fiancée (Dolores Moran) for representing a member of a despised outgroup. It's not by chance that the name of the lawyer protagonist is Douglas Madison. Director Don Siegel (1912-1991) skillfully blends this archetypal Fifties theme with that staple of Forties *noir*, the race to save the innocent man from the electric chair. As the countdown proceeds, the real killer (Jack Elam) takes steps to make sure the case stays closed. Shot in nine days, showing many signs of haste but many more of great directorial talent under pressure, *Count the Hours* is a low-budget gem, featuring some magnificent lighting effects by that prince of *noir* cinematographers, John Alton.

Please Read Before the Lights Dim

PICKUP ON SOUTH STREET (20th Century-Fox, 1953)

Producer	Jules Schermer
Cinematographer	Joe MacDonald
Film Editor	Nick DeMaggio
Music Score	Leigh Harline
Screenplay	Samuel Fuller
Original Story	Dwight Taylor
Director	Samuel Fuller
Skip McCoy	Richard Widmark
Candy	Jean Peters
Moe	Thelma Ritter
Capt. Dan Tiger	Murvyn Vye
Joey	Richard Kiley
Zara	Willis Bouchey
Winoki	Milburn Stone

Unbilled Bit Parts   Parley Baer, Virginia Carroll, Harry Carter, Clancy Cooper, George Eldredge, John Gallaudet, Frank Kumagi, Jay Loftin, Ray Montgomery, Ralph Moody, Roger Moore, Jerry O'Sullivan, Victor Perry, Stuart Randall, Maurice Samuels, Ray Stevens, George E. Stone, Wilson Wood

Copyright Date: 27 May 1953 Running Time: 80 min.

Film critics outraged by the McCarthyite and HUAC witch hunts of the early Fifties tend to dismiss the Red menace movies of that period as garbage. But the finest films of that sort integrate the reigning paranoia with the harsh lighting and violent shadows characteristic of *film noir* and form a legitimate subcategory of the genre. Among these finest is *Pickup on South Street*, written and directed by Samuel Fuller (1912-1997), in which a small-time pickpocket (Richard Widmark) inadvertently lifts a top secret microfilm from a woman (Jean Peters) who's the former lover of a Red spy (Richard Kiley). Hounded alike by Commies, local cops and the FBI, Widmark's Skip McCoy is a genuine *noir* protagonist, and the patriotically typical storyline, with its lower-depths trio of pickpocket and prostitute and lady stoolpigeon (Thelma Ritter) fighting for the good old U.S. of A., is played out in vividly created Mean Streets settings, photographed by Joe MacDonald in extreme chiaroscuro.

99 RIVER STREET (World Films/United Artists, 1953)

Producer	Edward Small
Cinematographer	Franz Planer
Film Editor	Buddy Small
Music Score	Emil Newman & Arthur Lange
Screenplay	Robert Smith
Original Story	George Zuckerman
Director	Phil Karlson

Ernie Driscoll	John Payne
Linda James	Evelyn Keyes
Victor Rawlins	Brad Dexter
Stan Hogan	Frank Faylen
Pauline Driscoll	Peggie Castle
Christopher	Jay Adler
Mickey	Jack Lambert
Lloyd Morgan	Glenn Langan
Pop Durkee	Eddy Waller
Bud	John Day
Waldo Daggett	Ian Wolfe
Nat Finley	Peter Leeds
Director	William Tannen
Chuck	Gene Reynolds

Copyright Date: 11 Sep 1953 Running Time: 82 min.

Phil Karlson (1908-1985) began his directing career with "B" quickies, including some less-than-stellar Charlie Chan and Bowery Boys flicks, and ended with the powerful and ultra-violent *Walking Tall* (1973). In between he made a number of offtrail specimens of Fifties *noir*. The plot of *99 River Street* has its full share of standard elements: Ernie Driscoll (John Payne), a failed boxer trapped in a corroded marriage, becomes involved with aspiring actress Linda James (Evelyn Keyes), tries to help her out of a murder mess in which she thinks she's implicated, and finds himself accused of the murder of his greedy and sluttish wife (Peggie Castle). John Payne, who also starred in Karlson's *Kansas City Confidential* (1952) and *Hell's Island* (1955), makes an effective *noir* protagonist, and the director weaves through his mean-streets melodrama a most unusual subtext, shooting scenes as "real" which turn out to be "unreal" and vice versa, giving us a fine example of *noir* on a shoestring.

THE BIG HEAT (Columbia, 1953)

Producer	Robert Arthur
Cinematographer	Charles Lang
Film Editor	Charles Nelson
Music Director	Mischa Bakaleinikoff
Screenplay	Sydney Boehm
Source Novel	William P. McGivern, *The Big Heat* (1952)
Director	Fritz Lang
Dave Bannion	Glenn Ford
Debby Marsh	Gloria Grahame
Katie Bannion	Jocelyn Brando
Mike Lagana	Alexander Scourby
Vince Stone	Lee Marvin
Bertha Duncan	Jeanette Nolan
Tierney	Peter Whitney
Lt. Wilkes	Willis Bouchey
Gus Burke	Robert Burton
Larry Gordon	Adam Williams
Commissioner Higgins	Howard Wendell

Unbilled Bit Parts   Chris Alcaide, Phil Arnold, Linda Bennett, Charles Cane, Phil Chambers, John Close, Sid Clute, John Crawford, John Doucette, Kathryn Eames, Al Eben, Douglas Evans, Edith Evanson, Robert Forrest, Michael Granger, Jimmy Gray, Dorothy Green, Carolyn Jones, Byron Kane, Lyle Latell, Harry Lauter, Herbert Lytton, Mike Mahoney, Paul Maxey, Joe Mell, John Merton, Pat Miller, Bill Murphy, Ezelle Poule, Norma Randall, Ric Roman, Mike Ross, Dan Seymour, Ted Stanhope, William Vedder

Copyright Date: 1 Oct 1953   Running Time: 90 min.

Generally considered Fritz Lang's best American film of the Fifties, *The Big Heat* is built around some of the quintessential motifs of *noir* as tough cop Dave Bannion (Glenn Ford) goes outside the law and recruits a vigilante force of fellow World War II veterans to break the mob's grip on the city and avenge the murder of his wife. As usual in Fifties *noir*, the mob has corrupted everything. Its boss is a wealthy and respectable man (Alexander Scourby) who, like all leaders, has insulated himself from the butchery by which he prospers. A Don Siegel or Sam Fuller would have crammed this picture with brutal confrontations but Lang directs in a cool outsider's style, downplaying the violence—so that when it comes, as in the scene where Lee Marvin throws a pot of boiling coffee in Gloria Grahame's face, it's unforgettable—and making it clear to us that the avenging angel who fights fire with fire inevitably gets contaminated by the soot.

THE BIG COMBO (Security & Theodora/Allied Artists, 1955)

Producer	Sidney Harmon
Cinematographer	John Alton
Film Editor	Robert Eisen
Music Score	David Raksin
Screenplay	Philip Yordan
Director	Joseph H. Lewis
Leonard Diamond	Cornel Wilde
Mr. Brown	Richard Conte
McClure	Brian Donlevy
Susan Lowell	Jean Wallace
Peterson	Robert Middleton
Fante	Lee Van Cleef
Mingo	Earl Holliman
Alicia	Helen Walker
Sam Hill	Jay Adler
Dreyer	John Hoyt
Bettini	Ted De Corsia
Rita	Helene Stanton
Audubon	Roy Gordon
Doctor	Whit Bissell
Bennie Smith	Steve Mitchell
Young Detective	Baynes Barron
Lab Technician	James McCallion
Photo Technician	Tony Michaels
Malloy	Brian O'Hara
Nurse	Rita Gould
Detective	Bruce Sharpe
Hotel Clerk	Michael Mark
Mr. Jones	Philip Van Zandt
Miss Hartleby	Donna Drew

Copyright Date: 13 Feb 1955 Running Time: 89 min.

The last *noir* classic of director Joseph H. Lewis (1907-2000) brings the explosive action and perverse sexual undertones of his *Gun Crazy* (1949) into the sleazy urban ambience customary in Fifties *noir*. The city, like all cities in the genre, is controlled by the Mob or, as Lewis prefers to call it, the Combo. At the head of the table of corruption sits the respectable Mr. Brown (Richard Conte). The brutal lone-wolf cop Diamond (Cornel Wilde) sets out to take away from Brown not only the city but Susan (Jean Wallace), the woman by whom both men are obsessed. Lewis and the great cinematographer John Alton fill the film with harsh, brutally memorable images, climaxing with an airport shootout that, like those of Lewis' *Gun Crazy* and *A Lady Without Passport* (1950), takes place in a dank mist. *The Big Combo* is both a gem of Fifties *noir* and a powerful demonstration of the influence of Mickey Spillane on all sorts of pictures with which he had not the least connection.

KISS ME DEADLY (Parklane/United Artists, 1955)

Producer	Robert Aldrich
Cinematographer	Ernest Laszlo
Film Editor	Michael Luciano
Music Score	Frank DeVol
Screenplay	A.I. Bezzerides
Source Novel	Mickey Spillane, *Kiss Me Deadly* (1952)
Director	Robert Aldrich
Mike Hammer	Ralph Meeker
Dr. Soberin	Albert Dekker
Carl Evello	Paul Stewart
Eddie Yeager	Juano Hernandez
Pat	Wesley Addy
Velda	Maxine Cooper
Christina	Cloris Leachman
Gabrielle/Lily Carver	Gaby Rodgers
Friday	Marian Carr
Manager	Marjorie Bennett
Piker	Mort Marshall
Carmen Trivago	Fortunio Bonanova
Truck Driver	Strother Martin
Singer	Madi Comfort
Super	James McCallion
F.B.I. Man	Robert Cornthwaite
Mover	Silvio Minciotti
Nick	Nick Dennis
Radio Announcer	Ben Morris
Charlie Max	Jack Elam
Attacker	Paul Richards
Mrs. Super	Jesslyn Fax
F.B.I. Man	James Seay
Morgue Doctor	Percy Helton
Girl at Pool	Leigh Snowden
Sugar	Jack Lambert
Sammy	Jerry Zinneman
Unbilled Bit Parts	Eddie Beal, Art Loggins, Mara McAfee, Keith McConnell, Bob Sherman

Please Read Before the Lights Dim

Copyright Date: 20 Apr 1955 Running Time: 105 min.

Five classic crime novelists—Dashiell Hammett, Raymond Chandler, James M. Cain, W.R. Burnett and Cornell Woolrich—had a profound impact on the *film noir* of the 1940s. During the Fifties the only crime writer crucial to *noir* was Mickey Spillane (1918-2006), whose early novels like *I, The Jury* (1947) and *Vengeance Is Mine* (1950) and *One Lonely Night* (1951) made all the difference in the look and feel of Fifties *noir*. Several negligible movies were based on Spillane but only one classic, *Kiss Me Deadly*. Alone among the directors who adapted Spillane material, Robert Aldrich (1918-1983) recognized and portrayed Mike Hammer not as a hero but as a cheap sadistic lout. Although he kept many of the bare bones of Spillane's plot, his objective evocation of Hammer joins with a bizarrely menacing visual style and apocalyptic story elements (which weren't in the novel at all) and unforgettably offbeat subsidiary characters to create one of the finest examples of *film noir* ever.

THE KILLING (Harris-Kubrick/United Artists, 1956)

Producer	James B. Harris
Cinematographer	Lucien Ballard
Film Editor	Betty Steinberg
Music Score	Gerald Fried
Screenplay	Stanley Kubrick
Source Novel	Lionel White, *Clean Break* (1955)
Director	Stanley Kubrick
Johnny Clay	Sterling Hayden
Fay	Coleen Gray
Val Cannon	Vincent Edwards
Marvin Unger	Jay C. Flippen
Randy Kennan	Ted De Corsia
Sherry Peatty	Marie Windsor
George Peatty	Elisha Cook, Jr.
Mike O'Reilly	Joe Sawyer
Track Parking Attendant	James Edwards
Nikki Arcane	Timothy Carey
Maurice Oboukhoff	Kola Kwariani
Leo	Jay Adler
Joe Piano	Tito Vuolo
Ruthie O'Reilly	Dorothy Adams
Airline Clerk	Herbert Ellis
Mr. Grimes	James Griffith
Lady with Small Dog	Cecil Elliott
Tiny	Joseph Turkel
Brown	Steve Mitchell
Woman	Mary Carroll
Airline Clerk	William Benedict
Plainclothesman	Charles R. Cane
Plainclothesman	Robert B. Williams
Unbilled Bit Parts	Franklyn Farnum, John George, Art Gilmore, Sol Gorss, Harry Hines, Kenner G. Kemp, Hal J. Moore, Harvey Parry, Richard Reeves, Frank Richards

Copyright Date: 19 May 1956 Running Time: 83 min.

The first major feature directed by Stanley Kubrick (1928-1999) was based on a novel by Lionel White, who was well known in the

Fifties as a specialist in Big Caper fiction. But the film owes at least as much to John Huston's *The Asphalt Jungle* (1949), even to the point of using the same star, Sterling Hayden. Huston presented all the front-line criminals as good-hearted proletarians but Kubrick is more objective and unromantic about small-time crooks, casting Hayden as the mastermind of the big racetrack robbery (more or less the equivalent of Sam Jaffe's part in *The Asphalt Jungle*), and giving the parts of the accomplices to grotesques like Elisha Cook Jr. and wolf-faced Timothy Carey. The most unusual aspect of *The Killing* is the way Kubrick juggles the time sequence, showing us scenes completely out of chronological order yet so well organized, like the crime itself, that we are never in doubt about what's happening at any given moment or why. *Noir* novelist Jim Thompson is credited with additional dialogue for the film.

NIGHTFALL (Copa/Columbia, 1956)

Producer	Ted Richmond
Cinematographer	Burnett Guffey
Film Editor	William A. Lyon
Music Score	George Duning
Screenplay	Stirling Silliphant
Source Novel	David Goodis, *Nightfall* (1947)
Director	Jacques Tourneur
James Vanning	Aldo Ray
John	Brian Keith
Marie Gardner	Anne Bancroft
Laura Fraser	Jocelyn Brando
Ben Fraser	James Gregory
Dr. Edward Gurston	Frank Albertson
Red	Rudy Bond
Unbilled Bit Parts	Arline Anderson, Monty Ash, Maria Belmar, Orlando Beltran, Art Bucaro, Robert Cherry, George Cisar, Lillian Culver, Joan Fotre, Annabelle George, Pat Jones, Lillian Kassan, Betty Koch, Jane Lynn, Eddie McLean, Gene Roth, Walter Smith, Maya Van Horn, Winifred Waring

Copyright Date: 1 Dec 1956   Running Time: 80 min.

David Goodis (1917-1967) was the most powerful writer of *noir* fiction after Cornell Woolrich. His first suspense novel, *Dark Passage* (1946), was the basis of a superb 1947 *film noir* with Bogart and Bacall, and in the Fifties two more of his compulsively readable novels were filmed. Director Jacques Tourneur (1904-1977) had brought the *noir* motifs into lush outdoor settings in his classic *Out of the Past* (1947) and does it again in *Nightfall*, much of which was shot on location in the snow-covered Wyoming mountains. It's a visually beautiful and harshly violent picture, with movie tough guy Aldo Ray cast against type as the hunted innocent and all-American nice guy Brian Keith as a sadistic thug. About half a year after the release of this film came *The Burglar* (1957), also based on a Goodis novel.

Please Read Before the Lights Dim

THE WRONG MAN (Warner Bros., 1956)

Producer	Alfred Hitchcock
Cinematographer	Robert Burks
Film Editor	George Tomasini
Music Score	Bernard Herrmann
Screenplay	Maxwell Anderson & Angus MacPhail
Original Story	Maxwell Anderson
Director	Alfred Hitchcock
Manny Balestrero	Henry Fonda
Rose Balestrero	Vera Miles
Frank O'Connor	Anthony Quayle
Lt. Bowers	Harold J. Stone
Detective Matthews	Charles Cooper
Tomasini	John Heldabrand
Manny's Mother	Esther Minciotti
Ann James	Doreen Lang
Constance Willis	Laurinda Barrett
Betty Todd	Norma Connolly
Gene Conforti	Nehemiah Persoff
Olga Conforti	Lola d'Annunzio
Robert Balestrero	Kippy Campbell
Gregory Balestrero	Robert Essen
Daniell	Richard Robbins
Judge Groat	Dayton Lummis
Miss Dennerly	Peggy Webber

Unbilled Bit Parts   Charles Aidman, Sammy Armaro, Barry Atwater, Michael Ann Barrett, John C. Becker, Henry Beckman, Ray Bennett, Harold Berman, Mary Boylan, Paul Bryar, Ed Bryce, John Caler, Leonard Capone, Paul Carr, Gordon Clark, William Crane, Spencer Davis, Mel Dowd, Josef Draper, Richard Durham, Olga Fabian, Bonnie Franklin, Chris Gampel, Earl George, Charles J. Guiotta, Will Hare, Cherry Hardy, Rhodelle Heller, Bill Hudson, Anna Karen, Barbara Karen, Mike Keene, Dave Kelly, Werner Klemperer, Walter Kohler, William Le Massena, Alexander Lockwood, Maurice Manson, Donald May, Marc May, Don McGovern, John McKee, Dallas Midgette, Silvio Minciotti, Pat Morrow, Thomas J. Murphy, Daniel Ocko, Natalie Priest, Allan Ray, Frances

Reid, Maria Reid, Rossana San Marco, Penny Santon, Frank Schofield, Elizabeth Scott, Helen Shields, Otto Simanek, Olive Stacey, Harry Stanton, John Stephen, Clarence Straight, Dino Terranova, Emerson Treacy, John Truax, Don Turner, John Vivyan, Tuesday Weld, Maurice Wells

Copyright Date: 26 Jan 1957 Running Time: 105 min.

The Wrong Man is less of a household title than Hitchcock's other *noir* classics of the Fifties but not a bit less powerful than *Vertigo* or *Psycho*. Through a totally meaningless quirk of fate, innocent nightclub musician Manny Balestrero (Henry Fonda) is mistaken for a violent criminal, sucked into a merciless criminal justice system and, along with his wife Rose (Vera Miles), all but destroyed. In this picture Hitchcock treats us to no showpiece "suspense" sequences and only a bare minimum of memorable shots. The effect of the film is much like that of a documentary, intensifying the *noir* insight that any of us could be these trapped people, that the beams fall where they will and we live only while blind chance spares us. The bizarre Jesus Saves motif near the end is put in its place by the unbearable final scene in which it's made clear that he didn't save much, and the printed postscript over the last shot is a flat lie that made Hitchcock furious. A case can be made, however, that it's akin to the image of the automobile being raised from the swamp at the end of *Psycho*, and justified as a way of lifting us out of the desolation which is the picture's theme.

THE BURGLAR (Columbia, 1957)

Producer	Louis W. Kellman
Cinematographer	Don Malkames
Film Editor	Herta Horn
Music Score	Sol Kaplan
Screenplay	David Goodis
Source Novel	David Goodis, *The Burglar* (1953)
Director	Paul Wendkos
Nat Harbin	Dan Duryea
Gladden	Jayne Mansfield
Della	Martha Vickers
Baylock	Peter Capell
Dohmer	Mickey Shaughnessy
Police Captain	Wendell Phillips
Sister Sara	Phoebe Mackay
Charlie	Stewart Bradley
News Commentator	John Facenda
News Reporter	Frank Hall
Newsreel Narrator	Bob Wilson
State Trooper	Steve Allison
Harbin as a Child	Richard Emery
Gladden as a Child	Andrea McLaughlin
Unbilled Bit Parts	John Boyd, Ruth Burnat, Ned Carey, Sam Cresson, Sam Elber, George Kane, Frank Orrison, Michael Rich

Copyright Date: 1 Jun 1957 Running Time: 90 min.

Noir novelist David Goodis (1917-1967) wrote both the screenplay for *The Burglar* and the source novel, so it's no surprise that the film's dominant theme is the utter hopelessness of the human condition. The obvious visual style for this story of thieves' honor, police corruption, love-hate and grim death would have been the style of a naturalistic documentary. Director Paul Wendkos (1925-2009), who went on to a long and prolific career in TV, shot the picture on location in Philadelphia and Atlantic City but in a bravura, visually ostentatious style similar to that of Orson Welles. Dan Duryea turns in his last great *noir* performance as the doomed thief Harbin, with ripe-breasted Jayne Mansfield cast as the heist artist Gladden. If ever there were an obscure *film noir* that should be better known, it's this one.

Please Read Before the Lights Dim

TOUCH OF EVIL (Universal, 1958)

Producer	Albert Zugsmith
Cinematographer	Russell Metty
Film Editor	Virgil W. Vogel & Aaron Stell
Music Score	Henry Mancini
Screenplay	Orson Welles
Source Novel	Whit Masterson, *Badge of Evil* (1956)
Director	Orson Welles
Ramon Miguel Vargas	Charlton Heston
Susan Vargas	Janet Leigh
Hank Quinlan	Orson Welles
Pete Menzies	Joseph Calleia
Uncle Joe Grandi	Akim Tamiroff
Marcia Linnekar	Joanna Moore
Tanya	Marlene Dietrich
Nightclub Owner	Zsa Zsa Gabor
Adair	Ray Collins
Motel Manager	Dennis Weaver
Pancho	Valentin de Vargas
Schwartz	Mort Mills
Manolo Sanchez	Victor Millan
Risto	Lalo Rios
Pretty Boy	Michael Sargent
Blaine	Phil Harvey
Blonde	Joi Lansing
Gould	Harry Shannon
Unbilled Bit Parts	Joe Basulto, Yolanda Bojorquez, Eleanor Corado, Joseph Cotten, Domenick Delgarde, Jennie Dias, Mercedes McCambridge, Arlene McQuade, Ken Miller, Raymond Rodriguez, Wayne Taylor, Rusty Wescoatt, Keenan Wynn

Copyright Date: 15 Mar 1958 Running Time: 95 min.

Bravura visuals, socially conscious storyline, characters as grotesque as the chiaroscuro—these are the hallmarks of all the American features of Orson Welles (1915-1980) from his first, *Citizen Kane* (1941), to his last, *Touch of Evil*. The car-bombing sequence with which the film opens consists of a single shot, lasting over three minutes, and the investigation of that crime pits Mexican detective Mike Vargas (Charlton Heston) against Welles himself as Texas cop Hank Quinlan, the most vivid anti-policeman in all *film noir*. Grossly obese, oozing sadism and corruption, both psychotic and pathetic, Quinlan as portrayed by Welles is at once the true original and the evil twin of the best-known Noir Cop of them all, Dirty Harry. In the Eastwood movies we are never in doubt that Harry is right and all the liberals who oppose his kick-em-and-kill-em methods are fools and clowns. One would expect the liberal Welles to have made Quinlan just as indefensible as Eastwood and his collaborators make the civil lib types in the Harry series. Surprise! Despite the stereo-liberal good-guy team of the Latino cop and the Jewish prosecutor (Mort Mills), Welles organizes the film so that Quinlan comes across not just as (dare I say it?) a fully-fleshed human being but also as one whose illegal methods maybe, just maybe, make sense.

THE LINE-UP (Pajemar/Columbia, 1958)

Producer	Jaime del Valle
Cinematographer	Hal Mohr
Film Editor	Al Clark
Music Score	Mischa Bakaleinikoff
Screenplay	Stirling Silliphant
Director	Don Siegel
Dancer	Eli Wallach
Julian	Robert Keith
Inspector Ben Guthrie	Warner Anderson
Sandy McLain	Richard Jaeckel
Dorothy Bradshaw	Mary La Roche
Larry Warner	William Leslie
Inspector Al Quine	Emile Meyer
Inspector Fred Asher	Marshall Reed
Philip Dressler	Raymond Bailey
The Man	Vaughn Taylor
Cindy	Cheryl Callaway
Staples	Robert Bailey

Unbilled Bit Parts: Jack Carol, Chuck Courtney, Francis De Sales, George Eldredge, Kay English, Bert Holland, Bill Marsh, Junius Matthews, John Maxwell, Al Merin, Jack Moyles, Kathleen O'Malley, Dee Pollock, Clayton Post, Billy Snyder, Charles Stewart, Frank Tang

Copyright Date: 17 Jun 1958 Running Time 86 min.

The Lineup (CBS, 1954-60) was a TV police series that more or less tried to do with San Francisco settings what Jack Webb's *Dragnet* on NBC was doing in Los Angeles. Don Siegel, who had directed the pilot episode, was invited by Columbia to helm the feature based on the series, and the result was another *noir* classic, with a bare minimum of footage devoted to police routine and with the TV series star, Warner Anderson, reduced to third billing in the cast. The core of Siegel's picture is the pair of sociopaths (Eli Wallach and Robert Keith) who leave a trail of blood and terror across the Bay Area as they hunt for three misplaced parcels of heroin. The climactic auto chase along the incomplete elevated freeway is a masterpiece of its kind, its pure physical excitement undimmed by the thousands of canned auto chases we've seen all our lives on TV cop shows.

POETIC PUZZLEMENT

Like every other student of my generation, I had great gobs of poetry shoved down my throat in my English classes, but I never developed a fondness for it except for what I discovered on my own, like the hilarious verses of Ogden Nash. I did live a block from Howard Nemerov between 1980 and his death, and every so often a poem has figured in one of my stories or novels—for example the toad quotations from Shakespeare, Kipling and Karl Shapiro in "Toad Cop"—but these facts hardly qualify me as an authority on poetry. So it was rather odd that a few years ago I was offered a princely fee by the Poetry Foundation, which has an endowment in the megamillions, to write an essay for its website (www.poetryfoundation.org) on the links between poetry and crime fiction. But that piece went through more drafts than infant octuplets go through diapers, and a slew of interesting interfaces between poetry and mystery fiction wound up on the electronic cutting-room floor. This book gives me a chance to resurrect them.

~ ~ ~ ~ ~

What we know as private eye fiction began in the early 1920s when Dashiell Hammett's tales of the fat hard-bitten Continental Op began to appear in the pages of the pulp magazine *Black Mask*. With no formal education beyond high school and a background as a Pinkerton detective, Hammett (1894-1961) seems an improbable devotee of poetry. But between early PI tales he wrote a few poems, and two of them, cynical takes on love and women, were published in periodicals of the Twenties. He also wrote a few short stories touching on poetry and even created a poet as protagonist and first-person narrator. "The Figure of Incongruity" was written around 1925 (although not published until shortly before Hammett's death, when it appeared in the March 1961 issue of *Ellery Queen's Mystery Magazine* as "A Man Named Thin") and introduces 30-year-old Robin Thin, who works in the San Francisco private detective agency run by his father but much prefers composing sonnets and rondeaus for that versifiers' Valhalla *The Jongleur*. The first few paragraphs leave us in no doubt that Robin is a twit. "Papa was, though I may be deemed an undutiful son for saying it, in an abominable mood." "[I]f now and then I garble Papa's remarks in reporting them, it is not, I beg you to believe, because he is addicted to incoherencies, but simply because he frequently saw fit to sacrifice the amenities of speech to what he considered vigor of expression." Thin Senior ridicules his son's efforts as "Mother Goose rhymes" but recognizes that the kid is coming along as a detective. The story opens with Robin learning that the editor of *The Jongleur* is displeased with the final lines of his latest sonnet, "Fictitious Tears":

> And glisten there no less incongruously
> Than Christmas balls on deadly upas tree.

At this juncture Papa sends Robin out to investigate the robbery of a jewelry store in the heart of the city and in broad daylight. The scar-cheeked thief described in detail by witnesses ran out of the store and was seen to jump into a moving car at the nearby corner of Powell and O'Farrell, but Robin picks up on some subtle inconsistencies in the testimony and deduces that both thief and loot are close at hand. I won't explain why or how, but the solution inspires him to replace that rejected couplet with:

> And shining there, no less inaptly shone
> Than diamonds in a spinach garden sown.

The most recent appearance of this first-rate detective tale was in the Hammett collection *Nightmare Town* (Knopf, 1999).

~ ~ ~ ~ ~

During the pit of the Depression Hammett became rich and famous and the darling of the literati thanks to classic private eye novels like *Red Harvest* (1929) and *The Maltese Falcon* (1930). "Too Many Have Lived" (*American Magazine*, October 1932), one of only three short stories featuring *Falcon*'s immortal Sam Spade, is a tightly plotted tale about the murder of Eli Haven, a poet with underworld connections and a penchant for blackmail. Spade quotes one complete specimen of Haven's work:

> Too many have lived
> As we live
> For our lives to be
> Proof of our living.
> Too many have died
> As we die

> For their deaths to be
> Proof of our dying.

"I don't like blackmailers myself," Spade remarks ironically as the story ends. "I think Eli wrote a good epitaph for them—'Too many have lived.' " This tale too was recently revived in the *Nightmare Town* collection.

~ ~ ~ ~ ~

A few years after Hammett went silent, Raymond Chandler (1888-1959) and his protagonist Philip Marlowe took over as PI author and character number one. Born in Chicago but raised by his divorced mother in England, where he lived until 1912, Chandler as a young man contributed essays and poetry to periodicals like *The Westminster Review* and *The Academy*. "My first poem was composed at the age of nineteen, in the bathroom," he wrote his English publisher in 1950, "and was published in *Chambers' Journal*. I am fortunate in not possessing a copy." Two stanzas are printed in Frank MacShane's *The Life of Raymond Chandler* (1976) but I shall be merciful and quote only the first.

> When the evening sun is slanting,
> When the crickets raise their chanting,
> And the dewdrops lie a-twinkling on the grass,
> As I climb the pathway slowly,
> With a mien half proud, half lowly,
> O'er the ground your feet have trod I gently pass.

"The less said about Chandler's early poems the better . . ." MacShane writes, going on to call his 27 published contributions to the form "cloying and saccharine. Whether intended or not, they are conventional in the worst sense. They are full of sadly noble subjects and sentiments like death, fairyland, melancholy, art, and meditation . . . [P]oetry for Chandler was an escape from the reality of daily life. It was a world populated by knights and ladies who achieve happiness only in death." That verdict is seconded by the Raymond Chandler Web Site, according to which his 27 published poems "show little literary merit. The forms are fixed and rigid, usually in quatrains or sestets . . . The writing is abstract and distant, focusing on grand concepts such as art, love, beauty, and loss." His poems offer "a strongly Romantic conception of art as the most noble human pursuit and of the poet as a suffering, tormented recorder of life." Anyone not deterred by these critiques may check out the work for themselves in *Chandler Before Marlowe: Raymond Chandler's Early Prose and Poetry, 1908-1912* (1973) and in *The Raymond Chandler Papers* (2001).

In 1932, long after he returned to the U.S. and as he was about to launch his second and far more rewarding literary career in pulps like *Dime Detective* and *Black Mask*, Chandler worked on one final poem, never finished and never published until MacShane's biography. It's not only superior to his early poetry but, in MacShane's words, "thematically central to his fiction . . ."

> There are no countries as beautiful
> As the England I picture in the night hours
> Of this bright and dismal land
> Of my exile and dismay.
> There are no women as tender as this woman
> Whose cornflower-blue eyes look at me
> With the magic of frustration
> And the promise of an impossible paradise.

~ ~ ~ ~ ~

Chandler's first contribution to the PI genre was "Blackmailers Don't Shoot" (*Black Mask*, December 1933), of which critic Julian Symons (who was also a poet and a novelist and so much more) wrote: "[I]t is emblematically right that in this first story the detective should be named Mallory, echoing the *Morte d'Arthur*. His carapace of iron . . . conceals a quivering core, and . . . he is truly a knight errant." After several years of turning out pulp stories about variously named PIs, Chandler made the leap into hardcover and both popular and critical success with his first novels, *The Big Sleep* (1939) and *Farewell, My Lovely* (1940), where for the first time his knightly protagonist/narrator is named Philip Marlowe. Chandler never claimed that he named his character after the author of *Doctor Faustus* nor even after the narrator of Conrad's *Heart of Darkness*. The most likely source of the name was Marlowe House, one of the buildings at Dulwich, the English boarding school Chandler attended in his teens. But it's a curious coincidence that both his first PI and his best known have names just one letter different from those of two famous figures in English literary culture. The only reference to a poem I've found in Chandler takes place in *The Little Sister* (1949) when Marlowe is menaced by a woman with a gun. "Never the time and the place and the loved one all together," he remarks. Seeing that she doesn't comprehend, he adds: "Browning. The poet, not the automatic. I feel sure you'd prefer the automatic."

At the height of his success Chandler remained modest about his early ventures into poetry. Of the verses he wrote for *The Westminster Gazette*, he told his English publisher, "most of [them] now seem to be deplorable, but not all . . ." To one of the many women he corresponded with late in life he wrote: "I never claimed to be a poet, although as a young man I wrote quite a lot of verse . . . I suppose it was fair or it would not have been published, but that is as far as I could go."

~ ~ ~ ~ ~

As Chandler had taken Hammett's place in PI fiction, he himself was succeeded by Kenneth Millar (1915-1983), who usually wrote as Ross Macdonald. Millar was born in California but lived in Canada from childhood till his late twenties. His early years were miserable but he found escape by reading omnivorously: Edgar Wallace, the Tarzan books, *Oliver Twist* (with whose protagonist he closely identified). By a turn of events worthy of Dickens and described in Tom Nolan's *Ross Macdonald: A Biography* (1999), he was taken under the wing of a well-to-do aunt and wound up at St. John's, an Anglican boarding school in Winnipeg, where he made up his mind to become a writer himself. As a teen he wrote poetry for the literary magazines of the various prep schools he attended and later for the publications of Waterloo College and the University of Western Ontario. A short sample from 1934:

Thou sad-voiced sky-born Fury, thou storm-child of the North,
Swift arrow of His vengeance, what Bowman launched thee forth?

The day after graduating with high honors from UWO, 22-year-old Millar married Margaret Sturm, who as Margaret Millar was to launch her own career as a mystery novelist a few years earlier than her husband. The first general periodical to publish his work was *Saturday Night*, a Toronto-based weekly which paid him a penny a word for contributions like these:

If light were dark
And dark were light,
Moon a black hole

In the blaze of night,

A raven's wing
As bright as tin,
Then you, my love,
Would be darker than sin.

In 1941 Margaret Millar completed and quickly found an American publisher for her first whodunit, *The Invisible Worm*, its plot contributed by her husband and its title borrowed of course from William Blake. That same year Kenneth accepted a teaching fellowship at the University of Michigan and he and Margaret moved to Ann Arbor. There he took a course on "Fate and the Individual in European Literature" offered by the already world-famous young poet W.H. Auden, who loved mystery fiction and took it seriously, reinforcing his student's growing belief that the genre was not unworthy of one who loved literature. Several years later, after reading Auden's essay "The Guilty Vicarage" which sought to interpret detective fiction as Christian allegory, Millar remarked to an old school friend that his mentor simply didn't know what he was talking about.

Pearl Harbor interrupted Millar's budding dual career as author and academic but he managed to complete his first novel, *The Dark Tunnel* (1944), before enlisting in the Navy and serving as communications officer on a sub in the Pacific. Following his discharge he returned to Ann Arbor and, after a few other non-series crime novels, created private eye Lew Archer. *The Moving Target* (1949) and the other early Archer novels were heavily influenced by Chandler but in the later books in the series, beginning with *The Galton Case* (1959), he found his own unique voice. He continued to work towards his Ph.D. and wrote a dissertation on Coleridge, but once having switched definitively to crime fiction he seemed to lose most of his interest in poetry. Not quite all of it. In the mid-1950s, when the Millars were among the top authors who were moving their genre (in Julian Symons' phrase) "from the detective story to the crime novel," Kenneth wrote Margaret the following lines about their transformative task:

We had to pioneer a novel land
And track the darkling wood behind the eyes.
But who was Psyche? Who analysand?
Who is the hero of our mysteries?

The echo of the rhyme in the third and fourth lines of Blake's best known poem is surely not an accident.

~ ~ ~ ~ ~

After Chandler's death in 1959 there could be no doubt that Ross Macdonald had taken over as the living master of PI fiction, but no reign lasts forever. It's questionable whether any of the countless PI novelists who came after Macdonald were of the same literary stature as the Big Three, but among the most popular and prolific was Robert B. Parker (1932-2009), who also began as an academic. He earned his Ph.D. at Boston University with a dissertation on Hammett and Chandler—a subject that no university would have allowed him to choose even a decade earlier—and taught at Northeastern until 1979. Parker's earliest novels, like those of Macdonald, were indebted to the Philip Marlowe cycle, but he too soon found his own voice, rejecting the Hammett-Chandler tradition that the PI must be a loner and a have-not and reconfiguring his protagonist Spenser (deliberately but for no thematic reason named after the *Faerie Queene* poet) as a yuppie/foodie/bodybuilder in a more or less stable long-term relationship with one woman. Of his dozens of crime novels the one most likely to appeal to poetryphiles is *The Widening Gyre* (1983), which contains allusions to Tennyson, Arnold, Hopkins, Eliot, Frost, Stevens and, I am not making this up, Kris Kristofferson.

~ ~ ~ ~ ~

Agatha Christie is almost certainly the world's best-selling mystery writer, but she was also a published poet. One of her first books, published the year before *The Murder of Roger Ackroyd*, was a volume of verse called *The Road of Dreams* (London: Bles, 1925). Included in this collection is "In the Dispensary":

From the Borgias' time to the present day, their power
    has been proved and tried:
Monkshood blue, called aconite, and the deadly cyanide.
Here is sleep and solace and soothing of pain—
    courage and vigour new;
Here is menace and murder and sudden death—in these
    phials of green and blue.

Okay, so it's doggerel. But I didn't want every writer discussed in this section to be male.

~ ~ ~ ~ ~

In *The League of Frightened Men* (1935), the second of Rex Stout's Nero Wolfe novels, Wolfe's adversary is Paul Chapin, who was crippled and apparently emasculated in a fraternity hazing incident at Harvard in 1909 that went horribly wrong. A quarter century later Chapin has attained something of a literary reputation. As members of the group that maimed him begin dying off, the survivors receive anonymous poems that send them scurrying to Wolfe in fright. The first, following the apparently accidental death of a judge in a fall over a cliff, begins:

> Ye should have killed me, watched the last mean sigh
> Sneak through my nostril like a fugitive slave
> Slinking from bondage.
> Ye should have killed me.
> Ye killed the man,
> Ye should have killed me!

Wolfe, who admits that he "cannot qualify as an expert in prosody" but claims to be "not without an ear," calls the poem "verbose, bombastic, and decidedly spotty." Suspecting that a few lines were influenced by Edmund Spenser, he has Archie Goodwin pull down the collected works of that poet: "dark blue, tooled . . . A fine example of bookmaking . . . Printed of course in London, but bound in this city by a Swedish boy who will probably starve to death during the coming winter." The hunt for parallel passages fails but in any event, says Wolfe, "it was pleasant to meet Spenser again, even for so brief a nod." The second death, the apparent poison suicide of an art dealer, triggers a second poem:

> Two.
> Ye should have killed me.
> Two;
> And with no ready cliff, rocks waiting below
> To rub the soul out; . . .
> I found the time, the safe way to his throat . . .
> Ye should have killed me.

Then comes the mysterious vanishing of a Columbia psychology professor and yet another effusion:

> One. Two. Three.
> Ye cannot see what I see;
> His bloody head, his misery, his eyes . . .
> One. Two. Three.
> Ye should have killed me.

We occasionally find Wolfe savoring a volume of poetry but in none of the full-length or short novels is poetry as central as in this longest and perhaps finest exploit of the obese and infuriating genius of West Thirty-Fifth Street.

~ ~ ~ ~ ~

Fatal Descent (1939) was the only collaboration between two of the giants of the golden age of detective fiction, John Rhode and Carter Dickson (John Dickson Carr). Its plot seems to have been devised by both men but the writing is all Carr, a fact for which anyone who's read Rhode's dryasdust prose will thank whatever gods there be. Investigating the impossible murder of a publisher while alone in a descending elevator, Scotland Yard's Inspector Hornbeam takes time out to read a newspaper account of a speech by one of the suspects entitled "A Peak in Darien." The inspector is unversed (sorry, couldn't resist) in poetic allusion. "What's Darien?" he asks Dr. Horatio Glass. "I'm not sure," that brilliant amateur sleuth replies. "It's a place where you're supposed to stand silent and look at the Pacific. Why are you interested in all that guff, anyway?"

~ ~ ~ ~ ~

In the first edition of Cornell Woolrich's *The Bride Wore Black* (1940), each of the novel's five parts opens with a motto, whose respective sources are Rodgers & Hart, Guy de Maupassant, Cole Porter, and de Maupassant twice more. In the first paperback edition (Pocket Books pb #271, 1945), the first and third of these are dropped and replaced by lines attributed respectively to Poe and the social philosopher Herbert Spencer. The Poe couplet at the beginning of Part One reads as follows:

> How silent is the night—how clear and bright!
> I nothing hear, nor aught there is to hear me.

A few years ago an Italian author who is preparing an anthology of essays on Woolrich E-mailed me to ask if I knew the source of that couplet, which doesn't appear in any known poem of Poe's. Splitting the first line into its component parts and calling on trusty Google produced just one hit. According to www.authorspot.com/poetry the quoted matter comes from the first verse of "The Murderer", which is billed as an unpublished poem by Edger (sic) Allen (sic) Poe, rewritten (with many other misspellings) by one coyote103 and posted in 2007. But the lines I quoted above must have been published before 1945; otherwise whatever copyright-paranoid munchkin at Pocket Books substituted them for Woolrich's Rodgers & Hart quotation couldn't have known about them. A later E-mail from my Italian correspondent solved the problem. The quoted couplet is part of a 70-line fragment first published almost forty years after Poe's death in George W. Conklin's *Handy Manual* (Chicago, 1887). No scholar today believes they were written by Poe but the first three lines ("Ye glittering stars! How fair ye shine tonight/And O, thou beauteous moon! Thy fairy light/Is peeping thro' those iron bars so near me") are quoted in Thomas Ollive Mabbott's definitive edition of Poe's poetry (Harvard University Press, 1969). How Pocket Books came across them more than a quarter century earlier remains a mystery.

~ ~ ~ ~ ~

Of all the 20th-century poets who made significant contributions to the whodunit, the most distinguished was Cecil Day-Lewis (1904-1972). He is best known today as the father of actor Daniel Day-Lewis, but in his lifetime he served as England's Poet Laureate and, as Nicholas Blake, the creator of amateur sleuth Nigel Strangeways, he was considered one of the finest crime novelists of his generation. He combined both interests in the Strangeways novel *Head of a Traveler* (1949), which Thomas M. Leitch summarized superbly in his chapter on Blake for Volume 1 of *Mystery and Suspense Writers: The Literature of Crime, Detection and Espionage* (1998). "The central figure is the distinguished poet Robert Seaton, whose household is destroyed by the unexpected discovery of his brother Oswald's decapitated corpse . . . [T]he real interest of the novel is in its impassioned examination of the costs of poetry—the lengths to which poets and those who love them will go in pursuit of their craft." Anthony Boucher, reviewing the novel in his "Speaking of Crime" column (*Ellery Queen's Mystery Magazine*, August 1949), suggested that "Blake knows so much about his theme, the nature of poetic creation, that he never quite conveys it convincingly to the reader." But those with twin passions for poetry and mystery fiction may well find *Head of a Traveler* the single most rewarding whodunit they've ever read.

~ ~ ~ ~ ~

Vincent Cornier (1898-1976) was an English author of French descent who inherited a neat pile of money as a young man and thereafter devoted himself to writing short stories of fantasy and mystery. Very few of them were published in the U.S. until, after World War II, Fred Dannay discovered his work in old British periodicals and began reprinting occasional Cornier stories in *Ellery Queen's Mystery Magazine*. Eventually Cornier began to send Fred a few originals. When I reread most of his *EQMM* stories recently, the one I found most intriguing was "O Time, In Your Flight" (September 1951). Why? Because it contains a uniquely beautiful clue to the solution: one that is available only to readers who recognize the title's poetic source and remember the three words in the poem that come just before the five in the title! The question all but asks itself: Was it Cornier or Fred who put that brilliant title on the story? Their correspondence, which is archived at Columbia University, doesn't indicate what title was on the tale when Cornier submitted it, but we know that Fred had a penchant for changing the titles of many of the stories he published. Also I find no evidence in Cornier's other stories that he had any particular interest in poetry, while Fred not only collected rare first editions of poetry but also wrote some of his own. It seems to me far more likely than not that the stroke of genius was Fred's. If further proof is needed, there's indisputable evidence that Fred knew the poem in question: he used the first three words of the line, the words that provide the clue to Cornier's story, as the title for another tale by another author that appeared in *EQMM* a few years later! The author was Dorothy Salisbury Davis, the issue June 1954. If you don't know the three words that precede "O Time, in your flight," google the phrase and you'll quickly find what I've been hinting at. But if you haven't found and read Cornier's story first, it may be spoiled for you.

~ ~ ~ ~ ~

Richard Hugo (1923-1982) published his first volume of poetry in 1961 but remained unknown to the mystery-reading world until the appearance of James Crumley's *The Last Good Kiss* (1978), one of the finest private-eye novels ever. Crumley dedicated the book to his friend and fellow Montanan, whom he called the "grand old detective of the heart," and took its title from Hugo's "Degrees of Gray in Philipsburg" ("The last good kiss/You had was years ago"). Hugo made his own pass at the crime genre with *Death and the Good Life* (1981), whose protagonist Al Barnes is a cop, based in western Montana but stopping over in Portland to look into the one ax murder that a recently apprehended serial killer didn't commit. Some cop! Overwhelmingly gentle, optimistic about human nature, feeling guilty for the world's woes, a klutz at police procedure (his idea of a Miranda warning being "You're under arrest. You know your rights because you're rich"), Barnes is *de facto* a variant of Ross Macdonald's Lew Archer, a PI investigating a crime of the present with deep psychological roots in the past. Hugo's prose is less colorful than Crumley's and his plotting more complex, but he shares his friend's genius for creating softly quirky incidental characters, like the tough Homicide captain and the wily criminal-defense lawyer who on the side are both published poets. If he hadn't died the year after his first novel came out he would surely have written more, with Barnes reconfigured as the Archeresque PI that he is in all but official title in *Death and the Good Life*. For those who want to check out Hugo's poetry, perhaps the best starting point is the posthumously published collection *Making Certain It Goes On* (1984).

~ ~ ~ ~ ~

What the young Hemingway was to the Lost Generation, Richard Brautigan (1935-1984) was to the counterculture of the Vietnam era. Both men ended up shooting themselves in the head. After several poetry collections and novels came Brautigan's *Dreaming of Babylon* (1977), whose protagonist is a porn-peddling sleazeball PI named C. Card who operates out of a San Francisco phone booth in 1942, a man so poor he can't even afford bullets for his gun. Amid his fantasies of being the Sam Spade of ancient Babylon he's hired to steal a body from the morgue and winds up in the soup: an exotic slumgullion indeed. Most traditionalists don't care for this one, and with reason, since it's less a PI novel than a literary experiment that takes off from Hammett and Chandler like a rocket from its launching pad.

~ ~ ~ ~ ~

Stephen Dobyns (1941-) had already published four volumes of poetry when in *Saratoga Longshot* (1976) he introduced PI Charlie Bradshaw. Critic George Grella has described Bradshaw as both a "lovable bumbler" and a man of "unsensational kindness and decency." Poor Charlie is only marginally successful at his job and, to make ends meet, often takes on temporary gigs like delivering milk or managing a hotel in the slow season. Over the past 35 years Dobyns has turned out ten Bradshaw novels, all with Saratoga in their titles, sandwiched between mainstream fiction and collections of poetry.

~ ~ ~ ~ ~

James Sallis (1944-), whose huge output includes poetry, criticism, anthologies, translations from French literature and books on the jazz guitar, stepped into the PI arena with *The Long-Legged Fly* (1992), first of six novels he now describes as one long story. In a non-linear style which (like Brautigan's) may be too "literary" for PI traditionalists, Sallis explores the world of Lew Griffin, a black man who has led three lives: alcoholic New Orleans street thug, sober professor of French literature, and offbeat private detective. The series came to an irrevocable end in *Ghost of a Flea* (2000). "I'd truly be surprised if many fans of my crime fiction turned to the poetry," Sallis has said. But much of it is easily accessible on the Web and well worth sampling.

~ ~ ~ ~ ~

After making his name as a poet, Paul Auster (1947-) found himself desperately short of what all poets need more than inspiration: money. The result was *Squeeze Play* (1982, as by Paul Benjamin), his first novel and the sole recorded case of baseball-loving New York PI Max Klein, whose client is a one-legged ex-ballplayer with eyes on a U.S. Senate seat and death threats in his mail. The first edition of this paperback quickie earned Auster a piddling $900 but copies have become highly collectible (and pricey) since the postmodern metaphysical crime novels known as the New York Trilogy (1985-87) put him on the literary map.

MEDIA

POINT BLANK

In August and September of 1961, very early in what was to prove a meteoric mystery-writing career, Donald E. Westlake wrote a novel which he provisionally entitled *The Hunter*. The book dealt with a professional thief who had been betrayed by his wife and some others over the proceeds of a robbery and who was determined to get even and recover the loot for himself. Westlake called this character Parker but wrote the book at such white heat that he forgot to give the thief a first name until he was halfway through, and by then he couldn't find a graceful way to insert a first name. At the end of the book Parker had gotten his revenge but was in the hands of the police.

Bucklin Moon, then an editor at Pocket Books, liked the manuscript but wanted Westlake to let Parker get away at the end so that he could become the protagonist of future novels. Westlake made the change and *The Hunter* was published by Pocket Books very late in 1962 under the pen name of Richard Stark.

Paperback originals had long been considered unworthy of notice by most reviewers of mystery fiction. This snobbishness was not shared by Anthony Boucher (1911-1968), conductor of the Criminals at Large column in the *New York Times Book Review*, but unfortunately *The Hunter* came out during the newspaper strike of late 1962 and early 1963 which shut down the *Times* for four months. Nevertheless, in his second Criminals at Large column after the strike (April 14, 1963) Boucher reviewed *The Hunter*, describing it as "a harsh and frightening story of criminal warfare and vengeance . . . written with economy, understatement and a deadly amoral objectivity—a remarkable addition to the list of shockers that the French call *romans noirs*."

Four years later the novel was very freely transformed into an equally harsh and frightening film, directed in a style completely at odds with Westlake's Hammett-like simplicity of language, and constituting a remarkable addition to the list of American movies that first the French and now the world call *film noir*.

Point Blank is a film full of dissonances, ambiguities, fragmentations. Its people have no values or emotions, no past to remember, no future to hope for and a jagged-edged present. In many respects, as some critics complained, it's an anti-human film, a creation of ice and stone with no trace of compassion or hope. But it's also a triumph of bleak cinematic vision on the part of its director, London-born John Boorman (1933-). Prior to *Point Blank* Boorman's only fiction film had been *Having a Wild Weekend* (1965), a little-noticed but very personal vest-pocket variation on the Beatles' and Richard Lester's *A Hard Day's Night*. In the decades since then Boorman has directed a number of fine films including *Deliverance* (1972), *Zardoz* (1974), *The Emerald Forest* (1985), *Hope and Glory* (1987), and *The General* (1998).

Boorman begins *Point Blank* with a series of Chinese puzzle boxes of consciousness. Walker (Lee Marvin), left for dead, is lying in a cell on deserted Alcatraz, thinking of how he was shot by Mal Reese (John Vernon); then he escapes; then we see him a year later on a sightseeing boat that passes the prison island, thinking of himself dying and thinking. With economy, visual brilliance and minimal dialogue Boorman has given us a viewpoint and a background, but now he proceeds to puzzle us with an enigmatic conversation between Walker and the godlike Yost (Keenan Wynn). We never learn how Yost found out that Walker was alive, or knew how to contact him, or came to choose as their rendezvous a boat that goes past the place where Walker was betrayed; until the end of the film neither we nor Walker even know who Yost is. This is not a movie for rationalists. It's enough for Boorman's purposes that we know Yost will be behind the scenes as Walker tears up the Organization, to whose good graces Walker's ex-partner Mal Reese returned thanks to the $94,000 Mal took from Walker. Yost's first service to Walker is to give him the present address of his wife Lynne (Sharon Acker), who had set him up for Mal's bullets.

Walker is next seen pounding through an endless corridor, at once brute fact and a fantasy of fear in Lynne Walker's mind that her husband is coming after her. The image accompanies her as she walks trancelike through her daily round while the harsh reality comes nearer. In a frenzied moment when Walker breaks into her house and empties his gun into her mattress, dream and reality become one. The burst of violence clears the air and leads to a quietly terrifying dialogue between Walker and Lynne, as emotionless and ritualistic and antiphonal as a solemn high mass. Through a flashback sequence we learn a bit more about the two, but as to how the longshoreman of the flashback became the skilled professional thief of the Alcatraz hijack there is no hint of an explanation. These people, drained of love and fear, capable only of hate, their past unconnected with their present which is a mess of unrelated fragments, may be Boorman's images of human nature.

The next morning Walker discovers that Lynne has killed herself during the night, and the "wake sequence" that follows is perhaps the most puzzling in the film. Stephen Farber in *Film Quarterly* (Winter 1968-69) wrote that after three viewings the sequence was still not quite clear to him.

> "After Walker . . . finds his wife dead and slips his ring onto her finger, he walks to the window of the living room, looks out and sees Yost . . . When Walker walks back into his wife's bedroom, her body is gone. He drops one of the bottles on her vanity table, and the camera moves in close on the spilt liquid; . . . now the bed is stripped, and all of the furniture of the living room has vanished. Walker sits down in a corner of the empty living room and recalls the moment of his betrayal on Alcatraz. The sound of the gunshot in the subliminal flashback becomes the sound of a doorbell, and Walker goes to answer the door of his wife's apartment. But the living room is now furnished exactly as it was when he arrived."

After seeing the film three times myself I found I agreed with Farber's tentative judgment: "Perhaps the stripping of the apartment is to be taken as only a fantasy, a visualization of Walker's forlorn state of mind." A letter Boorman wrote to me early in 1970 explains more fully what he was trying to do.

> "The oils and lotions represent the life-essence of Lynne draining away and the vestiges of human feeling ebbing away from Walker. He re-enters the room which is now barren—like his marriage. The room has become the prison cell that he now permanently inhabits. You may be interested in how the scene evolved. The book [Westlake's *The Hunter*] spoke of him waiting out three days in the apartment, a wake or meditation. We wanted to render this cinematically. [Alexander] Jacobs [one of the film's three screenwriters] had the idea of Walker slowly and systemati-

cally destroying everything in the apartment. But this seemed too heavy-handed and I decided to show Walker's mental disruption in terms of fractured time—forward/back/present. By the time I started shooting I had gone a step further by discarding rational progression and using each setting throughout the film boldly and primarily to externalise the mental state of this incommunicative man. Seen in this light, I think the apartment sequence become clearer."

In *The Hunter* Parker had taken Lynne's body out to the park, mutilated her face so it wouldn't be identified, then returned to her apartment and holed up there for three days. Boorman was not at all interested in the mechanics of moving a dead body and was able to achieve the results he wanted in this part of the film by fragmenting time, discarding rationality, and using something which he did not mention in his letter and for which there is no equivalent in Westlake's novel: the figure of Yost. The godlike aspect of this character, first suggested on the sightseeing boat, comes further into focus at the end of the wake sequence as he nods approvingly upward at Walker from the street, seemingly assuring him that everything will be taken care of. If one insists on asking what happened to Lynne's body, this is all the answer there is.

The sequence ends with the ringing doorbell and the arrival of the messenger with the monthly payoff for Lynne. Walker forces the messenger (John McMurtry) to name the source of the payoff, Big John Stedman (Michael Strong). As Walker arrives at Stedman's auto sales lot, Big John and an assistant are maneuvering with equal effort to sell a car to a swinging chick in a low-cut mod outfit (Susan Holloway) and to peer at her breasts. Walker manages to get Stedman into a car for a demonstration ride, then proceeds to demolish the auto and put a few dents in Stedman while Big John's "Love My Guarantees" commercial blares from the car radio.

What Stedman tells him leads Walker to the mixed-media club and the most savage scene in the film, the assault in the men's room, with the brutal attack counterpointed by the screaming singer, whirling lights, and hallucinatory images and sounds from the other side of the curtain. From the club Walker staggers to the home of Lynne's sister Chris (Angie Dickinson) who ostensibly owns the club, and in their quiet bedside dialogue we learn how their milieu is controlled by the Organization, which runs the club and Stedman's car lot, almost runs Chris, and has destroyed the man she loved. Only at the end of the film, however, will we see just how complete is the Organization's control. Chris decides—but it's not really a decision, just something she does for no adequate reason and with no discernible awareness that it means a change in her life—to help Walker nail Mal Reese.

Reese meanwhile has become aware, through the death of Lynne and the report of the battered Stedman, that Walker is alive and angry. On the advice of Carter, his superior in the Organization, Reese holes up in a penthouse at the Huntley Towers, a sumptuous apartment building owned by the Organization and now surrounded by a small army of guards waiting for Walker to show himself. Walker's strategy to get into the building is based on his having learned from Stedman that Mal Reese wants very badly to sleep with Chris, just as the year before he had desired her sister Lynne. Walker tells Chris to get herself invited up to the penthouse for a night in bed with the man who, as she had earlier told Walker, "makes my flesh crawl," and Chris casually consents.

The way Walker gets past or rid of the guards on the staircase leading up to the penthouse and overpowers the second set of guards on the roof is presented in a series of disconnected fragments that have never been clear to me. Boorman's long letter once again explains what has happened in the sequence and why.

> "As Chris and Walker case [the building] they establish that there are two rooftop penthouses, one reached by the outside elevator and one by the inside elevator. Walker gets into the inner elevator by distracting the guards. We next see him inside the second empty penthouse looking across at Reese and Chris in the other. The roof guards are leaning over the parapet also distracted by the police opposite. After cutting inside Reese's room, we next return to the roof where Walker has bound the guards and is disposing of their guns. I didn't want to spend footage on him hitting them on the head and tying them up. My theory is that the audience fills in these kinds of actions which they are intensely familiar with from hundreds of similar films—in other words, I jump over the clichés. Also it would have been a violent climax in a sequence which is smooth and dream-like. I

could allow nothing to impinge on the form and rhythm of the movie which was its very existence."

Walker enters the apartment via the sliding door left unlocked by Chris, separates Chris and Reese from their "love" making at gunpoint, and forces out of Reese the names of the three heads of the Organization: Carter, Brewster, Fairfax. Since Reese had used the Alcatraz loot to buy his way back into the Organization, Walker has decided that it owes him the $94,000. At the end of the scene Reese topples naked off the roof and into the stream of traffic two dozen or so stories below. Amid the crowd milling and screaming around the accident we see Yost, knowing, self-confident and supremely satisfied.

Walker's next target is the urbane executive Frederick Carter (Lloyd Bochner) and his approach is "If you don't pay me, I will kill you." The Carter episode's background of corporate conglomerates and ultra-modern directors' suites clarifies a theme that till now was merely implicit in the far-flung properties of the Organization. Its business is business. Free enterprise is not a front, it is the Organization itself. The assassin on the bridge (James Sikking), who casually kills two men with his telescopic rifle in full view of hundreds of passing motorists and then calmly returns his weapon to its case and blends into the stream of traffic, carries the theme even further, for we in those other cars know about and consent to the Organization's atrocities and the casual killers programmed into the system blend effortlessly into our milieu because they and we are one. At the end of the storm-drain sequence Carter and Stedman are dead and Walker is the proud possessor of a parcel full of blank paper rectangles.

The next man he tries to get the money from is Brewster (Carroll O'Connor a few years before he became Archie Bunker). The Brewster episode is set in the world of the Organization man at play, a luxury ranch complete with public address system, home Muzak and automated breakfasts. Yost takes Walker to the house and lets him know when Brewster is due there. The Organization having meanwhile demolished Chris's apartment, Walker takes her to the house with him. Chris begins the evening by physically attacking Walker, to which he reacts like a stone statue, and ends in bed with him, where from the little Boorman shows us he seems equally unmoved. The robotic sumptuousness of the ranch forms an ideal setting for the nonrelationship between the man with no first name and the woman with no last.

Next morning Brewster arrives at the airport and is accosted by the bridge sharpshooter, looking for someone to pay him. Brewster declines and suggests mockingly that maybe Fairfax would pay him. When Brewster reaches the ranchhouse and falls into Walker's hands, he protests that he can't pay Walker himself since in this age of checks and credit cards he never carries more than a few dollars in cash. Fairfax, the Organization's accountant, the man who writes the checks, is reached on the phone but refuses to send any money, leaving Brewster to Walker's tender mercies. Brewster saves himself by remembering that one Organization activity still involves large sums of cash—the Alcatraz run, the same operation that Walker and Reese originally hijacked although since that time it has become an Organization property.

So the circle completes itself and we return to Alcatraz where the film began. It is night, and a helicopter descends into the prison yard. Walker merges into the shadows while Brewster goes out into the yard to pick up the money. A shot, and Brewster falls, and two men emerge from the shadows. One is the sharpshooter from the bridge. The other is Fairfax, who has indeed paid the gunman, and we see with Walker that Fairfax is the man we have known as Yost.

How did he know that Brewster would take Walker to the Alcatraz drop before Walker could shoot him? Where has Chris gone between the ranch and Alcatraz scenes? Once again such matters are irrelevant to Boorman. The point of this final scene is Walker's realization that in every step he has taken as the ruthless lone-wolf individualist against the equally amoral bureaucracy he has been a pawn of that bureaucracy's top echelon. Fairfax has used him to eliminate rivals for supreme power in the Organization. He who lashes out at the system is just as trapped by it as he who does nothing. At the end of Boorman's earlier film *Having a Wild Weekend* the lovers learned that their island was linked at low tide to the corrupt mainland they had been trying to escape. The island and the protagonist's frustration reappear in *Point Blank*, reinforced by the fact that Walker is as evil as his enemies and that having learned the truth he does nothing.

In the script as originally written by Alexander Jacobs, Walker was nowhere near so passive. On learning the truth he

"becomes absolutely incensed, and he advances upon Yost who has a gun, and Yost is suddenly terrified by this mad force, because Walker is now completely insane. And

Walker just advanced upon him—he's going to kill him with his bare hands, a complete animal, he's frothing at the mouth. And Yost shoots him three times and the three bullets miss. Yost actually cannot shoot this force. He tries, his hands shake, and he suddenly realizes his age; suddenly his age sinks through him like a flood, like a great stone sucking him under, and he's a completely old man, and he steps backward and falls off the parapet and dies. And Walker comes to at the edge of the parapet, and shaken and quivering is led away by the girl out into the world again."

Boorman revised the ending radically to conform to his own concept of the film. Fairfax/Yost, shouting into the darkness, offers Walker a top slot in the Organization; Walker in outraged and frustrated silence blends into the deep shadows of the prison; Yost signals for the helicopter to pick him up. Walker has gained the $94,000 which lies in the prison yard waiting for him but has lost the illusion that he was in control of his own life. Point blank indeed. As Boorman put it in his letter to me, "Brutal predatory faceless forces crush the individual. The worst of it is that if he fights back, there is nothing he can grasp by the throat. He is left clutching a handful of smog."

All this of course is worlds removed from the simply told naturalistic crime novel that Donald Westlake had written back in 1961. And considering how many novelists have damned the movies for mauling and distorting their work, you might suppose that Westlake would not have been too happy with *Point Blank*. But in 1970, when I met him for the first but far from the last time, he told me he had liked the film very much. Truly he was a rare bird among writers and also a moviegoer of excellent taste.

BERNARD HERRMANN

My parents had little interest in either movies or music but they bought their first TV set around 1952, and that 12½-inch screen exposed me to both those worlds at the tender age of nine. My first experience of great music was in the form of the scores for cliffhanger serials like *Flash Gordon* and TV series like *Captain Video* and *The Lone Ranger*. Little did I know at the time that I was listening to Liszt, Wagner and Tchaikovsky! My first experience of great music written directly for the screen came when I was around 14 and spent many a Friday and Saturday evening watching CBS series like *Perry Mason, Have Gun Will Travel, Rawhide*, and *The Twilight Zone*. Little did I know at the time that I was listening to Bernard Herrmann (1911-1975), who wasn't even listed in the credit crawls of the countless episodes of those superb series. More precisely, he was credited as composer of the score for *Have Gun's* debut episode, but with his name misspelled. Even had I seen his name several times a weekend as by rights I should have, it would have meant nothing to me. Discovering him by name didn't come until several years later, when I had become entranced by classic Alfred Hitchcock films like *Vertigo* and *Psycho*—not only the films but the haunting scores, which of course Herrmann had composed. By the time I finished my education I should have had enough musical savvy to recognize the unique Herrmann sound whenever I heard it, but I was well into adulthood before I learned that much of the TV music of my formative years came from the man who had scored Hitchcock's greatest hits.

All this is by way of introduction to *Bernard Herrmann: The CBS Years*, a 2-CD set released late in 2003 by the Belgium-based Prometheus label and already a scarce item. I had to turn handstands to get my copy, but the hassle was well worth it. Listen to that music—some of it written in the form of scores for specific episodes, some of it as "suites" written for the CBS Music Library and later "tracked" into episodes by editors—and you'll understand part of the reason why the first seasons of *Raw-

hide and *Have Gun* and *The Twilight Zone* remain so green in the memories of those who grew up on them.

You'll also understand why the early *Perry Mason* segments, when offered on video by Columbia House a few years ago, were touted as having been shot "in the *film noir* style"—a ridiculous claim but one that almost makes intuitive sense if you know that the *Mason* background themes came from the same pen that had scored *Vertigo* and *Psycho*, and earlier noirs like *On Dangerous Ground*, and that spiritual grandfather of so much *film noir, Citizen Kane*. No one does ominous like Herrmann does ominous. Much of the remaining music for the early *Mason* episodes was composed by René Garriguenc (1908-1998), whose sound, when he wanted it to be, was so much like Herrmann's that even experts are sometimes fooled. The first several minutes of "The Case of the Restless Redhead" (September 21, 1957), the earliest broadcast *Mason* episode, are especially rich in Herrmann/Garriguenc themes, as are several sequences in "The Case of the Nervous Accomplice" (October 5, 1957).

My favorite example of the music's contribution comes at the climax of "The Case of the Sulky Girl" (October 19, 1957). Cross-examining a crucial witness against his innocent client, Mason approaches, hands him a set of flash cards and asks him to read from them. Chord. "The quick brown fox jumps over the lazy dog." Mason takes a few steps back. Chord. "The early bird catches the worm." Mason, stepping further back: "Louder, please, Mr. Graves." Chord. "A bird in the hand is worth two in the bush." Mason steps even further back. Chord. "In a democracy all men are created equal." Mason, shouting: "What was that? I can't hear you, Mr. Graves!" He repeats the line. Chord. He turns to the next card. "As the twig is bent, so grows the tree." Mason: "Louder, please!" Chord. "A stitch in time saves nine." Mason, now at the courtroom door: "The next card!" The witness starts to read, then stops. Music floods the soundtrack from this point on. "GO ON, MR. GRAVES!" "Crinston, I want Graves to go with you." "Read it again, Mr. Graves. LOUDER, MR. GRAVES! GO ON!" "CRINSTON, I WANT GRAVES TO GO WITH YOU!" That is all Mason needs to break down the witness and expose the plot to frame his client. Thanks in part to the music, but also of course to director Christian Nyby and scriptwriter Harold Swanton, it's the most dramatic climax in any episode of the *Mason* series, and nothing at all like the denouement in Erle Stanley Gardner's 1933 novel of the same name.

Soon after finding the *CBS Years* set, I typed Herrmann's name into ever-faithful Google and was rewarded with two discoveries: a Bernard Herrmann Society with its own website, and an excellent Herrmann biography by Steven C. Smith (*A Heart at Fire's Center: The Life and Music of Bernard Herrmann*, University of California Press 1991) which taught me much about the composer that I had never dreamed of. Let me quote a few passages and then, in the best Ellery Queen manner, challenge you to spot the connection I made.

"Explosive, insecure, paranoiac, Herrmann was, as many observed, his own worst enemy." (1)

"Herrmann's life was an ongoing battle with demons . . ." (3)

"[He had] a lifelong fascination with—and fear of—death, a subject Herrmann . . . studied obsessively in his art." (3)

"[His] vision of life . . . recognized both the beauty and horror in the human condition . . . [He] excelled in capturing the psychological bond between love and anxiety." (4)

"[He was] a lost child who wanted affection desperately . . . [E]verything about him said, 'Love me, please.' Yet his behavior drove people away, the very people he wanted to love him." (204)

"[His] favorite dramatic themes [were] romantic obsession, isolation, and the ultimate release of death." (219)

Sound familiar? These passages, and countless more in Smith's biography, describe another man precisely as well as they describe Herrmann. A man whom I've called the Hitchcock of the written word and the director's spiritual brother. A man who like Herrmann was born and raised in New York City and had Jewish roots that were meaningless to him and who, like Herrmann, died at age 64. I refer, as if you hadn't guessed by now, to Cornell Woolrich. We don't ordinarily think of an author having any special affinity with a composer, and no one would dream of trying to identify most crime-suspense novelists with particular composers. But if you've read enough Woolrich and heard enough Herrmann, I bet you will also hear the CLICK in your head just as I did. Woolrich-Hitchcock, Hitchcock-Herrmann, Herrmann-Woolrich. Like Jules and Jim and Catherine in Truffaut's film: round and round, together bound.

Francis M. Nevins

ANTHONY BOUCHER ON RADIO'S HOLMES

As all mysteryphiles know, "Ellery Queen" was both the joint byline of first cousins Frederic Dannay (1905-1982) and Manfred B. Lee (1905-1970) and the brilliant sleuth who starred in most of their mysteries. It's also well known that, for all but the first years of their long joint career, Fred's function was to devise lengthy plot synopses which Manny would flesh out to novel or story length. This was their division of labor when the *Ellery Queen* radio series debuted on CBS in the summer of 1939. What was not known outside the inner circle was that, after his first wife died of cancer in 1945, Fred was so overwhelmed with raising their two small children and keeping *Ellery Queen's Mystery Magazine* afloat that he simply couldn't continue coming up with new plots. After a few false starts, the writer chosen to take over much of Fred's function on the series was Anthony Boucher (1911-1968). Since Tony lived in Berkeley, California and Manny on the East Coast, the arrangement required correspondence between them on almost a daily basis. That correspondence, which rivals *Gone with the Wind* in word count, is preserved at Indiana University's Lilly Library. I've made several trips to Bloomington to immerse myself in those letters. Some of them are close to indecipherable since they deal with the plot minutiae of radio dramas that have apparently ceased to exist in audio form. But the rest! Working at opposite ends of the country and under wartime and immediate post-war traveling conditions, Tony and Manny almost never met in person. But from their correspondence alone the devout Catholic and the agnostic Jew grew to be closer than brothers, and their letters range all over the map, from the health problems of their children to Hiroshima and the Cold War and anti-Semitism. Manny's letters tend to be much longer and more irascible and clearly he was using them to vent. His rants about the confederacy of dunces he had to deal with in the broadcasting world offer some remarkable insights into the medium—as long as one keeps in mind that, being a classic type A personality and a past master at getting hot under the collar, he may not have been the most objective witness in the world.

During much of his time collaborating with Manny, Boucher was also writing scripts for the *Sherlock Holmes* radio series, which between 1939 and 1946 starred Basil Rathbone and Nigel Bruce, the Holmes and Watson of Universal's movie series. "Compared to EQ, Holmes scripts practically write themselves," he told Manny in one letter (September 13, 1945), "and the EQ occupies by far the major portion of my working week . . . You have no idea of the number of ideas that I worked on for days only to reject because I discovered an ineradicable flaw that would exasperate you . . ."

As if to reassure Manny that he wasn't the only man in radio who was surrounded by jerks, Boucher in his letters often recounted his travails with the *Holmes* program. "On Holmes, either my collaborator [Denis Green] or I am—is—I hate that kind of sentence—one of us is present at every rehearsal-and-broadcast. And a good thing we find: not only directors but star actors can get the damndest ideas they have to be gently talked out of." (January 28, 1945) "We do at least have a firstrate man at the control board; but our sound technicians are two of the clumsiest louts that ever held a union card and all the things about time for commercials and cutting dialog to the bone—God does all that happen regularly to us. Especially since the sponsor switched announcers on us because the new one reads slower!" (July 5, 1945)

But these problems were as nothing compared with what happened at the beginning of the 1946-47 season, when Rathbone left the series for the Broadway stage and was replaced by Tom Conway. "The new producer on the show . . . is a pretentious and arrogant boor with a great deal of very real talent for production and writing—in some ways the ablest (and also the most offensive) man I have known in radio. He is convinced that only he knows anything about Holmes . . . He is bent on reducing Holmes to the simple formula of heavy melodrama and heavier low comedy that has driven Holmes enthusiasts screaming from their radios and theaters. And he assumes automatically that his duties as producer include replotting and rewriting of all scripts . . ." (October 14, 1946) "My favorite enemy, . . . with his constant miscasting, his incredibly inept music, and his campaign of forcing me [and Denis Green] off and replacing us by astonishing scripts from his ex-wife and a protégé, has succeeded finally in driving Holmes off the air . . . I don't know what this will mean. The director will try to argue that this is all simply due to Rathbone's absence. But if [he] is kept on the show, . . . I'm pretty certain to be entirely off Holmes in the fall." (June 30, 1947) "Did you read in the trades what's happened to Holmes? It's been sold to a cheap NY outfit, to be an extreme low-budget show—cheap production, no actors over scale (including Holmes & Watson), scripts for pennies—and $1,000 a week to Denis PS Conan Doyle [who was Sir Arthur's son and one of his literary executors]." (July 25, 1947) Taking over the parts of Holmes and Watson were the long-forgotten John Stanley and Alfred Shirley. "I'm definitely out on Holmes—not even a hope of some income from repeats . . . I think this may be the most severe fatality Holmes has suffered since the Reichenbach Falls—but then he survived even that . . ." (August 12, 1947)

As far as I know, no Sherlockian has ever delved into Boucher's running commentary on the Holmes radio series, but it's a job eminently worth doing. And so is the assembling of a full-length book of the Boucher-Lee correspondence, which chronicles one of the strongest, deepest, most fascinating literary friendships of the 20th century.

NOTES ON CRIME SHOWS
OF TV'S GOLDEN AGE

In the decades before the first 19 episodes of the *Perry Mason* TV series (1957-66) came out on DVD, millions had seen this old series on WTBS, but every episode had been cut to shreds to accommodate far more commercials than were the norm back in the Fifties. The DVD copies were complete and remastered and lovely to look at. Whether the series stood up well after almost half a century was another question entirely. All the early episodes were supposedly based on Erle Stanley Gardner's novels but—as I confirmed by rereading several of the books after watching their TV incarnations—it would be more accurate to describe most of them as using parts of Gardner's plots and some of his characters in new and much simpler stories, completely lacking the breakneck pace and dynamism of the novels. I've heard that Gardner, happening to be in the room when overweight Raymond Burr read for the part of District Attorney Hamilton Burger, jumped up and cried "That's Mason!"—and that Burr lost more than 100 pounds before the cameras rolled. But most of us who grew up on the dozens of Mason novels predating the TV series find it all but impossible to visualize Burr's ponderous bureaucrat as the reckless lawyer-adventurer Gardner created. For my money the finest episodes of the series are the first few, especially "The Case of The Nervous Accomplice" (October 5, 1957) and "The Case of the Sulky Girl" (October 19, 1957). The former features a script by TV writing legend Stirling Silliphant and the latter climaxes far more dramatically than any other episode of the series—or than Gardner's 1933 novel of the same name. Both of these and a few other very early episodes are further distinguished by the haunting background music of a never-credited Bernard Herrmann. I might think twice about picking up any additions to the package but on the whole I'm glad I bought this first DVD release of one of the most successful TV detective series of all time.

Of the detective-crime series that were on TV in the early 1950s when my parents bought their first set, the two I'd most like to see restored and on DVD like *Perry Mason* are a sort of matched pair. *Man Against Crime*, starring Ralph Bellamy as PI Mike Barnett, usually involved extended chases through signature locales of the New York City metro area like the subway and the Staten Island ferry and the Statue of Liberty. Principal director Edward J. Montagne (1912-2003) was basically a documentary film-maker without much in the way of visual flair, but he sure know how to choose evocative places to shoot in. *Boston Blackie*, with Kent Taylor in the title role, relied even more heavily on chase sequences through picturesque Los Angeles locations. As chance would have it, the name of its first and foremost director kept popping up in the credits of almost every TV series kids of my generation were watching. *The Cisco Kid, The Lone Ranger, Ramar of the Jungle, Cowboy G-Men, Adventures of Kit Carson, Brave Eagle*—Paul Landres (1912-2001) contributed to them all and usually directed their finest episodes. I never imagined that almost half a century after I began watching all those series, plus of course *Boston Blackie*, I'd be in Paul's home, taping with him, working on a book about him that fortunately came out a year before he died. For one of his best *Blackie* segments ("Roller Coaster Murder" January 7, 1952) he took over a deserted amusement park and staged some fantastically exciting action sequences, some of them shot from the front of a runaway roller coaster so as to create an amazing 3-D effect. As chance would have it, one of the *Man Against Crime* episodes ("Free Ride", April 8, 1953) was also shot at an amusement park, this one in New Jersey across the Hudson from Mike Barnett's home base, but that director was content to do the roller-coaster action in long shot and his segment isn't in the same league with Paul Landres' counterpart for *Blackie*. Today the episodes of both series are like time machines, permitting the lucky few who find them to see what New York and LA looked like more than half a century ago.

~ ~ ~ ~ ~

Of the TV crime-detective shows of my adolescence, the one I'd especially love to revisit on DVD is *The Naked City*, especially the 30-minute episodes of its first season. These too were shot on location in the streets of New York and often culminate in a chase through an exotic location. Perhaps my favorite is "The Bird Guard" (November 18, 1958), a perfect blend of emotion and violent action as the young cop played by James Franciscus tries to save a murder witness who's taken refuge in a remote lighthouse from the thugs who are out to shut her up. The script was written by our old friend Stirling Silliphant and, though I didn't know it back in 1958 when I first saw this episode on our tiny screen, the background music was lifted—legally since written for the same studio employer—from Leonard Bernstein's score for *On the Waterfront*. I am lucky enough to have this episode on DVD. The later 60-minute incarnation of *Naked City* I also watched regularly but found it slow and dull and mainly devoted to character sketches of the big city's wistful little people. Once in a while however an hour-long episode was as powerful as the best 30-minute segments. I especially recommend "A Hole in the City" (January 25, 1961), in which the cops (including a young Ed Asner) trap a psychotic murderer (a young Robert Duvall) in an apartment house with hostages (including Sylvia Sidney). This superb *telefilm noir* is worth whatever trouble you may have tracking it down.

~ ~ ~ ~ ~

Naked City's policemen were mush-hearted humanists next to Lee Marvin's Lt. Frank Ballinger of Chicago's *M Squad*, the definitive tough-cop series of the Eisenhower era, which was shot not in Chicago but on Hollywood's back lots. I recently discovered that several early episodes of the series were based on previously published short stories. "Neighborhood Killer" (October 4, 1957) was scripted by ubiquitous Stirling Silliphant from William Holder's short story (*Argosy*, August 1948). "Face of Evil" (October 18, 1957) and "Street of Fear" (November 1, 1957) came respectively from stories of the same names by David Alexander (*Manhunt*, January 1957) and Thomas Walsh (*Saturday Evening Post*, March 30, 1957). How many others of Lt. Ballinger's cases were originally cracked in the print media by different cops is anyone's guess.

BITS AND PIECES

No one ever heard of regional mystery novels back in the 1930s, but I've recently reread four superb specimens from that period, all of them written by Baynard Kendrick (1894-1977), who is best known as creator of the blind detective Captain Duncan Maclain. *Blood on Lake Louisa* (1934) is a non-series whodunit, while *The Iron Spiders* (1936), *The Eleven of Diamonds* (1936) and *Death Beyond the Go-Thru* (1938) feature the lanky and ever-hungry PI Miles Standish Rice, a character who might have been played effectively by the young Jimmy Stewart if he rather than Duncan Maclain had made it into the movies. Much of *The Eleven of Diamonds* takes place in and around Miami but the others are set in the rural Florida of the Thirties and are full of local atmosphere. I am lucky enough to own copies of all four, which are hard to come by today and haven't been reprinted in generations. *The Iron Spiders* takes place on Broken Heart Key, a coral islet 50 miles north of Key West which serves as winter quarters for a paralyzed millionaire banker and an assortment of his relatives and hangers-on. Two detailed diagrams of the upper and lower stories of the main house are supplemented (if you're lucky enough to own the Dell mapback edition) by an artist's rendition of the entire Key that seems quite faithful to Kendrick's descriptions. There are plenty of enigmatic clues and suspects (perhaps a few too many?) and much less fairness to the reader than in, say, an Ellery Queen novel of the same period. On the other hand most of the minority characters are treated with great respect. In the last paragraph of the novel, Stan Rice describes the half-black half-Seminole who's been prominent from the early chapters. "This is his country," Rice says. "It belongs to him and his people. They understand its colors, its heat, its storms, and its death. The whites have never really taken it away. With his tribe dwindling, and everything he worshiped gone, he is still a man . . .." It's hard to believe that such contemporary-sounding words were written more than seventy years ago.

~ ~ ~ ~ ~

Who perpetrated the following lines? 1. "Once he got settled he didn't move and looked like a big toad squatting in his ambush." 2. "' . . . (H)e's got no more honor than a toad . . . ' " 3. "It was twenty minutes to four when I finally scored. The cabby I scored with looked like a toad." 4. " . . . Wally looked considerably like a toad." 5. "He looked sort of like a toad, but his voice had the rich timbre that professional voices have." All five were written by the late Robert B. Parker and can be found respectively in *Mortal Stakes, Promised Land, Ceremony, Pale Kings and Princes* and *Crimson Joy*. What Parker had against those useful and sweet-singing little amphibians, and why the toad is still the most hated animal in literature, remain mysteries.

~ ~ ~ ~ ~

In an idle moment awhile ago I pulled down my copy of the anthology *Classic Mystery Stories*, ed. Douglas G. Greene (1999), and reread "The Archduke's Tea", the first of H.C. Bailey's dozens of Reggie Fortune stories and one that I hadn't glanced at in more than thirty years. The story seems to take place before World War I but first appeared in book form in *Call Mr. Fortune* (1920), the earliest collection of Fortune shorts. I wouldn't rank it among Reggie's top detective exploits but it's certainly one of the most historically important in the series. Why? Because the climax, where Reggie creates a diversion and switches a poisoned cup of tea so that the legally untouchable murderer inadvertently poisons himself, was so obviously S.S. Van Dine's inspiration for the denouement of *The Bishop Murder Case* (1929), where art connoisseur and amateur sleuth Philo Vance creates a similar distraction—having to do with an artwork of course—to switch wineglasses so that the serial killer poisons himself rather than his next intended victim. "You took the law in your own hands!" says Vance's outraged friend District Attorney Markham. "I took it in my arms—it was helpless," Vance replies. " . . . Do you bring a rattlesnake to the bar of justice? Do you give a mad dog his day in court? . . . I say, am I by any chance under arrest?" He isn't, of course, any more than Reggie Fortune was. In Markham's shoes I would have declined to put the cuffs on Vance also, if only because he didn't refer to the murderer as a toad.

~ ~ ~ ~ ~

The first murder in Rex Stout's *Over My Dead Body* (1940) takes place in a fencing academy. The weapon is a *col de mort*, a doohickey that when slipped over the usually blunt end of an epee turns it into a lethal weapon. Whether Stout made up this device out of whole cloth (if I may coin an Avalloneism) or whether it exists in the real world I have no idea and couldn't care less. What intrigues me is whether among the readers of this Nero Wolfe adventure might have been one J.K. Rowling. Is it coincidence that the king toad of the Harry Potter books is named Lord Voldemort?

~ ~ ~ ~ ~

Not every edition of every mystery reads the same. Some changes are motivated by Puritanism, others by something more interesting. Take John Dickson Carr's *Hag's Nook* (1932), the first novel about Dr. Gideon Fell. About midway through Chapter One, when Tad Rampole meets Dorothy Starberth while they're both buying books at a railway station bookstall, comes the following passage:

> He made the discovery that both the book he had just bought and the book he had knocked out of her hands had been written by the same author. As the author was Mr. Edgar Wallace, this coincidence was hardly stupefying enough to have impressed an outsider, but Rampole made much of it.

That's how the passage appears in the original 1932 edition and also in the 1962 Collier paperback, which features an introduction by Anthony Boucher. But if you happen to have a copy of the 1951 Dell mapback edition, you find the second sentence beginning differently: "As the books were thrillers, this coincidence" etc. I suppose someone at Dell decided they shouldn't be promoting an author whose books weren't being published by Dell!

~ ~ ~ ~ ~

More than seventy years ago the English writer Peter Cheyney, who knew the U.S. about as well as a toad knows existentialism, launched a series of thrillers starring two-fisted FBI agent Lemmy Caution, whose first-person narrative in Cheyney's version of American English is of a unique eyeball-popping awfulness. At least I thought it was unique until I stumbled upon Michael C. Peacock's "Bait" (*Clues*, May 10, 1931) and its protagonist Whisper Timkins, a good-hearted pickpocket who narrates not only in first person present tense like a Damon Runyon street character but also in dialect like a Harry Stephen Keeler ethnic. "I lowers me hands and flops back onta the chair. Everythin' is as plain as me Aunt Maggie's face." He also uses nouns for verbs and all sorts of other silly said substitutes as if, as he might have put it, there wuz no tomorrah.

> "Rule me out," I lips.
> "You're ruled in . . ." he menaces.
> "This way," chills a icy voice.
> "As for you, Garvin," he threats.
> "Now use your ears!" he grits . . .
> "Mr. Wade," Hope yodels, fondlin' the gat, "have you ever been to Coney Island?"
> He . . . oaths, "We're leaving for there right away!"
> "Terrible," I throats, mournful.
> "Sorta mixed up," I warbles.

More than half a century after the tale got published for the first and only time, I met the author, who had lived in the States only a few years before perpetrating this collage of howlers. I got to like him and he's dead now so I'll leave his real name unmentioned. No, he didn't become a professional mystery writer.

~ ~ ~ ~ ~

Of all the silly lines in mystery fiction, one in particular has clung like a barnacle to the underside of my memory for more decades than I care to count. It's in *The Black Gold Murders* (1959), a long-forgotten novel by a long-forgotten author—John B. Ethan, if you must know—in which a woman introducing the narrator to two beatniks says: "The one on the right thinks he's Zen Buddha." You remember Zen from World Religions 101, right? Wasn't he Prince Gautama's kid brother?

~ ~ ~ ~ ~

Just about everyone knows about the sign on Harry Truman's desk, but how many know of its possible link with mystery fiction? The story is briefly told on page 48 of David McCullough's 1992 biography *Truman*. "In the fall [of 1945, soon after FDR's death and Truman's unexpected rise to the presidency], Fred Canfil had given him a small sign for his desk. 'The Buck Stops Here,' it said. Canfil had seen one like it in the head office of a federal reformatory in El Reno, Oklahoma, and asked the warden if a copy might be made for his friend the President, and though Truman kept it on his desk only a short time, the message would stay with him permanently." The obvious follow-up questions are: Where did the warden get the sign? Was he or the person who had it made for him aware that a sign with an almost identical message figures in a mystery novel published just a few years before FDR's death? *Five Alarm Funeral* (1942) was the first novel in what became a long series about New York fire marshal Ben Pedley, written by super-prolific pulpster Prentice Winchell (1895-1976) under his most frequently used pseudonym, Stewart Sterling. At the beginning of Chapter Three, Pedley tells his assistant Barney that on the arson murder he's currently investigating the Police Commissioner "has to pass the buck to somebody." Barney: "You'd ought to have a new sign up on the door there . . ." Pedley: "What kind of a sign?" Barney: " 'The Buck'—it oughta read— 'Stops Right Here.' " Perhaps Truman's next biographer will look into the connection, if any, between this passage and the most famous sign in recent presidential history.

~ ~ ~ ~ ~

Has anyone ever heard of a spy novel by Ian Fleming called *You Asked for It*? It's the Popular Library paperback edition of *Casino Royale*, published in 1955 when Fleming was all but unknown. "If he hadn't been a tough operator, Jimmy Bond would never have risked" something or other, we are informed by the blurb on the back cover. "But it was toughness that had landed Jimmy his job with the Secret Service." I suspect that the blurb alone makes this rare softcover worth a pretty penny more than the 8 1/3 cents I paid for it forty years ago in a secondhand store in upstate New York. I wish I had a few paperbacks with blurbs extolling the toughness of other hard-boiled ops like Hank Merrivale, Al Campion and Herc Poirot.

~ ~ ~ ~ ~

What world-famous mystery writer first created James Bond? Who wrote the story that begins: "With a serious effort James Bond bent his attention once more on the little yellow book in his hand. On its outside the book bore the simple but pleasing legend, 'Do you want your salary increased by £300 per annum?' " No, 007 is not about to hit M for a raise and the author of these lines is not Ian Fleming, it's Agatha Christie. Her Bond is a silly-ass young Brit with a hoity-toity fiancée and a stolen jewel on his hands, and "The Rajah's Emerald" (first collected in England in *The Listerdale Mystery*,

1934, and over here in *The Golden Ball*, 1971) tells how he disposes of both.

~ ~ ~ ~ ~

Have you heard the one about the dyslexic hit man? A character in one of Lawrence Block's novels about PI Matthew Scudder tells the story. Seems this guy was hired to walk into a certain restaurant with an AK-47 and whack everyone at the first table to the left of the door but, being dyslexic, blew away all the poor schmucks at the first table to the right. "You idiot!" his employers told him when he went to collect his fee. "You wiped out the wrong table!" To which the hit man, shrugging, replied: "Well, everyone makes miskates."

Certainly every mystery writer makes them. In Stuart Palmer's "The Riddle of the Brass Band" (*Mystery*, March 1934; collected in *Hildegarde Withers: Uncollected Riddles*, 2002), the murder takes place during a St. Patrick's Day parade on which the APRIL sun is shining down. How did that one slip past the editors? The egregious Michael Avallone informed the readers of his paperback political thriller *Missing!* (1969) that Washington, D.C. was burned down by the British during the Revolutionary War. In Ellery Queen's *The Greek Coffin Mystery* (1932) the pedantic young sleuth quotes an ancient proverb he renders as *Ne quis nimis*. This is bad Latin and ought to be *Ne quid nimis*, meaning Nothing too much, Everything in moderation. Ellery then adds insult to injury by translating the phrase as a totally different ancient proverb: Know thyself! Cornell Woolrich in *Rendezvous in Black* (1948) has the International Date Line running the wrong way. If you read enough mysteries and keep a halfway reasonable fund of background knowledge in your head, you can build up a huge collection of gaffes like these.

I am no more infallible than any of my colleagues. In the hardcover edition of my novel *The 120-Hour Clock* (1986) a woman in New York City offers Milo Turner some wine from her fridge, "if you don't mind Almaden from the supermarket." That boner slipped past the hardcover publisher even though its offices were in New York, where you can't buy liquor or wine at a supermarket but only in state stores. (It slipped past me first of course, but during the years when I lived in Greenwich Village and attended NYU Law School I was a serious student and hardly drank a drop.) A friend of mine at Fordham Law School read *Clock* in hardcover and politely pointed out my blunder to me just in time for me to call the editor at Penguin, which was about to reprint the book in paperback. This is why the softcover substitutes for "supermarket" the words "corner store," which luckily have the same number of letters.

Everybody makes miskates. Me too.

~ ~ ~ ~ ~

Steven Slutsky, a professor of economics at the University of Florida, recently told me about a little book that will fascinate all fans of old-time radio and of Ellery Queen. The 107-page *Chillers & Thrillers* was published in 1945 by Street & Smith and exclusively distributed by the Special Services Division of the Army Service Forces. It appeared as Volume 18 of the "At Ease" series, whose purpose was "to assist the Special Service Officer, the Theatrical Advisor and all other military personnel concerned with the development of the Army recreation program." These volumes were "not to be resold or made available to civilians." Pages 40 through 107 of *Chillers & Thrillers* are devoted to three episodes of the long-running *Ellery Queen* radio series: "The Blue Chip" [June 15/17, 1944], "The Foul Tip" [July 13/15, 1944], and "The Glass Ball" [March 23/25, 1944; based on "The Man Who Wanted To Be Murdered", December 3, 1939]. Each episode was adapted for live impromptu staging in GI recreation halls, "with the performers reading from scripts and acting out the action without the use of scenery, costumes or props." It was expected that these unrehearsed performances would include plenty of boners, which were supposed to "add to rather than detract from the audience's enjoyment." In charge of each staging was a Master of Ceremonies, who "helps the players, prompts them and carries the action when it shows any signs of faltering. He bridges the scene changes and time passages by telling the audience what is happening. He pantomimes such actions as swimming, climbing stairs, walking, running, etc. He simulates sounds when necessary. He may in the course of a sketch become a prop, a corpse, a ferryboat, a radiator or any of a dozen things that are required for the action." In lieu of the guest armchair detectives of the radio series, these versions call for "a jury composed of members of the audience. These jurors should be the men in the unit who would be most amusing on the stage, such as the CO, the mess sergeant, the company clerk, and any other 'characters' among the men ... The jury should be an odd number of men, to avoid a tie vote." After the GI playing Ellery announces that he knows who the murderer is, "the jurors are called onstage and polled individually ... As they give their choice[s], the MC should question them on the reason for such selection . . . After the last juror has been polled, the jury is told that it must decide among them which [suspect] is the criminal. All discussion of the case takes place in front of the audience. When the MC thinks the discussion has reached the ballot-taking stage, he directs them to vote. After the vote has been taken, the play is resumed and the true solution is unveiled. Prizes are then awarded to the members of the jury who have guessed the correct culprit." None of the three EQ scripts has ever been published elsewhere, although "The Foul Tip" is available on audio. *Chillers & Thrillers* is a must-read volume not only for Queen fans but also for anyone interested in how the men of "The Greatest Generation" were entertained as they fought their war.

~ ~ ~ ~ ~

In the early 1950s, at the end of his first period as a novelist and the beginning of his career as a writer of live television drama, Gore Vidal (1925-) turned briefly to detective fiction. Under the pseudonym of Edgar Box he published a trilogy of mystery novels narrated by and starring Peter Cutler Sargeant II, young public relations expert, sexual gymnast (hetero only), and amateur sleuth. The books were reprinted in paperback regularly over the quarter century following their first appearance, often with a glowing encomium from Vidal himself on their covers, and in 1978 were reissued as a hardcover omnibus. Judged as detective novels all three are mediocre, but Vidal's guided tour through the worlds of art, politics and high society entertains us royally with countless gleefully sardonic jabs at every target in sight.

In *Death in the Fifth Position* (1952) Peter is hired to procure favorable media coverage for a ballet company which is being harassed by a right-wing veterans' group for having a "Communist" choreographer. Then the company's prima ballerina is murdered onstage and we are treated to pages of superb satire about professional dancers and hangers-on and much tedious speculation about homicidal motives, interspersed with two more gruesome deaths. *Death Before Bedtime* (1953) finds Peter in Washington as PR adviser to an ultra-conservative senator angling for the presidential nomination—until he's blown to bits by a gunpowder charge in his fireplace. Once again a lackluster detective plot is saved by Vidal's mocking gibes at politics, journalism, sex and society. And in *Death Likes It Hot* (1954) Peter is invited to a weekend house party at a Long Island beachfront mansion and encounters tangled emotions and murder among a cast of ludicrous plutocrats and talentless pseudo-artists. Its fairly complex plot, a few deft clues and a dramatic climax make this one the best of the trio, but as with the others it's the pungent satire that brings the book to life.

Clever deductions, fair play with the reader and the Carr-Christie-Queen bag of tricks are not Vidal's strong points. But his mastery of the language did not fail him, even in these mysteries that he himself regarded as potboilers, and his tone of cynical good-humored tolerance towards an America populated exclusively by crooks, opportunists and buffoons is the closest thing to the authentic spirit of H.L. Mencken that I've ever encountered in mystery fiction.

~ ~ ~ ~ ~

Why was a visitor to a college campus, just before he was murdered, searching for the elevator in a building that had none? You'll find the answer in Jon L. Breen's "The Missing Elevator Puzzle" (*Ellery Queen's Mystery Magazine*, February 2007), which may just be the finest short whodunit with an academic setting I've ever read. I've known Jon and admired his work for more than forty years. His contributions to the mystery field fall neatly into four categories: book reviews and editorial-critical work, short parodies of other writers, "serious" short mysteries, and detective novels. His periodical articles, especially those for *The Weekly Standard*, and his review columns for *Wilson Library Bulletin* (1972-83) and *EQMM* (1977-83, 1988-present), rank with the finest mystery criticism since the death of Anthony Boucher. His reference volumes *What About Murder?* (1981, 2nd ed. 1993) and *Novel Verdicts* (1984, 2nd ed. 1999) are indispensable guides, the one to earlier nonfiction books on the genre, the other to courtroom crime fiction. His parodies, collected in *Hair of the Sleuthhound* (1982), are masterpieces of this most difficult form, capturing in about ten pages apiece both what is memorable and what is laughable in the styles and shticks of Van Dine, Queen, Carr, Christie, McBain, MacDonald, Macdonald and the outrageous Avallone. His "straight" short mysteries, collected in *The Drowning Icecube* (1999) and *Kill the Umpire* (2003), reflect his love of the old-fashioned whodunit and of horse-racing, baseball and other sports. His novels likewise pay homage to both sports and the traditions of the Golden Age whodunit, with his series characters (racetrack announcer Jerry Brogan in four titles, bookshop owner Rachel Hemmings in two) proving themselves as amateur detectives in cases that spring from their occupations and feature neat plots, likable characters, unpretentious prose, a soft-spoken leisurely ambience—precisely as if the ghost of Earl Derr Biggers, the creator of Charlie Chan, were hovering over Jon's word processor. His most recent novels are *Eye of God* (2006), a serious whodunit set in the world of televangelism, and *Probable Claus* (2009), a comic legal thriller. Jon once called me the closest counterpart to Anthony Boucher who was still alive, but it seems to me that if he wants to find Boucher's living heir he should look in a mirror.

FOR THE ABSENT

CHRISTIANNA BRAND

Under her pen name she became one of the great masters of English detective fiction. She was born Mary Christianna Milne in Malaya on December 17, 1907, began writing whodunits a couple of years after the start of World War II, and is best known as the author of *Green for Danger* (1944), a classic of fair-play detection set in a military hospital in Kent during the Blitz. I got to meet her when she was around 70 and quickly discovered that she was as perfect in the role of the dotty English lady as was Basil Rathbone playing Holmes. Who can ever forget the MWA dinner where she was asked to present one of the Edgar awards? "The nominees are: Emily Smith, James Quackenbush . . . Hahaha, Quackenbush, what a funny name!" The audience, except perhaps for poor Quackenbush, was left rolling in the aisles. On my first visit to England, to serve as an expert witness at a trial in the Old Bailey during the summer of 1979, Christianna and her husband Roland Lewis, one of England's top ear-nose-and-throat surgeons, took me to dinner at Simpson's in the Strand, the famous old eatery where one tips the server who carves your roast beef tableside. A few years later I edited *Buffet for Unwelcome Guests* (1983), the first collection of her short stories published in the U.S. On my next visit to England after the book came out I could hardly lift my suitcases, which were packed to bursting with copies for her. She died on March 11, 1988, and everyone who knew her still misses her. The 1946 movie version of *Green for Danger*, starring Alastair Sim as the insufferable Inspector Cockrill and featuring superb English actors like Trevor Howard and Leo Genn, has long been considered one of the finest pure detective films ever made, but it was very hard to access over here until it came out on DVD. Anyone who loves classic whodunits but has never seen the film nor read the book has a double treat in store.

RAY B. BROWNE

The news was no surprise. His wife had prepared me several days earlier: "His heart and kidneys are failing. We have brought him home from the hospital.... I think he won't live much longer." He died on October 22, 2009, at age 87. You may never have heard of Ray Browne, but I had known him for forty years and he wonderfully shaped my life and that of every other mystery writer of the last four decades who sported academic credentials.

To begin explaining what he accomplished for us I must go back 75 years. A brilliant young man named William Anthony Parker White had completed his academic work and was more than eminently qualified to become a professor at any university in the country but he chose not to. Why? One main reason, as his widow explained long after his all too early death, was "that he was surrounded by people who took no interest in contemporary popular literature but at the same time were trying to research the popular literature of a few centuries back." Instead he decided to become a professional writer. And, because there were already 75 authors named William White, he chose to adopt a pen name: Anthony Boucher.

Academic contempt for anything contemporary and popular was still alive and well thirty years later. In my college years, which roughly corresponded with JFK's presidency, there wasn't a single "popular culture" course in the entire curriculum. I vividly recall one of my professors bewailing the fact that William Faulkner was forced by a Philistine reading public to support himself by writing for (YUCCH!) the movies. Carolyn Heilbrun, a young professor of English at Columbia University, had begun writing mystery novels but had to do it under a pseudonym (Amanda Cross) because, as she explained years later, she would never have gotten tenure if her colleagues had known of her sideline.

This was the academic environment when Ray Browne came into the picture. With a Ph.D. in English and Folklore and twenty years of university teaching under his belt, he moved from Purdue to Ohio's Bowling Green State University and, with the support of the administration, launched the movement that made it academically respectable to teach and study popular culture (a term it's said he invented). If aging memory serves me, I met him in 1969. We hit it off immediately. He invited me to write for the *Journal of Popular Culture*, which he had launched at Bowling Green two years earlier, and after he founded the Popular Culture Association, he encouraged me to attend annual meetings. (Both my first presentation for the PCA and much of my writing for the JPC dealt with a writer I was entranced by then and still am today: that great mad genius of 20th century American fiction, Harry Stephen Keeler.) Knowing that countless colleges around the country were beginning to offer courses on mystery fiction, and that I knew a bit about the subject, he asked me to put together a book of readings for publication by Bowling Green University Popular Press. The result was *The Mystery Writer's Art* (1970), which remained in print for well over 20 years, long after I thought it had outlived its usefulness. A few years later the same press published *Royal Bloodline: Ellery Queen, Author and Detective* (1974), for which I received an Edgar. By that time I was a professor myself, having accepted a position at St. Louis University School of Law which I kept until retiring 34 years later. I had also begun writing mysteries of my own but, thanks to the influence of Ray Browne and a handful of like-minded colleagues of his who had made popular culture respectable, I didn't have to use a pen name.

JOE L. HENSLEY

One of my closest mystery-writing friends died on August 27, 2007, at age 81. Joe Hensley had been a private attorney, a member of the Indiana legislature, a prosecutor, a judge, a dealer in rare coins and paper money, a writer of science fiction since the early 1950s and more recently of 20-odd mystery novels. For the last several decades of his life his home was Madison, Indiana, a charming town on the Ohio River just across from Kentucky and about 300 miles from St. Louis. Whenever I was driving east he'd invite me to stay over for drinks, dinner, dialogue and the use of his guest bedroom. How he could tell stories! Hoosier politics, the judiciary, colleagues in the s.f. and mystery fields ranging from Harlan Ellison to Avram Davidson to John D. MacDonald, encounters over the years with everyone from Robert Frost to Bob Hope—the anecdotes poured out of him like the water over Niagara Falls, especially when we'd drive together from Madison to the annual Pulpcon in Dayton, Ohio, where he was guest of honor one year and I the next. I reviewed several of his novels for St. Louis newspapers and wrote the entry on him for the reference book that used to be called 20th *Century Crime and Mystery Writers* and is now for obvious reasons known as the *St. James Guide to Crime and Mystery Writers*. His final novel, *Snowbird's Blood*, was published posthumously. Driving east will never again be so pleasant for me.

For the Absent

EDWARD D. HOCH

On Thursday morning, January 17, 2008, I lost another of my closest friends in the mystery-writing community. Ed Hoch's death was the sort we wish for ourselves and those we care about, instant, without pain. He got up and went to take a shower and his wife heard a *thump* from the bathroom and he was already gone, apparently a massive heart attack. He would have been 78 in another month. His ambition was to write 1000 short stories but he died something like 50 short of that goal.

I first met him in the late Sixties, a year or two after he had left his advertising job to write full time. Over the decades we corresponded endlessly, appeared on panels together, did things for each other. I edited two collections of his short stories, recommended him for Guest of Honor at the Pulpcon the year after I had that slot (he should of course have been asked long before I was), gave him my extra copy of Fred Dannay's all but impossible to find autobiographical novel *The Golden Summer* (1953, as by Daniel Nathan). The morning after each year's MWA dinner, I'd have breakfast with Ed and Pat at the Essex House on Central Park South, where they habitually stayed on their frequent visits to town, and we would talk the morning away. All the things he did for me would fill a book even if one didn't mention the countless hours of reading pleasure his stories gave me.

He was such a kind man, so generously giving of himself to so many others, so modest and tolerant and thoughtful. It was typical of him that when an interviewer wanted to describe him as a devout Catholic, Ed said it would be presumptuous to apply that adjective to himself and that he preferred "observant," a word generally associated with the Jewish tradition. If there was anyone remotely like him in the genre, it was Anthony Boucher. Both men loved and were immensely knowledgeable about mystery fiction, both wrote far more short stories than they did novels, both edited superb anthologies of short fiction in their genre, both combined deep religious feeling with total openness of mind and heart and deep respect and appreciation for those of another faith or none.

Ed was the polar opposite of a stereotypical Type A personality.

He never seemed harried or rushed, never lost his temper, always had time for others' concerns and yet never fell behind schedule with his own work. His ability to devise mystery plots was astonishing. Where did they come from? Wide and constant reading—almost anything he came across in a novel or story or nonfiction book might become a springboard for him—coupled with a mind like no other. About twenty years ago we attended a cocktail party at a New York publisher's office whose roof garden offered a fine view of the then new Marriott Marquis hotel with its glass-walled elevator traveling nonstop up and down the side of the building from top floor to street and back again. "What if someone was seen entering that elevator," I asked Ed idly, "and wasn't there when it stopped at the other end?" Almost anyone could come up with a wild premise like that. Ed made it work, made one of his neatest impossible crime stories out of it ("The Way Up to Hades", *Alfred Hitchcock's Mystery Magazine*, January 1988).

He's gone now. The genre he loved and to which he contributed so much will never again see anyone like him. But maybe in a sense he's still with us. There's a Jewish saying that you haven't really died until the death of the last person with fond living memories of you. In that sense Ed Hoch will live for generations as his finest stories will.

For the Absent

STUART M. KAMINSKY

His field was film and mine was law but we had so much in common that I wish I had known him better. Stuart Kaminsky was one of the young academics who, after the revolution launched by Ray Browne and his colleagues, were hired to teach university-level courses on movies, science fiction, mysteries and countless other "popular culture" subjects. Stu was born in 1934 and grew up in Chicago. Drafted into the Army, he served as a medic in France and developed Hepatitis C, which plagued him for the rest of his life. After completing graduate work he began teaching film and film history at Chicago's Northwestern University. His early books dealt with directors like John Huston and Don Siegel. In 1977 he published *Bullet for a Star*, the first of two dozen novels set in Hollywood's golden years and starring PI Toby Peters.

I can't remember where I first met Stu but we did a lot of Bouchercons and Midwest MWA programs together. My most vivid memories of him come from the summer of 1986 when we were both among the guests at an international festival on Italy's Adriatic coast. It was in Stu's hotel room that I met the great French director Claude Chabrol, and the three of us were among the festival guests who, a day or two later when none of us were on duty, piled into a couple of vans and were taken to San Remo for a tour of the castle of Cagliostro. On the way back we stopped at a country inn whose kitchen staff, with no prior notice (this was before the cellphone era), put together perhaps the finest lunch I've ever eaten. One course after another without end, as if we'd all died and gone to culinary heaven—Mamma Mia!

A few years after our Italian junket, Mystery Writers of America awarded the Edgar for best mystery novel of 1988 to *A Cold Red Sunrise*, Stu's fifth book about Russian police detective Porfiry Rostnikov. Soon afterwards he left Northwestern and took a position at Florida State University, where on top of teaching and administrative duties he began a third series, this one about sixtyish Chicago PI Abe Lieberman. In 1994 he left academia to write full-time, as if he hadn't been doing more than that while still holding his day job. A few years later, while serving a term as president of MWA, he created Florida process server Lew Fonesca and started his fourth and final series. MWA named him a Grand Master in 2006. Early in 2009 he moved from Sarasota to University City, Missouri, where I hang my own hats, to await the liver transplant which his half-century-old hepatitis had made necessary, but 36 hours after arriving he suffered a stroke which disqualified him for the transplant. He died in a St. Louis hospital on October 9, at age 75.

Thanks to the success of Ray Browne and his colleagues at bringing contemporary popular culture into higher education, any number of us—Stu and I and Jeremiah Healy and Bill Crider, just to name four off the top of my head—were able openly to lead double lives as professors and mystery writers. Who could have dreamed of that when we were all young?

For the Absent

JOSEPH H. LEWIS

The last time I saw the man who directed *Gun Crazy*, we had lunch on the terrace of the Del Rey Yacht Club. It was the summer of 1999 and he was a small trim man 92 years old who walked very tentatively as if he were afraid at every step of falling. He had actually taken a fall a few months ago, he said, and still needed to go in for therapy two or three times a week. He didn't eat much, just a little fruit salad with cottage cheese. After lunch he felt like strolling over to the slip where his boat was moored. He hadn't seen the Buena Vista since his fall, he said. We wove along walkways amid the fleet of small craft glistening in their berths under the bright sun but when we reached his boat he couldn't find the key. He had been losing any number of small objects lately, he told me. We walked back to his car and searched and I found a key in the glove compartment. "That's not it," he said. Somehow I thought it might be. I left him in the yacht club lounge and went out again to the Buena Vista's slip and tried the key in the door and it fit. On the dining table was the book he'd been reading the last time he was on board: one of Lawrence Block's Burglar novels. I went back to the clubhouse and gave him the good news, which meant that he was spared an expensive appointment with a locksmith, and the two of us returned to the cabin where several years before we had taped the conversations that had become the first book about his life and world. He had owned and loved the Buena Vista for more than thirty years but had recently put it up for sale because he knew that at his age he could never take it out again. But he wasn't too old to drive and at the end of my visit he tucked me into his tiny sports car and sped me unerringly back to my hotel. That was the last time I saw Joseph H. Lewis.

He was born in New York City to Russian Jewish émigré parents on April 30, 1907 and grew up on the upper East Side, within walking distance of Columbia University. In his teens he may well have crossed paths with another youth of Russian Jewish roots who lived in that neighborhood and would also make huge contributions to the creative genre we call *noir*: Cornell Woolrich. During the late 1940s when he was directing films at Columbia, Joe told me, he spent several months preparing a feature based on a Woolrich novel but was never able to adapt the book into a viable screenplay. It was well over forty years later when we had this conversation and he had forgotten the novel's title but I suspect it must have been *Rendezvous in Black* (1948), Woolrich's then most recent book and his only suspense novel that hadn't already been filmed. (It still hasn't.) I can't help feeling that a picture based on this novel and directed by Joe might well have become one of the cornerstone works of *film noir*.

I met him when he was in his early eighties. Before long, whenever I was in southern California we would hang out on his boat and tape the conversations that eventually became the nucleus of our book. The words he used most often in discussing his life were pride, dignity, respect. As a director a compulsive perfectionist and tough taskmaster, off the set a loving husband and father and grandfather and a generous and thoughtful friend—these impressions that I formed of him during our tapings were confirmed again and again over the rest of his life.

The last time I talked to Joe was about a year after my lunch with him at the Yacht Club. I had been invited to Canada by a filmmaker who wanted to discuss working with me on a documentary about Woolrich. One thing we needed for the film we had in mind was just the right person to serve as the Woolrich voice, reading from that haunted man's autobiographical writings. I had brought with me a copy of Christian Bauer's 1987 documentary on Lewis, and as we watched Joe and listened to his marvelously expressive voice and remembered how much he and Woolrich had in common—virtually the same age, the same ethnic roots and Upper East Side adolescence and of course the same enormous significance in the literature and film we have come to call *noir*—we both knew who our Woolrich should be. We called Joe that day. He seemed interested but of course nothing could happen until our documentary was funded. A few weeks later and back in St. Louis I called Joe again. He was in bed, he said; just the flu, nothing serious. That was on August 20. I never heard his voice again.

Gail Reingold, a psychoanalyst and Joe's close friend for more than forty years, told me about the director's last few weeks.

"There had been an invitation to a *Gun Crazy* screening at UCLA and Joe and Buena came to that screening along with my wife and myself. He was pretty enfeebled at that point. I had been taking him to lunch on maybe a two-times-a-month basis but at that time he seemed weaker and a little disoriented, and he got into a very irascible discussion with the moderator and gave her a hard time. And I thought to myself: I wonder if he's ever going to do this again. Looks to me like he's sort of come to the end of the road.

"About a week later I called him and asked him if he'd like to go to lunch and he said, 'Well, not this particular week, I'm tired, but next week let's do it.' So I called about a week later and he said: 'No, I have something to do today, but I'll call you.'

"Maybe it was three or four days later when I got a message to call Georgia Sangster, his granddaughter, and I knew something must have happened. She said: 'My grandmother wanted me to call you that my grandfather died yesterday.' I said: 'My God, what happened?' She said: 'Well, he was at the Yacht Club and evidently he had a heart attack at the Yacht Club.' And she said they were just marvelous to him there, they rushed right over to him and they got 911 and the ambulance came and I believe they took him to Cedars-Sinai . . .

"She was a little confused, I thought, but she said to me: 'They thought my grandfather was okay and they were going to send him home.' And I understood her to say that he was about to be put in the wheelchair and they would wheel him downstairs where the car would be brought around to pick him up, and suddenly he collapsed and they were right there on top of him immediately and he went into unconsciousness and they couldn't resuscitate him and he passed away."

It could almost have been a scene out of a Woolrich novel or for that matter a Lewis *film noir*. Joe's granddaughter is waiting downstairs to take him home and the doctors have to tell her that Joe is dead and she has to go back and tell Joe's wife.

Another of the founding fathers of *film noir* is gone. I mourn his passing but can't help considering how lucky he was. To have lived so long, to have enjoyed health and wealth and honors and a loving family and to die with so little pain—who wouldn't wish to have had his life?

For as long as I remember anything I'll remember him fondly.

Francis M. Nevins

AARON MARC STEIN

There's a general rule to which the most conspicuous exception in our genre is Agatha Christie: when an author dies, his work dies too. Certainly Aaron Marc Stein's has. He was born in 1906, graduated *summa cum laude* from Princeton, wrote a couple of avant-garde novels which were published thanks to endorsements from Theodore Dreiser, then turned to mystery fiction under the pseudonym of George Bagby and, a few years later, under his own name too. He quickly learned how to parlay his day jobs and other activities into backgrounds for the early Bagby novels, using his time as radio critic for a New York paper to create his own station in *Murder on the Nose* (1938), dipping into his memories of apparently liquor-soaked Princeton reunions for *The Corpse with the Purple Thighs* (1939), employing his stint at the madhouse known as *Time* magazine in *Red Is for Killing* (1941). During World War II he abandoned fiction to serve as an Army cryptographer, but after the war he became a fulltime author and wrote so prolifically and skillfully that in the early 1950s, when he was turning out four or more titles a year, New York *Times* mystery critic Anthony Boucher called him the most reliable professional detective novelist in the United States. Between 1935 and his death half a century later he produced an astounding 110 book-length mysteries: 51 as Bagby chronicling the cases of the NYPD's sore-footed Inspector Schmidt; 18 as Hampton Stone about New York Assistant District Attorneys Gibson and Mac; 18 under his own name with the archaeologist-detective duo of Tim Mulligan and Elsie Mae Hunt as protagonists and, when his publishers demanded stronger beer in their Steins, 23 with adventurous civil engineer Matt Erridge in the lead. Factor in his one non-crime novel as Bagby plus one stand-alone crime novel under his own name and those two early literary experiments and you have a total of 114 books. He also wrote occasional short stories, which cry out to be collected. Most of his Bagby and Stone novels are set in and around New York, which Aaron knew and loved and characterized as vividly as any of his human beings, while most of his orthonymous books feature exotic locales in Central and South America or Europe. I had been reading him since my teens but never got to spend quality time with him until the mid-1970s when we both joined the board of the University of California's Mystery Library, and we remained friends for the rest of his life. In 1979 he received the Grand Master award from Mystery Writers of America. Later he and I served together on the board of Bantam's Collection of Mystery Classics. His health was failing but he continued to turn out a book or two a year well into his seventies. Acclaimed by colleagues and connoisseurs, he never attained the popular success he so richly deserved. He died of cancer in 1985. I still remember him fondly.

Since the early 1960s he had lived in a co-op on Park Avenue and 88th Street with his sister Miriam-Ann Hagen (who also wrote a few whodunits of her own) and her husband Joe. They had bought it for $34,000 which they'd won gambling at Las Vegas in a single night. At the time of his death the unit was worth well over a million. In effect he had an apartment inside the apartment, and after he and Miriam had died Joe invited me to stay in Aaron's quarters whenever I was in New York—which allowed me the unique experience of reading several of Aaron's later novels in the room where he'd written them. For most readers today his huge body of work remains an undiscovered treasure. Any who care to remedy that loss would do well to begin with his books from the years when he earned that accolade from Boucher: perhaps the Bagby titles *Drop Dead* (1949) and *Dead Drunk* (1953), or *The Girl with the Hole in Her Head* (1949) as by Stone, or *Days of Misfortune* (1949) under his own name. I still reread him regularly and with pleasure.

TWO WOMEN

They never met and eight years passed between the departure of the one from my life and the entrance of the other. What connects them is that they were the real-world originals of the most important women in my first novel.

Gael was the younger but she died first. The day we met is commemorated, distorted, whatever, in the first scene of *Publish and Perish* (1975) when Loren Mensing, young firebrand of a law professor and Gael, younger firebrand of a law student, join a box brigade taking outdated stuff down several flights of stairs from the law library to be put into storage. The real Gael and I were on that staircase that day in the late summer of 1971. A day or two later I discovered that she was in a class I was teaching. It was a huge class but she would have stood out in a group much larger. Before long I had kidnapped her from the real world and imprisoned her in the world of my imagination. Within a few years after she'd graduated and moved to San Francisco, a city so lovely she could never live elsewhere, she told me she had gotten jobs by truthfully telling potential employers: "I am a fictional character." In a state crawling with intellectual property lawyers I became her long-distance adviser whenever she had a copyright problem, whether she was working for the Bar Association or the American Cancer Society or somewhere else. Like all the characters in my fictional world including the series detectives, she got older, although nowhere near as fast as we both did in real time. I believe we still pictured each other as we were in those turbulent days when we first came together. Her last bow as a fictional character was in *Into the Same River Twice* (1996) when Loren encounters her again: older, less mercurial, practicing law in an old established firm and about to marry a wealthy WASP in front of an Episcopal bishop. Nothing like that happened to the Gael of the real world, where she was rear-ended by a drunk driver and spent years in constant pain. Then she was invaded by something infinitely worse which, on March 7, 2004, took her.

My God! How could she have died before me? She was so much younger, so much more alive and vibrant and worthy of living a long full life. Thank you, Lou Gehrig. Not.

Lucy was the older but she outlived Gael by almost four years. She was the first love of my life. I met her when JFK was in the White House and we were in college. We were separated for almost thirty years—my fault, I fear—and during that endless hiatus she became the model for the doomed Lucy in *Publish and Perish*. How we reunited is a story too complex and personal to be told here or anywhere else, but it happened in December 1990. The second phase of our relationship lasted a little over seventeen years.

She looked very much as I described her in *Publish and Perish*: petite and "uncannily attractive" and living with "a birth gift from blind chance."

> As she shrugged out of an oyster-white raincoat, half turned away from him, he watched the movement of her shoulders, her right held stiffly about two inches higher than her left, the outline of the finlike ridge running from below the neckline of her simple black dress to below her right shoulder blade plainly visible to anyone behind her. The childhood operation had corrected the spinal curvature she had brought into the world with her but at a price.

The real Lucy had many health problems besides the one she shared with the fictional Lucy. In January 2008 they claimed her.

For six months she had been in medical facilities near her home on the Jersey shore. Even after a tracheotomy she could never get back to breathing normally. She couldn't speak and had to be tube-fed for months. Then she improved and was moved from the ICU to a rehab center but at best she could say only a few words. I spoke with her on Thanksgiving and her birthday and Christmas. I went east early in January 2008 and was to have seen her on the 6th but she had a major relapse on the night of New Year's Day and almost died. Then she improved again and I arranged to visit her three days later, on the 9th. She had another relapse on the evening of the 8th and from then on she was out of it. She died three days later. What hideous timing: I never got to say goodbye to her.

Looking at *Publish and Perish* today, I am shaken by how many passages written more than 35 years ago capture how I thought and felt about her. Perhaps the last line says it best. "He knew that she would come to life as a sudden stab of loss within him, whenever he saw the gleam of starlight on dark water."

INDEX

Abbot, Anthony (Oursler pseudonym), 9, 107-113, 275, 276
"About the Disappearance of Agatha King" (Abbot), 112
About the Murder of a Man Afraid of Women (Abbot), 112
About the Murder of a Startled Lady (Abbot), 111
About the Murder of Geraldine Foster (Abbot), 108, 111, 275
About the Murder of the Circus Queen (Abbot), 111
About the Murder of the Clergyman's Mistress (Abbot), 110
About the Murder of the Night Club Lady (Abbot), 110-111, 275
"About the Perfect Crime of Mr. Digberry" (Abbot), 112-113
"Abraham Lincoln's Clue" (Queen), 80
"Absence of Emily, The" (Ritchie), 227
Academy, The (magazine), 357
Ace Books (paperback publisher), 128
Acker, Sharon, 372
Adam, Ronald, 321
Adams, Cleve F., 20, 86, 114-129, 313, 342
Adams, Dorothy, 342
Addy, Wesley, 340
Adler, Jay, 332, 338, 342
Adler, Luther, 325
Adventure of the Murdered Moths, The (Queen), 80
Adventures of Ellery Queen, The (Queen), 74, 78
Adventures of Ellery Queen, The (radio series), 80, 82, 189
Adventures of Henry Turnbuckle, The (Ritchie), 226
Adventures of Kit Carson, The (TV series), 386
Adventures of Paul Pry, The (Gardner), 28
Adventures of Sam Spade, The (radio series), 126
Adventures of Sherlock Holmes, The (Conan Doyle), 72
Affair of the Bottled Deuce, The (Keeler), 207
Agee, Philip, 255, 256, 261, 268
Air Adventure (magazine), 25
Albertson, Frank, 344
Aldrich, Robert, 340, 341
Alexander, David, 387
"Alexandrian Solution, The" (Hoch), 196
Alfred Hitchcock Hour, The (TV series), 226
Alfred Hitchcock Presents (TV series), 65, 126, 224
Alfred Hitchcock's Mystery Magazine(AHMM), 191, 192, 193, 194, 195, 200, 210, 211, 212, 224, 225, 226, 408
Alice in Wonderland (Carroll), 78
"All at Once, No Alice" (Woolrich), 63
All I Can Get (Ard), 163, 171-172
Allan, Elizabeth, 281
Allen, Woody, 175
Allende, Salvador, 251, 254, 259
Allied Artists (film production company), 338
Allingham, Margery, 20
Allison, Steve, 347
Alper, Murray, 307
Alton, John, 331, 332, 338, 339
"Always the Season" (Ritchie), 223
Alwyn, William, 321
Amazing Adventures of Lester Leith, The (Gardner), 27
Amazing Web, The (Keeler), 203
American Cancer Society, 416
American Gun Mystery, The (Queen), 78
American Magazine, 356
Amin, Idi, 253
"Among Thieves" (Gardner), 42, 44
And on the Eighth Day (Queen), 90
"And So to Death" (Woolrich), 63

419

And Sudden Death (Adams), 121
Anderson, Maxwell, 345
Anderson, Warner, 351
Ankers, Evelyn, 126
Anthony Boucher Chronicles, The (Nevins), 101, 123
Arbenz, Jacobo, 251, 253
Archainbaud, George, 277
"Archduke's Tea, The" (Bailey), 392
Ard, Eileen (Kovara), 161
Ard, William, 161-180
Ardell, Alice, 293
Argosy (magazine), 25, 26, 27, 58, 63, 196, 235, 240, 387
Arlen, Michael, 309
Armchair Detective, The (magazine), 15, 115
Armour (later Illinois) Institute of Technology, 201
Armstrong, Robert, 277, 293, 297
Arnold, Edward, 119, 293, 294
Arnold, Matthew, 361
Art of the Mystery Story, The (Haycraft), 114, 149
Arthur, Jean, 297, 298
Arthur, Robert, 336
As Bad As I Am (Ard), 169-170, 175
Asher, E.M., 289
Asner, Ed, 387
Asphalt Jungle, The (film), 343
Assassins Don't Die in Bed (Avallone), 185
"Assignment: Enigma" (Hoch), 198
Astor, Mary, 279, 287, 288, 307, 308, 316
Atlantic Monthly (magazine), 129
Atlee, Philip (J. Phillips pseudonym), 231
Auden, W.H., 360
Auer, Mischa, 285
Auster, Paul, 367
Aurora, 311
Authors League, 115
Autry, Gene, 234
Avallone, Michael, 9, 166, 183-188, 393, 396, 399
Avengers, The (TV series), 197
Award Espionage Reader, The (Santesson), 200

Axt, Dr. William, 283, 305
Aylesworth, Arthur, 287
Aylmer, Felix, 299
Babcock, Dwight, 319
Bacall, Lauren, 344
Backus, Jean, 97
Badge of Evil (Masterson), 349
"Bag of Tricks" (Hoch), 195
Bagby, George (Stein pseudonym), 414
Baggett, Lynn, 325
Bailey, H.C., 392
Bailey, Raymond, 351
Bailey, Robert, 351
"Bait" (Peacock), 393-394
"Baja" (Hoch), 200
Bakaleinikoff, Constantin, 309
Bakaleinikoff, Mischa, 336, 351
Ballard, Lucien, 342
Ballard, Willis Todhunter, 115, 127, 128, 129
Bancroft, Anne, 344
Banks, R. Jeff, 248
"Banquo's Chair" (Croft-Cooke), 126
Bantam Books (paperback publisher), 415
Barbier, George, 295
Bard, Ben, 317
Bari, Lynn, 309
Barnes, Barry K., 301
Barrat, Robert, 279
Barrett, Laurinda, 345
Barrier, Edgar, 331
Barron, Baynes, 338
Bartok, Bela, 183
Barzun, Jacques, 114, 122, 149
Batjac (film production company), 238
Bauer, Christian, 412
"Bearded Lady, The" (Queen), 78
Beatles, The, 372
Beaudine, William, 113
Beck, Reginald, 301
Beck, Thomas, 291
"Bedlam at the Budgie" (Ritchie), 226
"Bedside Murder" (J.D. MacDonald), 219
Begley, Ed, 329

Behold This Dreamer! (Oursler), 108
Bellamy, Ralph, 313, 386
Bellem, Robert Leslie, 125, 127, 128
Beloin, Edmund, 313
Bendix, William, 119
Benedict, Howard, 309
Benedict, William, 342
Benet, Stephen Vincent, 234
Benjamin, Paul (Auster pseudonym), 367
Bennett, Marjorie, 340
Benson Murder Case, The (Van Dine), 13, 279
Bercovici, Leonardo, 323
Berkeley Democratic Club, 103
Berkeley Lawn Bowling Club, 98
Berkeley, Martin, 319
Bernard Herrmann: The CBS Years (CD set), 379, 381
Bernard Herrmann Society, 381
Bernstein, Leonard, 387
Bernstein, Walter, 323
Best Detective Stories of the Year (anthology series), 102
Best of Fantasy and Science Fiction (anthology series), 101
Beware the Curves (Gardner), 47
Beyond the Night (Woolrich), 66
Bezzerides, A.I., 329, 340
Big Combo, The (film), 338-339
Big Heat, The (McGivern), 336
Big Heat, The (film), 336-337
Big Jim McLain (film), 237, 238, 245
"Big Rig, The" (J. Phillips), 240
Big Sleep, The (Chandler), 18, 165, 306, 358
Big Sleep, The (film), 306
Bigger They Come, The (Gardner), 45-47
Biggers, Earl Derr, 291, 400
"Bird Guard, The" (TV film), 387
Bishop Murder Case, The (Van Dine), 392
Bissell, Whit, 338
Black Alibi (Woolrich), 62
Black Angel, The (Woolrich), 62, 69, 317
Black Angel (film), 317-318

Black Book Detective (magazine), 57
Black Cat (magazine), 203
Black Curtain, The (Woolrich), 61-62
"Black Curtain, The" (radio drama), 63
Black Door, The (Adams), 121-122, 126
"Black Feather, The" (Gardner), 30
Black Gold Murders, The (Ethan), 394
Black Mask (magazine), 25, 26, 27, 30, 42, 43, 57, 59, 60, 63, 130, 133, 144, 215, 218, 355, 358
Black Path of Fear, The (Woolrich), 62
"Blackmail with Lead" (Gardner), 32
"Blackmailers Don't Shoot" (Chandler), 358
Blackmer, Sidney, 113, 303
Blackton, Gloria, 55
Blackton, J. Stuart, 55
Blake, Nicholas, (Day-Lewis pseudonym), 20, 305, 364
Blake, William, 360, 361
Bles, Geoffrey (publishing house), 361
Blish, James, 138
Block, Lawrence, 173, 396, 411
Blonde and Johnny Malloy, The (Ard), 179
Blonde in Lower Six, The (Gardner), 27
Blood in Their Ink (Scott), 149
Blood on Lake Louisa (Kendrick), 391
Blood Transfusion Murders, The (Propper), 159
Bloodfire (Lutz), 213
Blore, Eric, 297
Blue Book (magazine), 235
"Blue Chip, The" (Queen radio play), 397
Blues of a Lifetime (Woolrich), 67
Bochner, Lloyd, 376
"Body in Waiting" (Lawrence), 145
Boehm, Sydney, 336
Boetticher, Budd, 167

Bogart, Humphrey, 111, 116, 121, 187, 276, 307, 308, 315, 344
Bogeaus, Benedict, 331
Bolvary, Geza von, 299
Bonanova, Fortunio, 340
Bonanza Books (publishing house), 196
Bond, Rudy, 344
Bond, Ward, 307, 329
Bonegrinder (Lutz), 211
Boorman, John, 372, 373, 374, 375, 377, 378
Borden, Eugene, 319
Borges, Jorge Luis, 100
Boston Blackie (TV series), 386
Boston University, 361
Boucher, Anthony, 14, 15, 19, 82, 91, 92-104, 114, 123, 128, 161, 164, 167, 170, 176, 222, 364, 365, 371, 382-384, 393, 399, 400, 404, 407, 414, 415
Bouchey, Willis, 333, 336
Boudoir Murder, The (Propper), 150-151, 152, 154, 160
Bourdelle, Thomy, 299
Bowling Green State University, 404, 405
Bowling Green University Popular Press, 405
Bowman, Lee, 315, 316
Box, Edgar (Vidal pseudonym), 398
Box from Japan, The (Keeler), 203
Boys' High, 72
Brackett, Leigh, 126
Bradley, Stewart, 347
Brand, Christianna, 20, 321, 322, 403
Brand, Neville, 325, 326
Branden, Michael, 317
Brando, Jocelyn, 336, 344
Brautigan, Richard, 366, 367
Brave Eagle (TV series), 386
Brecher, Egon, 319
Bredell, Elwood, 311, 312, 313, 314
Breen, Jon L., 7, 40, 95, 96, 97, 199, 399
Breezy Stories (magazine), 25
Bride of Frankenstein (film), 294
Bride Wore Black, The (Woolrich), 61, 62, 67, 69, 218, 363
Briggs, Harlan, 305
Brigham Young University, 126
Brissac, Virginia, 311
Britton, Layne, 237
Britton, Pamela, 325
"Broadway Malady" (Lawrence), 142
Brock, Major General Sir Isaac, 131
Broderick, Helen, 278
Bromberg, J. Edward, 315
Brophy, Edward, 283, 393
Brown, John, 327
Browne, Ray B., 16, 404-405, 409, 410
Browning, Robert, 359
Bruce, David, 313
Bruce, Nigel, 111, 276, 318, 383
Buchanan Advertising Agency, 161
Buchanan, Edgar, 315
Buchanan Rides Alone (film), 167
Buckley, Kenneth, 301
Buffet for Unwelcome Guests (Brand), 403
Bull-Dog Drummond (McNeile), 285
Bulldog Drummond (film), 286
Bulldog Drummond Strikes Back (McNeile), 285
Bulldog Drummond Strikes Back (film), 285-286
Bullet for a Star (Kaminsky), 409
"Bullet-Proof" (Ritchie), 224
Burger, Knox, 241, 243, 244
Burglar, The (Goodis), 347
Burglar, The (film), 344, 347-348
"Burial Is Arranged, A" (Lawence), 140-141
Burke, James, 307
Burks, Robert, 327, 345
Burlingham, Carlos, 53
Burn (Lutz), 213
Burnett, Hallie, 214
Burnett, W.R., 341
Burnett, Whit, 57, 63, 214
Burr, Raymond, 50, 385
Burtis, James, 287
Burton, Robert, 336
Butler, Gerald, 323, 324, 329

Butterworth, Charles, 285
Buyer Beware (Lutz), 211
CBS Music Library, 379
CIA and the Cult of Intelligence, The (Marchetti & Marks), 256
CIA Diary (Agee), 255
"C-Jag" (Woolrich), 63
"Cactus Killer, The" (Hoch), 200
Cagliostro, Count, 409
Cagney, James, 156, 187
Cain, James M., 56, 323, 341
Caine, Michael, 196
Calamity Town (Queen), 81, 91
Calendar of Crime (Queen), 85
Call Mr. Fortune (Bailey), 392
Callaway, Cheryl, 351
Calleia, Joseph, 349
Callejo, Cecilia, 303
Campbell, Beverly, 325
Campbell, Judy, 321
Campbell, Kippy, 345
Canadian Advertising Agency, 138
Canadian Bomber Contract, The (J. Phillips), 245
"Candy Kid, The" (Gardner), 29
Cane, Charles R., 342
Canfil, Fred, 394
Cansino, Rita (Rita Hayworth), 291, 292
Capell, Peter, 347
Capra, Frank, 111, 144, 304
"Captain Leopold Beats the Machine" (Hoch), 195
"Captain Leopold Gets Angry" (Hoch), 194
"Captain Leopold Goes Home" (Hoch), 194
"Captain Leopold Looks for the Cause" (Hoch), 195
"Captain Leopold Plays a Hunch" (Hoch), 195
Captain Video (TV series), 379
Cardinal (film production company), 325
Carey, Macdonald, 331
Carey, Olive, 329
Carey, Timothy, 342, 343
Carle, Richard, 303
Carlos (terrorist), 260, 266
Carlos Contract, The (D. Phillips), 250, 266, 267

Carr, John Dickson, 13, 18, 19, 41, 42, 77, 91, 94, 95, 96, 100, 110, 190, 191, 198, 207, 226, 331, 340, 363, 393, 399
Carr, Marian, 340
Carradine, John, 41
Carroll, Leo G., 327
Carroll, Lewis, 78, 79
Carroll, Mary, 342
Carruth, Milton, 323
Carter, Jimmy, 257
Casablanca (film), 185
Case Book of Gregory Hood, The (radio series), 97
Case of Erle Stanley Gardner, The (Johnston), 24
Case of the Amorous Aunt, The (Gardner), 50
Case of the Barking Clock, The (Keeler), 19, 207
Case of the Beautiful Beggar, The (Gardner), 51
Case of the Bigamous Spouse, The (Gardner), 50
Case of the Careless Kitten, The (Gardner), 40
Case of the Caretaker's Cat, The (Gardner), 37
Case of the Cheating Bride, The (Propper), 157-158
Case of the Counterfeit Eye, The (Gardner), 34, 35, 38
Case of the Crooked Candle, The (Gardner), 40
Case of the Daring Divorcee, The (Gardner), 50
"Case of the Drowned Coroner, The" (Hoch), 197
Case of the Fabulous Fake, The (Gardner), 51
Case of the Fiery Fingers, The (Gardner), 40
Case of the Half-Wakened Wife, The (Gardner), 40
Case of the Hesitant Hostess, The (Gardner), 48
Case of the Howling Dog, The (Gardner), 35, 36, 287
Case of the Howling Dog, The (film), 287-288

Case of the Ice-Cold Hands, The (Gardner), 50
Case of the Lavender Gripsack, The (Keeler), 204-205
Case of the Lucky Loser, The (Gardner), 48, 49, 51
Case of the Mischievous Doll, The (Gardner), 50
"Case of the Nervous Accomplice, The" (TV film), 380, 385
Case of the Perjured Parrot, The (Gardner), 38-39
Case of the Phantom Fortune, The (Gardner), 50
Case of the Reluctant Model, The (Gardner), 50
"Case of the Restless Redhead, The" (TV film), 380
Case of the Rolling Bones, The (Gardner), 40
Case of the Seven of Calvary, The (Boucher), 94-95
Case of the Shapely Shadow, The (Gardner), 50
Case of the Shivering Chorus Girls, The (J. Phillips), 233, 234
"Case of the Sulky Girl, The" (TV film), 380, 385
Case of the Terrified Typist, The (Gardner), 48
"Case of the Third Apostle, The" (Hoch), 197
Case of the Transparent Nude, The (Keeler), 207
Case of the Transposed Legs, The (Keeler), 207
Case of the Troubled Trustee, The (Gardner), 50
Case of the Velvet Claws, The (Gardner), 23, 32, 33, 34, 36, 51
Case of the Worried Waitress, The (Gardner), 50
Casino Royale (Fleming), 395
Castle, Peggie, 334
Castle, William, 102
Castro, Fidel, 252, 253, 270
Cat of Many Tails (Queen), 83-84, 86, 89
Catalogue of Crime, A (Barzun & Taylor), 114, 122, 149
Catch-22 (Heller), 203

Cavalier (magazine), 210
Cavanagh, Paul, 279
Cavanaugh, Hobart, 305, 317
Cavett, Dick, 91
Central Intelligence Agency (CIA), 214, 242, 246, 247, 249, 250, 252, 253, 255, 256, 257, 258, 260, 261, 264, 265, 266, 267, 268, 269
Ceremony (Parker), 392
Chabrol, Claude, 409
Chambers' Journal (magazine), 357
Chameleon, The (Keeler), 204
Chandler Before Marlowe: Raymond Chandler's Early Prose and Poetry, 1908-1912, 358
Chandler, Raymond, 17, 19, 114, 116, 118, 127, 129, 130, 156, 162, 164, 165, 187, 215, 218, 231, 244, 245, 279, 303, 309, 310, 327, 341, 357, 358, 359, 360, 361, 366
Chanslor, Roy, 317, 318
Chaplin, Charlie, 212
Chapman, Marguerite, 315, 316
Charles, Franklin (Adams pseudonym), 125
Charlie Chan in Egypt (film), 291-292
Charteris, Leslie, 13, 309, 313, 314
Charters, Spencer, 295
Chastain, Thomas, 199
Cheirel, Micheline, 319
Chesterton, G.K., 18, 20, 95, 104, 190, 194, 195
Cheyney, Peter, 393
Chicago *Sun-Times*, 100, 102
Children of the Ritz (Woolrich), 54
Chillers & Thrillers, 397, 398
Chinese Orange Mystery, The (Queen), 78, 189, 190
Ching, William, 325
Chodorov, Edward, 305
Christie, Agatha, 13, 20, 91, 94, 100, 190, 191, 198, 226, 321, 361, 395, 399, 414
"Christmas Egg, The" (Hoch), 192
Church, Senator Frank, 257
"Circus" (Hoch), 193, 195

Circus, Anthony (Hoch pseudonym), 198
Circus Queen Murder, The (film), 111, 276
Cisco Kid, The (TV series), 386
Citizen Kane (film), 349, 380
City of Brass (Hoch), 192
Clarence, O.B., 299
Clark, Al, 351
Clark, Cliff, 303
Clark, Daniel B., 291
Clarke, Mae, 277
Classic Mystery Stories (Greene), 392
Clean Break (White), 342
Clifford, Clark, 257
Clive, E.E., 285
Clork, Harry, 289, 293
"Close Call" (Gardner), 31
"Club Fighter" (Lawrence), 144
Club 17 (Ard), 178, 179
Clues (magazine), 25, 27, 116, 395
Clyde, Andy, 303
"Cocaine" (Woolrich), 63
Codee, Ann, 319
"Coffin a Day, A" (J.D. MacDonald), 217-218
Cohen, Albert J., 315
Colbert, Claudette, 303, 304
Cold Red Sunrise, A (Kaminsky), 409
Coleridge, Sauel Taylor, 360
College Humor (magazine), 54
College Life (magazine), 54
Collegiate Institute, 131
Collier, John, 209
Collier Books (paperback publisher), 393
Collier's (magazine), 235, 237, 240, 241, 244
Collins, Michael (Lynds pseudonym), 19, 289, 297, 305, 313, 327, 349
Collins, Ray, 349
Collins, Tom, 305
Colman, Ronald, 285, 286
Columbia (pulp magazine chain), 192
Columbia Broadcasting System (CBS), 66, 80, 189, 382
Columbia College, 54

Columbia House, 380
Columbia Pictures (movie studio), 80, 111, 275, 276, 315, 336, 344, 347, 351
Columbia University, 67, 194, 362, 365, 404, 411
"Come Die with Me!" (J.D. MacDonald), 218
Comfort, Mady, 340
"Computer Cops" (Hoch), 197
Conan Doyle, Denis P.S., 384
Conan Doyle, Sir Arthur, 20, 72, 77, 97, 113, 190
Conklin, George W., 364
Connell, Allen, 239
Connolly, Norma, 345
Conrad, Joseph, 358
Conried, Hans, 303
Conroy, Frank, 279
"Construction of a Short Story" (Lawrence), 133-134
Conte, Richard, 338, 339
Conti, Albert, 275
Contraband (Adams), 128
Conway, Tom, 310, 383
Cook, Donald, 277
Cook, Elisha, Jr., 307, 311, 342, 343
Cook, Whitfield, 327
Cooper, Charles, 345
Cooper, Gary, 185, 187
Cooper, Jackie, 240
Cooper, James Fenimore, 194
Cooper, Maxine, 321
Copa (film production company), 344
Copelin, Campbell, 323
Cornier, Vincent, 365
Cornthwaite, Robert, 340
"Corpse in His Dreams, A" (J.D. MacDonald), 217
"Corpse Next Door, The" (Woolrich), 58
Corpse with the Purple Thighs, The (Stein), 414
"Corpse-Maker Goes Courting, A" (J.D. MacDonald), 220
"Corpus Delicti, The" (Post), 45, 49
Cortez, Ricardo, 307

Cosmopolitan (magazine), 79, 112-113, 215
Coulouris, George, 313
Count the Hours (film), 331-332
"Courier and Ives" (Hoch), 200
Cover Charge (Woolrich), 54, 67
Cowan, Jerome, 307
Cowboy G-Men (TV series), 386
Crack Detective Stories (magazine), 219
Craven, John, 331
Crawford, Broderick, 317
"Credit Card Caper, The" (Hoch), 197
Creeps, The (Abbot), 113
Crehan, Joseph, 305, 311
Crider, Bill, 410
Crime and Justice (magazine), 192
"Crime of Omission" (J.D. MacDonald), 221
Crime Prevention in the 30th Century (Santesson), 197
"Criminals at Large" (Boucher review column), 100, 371
Crimson Joy (Parker), 392
Crippen & Landru (publishing house), 192, 196, 198, 199
Criss Cross (film), 312
Croft-Cooke, Rupert, 126
Crofts, Freeman Wills, 149
Crooking Finger, The (Adams), 124
Crosland, Alan, 287, 288, 289, 290
Cross, Amanda (Heilbrun pseudonym), 404
Crumley, James, 366
Cry of the City (film), 312
Cry Scandal (Ard), 166, 170, 175
Cummings, Constance, 293, 294, 299, 300
Cummings, Irving, 111, 275, 276
Cunningham, Cecil, 303
Curtis, Alan, 311
Curtis, Tony, 170
Curtiz, Michael, 279, 280
D.A. Draws a Circle, The (Gardner), 41
D.A. Takes a Chance, The (Gardner), 42
D.O.A. (film), 325-326
Dahl, Roald, 209

Dale, Esther, 305
Damned If He Does (Ard), 177, 179
Dannay, Frederic, 16, 18, 65, 72-91, 100, 103, 113, 148, 190, 196, 197, 198, 199, 226, 365, 382, 407
Dannay, Hilda (Wiesenthal), 86
Dannay, Mary (Beck), 80
Dannay, Rose (Koppel), 91
Dannay, Stephen, 86
d'Annunzio, Lola, 345
Dark Passage (Goodis), 344
Dark Passage (film), 344
Dark Side of Love, The (Woolrich), 66-67
Dark Tunnel, The (K. Millar), 360
Darkness at Dawn (Woolrich), 56
Dartmouth University, 161
Darwin, Charles, 85
"Dauphin's Doll, The" (Queen), 85
David, Charles, 313, 314
Davidson, Avram, 89, 90, 406
Davis, Dorothy Salisbury, 365
Davis, Frank, 303
Davis Publications, 196, 199
Day, John, 334
Day, Laraine, 66
Day-Lewis, Cecil, 364
Day-Lewis, Daniel, 364
Days of Misfortune (Stein), 415
De Corsia, Ted, 338, 342
de Courville, Albert, 299
de Gaetano, Al, 291
de Vargas, Valentin, 349
de Vol, Frank, 340
De Wit, Jacqueline, 313
De Wolf, Karen, 331
Dead Drunk (Stein), 415
"Dead Man" (Lutz), 211
Dead Men's Letters (Gardner), 27
"Dead on Her Feet" (Woolrich), 59
"Dead to the World" (J.D. MacDonald), 221
Deadline at Dawn (Woolrich), 64, 68
Deadly Mermaid, The (J. Phillips), 239
"Dear Dorie" (Lutz), 211
Dearden, Basil, 301

Death and the Good Life (Hugo), 366
Death Before Bedtime (Vidal), 398
Death Beyond the Go-Thru (Kendrick), 391
Death Dives Deep (Avallone), 185, 186
"Death in the Air" (Woolrich), 314
Death in the Fifth Position (Vidal), 398
Death Is Like That (Adams), 125
Death Likes It Hot (Vidal), 398
"Death Sits in the Dentist's Chair" (Woolrich), 56
Decoy (Adams), 118, 121
"Deed of Gift" (Lawrence), 145
Defrauded Yeggman, The (Keeler), 203-204, 205
"Degrees of Gray in Philipsburg" (Hugo), 366
Deighton, Len, 196, 247
Dekker, Albert, 340
Del Ruth, Roy, 285, 286
Del Valle, Jaime, 351
Deliverance (film), 372
Dell (paperback publisher), 170, 239, 393
DeMaggio, Nick, 333
Dennis, Nick, 340
Denny, Reginald, 293, 295
Dentinger, Stephen (Hoch pseudonym), 192, 193, 195, 200
Department of Queer Complaints, The (Carr), 97
Derek, John, 177
Detective Action Stories (magazine), 25, 27, 133, 139, 140
Detective Fiction Weekly (magazine), 25, 27, 29, 56, 57, 58, 59, 60, 63, 119, 120, 121
Detective Tales (magazine), 215, 221
Detectives A to Z, (McSherry, Greenberg & Waugh), 195
"Detour to Death" (Lawrence), 144
Deutsch, Adolph, 307
"Devil and Daniel Webster, The" (Benet), 238
Devil Is a Woman, The (film), 296
Devil to Pay, The (Queen), 80

"Devil's Fire" (Gardner), 32
Dexter, Brad, 334
Diagnosis: Impossible (Hoch), 198
Dial Press (publishing house), 233
Diary, The (Ard), 163-164
Dick, Philip K., 97
Dickens, Charles, 96, 203, 208, 359
Dickinson, Angie, 374
Dickson, Carter (Carr pseudonym), 97, 363
Dietrich, Marlene, 296, 349
Dig Me a Grave (Adams), 125
"Dime a Dance" (Woolrich), 59
Dime Detective (magazine), 25, 28, 58, 130, 133, 138, 140, 142, 143, 144, 145, 215, 220, 221, 358
Dime Detectives, The (Goulart), 116
Diskant, George A., 329, 330
Disney (film production company), 324
Divorce Court Murder, The (Propper), 152, 155
Dixon, Jean, 289
Dobkin, Lawrence, 325
Dobyns, Stephen, 367
Doc Savage (magazine), 215, 217, 220
Doctor Faustus (Marlowe), 358
"Dog That Barked All Day, The" (Hoch), 198
Donlan, James, 277
Donlevy, Brian, 338
Don't Come Crying to Me (Ard), 162, 165
Double Blind (J. & D. Phillips), 267
Double Cross (Ard), 176, 177
"Double Deal in Diamonds, A" (Gardner), 28
Double Detective (magazine), 125
Douglas, Melvyn, 305, 306
Dowling, Constance, 317
Down I Go (Ard), 176, 177
Drake, Frances, 295, 303
Dragnet (TV series), 351
Dreaming of Babylon (Brautigan), 366
Dreiser, Theodore, 414
"Dressed to Kill" (Gardner), 28
Drew, Bernard, 116

Drew, Donna, 338
Drop Dead (Stein), 415
Drowning Icecube, The (Breen), 399
Drury Lane's Last Case (Queen), 77
"Duality of Impressionism in the Recent German Drama, The" (Boucher), 94
Dulwich (preparatory school), 358
Dumbrille, Douglas, 305
Duncan, David, 97
Duning, George, 344
Durbin, Deanna, 313, 314
Duryea, Dan, 313, 314, 317, 347
"Dusk to Dawn" (Woolrich), 59
Dutton, E.P. (publishing house), 120, 121, 122, 125, 206
Duvall, Robert, 213, 387
Dyne, Aminta, 323
Eastwood, Clint, 350
Edeson, Arthur, 307
Edwards, Blake, 192
Edwards, Henry, 321
Edwards, James, 342
Edwards, R.T. (Hoch pseudonym), 199
Edwards, Vincent, 342
Egyptian Cross Mystery, The (Queen), 78
"Eight Dozen Agents" (J.D. MacDonald), 220
Eilers, Sally, 293
Eisen, Robert, 338
Eisenhower, Dwight D., 239, 387
Eisinger, Jo, 315
El Greco, 183
Elam, Jack, 331, 332, 340
Election Booth Murder, The (Propper), 155, 160
Eleven of Diamonds, The (Kendrick), 391
Eliot, T.S., 361
Ellery Queen (radio series), 382, 397
Ellery Queen (TV series), 91
Ellery Queen's Anthology, 197
Ellery Queen's Mystery Magazine (EQMM), 16, 18, 66, 67, 81, 82, 85, 87, 88, 90, 96, 97, 100, 102, 170, 189, 192, 193, 194, 195, 196, 197, 198, 199, 210, 211, 227, 355, 364, 365, 382, 399
Ellery Queen's Prime Crimes, 199
Elliott, Cecil, 342
Elliott, Laura, 327
Elliott, Wild Bill, 146
Ellis, Edward, 283
Ellis, Herbert, 342
Ellis, Robert, 291
Ellison, Harlan, 406
Emerald Forest, The (film), 372
Emery, Richard, 347
Encyclopaedia Britannica, 102
Encyclopedia of Mystery and Detection (Steinbrunner & Penzler), 114, 149
Esquire (magazine), 215
Essen, Robert, 345
Ethan, John B., 394
Ethnic Detectives, The (Pronzini & Greenberg), 199
Everson, William K., 274
Evil Star, The (Adams), 125
Ex-Mrs. Bradford, The (film), 297-298
Exeunt Murderers (Boucher), 96
Eye, The (Pronzini & Lutz), 212, 213
Eye of God (Breen), 400
Eye of Violence, The (D. Phillips), 266
FBI Detective (magazine), 217, 219
"Face of Evil" (TV film), 387
Face of the Man from Saturn, The (Keeler), 203
Face to Face (Queen), 90
Facenda, John, 347
Faerie Queene, The (Spenser), 361
Fair, A.A. (Gardner pseudonym), 44
Falcon Takes Over, The (film), 309-310
Family Burial Murders, The (Propper), 151, 155, 160
Famous Detective Stories (magazine), 192
Farber, Stephen, 373
Farewell, My Lovely (Chandler), 18, 309, 310, 358
Farnum, Franklyn, 295
Farrell, Roy, 236, 246

"Fast Break" (J. Phillips), 240
Fat Death, The (Avallone), 185
Fatal Descent (Rhode and Carr), 363
Fatal Witness, The (film), 126
Faulkner, William, 233, 404
Fawcett Gold Medal (paperback publishing house), 167, 176, 241, 243, 244
Fax, Jesslyn, 340
Faylen, Frank, 334
Fear and Desire (film), 239
Federal Bureau of Investigation (FBI), 260, 268, 333
Fellowship of the Hand, The (Hoch), 197
Fenton, Frank, 309
Fenton, Leslie, 305, 306
Fenwick, Jean, 305
Ferguson, Frank, 329
Fetchit, Stepin, 157, 291, 292
Fictioneers, The (writers' club), 115
15 Mystery Stories (magazine), 220
"Figure of Incongruity, The" (Hamnett), 355
Film Quarterly (magazine), 373
"Final Problem, The" (Conan Doyle), 113
"Finding Joe Finch" (Hoch), 195
Fine and Private Place, A (Queen), 90-91
"Finger of Doom" (Woolrich), 63
Finishing Stroke, The (Queen), 87-88, 89
"Finishing Touch, The" (Gardner), 28
Fireside Theatre (TV series), 240
"First Blood" (J. Phillips), 235
First National Pictures (movie studio), 54
First You Dream, Then You Die (Woolrich), 67
Fisher, Steve, 61
Fitzgerald, F. Scott, 54
Five Alarm Funeral (Winchell), 395
Five Star (publishing house), 200
"Five-Day Forecast" (Hoch), 198
Flame (Lutz), 213
Flash Gordon (film), 379

Fleming, Ian, 231, 246, 395
Flippen, Jay C., 342
"Floater" (Lawrence), 144
Florey, Robert, 295, 296
Florida State University, 410
Flynn, Errol, 136, 137
Flynn's Detective Fiction (magazine), 30
Fonda, Bridget, 213
Fonda, Henry, 345, 346
Fontaine, Joan, 323, 324
"For the Rest of Her Life" (Woolrich), 67
Forbes, Louis, 331
Forbes, Ralph, 281
Ford, Glenn, 336
Ford, John, 282
Ford, Wallace, 317
Ford Theater (TV series), 65
Fordham Law School, 396
Forrester, Cay, 325
Forsythe, John, 240
Foster, Norman, 323, 324
"Foul Tip, The" (Queen radio play), 397, 398
Foulger, Byron, 113
"Four O'Clock" (TV drama), 66
Four of Hearts, The (Queen), 80
Fox (film production company), 291
"Fractions" (Lutz), 210
"Frame for the Marquis, A" (Lawrence), 145, 146
Francis, Alec B., 281
Franciscus, James, 387
Franco, Generalissimo Francisco, 207
Frankenheimer, John, 66, 240
Frankenstein (film), 293
Frankenstein Factory, The (Hoch), 197
Fraser, Richard, 126
Frawley, William,. 313
Frederici, Blanche, 275
"Free Ride" (TV film), 386
Freeman, Helen, 319
Fried, Gerald, 342
Friedhofer, Hugo, 319
Frost, Robert, 361, 406
Fugitive, The (TV series), 200
Fuller, Samuel, 166, 333, 337

Funk, Wilfred (publishing house), 125
Gabel, Martin, 97
Gable, Clark, 187
Gabor, Zsa Zsa, 349
Gael, 416, 417
Gainsborough Pictures (film production company), 299
Galaxy (magazine), 210
Gall, Bobby, 301
Gallagher, Skeets, 275
Galton Case, The (K. Millar), 360
Gambling, Gambling! (stage play), 93
Gang World (magazine), 25, 28, 132, 133
Gangland Stories (magazine), 25
"Garden of Forking Paths, The" (Borges), 100
Gardner, Erle Stanley, 13, 18, 23-52, 102, 130, 139, 156, 215, 287, 288, 380, 385
Garriguenc, René, 380
"Gateway to Heaven, A" (Hoch), 199
Gaumont-British (film production company), 299
Gehrig, Lou, 416
General, The (film), 372
Genn, Leo, 321, 403
George, Florence, 305
George, Gladys, 307
Geray, Steven, 319
Gerrard, Douglas, 285
Gerrard, Henry, 277
Gerstle, Frank, 325
Ghost of a Flea (Sallis), 367
"Giant Moth, The" (Keeler), 202
Gibbon, James, 287
Gilbert, Helen, 309
Gilbert & Sullivan, 102
Gilliat, Sidney, 299, 300, 321, 322
Girardot, Etienne, 270
Girl for Danny, A (Ard), 168
Girl with the Hole in Her Head (Stein), 415
Gist, Robert, 327
"Glass Ball, The" (Queen radio play), 397
Glass Key, The (Hammett), 17, 31, 119, 125, 176, 177, 283

Glass Village, The (Queen), 86-87
"Glass-Domed Clock, The" (Queen), 78
Gleason, James, 277, 278, 297, 309
Gleason, Lucille, 297
Gleckler, Robert, 289
Goldbeck, Willis, 277
Goldberg, Rube, 216, 217
Golden Ball, The (Christie), 396
Golden Books, 131
Golden Summer, The (Nathan), 86, 407
Golden Voices (Boucher radio program), 103
Goldsmith, Harold, 133, 138
Gombell, Minna, 283
Gomez, Thomas, 311
Gone with the Wind (Mitchell), 382
Good Old Stuff, The (J.D. MacDonald), 221
"Goodbye, New York" (Woolrich), 58
Goodis, David, 14, 18, 19, 344, 347
Goodkind, Saul A., 317
Goodrich, Frances, 283
Gordon, Gale, 97
Gordon, Michael, 299
Gordon, Roy, 338
Goulart, Ron, 97, 116, 199
Gould, Rita, 338
Grahame, Gloria, 336, 337
Granger, Farley, 327
Granstedt, Greta, 275
Grant, Cary, 63
Grant, James Edward, 297
Gray, Coleen, 342
Gray, Sally, 321
Great American Detective Stories (Boucher), 97
Great Insurance Murders, The (Propper), 157, 160
Greatest Story Ever Told, The (Oursler), 107, 113, 275
Greek Coffin Mystery, The (Queen), 13, 75, 76, 396
Green, A.C., 233
Green, Clarence, 325
Green, Denis, 97, 383
Green for Danger (Brand), 321, 403
Green for Danger (film), 321-322

"Green Heart, The" (Ritchie), 226
Green Wound, The (J. Phillips), 232, 241, 245
Greenbaum, Mutz, 299
Greenberg, Martin H., 27, 196, 199
Greene, Douglas G., 392
Greene, Graham, 14, 20, 193, 200, 242, 270
Greenstreet, Sydney, 119, 185, 307, 316
Gregory, James, 344
Grella, George, 367
Griffies, Ethel, 285
Griffith, D.W., 296
Griffith, James, 342"
"Griggsby Papers, The" (Ritchie), 226
Gross, Roland, 329
Grosset & Dunlap (publishing house), 198
Guffey, Burnett, 319, 344
"Guillotine" (Woolrich), 60
"Guilty Vicarage, The" (Auden), 360
Guinness, Alec, 270
Gun Crazy (film), 338, 339, 411
Guns of Revenge (Ard), 168
Gurney, Claud, 321
"Gypsy Gold" (Hoch), 199
Hackett, Albert, 283
Haden, Sara, 305
Hag's Nook (Carr), 393
Hagen, Joe, 415
Hagen, Miriam-Ann, 415
Hair of the Sleuthhound (Breen), 399
Hale, Jonathan, 315, 327, 328
Hall, Frank, 347
Hall, Porter, 283
Hall-Mills murder case, 110
Halperin, Morton, 257
Hamilton, John, 307
Hamlin, Ken (Ard pseudonym), 168, 173
Hammett, Dashiell, 17, 19, 30, 31, 36, 43, 102, 114, 116, 119, 127, 130, 162, 176, 177, 187, 215, 218, 231, 283, 284, 287, 289, 290, 307, 308, 309, 341, 355, 356, 357, 359, 361, 366, 371

"Handel and Gretel" (Hoch & Breen), 199
Handi-Books (paperback publisher), 127
Handwriting on the Wall, The (Propper), 158
Handy Manual (Conklin), 364
Hangover Murders, The (Hobhouse), 293
Hard Day's Night, A (film), 372
Hard-Boiled Dames (Drew), 116
Harline, Leigh, 333
Harmon, Sidney, 338
Harris, Henry, 301
Harris, James B., 342
Harris-Kubrick (film production company), 342
Harrison, Joan, 311, 312
Hart, Henry, 325
Hart House Theater, 132
Hart, Lorenz, 363, 364
Hart, William S., 27, 78
Harvard Business School, 214
Harvard University, 74, 260, 362
Harvard University Press, 364
Harvey, Forrester, 281
Harvey, Phil, 349
Have Gun—Will Travel (TV series), 379, 380
Havelock-Allan, Anthony, 301
Having a Wild Weekend (film), 372, 377
Havlick, Gene, 315
Hawks, Howard, 126, 186
Haycraft, Howard, 114, 148
Hayden, Sterling, 342, 343
Hayes, W. Donn, 305
Hayworth, Rita, 292, 292
Head of a Traveler (Day-Lewis), 364, 365
Healy, Jeremiah, 410
Heart at Fire's Center: The Life and Music of Bernard Herrmann, A (Smith), 381
Heart of Darkness (Conrad), 358
Hecht, Ben, 303
Heckelmann, Charles, 173
Hegel, G.W. F., 14
Heilbrun, Carolyn, 404
Heldabrand, John, 345

Hell Is a City (Ard), 162, 163, 165, 167, 169, 170, 171, 175, 176, 177
Hell's Island (film), 334
Hellman, Lillian, 283, 284
Helm, Fay, 311
Helms, Richard, 252, 259
Helton, Percy, 340
Hemingway, Ernest, 194, 231, 233, 277, 366
Henry, Louise, 293
Henry, O., 201
Henry, William, 283
Hensley, Joe L., 406
Henty, G.A., 147
Here Comes McBride (radio series), 127
"Heritage of Hate" (J.D. MacDonald), 218
Hermelin, Baroness, 237
Hernandez, Juano, 340
Herostratus, 259
Herrmann, Bernard, 329, 330, 345, 379-381, 385
Hers (magazine), 198
Hersh, Seymour, 267
Hervey, Grizelda, 323
Heston, Charlton, 349, 350
Hicks, Russell, 287
Hide the Body! (Propper), 158
High Noon at Midnight (Avallone), 187-188
"High Stakes" (Lutz), 211-212
Highsmith, Patricia, 327
Hildegarde Withers: Uncollected Riddles (Palmer), 396
Hillie, Verna, 289
Hilton, Arthur, 311
Hilton, James, 190
Hinds, Samuel S., 313
Hitchcock, Alfred, 18, 53, 62, 65, 66, 68, 122, 126, 185, 282, 286, 299, 300, 304, 311, 312, 314, 317, 321, 327, 328, 345, 346, 379, 381
Hitchcock, Patricia, 327
Hitler, Adolf, 321
Hoag, Doane R., 331
Hobbes, Halliwell, 285, 305
Hobbes, Peter, 323
Hobhouse, Adam, 293

Hobson, Thayer, 33
Hobson, Valerie, 301
Hoch, Earl G., 189
Hoch, Edward D., 189-201, 407-408
Hoch, Patricia (McMahon), 190, 407
Hodgson, Leland, 323
Hohl, Arthur, 279, 285
Holder, William, 387
"Hole in the City, A" (TV film), 387
Holles, Antony, 299
Holliman, Earl, 338
Holloway, Susan, 374
Holmes, H.H. (Boucher pseudonym), 95, 102
Holt, Henry (publishing house), 174
"Homesick Chicken, The" (Hoch), 198
"Homicide: Honolulu Bound" (Adams), 121
"Honest Money" (Gardner), 31
Honest Money (Gardner), 30-31
Honeymooners, The (TV series), 15
Hope, Bob, 406
Hope and Glory (film), 372
Hopkins, Gerard Manley, 361
Hopley, George (Woolrich pseudonym), 64
Hopley-Woolrich, Genaro, 53
Horn, Herta, 347
Horrible Man, The (Avallone), 185
Horton, Edward Everett, 313
Hot (Lutz), 213
Hotel Room (Woolrich), 66
House of Brass, The (Queen), 226
House Un-American Activities Committee (HUAC), 86, 101, 333
Houseman, John, 329
Houser, Lionel, 305
Howard, Trevor, 321, 403
Hoyt, John, 338
Huber, Harold, 283
Hubin, Allen J., 15
"Hudson Chain, The" (Hoch), 199
Hughes, Carol, 325
Hughes, Howard, 240
Hugo, Richard, 365

Hugo, Victor, 222
Human Zero, The (Gardner), 27
Hume, David, 14
Hunt, J. Roy, 287
Hunter, The (Westlake), 371, 373, 374
Hurley, Harold, 295
Huston, John, 185, 307, 308, 309, 315, 316, 343, 409
Hutchins Advertising Agency, 190
Hutton, Jim, 91
Hymerling, Madelyn, 147
I Confess (film), 328
I Fear You Not (Ard), 176, 177, 179
I Love You, Paris (Woolrich), 56
I Married a Dead Man (Woolrich), 65
I, The Jury (Spillane), 341
I Wake Up Screaming (Fisher), 61
I Was a Communist for the FBI (film), 331
I Was Waiting for You (Woolrich), 67
"I Wouldn't Be in Your Shoes" (Woolrich), 59-60
I Wouldn't Be in Your Shoes (Woolrich), 14, 59
Ickes, Harold, 255
Idris, King, 259
In a Lonely Place (film), 329
In re Patterson, 47
In re Whittington, 46
In Search of Enemies (Stockwell), 256
"In the Dispensary" (Christie), 361
Indiana University, 382
Inheritors, The (J. Phillips), 233
"Inner Circle, The" (Queen), 85
Innes, Michael, 20
"Interlude in India" (J.D. MacDonald), 214
Into the Night (Woolrich), 67
Into the Same River Twice (Nevins), 416
Invisible Worm, The (M. Millar), 360
Irish, William (Woolrich pseudonym), 54, 63, 311
Iron Angel and Other Tales of the Gypsy Sleuth, The (Hoch), 199

Iron Spiders, The (Kendrick), 391
Irving, Richard, 329
Irwin, Charles, 281
Isaac Asimov's Science Fiction Magazine, 198
It Happened One Night (film), 304
It's a Wonderful Life (film), 304
It's a Wonderful World (film), 303-304
"It's the McCoy" (Gardner), 28
Ivano, Paul, 317, 318
Jackson, Ambassador, 266
Jackson, Felix, 313
Jackson, Joseph Henry, 97
Jackson, Thomas, 295
Jacobs, Alexander, 373, 377
Jaeckel, Richard, 351
Jaffe, Sam, 343
Jakes, John, 173
James, P.D., 20
Jaquet, Frank, 325
Jaws (film), 211
"Jealous Lover" (Hoch), 192
Jeayes, Allan, 299
Jenkins, Allen, 287, 309, 313
Jenkins, Megs, 321
Jericho Man (Lutz), 211, 213
Jesus, 70, 346
John, Rosamund, 321
"John Jones' Dollar" (Keeler), 203
"Johnny on the Spot" (Woolrich), 57-58
Johnson, Nunnally, 285
Johnson, Owen, 234
Johnston, Alva, 24
Journal of Commerce, 243
Journal of Popular Culture, 405
Journey into Fear (film), 324
Joyce, Rev. Brian, 104
Judges of Hades, The (Hoch), 192
"Just Like I Hate Money" (J. Phillips), 237
KPFA (public radio station), 102, 103
KQED (TV station), 103
Kafka, Franz, 211
Kai-Shek, Chiang, 239
Kaiser Foundation Hospital, 104
Kaminsky, Stuart M., 19, 409-410
Kansas City Confidential (film), 334

Kaplan, Sol, 347
Karloff, Boris, 66, 184
Karlson, Phil, 334
Kaufman, Edward, 297
Kaylin, Samuel, 291
Keeler, Harry Stephen, 15, 19, 174, 201-208, 393, 405
Keeler, Hazel Goodwin, 202, 204, 207
Keeler, Thelma Rinaldo, 208
Keene, Day, 146
Keith, Brian, 344
Keith, Ian, 295
Keith, Robert, 351
Keith-Johnston, Colin, 323
Kellman, Louis W., 347
Kemper, Charles, 329
Kendrick, Baynard, 391
KenKnight, Brian, 128
Kennedy, Edgar, 277, 303
Kennedy, John F., 107, 195, 270, 277, 303, 404, 417
Kennedy, Joyce, 299
Kennel Murder Case, The (Van Dine), 279
Kennel Murder Case, The (film), 279-280
Kent, Ted, 293, 313
Kern, Jerome, 172
Kern, Robert J., 283
Kerr, Ben (Ard pseudonym), 167, 173, 174, 175, 176, 177, 178, 179
Kersh, Gerald, 209
Kesey, Ken, 19, 208
"Key to Room 537, The" (Gardner), 139
Keyes, Evelyn, 334
Khadafy, Moammar, 253, 259
Kibbee, Guy, 303
Kibrick, Leonard, 303
Kiley, Richard, 333
Kilgallen, Dorothy, 233
Kill the Umpire (Breen), 399
"Killer and the Clown, The" (Hoch), 193
Killer on the Keys (Avallone), 186
Killers, The (film), 312
Killing, The (film), 343
King, Louis, 291
King, Dr. Martin Luther, Jr., 253

Kipling, Rudyard, 331, 355
Kirkpatrick, Jess, 325
Kiss (Lutz), 213
Kiss Before Dying, A (Levin), 100
Kiss Me Deadly (Spillane), 340
Kiss Me Deadly (film), 340-341
Kiss of Death (film), 326
Kiss the Blood Off My Hands (Butler), 323
Kiss the Blood Off My Hands (film), 323-324
Kissinger, Henry, 252
Kitchin, Jack, 277
Knight (magazine), 210
Knock on Any Door (film), 329
Knopf, Alfred A. (publishing house), 128
Kress, Harold F., 303
Kristofferson, Kris, 361
Kubrick, Stanley, 239, 342, 343
Kwariani, Kola, 342
Lady for a Day (film), 144
"Lady of the Impossible" (Hoch), 198
Lady on a Train (film), 313-314
Lady Vanishes, The (film), 300, 321
Lady Without Passport, A (film), 339
Laemmle, Carl, Jr., 293
Lambert, Jack, 334, 340
"Lamp of God, The" (Queen), 79, 80
Lancaster, Burt, 323, 324
Lancer Books (paperback publisher), 197
Landres, Paul, 386
Lang, Charles, 336
Lang, Doreen, 345
Lang, Fritz, 299, 301, 336, 337
Langan, Glenn, 334
Lange, Arthur, 334
Lansing, Joi, 349
LaRoche, Mary, 351
LaRocque, Rod, 295
LaRouche, Lyndon, 256
LaRue, Jack, 279, 293
Last Domino Contract, The (J. Phillips), 246
Last Good Kiss, The (Crumley), 366

"Last Man Club, The" (Queen radio play), 80
Last Woman in His Life, The (Queen), 90
Laszlo, Ernest, 325, 340
Launder, Frank, 299, 300, 321
Lawrence, Gertrude, 131, 132, 134, 135, 136
Lawrence, John (Jack), 20, 130-146
Lawrence, Judith (J.A.), 134, 135, 136, 137, 138
Lawrence, Muriel (Bodkin), 134, 135, 136, 137, 138, 141
Lawton, Charles, Jr., 315
Layman, Richard, 290
Lazarus Man (Lutz), 211
Le Carré, John, 20, 194, 196, 198, 200, 232, 246, 247, 265
Le Morte d'Arthur (Malory), 358
Leachman, Cloris, 340
League of Frightened Men, The (Stout),362
Leatherneck, The (magazine), 235
Lee, James, 279
Lee, Kaye (Brinker), 82
Lee, Lila, 297
Lee, Manfred B., 16, 18, 72-91, 97, 148, 190, 226, 382, 383, 384
Lee, Rand, 74
Lee, Robert N., 279
Leeds, Peter, 334
"Leg Man" (Gardner), 43
Lehrman, Henry, 285
Leicester, James, 331
Leigh, Janet, 349
Leigh, Jennifer Jason, 213
Leisure Books (paperback publisher), 192
Leitch, Thomas M., 364
"Lend-Lease Christmas Tree" (J. Phillips), 235
Lenniger, August, 125
Leopold, Jules, 193
"Leopold Locked Room, The" (Hoch), 194
"Leopold Undercover" (Hoch), 195
Leopold's Way (Hoch), 193
Lepofsky, Manford (Manfred B. Lee), 72
Les Miserables (Hugo), 222
Leslie, William, 351

Lester, Mark, 299
Lester, Richard, 372
Letterman, David, 17
Lever, Philip, 301
Levin, Ira, 100
Levy, Louis, 299
Lewis, Buena (Mrs. Joseph H.), 412
Lewis, Elliot, 97
Lewis, Freeman, 26
Lewis, Joseph H., 319, 320, 338, 339, 411-413
Lewis, Roland, 403
Lexy, Edward, 301
Liberty (magazine), 107, 215, 275
Liddy, G. Gordon, 211
Life of Raymond Chandler, The (MacShane), 357
Lightning (Lutz), 213
Like Ice She Was (Ard), 172
Lincoln, Abraham, 90
Line-Up, The (film), 351-352
Line-Up, The (TV series), 351
Ling, Frank, 321
Lion Books (paperback publisher), 174
Listerdale Mystery, The (Christie), 395
Liszt, Franz, 379
Little Boxes of Bewilderment (Ritchie), 225
"Little People, The" (J.D. MacDonald), 220
Little Sister, The (Chandler), 358-359
"Live Man's Shoes" (Lawrence), 142-143
Living Bomb, The (Avallone), 185
Lloyd, Doris, 311
Lockhart, Gene, 305
Logan, Helen, 291
"Lollipop Cop, The" (Hoch), 197
London, Pauline, 305
Lone Ranger, The (TV series), 379, 386
Long Goodbye, The (Chandler), 18
"Long Way Down, The" (Hoch), 200
Long-Legged Fly, The (Sallis), 367
"Loot for the Unlucky Lady" (J.D. MacDonald), 219

Lorne, Marion, 327
Lorre, Peter, 187, 307, 316, 317
Loser, The (Woolrich), 49, 67
Lost Horizon (Hilton), 190
Lost Patrol, The (film), 282
Lovejoy, Frank, 126
Lowe, Edmund, 289, 299, 300
Lowe, Edward T., 291
Lowell, Helen, 287
Lowndes, Robert A.W., 192
Loy, Myrna, 283, 284
Luciano, Michael, 340
"Luck of a Gypsy, The" (Hoch), 199
Lucy, 417
Luez, Laurette, 325
Lugosi, Bela, 113
Lummis, Dayton, 345
Lumumba, Patrice, 252
Lupino, Ida, 329, 330
Lutz, Barbara (Jean Bradley), 209, 210, 213
Lutz, John, 209-213
Lynds, Dennis, 19
Lyman, Frank, 289
Lyon, William A., 344
Lyons, Leonard, 233
M Squad (TV series), 387
Mabbott, Thomas Ollive, 364
Macabre (film), 102
MacDonald, David, 301
MacDonald, George, 281
MacDonald, Joe, 333
MacDonald, John D., 14, 209, 214-222, 234, 399, 406
MacDonald, Philip, 281
Macdonald, Ross (K. Millar pseudonym), 162, 209, 359, 361, 366, 399
MacDougal, Roger, 301
MacGowan, Kenneth, 277
Mackay, Phoebe, 347
Mackey, Percival, 301
MacKinnon, Allan, 301
MacLane, Barton, 307
MacPhail, Angus, 345
Macready, George, 315, 316
MacShane, Frank, 357, 358
"Mad Tea Party, The" (Queen), 78
Mad with Much Heart (Butler), 329
"Madam Sing's Gold" (Hoch), 193

Madama Butterfly (Puccini opera), 53, 54
Maddow, Ben, 323
Madison Square Garden, 111
Magazine of Fantasy and Science Fiction, The, 101
"Magic Bullet, The" (Hoch), 196
"Mail Order" (Lutz), 210
Making Certain It Goes On (Hugo), 366
"Making the Breaks" (Gardner), 31
Malkames, Don, 347
Malloy, Doris, 289, 293
Maltese Falcon, The (Hammett), 17, 36, 37, 188, 283, 307, 309, 356
Maltese Falcon, The (film), 307-308, 309, 315
Mammoth Mystery (magazine), 215
Man Against Crime (TV series), 386
"Man Named Thin, A" (Hammett), 355
Man Who Changed His Skin, The (Keeler), 207
"Man Who Wanted To Be Murdered, The" (Queen radio play), 397
Man with the Crimson Box, The (Keeler), 204-205
Man with the Magic Eardrums, The (Keeler), 204-205
Man with the Wooden Spectacles, The (Keeler), 204-205
Mancini, Henry, 349
Mander, Miles, 315
Mandrake the Magician (radio series), 131
Manhattan Love Song (Woolrich), 55-56
Manhunt (magazine), 192, 224, 387
Mankiewicz, Herman J., 303
Mansfield, Jayne, 347-348
Mapp v. Ohio, 153
Mara, Adele, 331
Marble Forest, The (Boucher et al.), 102
Marceau Case, The (Keeler), 203
Marchetti, Victor, 256
Mark, Michael, 338
Marker, Harry, 309

Marks, John, 256
Markson, Ben, 287
Marley, Peverell, 285
Marlowe, Brian, 295
Marlowe, Hugh, 80
Marriott, Moore, 321
Marsh, Gary, 301
Marsh, Oliver (T.), 281, 303
Marshall, E.G., 66
Marshall, Mort, 340
Martin, Dean, 170
Martin, Marion, 317
Martin, Strother, 340
Marvin, Lee, 336, 337, 372, 387
Masterson, Whit, 349
Maté, Rudolph, 325, 326
Matilda Hunter Murder, The (Keeler), 203, 207
Matthau, Walter, 226
Matthews, Junius, 317
Maupassant, Guy de, 363
May, Elaine, 226
McBain, Ed (Hunter pseudonym), 19, 399
McCallion, James, 338, 340
McCarry, Charles, 270
McCarthy, Senator Joe, 86, 101, 168, 237, 331, 333
McClure's (magazine), 54, 73
McComas, J. Francis, 101, 102
McCullough, David, 394
McGivern, William P., 336
McKnight, Tom, 317-318
McLaughlin, Andrea, 347
McLernon, Harold, 279
McMillan and Wife (TV series), 113
McMurtry, John, 374
McNeile, H.C. (Sapper), 285, 286
McNeill, Allen, 285
McSherry, Frank D. Jr., 196
Meeker, George, 293
Meeker, Ralph, 340
"Men Must Die" (Woolrich), 60-61
Mencken, H.L., 399
Mendes, Lothar, 315, 316
Menjou, Adolphe, 111, 275, 276
Merchant of Venice, The (Shakespeare), 41
Merivale, Bernard, 299
Merkel, Una, 285

Mertz, Stephen, 115, 127, 128, 129
Metal Forest, The (J. Phillips), 233
Methot, Mayo, 111, 275, 276
Metro-Goldwyn-Mayer) MGM) (movie studio), 80, 281, 282, 283, 284, 297, 303, 304, 305, 306
Metty, Russell, 323, 349
Meyer, Emile, 351
Michaels, Tony, 338
Middlesex County Legal Services Corporation, 16
Middleton, Robert, 338
Midsummer Night's Sex Comedy, A (film), 175
Mike Shayne Mystery Magazine, 210, 211, 226
Miles, Vera, 345, 346
Mill, M.S. (publishing house), 163
Millan, Victor, 349
Millar, Kenneth (Ross Macdonald), 359, 360
Millar, Margaret (Sturm), 359, 360
Miller, Arthur, 88
"Million-Dollar Jewel Caper, The" (Hoch), 197
Mills, Mort, 349, 350
Milne, Peter, 279
Milwaukee State Teachers College, 222
Minciotti, Esther, 345
Minciotti, Silvio, 340
Mine to Avenge (Ard), 176, 177
"Miranda" (J.D. MacDonald), 220
Miranda v. Arizona, 195
Mirror Theater (TV series), 65
Missing! (Avallone), 396
"Missing Diamonds, The" (radio play), 127
"Missing Elevator Puzzle, The" (Breen), 399
Mister Dynamite (film), 289-290
Mitchell, Grant, 338, 342
Mitchell, Roy, 132, 134
Mitchell, Steve, 338, 342
Mitchum, Robert, 237, 240, 310
Mohr, Hal, 351
Mok, Michael, 232
Mollé Mystery Theatre (radio series), 63

Monarch Books (paperback publisher), 168, 171, 172
Monkey's Clue and the Stolen Sapphire, The (Hoch), 198
Montagne, Edward J., 386
Montgomery, Robert, 281, 282
Moon, Bucklin, 371
Moore, Cleo, 329
Moore, Joanna, 349
Moorhead, Natalie, 283
Moran, Dolores, 331
Moran, Mike (Ard pseudonym), 167, 173, 175
More Good Old Stuff (MacDonald), 221
More Things Impossible (Hoch), 198
Morgan, Ralph, 279, 297
Morison, Patricia, 313
Morris, Ben, 340
Mortal Consequences (Symons), 148
Mortal Stakes (Parker), 392
"Most Dangerous Man Alive, The" (Hoch), 193
"Motivation in Mystery Fiction" (Adams), 119
Moving Target, The (Millar), 360
Mr. Trouble (Ard), 163, 165-166
Mudie, Leonard, 281
Mudgett, Herman W., 95
Mulhall, Jack, 295
"Murder at the Automat" (Woolrich), 58
Murder for Pleasure (Haycraft), 114, 148
"Murder Goes Unshod" (Adams), 120
"Murder in Mind" (J.D. MacDonald), 220
Murder in the Calais Coach, (Christie), 13
Murder of Roger Ackroyd, The (Christie), 190, 361
"Murder on Margin" (Lawrence), 140
Murder on the Nose (Stein), 414
"Murderer, The" (Poe?), 364
Murderer Is a Fox, The (Queen), 82
Murnau, F.W., 296

Mutual Broadcasting Co. (radio network), 97
"My Queer Dean!" (Queen), 87
Myers, Greta, 289
Myers, Thelma, 321
Mysterious Mr. I, The (Keeler), 204
Mysterious Press, 192, 196
Mystery (magazine), 396
Mystery and Suspense Writers: The Literature of Crime, Detection and Espionage (Winks), 364
Mystery Book (magazine), 215, 217, 219, 220
"Mystery in Room 913" (Woolrich), 60
Mystery Library, 415
Mystery of Mr. X, The (film), 281-282
Mystery of the Dead Police (P. MacDonald), 281, 282
Mystery Writer's Art, The (Nevins), 16, 405
Mystery Writers of America (MWA), 97, 102, 189, 190, 191, 197, 212, 227, 231, 403, 407, 409, 410, 415
Nadel, Arthur H., 325
Nader, Ralph, 211
Naked City, The (TV series), 386-387
Name's Buchanan, The (Ard), 167
Nash, Millard K., 239
Nash, Ogden, 355
Nathan, Daniel (Frederic Dannay), 72, 407
Nathan, Meyer, 72
Nation's Business, The (magazine), 240
National Broadcasting Company (NBC), 66, 82, 91, 113, 126, 240, 351
Native Son (Wright), 59
"Natural Killer" (Lawrence), 143
Nazareth Hall Military Academy, 147
"Neighborhood Killer" (TV film), 387
Neill, Roy William, 111, 276, 317, 318
Nelson, Charles, 336
Nemerov, Howard, 355

Nevins, Francis M., 6, 20
New Adventures of Ellery Queen, The (Queen), 80
New Detective (magazine), 145, 218
New Leaf and Other Stories, A (Ritchie), 225
New Leaf, A (film), 226
New York *Daily News*, 224
New York *Herald-Tribune*, 102
New York *Times*, 14, 19, 128, 161, 267, 414
New York Times Book Review, 100, 128, 371
New York University (NYU), 72, 132, 274
New York University School of Law, 396
Newman, Alfred, 285
Newman, Emil, 334
Newton, Robert, 323, 324
Night Caller, The (Lutz), 213
Night Club Lady, The (film), 111, 275-276
Night Forms (Nevins), 17
Night Has a Thousand Eyes (Woolrich), 64
Night My Friend, The (Hoch), 200
Night People and Other Stories, The (Hoch), 200
"Night Reveals, The" (Woolrich), 57
Night Watch, The (D. Phillips), 250, 251, 266
Nightfall (Goodis), 344
Nightfall (film), 344
Nightlines (Lutz), 212
"Nightmare" (Woolrich), 63
Nightmare Town (Hammett), 356, 357
"9 from 12 Leaves 3" (Ritchie), 225
99 River Street (film), 334-335
Nixon, Richard M., 211, 259
No Angels for Me (Ard), 168-169
No Wings on a Cop (Adams), 127
Nolan, Jeanette, 336
Nolan, Tom, 359
Norma (film production company), 323
Northwestern University, 409

Novel Verdicts: A Guide to Courtroom Fiction (Breen), 40, 399
Novello, Jay, 323
"Number's Up, The" (Woolrich), 66
Nyby, Christian, 380
"O Time, In Your Flight" (Cornier), 365
"Oblong Room, The" (Hoch), 191
O'Brien, Edmond, 325
O'Brien-Moore, Erin, 297
O'Connor, Carroll, 376
"Odds on a Gypsy" (Hoch), 199
Oedipus Tyrannus (Greek tragedy), 319
Office of Strategic Services (OSS), 214, 264
O'Hara, Brian, 338
O'Hara, John, 162, 172, 173, 178
O'Hara, Scott (house byline), 215
Ohio University Press, 200
Oland, Warner, 285, 291
Old Spies Club, The (Hoch), 196
Oliver, Edna May, 277, 278
Oliver Twist (Dickens), 359
Olivier, Sir Laurence, 270
Olsen, Moroni, 315
On Dangerous Ground (film), 324, 329-330, 380
"On the Make" (Hammett), 289-290
On the Waterfront (film), 387
101 Years' Entertainment (Queen), 81
120-Hour Clock, The (Nevins), 396-397
One Lonely Night (Spillane), 341
One Murdered: Two Dead (Propper), 156-157, 159
1001 Midnights (Pronzini & Muller), 114
Only Angels Have Wings (film), 186
Oops! (Lutz), 212
Opera News (magazine), 103
"Operator, The" (Ritchie), 225
Orczy, Baroness, 96
Origin of Evil, The (Queen), 84
Ormonde, Czenzi, 327
Osato, Sono, 240

Oscar, Henry, 299
O'Sullivan, Maureen, 283
"Other Runner, The" (Lutz), 211
Ottiano, Rafaele, 293
Our Man in Havana (film), 270
Oursler, Fulton, 107, 108, 109, 111, 113, 275
Over My Dead Body (Stout), 392
PRC Picrtures (movie studio), 113
Pacifica (public radio network), 102
Pagoda (J. Phillips), 236, 237, 240
Pajemar (film production company), 351
Pal Joey (stage musical), 173
Pale Kings and Princes (Parker), 392
Pallette, Eugene, 279
Palmer, Maria, 313
Palmer, Stuart, 277, 278, 396
Panther's Claw, The (film), 113
Paramount Pictures (movie studio), 80, 119, 161, 279, 295, 296, 297, 301
Parker, Robert B., 19, 361, 392
Parklane (film production company), 340
Paterson, Pat, 291
Patrick, Gail, 295
Patrick, Lee, 307, 315
Patterson, Elizabeth, 313
Pay Dirt and Other Whispering Sands Stories (Gardner), 27
Payne, John, 334
Peach, L. DuGarde, 299
Peacock Fan, The (Keeler), 206
Peacock, Michael C., 393-394
Pendleton, Nat, 275, 283, 303
Penguin Books (paperback publishing house), 396
Penguin Pool Murder, The (Palmer), 277
Penguin Pool Murder (film), 277-278
Penkovsky, Col. Oleg, 265
"Penny-a-Worder, The" (Woolrich), 66
Penzler, Otto, 149
People (magazine), 91
People v. Jones, 46
Perfect Frame, The (Ard), 163

Perry Mason (TV series), 49-51, 379, 380, 383, 385, 386
Persoff, Nehemiah, 345
Peters, Jean, 33
Pettet, Wilfrid H., 315
Phantom Lady (Woolrich), 64, 68, 69, 304, 311, 318
Phantom Lady (film), 311-312
Philadelphia *Public Ledger* (newspaper), 148
Philadelphia *Record* (newspaper), 148
Phillips, David Atlee, 242, 249-270
Phillips, James Atlee, 231-248, 249, 250, 267
Phillips, John, 317
Phillips, Shawn, 236
Phillips, Wendell, 347
Phoenix Press (publishing house), 206
Pickup on South Street (film), 331, 333
Pictorial Review (magazine), 153
Pitts, ZaSu, 278
Planer, Franz, 334
Platt, Louise, 305
Playboy (magazine), 91
Player on the Other Side, The (Queen), 89
Playhouse 90 (TV series), 66
Pocket Book of True Crime Stories, The (Boucher), 97
Pocket Books, Inc. (paperback publisher), 189, 190, 199, 363, 364, 371
Poe, Edgar Allan, 18, 56, 58, 79, 81, 90, 96, 234, 311, 363, 364
Poetry Foundation, 355
Point Blank (film), 9, 371-378
"Politics Is Simply Murder" (Ritchie), 225
Popkin, Leo C., 325
Popular Publications, Inc., 132-133, 139
Porlock, Martin (P. MacDonald pseudonym), 281
Porter, Cole, 172, 363
Post, Melville Davisson, 38, 39, 45, 47, 49
Powell, Dick, 310

Powell, William, 279, 283, 284, 287, 289, 297, 298
Prest, Pat, 329
Preview Murder Mystery, The (film), 295-296
Price, Prof. Lawrence Marsden, 93
Princeton University, 414
"Private Enemy Number One" (Lawrence), 133, 139
Private Eye, The (Adams), 122, 127
Private Party, A (Ard), 164-165
"Private War" (Adams), 119-120, 122
"Private War" (J.D. MacDonald), 220
Prize Detective (magazine), 25
Prize Meets Murder (Hoch), 199
Probable Claus (Breen), 400
"Problem of the Covered Bridge, The" (Hoch), 198
Prometheus (CD label), 379
Promised Land (Parker), 392
Pronzini, Bill, 199, 212
Propper, Milton, 20, 147-160
Psycho (film), 328, 346, 379
Publish and Perish (Nevins), 187, 416, 417
Puccini, Giacomo, 53, 59
Purdue University, 404
"Pure Rotten" (Lutz), 211
"Purloined Letter, The" (Poe), 90
Q.B.I.: Queen's Bureau of Investigation (Queen), 87
Q.E.D.: Queen's Experiments in Detection (Queen), 90, 226
Quayle, Anthony, 345
Queen, Ellery (Dannay & Lee pseudonym), 13, 16, 18, 65, 66, 72-91, 94, 95, 100, 108, 110, 113, 147, 148, 149, 156, 159, 187, 189, 190, 191, 192, 193, 199, 396, 397, 398, 399
Quests of Simon Ark, The (Hoch), 192
RKO Radio Pictures (movie studio), 237, 240, 277, 297, 309, 310, 329
Rae, John, 321
Raines, Ella, 311, 312

"Rajah's Emerald, The" (Christie), 395-396
Raksin, David, 338
Ralston, Esther, 289
Ramar of the Jungle (TV series), 386
Randall, Tony, 225
Rathbone, Basil, 111, 276, 318, 383, 403
Rasp, The (P. MacDonald), 281
Rathbone, Basil, 276, 318
Ratoff, Gregory, 293
Rawhide (TV series), 379, 380
Rawson, Clayton, 100, 190
Ray, Aldo, 344
Ray, Nicholas, 324, 329, 330
Raymond Chandler Papers, The (Chandler), 358
Raymond Chandler Speaking (Chandler), 114
Raymond, Jack, 295
Reader's Digest (magazine), 107, 275
Reader's Digest Books, 131
Reagan, Ronald, 214
"Real Shape of the Coast, The" (Lutz), 211
"Rear Window" (Woolrich), 314
Rear Window (film), 18, 65, 328
Rebecca (film), 282
Red Harvest (Hammett), 17, 30, 43, 119, 120, 122, 124, 125, 356
Red Is for Killing (Stein), 414
Redbook (magazine), 79
Reed, Carol, 270
Reed, Marshall, 351
Reed, Peter (house byline), 217
Rees, William, 287
Reese, William, 279
Regas, George, 285
Reicher, Frank, 287
Reilly, John, 232
Reingold, Gail, 412
Reis, Irving, 309
Reitci, John George (John Ritchie), 222
Remember Last Night? (film), 293-294
Rendell, Ruth, 20
Rendezvous in Black (Woolrich), 62, 66, 69, 396, 412

Republic Pictures (movie studio), 126
Resignation in Protest (Weisband), 255
Reynal & Hitchcock (publishing house), 122, 123, 124
Reynolds, Gene, 334
Rhode, John, 100, 363
Richards, Addison, 287
Richards, Paul, 340
Richards, Thomas, 307
Richardson, Elliott, 255
Richmond, Ted, 319, 344
Rickey, Branch, 254
"Riddle of the Brass Band, The" (Palmer), 396
Riddle of the Wooden Parakeet, The (Keeler), 207
Ridley, Arnold, 299
"Ride the Lightning" (Lutz), 212
Ride the Lightning (Lutz), 212
Rinehart (publishing house), 163, 164, 165, 166, 167, 169
Rinehart, Mary Roberts, 159
Rios, Lalo, 349
"Ripper of Storyville, The" (Hoch), 192
Ripper of Storyville and Other Ben Snow Tales, The (Hoch), 192
Risdon, Elisabeth, 315
Riskin, Robert, 111, 275
Ritchie, Jack (John G. Reitci), 9, 222-227
Ritchie, Rita (Krohne), 224, 227
Ritter, Thelma, 333
Road of Dreams, The (Christie), 361
Robbins, Frank E., 44
Robbins, Richard, 345
Roberts, Arthur, 297
Roberts, Stephen, 297
Robinson, George, 289, 309
Rodgers, Gaby, 340
Rodgers, Richard, 363
Rodriquez, Carlos Rafael, 253
Rogers, Ginger, 297
Rogers, Howard Emmett, 281
Rohmer, Sax, 113
"Roller Coaster Murder" (TV film), 386
Roman, Ruth, 327, 328
Roman Hat Mystery, The (Queen), 73, 74, 87, 91
Romero, Cesar, 283
Roosevelt, Franklin Delano, 107, 156, 394
Root, Lynn, 309
Root of His Evil, The (Ard), 163, 166
Rose, Billy, 232, 233
Roselle Park Public Library, 13, 20
Rosmond, Babette, 216
Ross, Anthony, 329
Ross, Barnaby (Dannay & Lee pseudonym), 74, 76
Ross, Michael, 325
Ross Macdonald: A Biography (Nolan), 359
Rouse, Russell, 325
Rowling, J.K., 393
Royal Bloodline: Ellery Queen, Author and Detective (Nevins), 405
Royal Military College, 131
Rosza, Miklos, 313, 314, 323
Ruehlmann, William, 114
Rumour at Nightfall (Greene), 14
Runyon, Damon, 57, 120, 144, 393
Russell, Jane, 240
Russell, Lewis L., 323
"Rusty Rose, The" (Hoch), 194
Ruttenberg, Joseph, 305
Ryan, Robert, 329
Ryder, Prof. Arthur William, 94
Sabatini, Rafael, 187
Sabotage (Adams), 114, 120
Sackheim, Jerry, 126
Saint Magazine, The, 191
Saint Mystery Magazine, The, 192, 193, 195, 200, 211-212
Saint with a Gun: The Unlawful American Private Eye (Ruehlmann), 114
Sallis, James, 367
Salter, Hans J., 311
San Francisco *Chronicle*, 19, 96, 87, 19\00, 101, 123
San Francisco Opera, 103
Sanborn, Donna, 325
Sanders, George, 309, 310
Sanders, Lawrence, 211, 212
Sanford, Ralph, 331

Sangster, Georgia, 413
Santesson, Hans Stefan, 192, 197, 200
Saratoga Longshot (Dobyns), 367
Sargent, Michael, 349
Saturday Evening Post (magazine), 38, 41, 42, 235, 244, 387
Saturday Night (magazine), 359
Sawyer, Joe, 342
Sayers, Dorothy L., 20, 104
Scarlet Claw, The (film), 318
"Scarlet Coat, The" Lawrence), 140
Scarlet Mummy, The (Keeler), 208
"Scarlet Stakes" (Lawrence), 133
Schermer, Jules, 333
Schilling, Gus., 329
Schisgall, Oscar, 113
Schlitz Playhouse of Stars (TV series), 65, 240
Schoenfeld, Bernard, 311
Schroeder, Barbet, 213
Scorcher (Lutz), 213
Scott, Randolph, 167
Scott, Sutherland, 149
Scott Meredith Literary Agency, 88, 89, 173
Scourby, Alexander, 336
Seay, James, 340
Security & Theodora (film production company), 338
Selander, Lesley, 126
Seldeen, Murray, 289
Selected Letters of Raymond Chandler, 114
Selwyn, Edgar, 281
Selznick, David O., 277
Seven Sinners (film), 299-300
Seyffertitz, Gustav von, 277, 293
Seymour, Harry, 287
Shadow, The (radio series), 84
Shadow Man, The (Lutz), 211, 290
Shadow Man: The Life of Dashiell Hammett (Layman), 290
Shadow Mystery Magazine, 215, 216
Shady Lady (Adams), 118, 128
Shakedown (Ard), 174
Shakespeare, William, 41, 76, 355
Shannon, Harry, 349
Shapiro, Karl, 355
Sharpe, Bruce, 338

Shattered Raven, The (Hoch), 196
Shaughnessy, Mickey, 347
Sheffield, Reginald, 323
Sherlock Holmes (radio series), 97, 383
Sherry, Norman, 270
Shibuk, Charles, 149
Shirley, Alfred, 384
Shirley, Lorraine, 233
Shockley, Marian, 80
Shoot It Again, Sam (Avallone), 187
Shortz, Will, 200
Shostakovich, Dmitri, 186
"Shrieking Skeleton, The" (Gardner), 25
Shubert, Eddie, 287
Shudders, The (Abbot), 113
Shumway, Lee, 295
Siamese Twin Mystery, The (Queen), 78
Sidney, Sylvia, 387
Siegel, Don, 331, 337, 351, 409
Signature (magazine), 210
Sikking, James, 376
Silken Baroness, The (J. Phillips), 243
Silliphant, Stirling, 344, 351, 385, 387
Silverberg, Robert, 167
Sim, Alastair, 301, 321, 322, 403
Simenon, Georges, 20, 97, 173, 193, 194, 234, 319
Simon & Schuster (publishing house), 94
"Simple Art of Murder, The" (Chandler), 129
Simpson, Ivan, 281
Sinatra, Frank, 170, 172
Sing Sing Nights (Keeler), 202
Single White Female (film), 213
Sins of Billy Serene, The (Ard), 172-173
Siodmak, Robert, 311, 312
Six from Nowhere, The (Keeler), 207
Skiles, Marlin, 315
Skinner, Frank, 317
Slutsky, Steven, 397
Small, Buddy, 334
Small, Edward, 334

Smart Set, The (magazine), 54
Smith, C. Aubrey, 285
Smith, Emily, 403
Smith, James, 295, 296
Smith, Robert, 334
Smith, Steven C., 381
Snepp, Frank, 256
"Snowball in July" (Queen), 87
Snowbird's Blood (Hensley), 406
Snowden, Leigh, 340
So Dark the Night (film), 319-320
Social Security Administration, 159
Socrates, 154
"Something Like a Pelican" (Gardner), 30
"Song of Hate" (Adams), 125
Sophocles, 319
South Pacific (stage musical), 169
South Pacific Mail (newspaper), 249
Southern Illinois University Press, 193
Southwest High School, 209
Spain, John (Adams pseudonym), 125
Spanish Cape Mystery, The (Queen), 74
Spark (Lutz), 213
"Speaking of Crime" (Boucher column), 364-365
Spectacles of Mr. Cagliostro, The (Keeler), 19, 202
Spencer, Herbert, 363
Spenser, Edmund, 361, 362
Spillane, Mickey, 101, 123, 162, 163, 164, 165, 173, 174, 175, 176, 183, 339, 340, 341
Spivak, Lawrence E., 81
Spotlight (magazine), 256
Spy and the Thief, The (Hoch), 196
Spy Who Came In from the Cold, The (LeCarré), 196
"Spy Who Did Nothing, The" (Hoch), 196
Squeeze Play (Auster), 367
St. Clair & Vilova (dance team), 317
St. James Guide to Crime and Mystery Writers, 406
St. John, Howard, 327

St. Louis University School of Law, 17, 405
Stalin, Josef, 250
Stand By—London Calling (Keeler), 207
Standish, Burt L., 147
Stanley, John, 384
Stanton, Helene, 338
Star of Midnight (film), 297
Star Ruby Contract, The (J. Phillips), 243-244
Star Trek (TV series), 138
Stark, Richard (Westlake pseudonym), 371
"Startled Face of Death, The" (J.D. MacDonald), 215-216
Station Wagon Murder, The (Propper), 158
Steeger, Harry, 133, 134, 138
Steele, Freddie, 317
Stein, Aaron Marc, 9, 414-415
Steinberg, Betty, 342
Steinbrunner, Chris, 149
Steiner, Max, 277
Stell, Aaron, 349
Stella Dallas (radio series), 84
Stephenson, Henry, 281
Sterling, Stewart (Winchell pseudonym), 395
Sternig, Larry, 223, 224
Stevens, Ruthelma, 275
Stevens, Wallace, 361
Stevenson, Robert Louis, 194
Stewart, James, 303, 304, 391
Stewart, Paul, 340
"Stiletto" (film script), 126
Stockwell, John, 256
Stokes, Frederick A. (publishing house), 73
"Stolen Finger, The" (Keeler), 202
Stone, Hampton (Stein pseudonym), 414
Stone, Harold J., 345
Stone, Lewis, 281
Stone, Milburn, 311, 333
Story (magazine), 57, 58, 63, 214
Stout, Rex, 13, 19, 44, 91, 116, 234, 362, 392
Strands of the Web (Keeler), 202
Strange Disappearance of Mary Young, The (Propper), 153-154

Strange Journey (Keeler), 208
Strangers on a Train (Highsmith), 327
Strangers on a Train (film), 327-328
Stravinsky, Igor, 186
Street & Smith (publishing house), 397
"Street of Fear" (TV film), 387
Stromberg, Hunt, 283
Strong, Michael, 374
Struss, Karl, 295, 296
Student Fraternity Murder, The (Propper), 152, 153, 154-155
Studio One (TV series), 240
Sturgeon, Theodore, 89
"Subway" (Woolrich), 58
"Suddenly in September" (Hoch), 193
Suitable for Framing (J. Phillips), 236
Sullivan, Eleanor, 198
Sunrise (film), 296
Suspense (radio series), 63, 189, 366
Suspicion (TV series), 66
Sutton, Grady, 303
Swank (magazine), 210
Swanton, Harold, 380
"Sweating Statue, The" (Hoch), 195
"Sweet Leilani" (song), 117
SWF Seeks Same (Lutz), 213
"Swift Among the Pirates" (Hoch), 199
Symons, Julian, 148, 358, 360
Syracuse University, 214
"Take Another Look" (Ritchie), 225-226
"Take It Or Leave It" (Gardner), 43, 44
Tales of the Unexpected (TV series), 226
Tall Dolores, The (Avallone), 183-184, 187
Tamiroff, Akim, 349
Tannen, William, 334
Tapley, Colin, 295
Tarler, George, 53, 54
"Tattooed Priest, The" (Hoch), 195
Taylor, Alfred, 305

Taylor, Dwight, 333
Taylor, Kent, 386
Taylor, Vaughn, 351
Taylor, Wendell Hertig, 114, 122, 149
Tchaikovsky, Peter Ilyich, 379
Tearle, Conway, 295
Tell No Tales (film), 305-306
"Tell-Tale Heart, The" (Poe), 58
Ten Days' Wonder (Queen), 82, 83, 89
10 Hours (Keeler), 203-204, 205
10-Story Book (magazine), 202
Tennyson, Alfred Lord, 361
Terror Brigade, The (D. Phillips), 270
Texas Christian University, 232, 233
Texas Monthly (magazine), 233
Tetzlaff, Ted, 275, 276
"Theft of the Clouded Tiger, The" (Hoch), 196
"Theft of the Ostracized Ostrich, The" (Hoch), 196
Thefts of Nick Velvet, The (Hoch), 196
They Live by Night (film), 329, 330
"Thieves' Honor" (Lutz), 210
Thieves' Nights (Keeler), 202-203
.38 (Ard), 162, 163, 164
Thin Man, The (Hammett), 283
Thin Man, The (film), 283-284, 290, 293, 294, 297, 298, 300, 304
Third Man, The (film), 324
Thirty-Nine Steps, The (film), 299-300, 304
This Man in Paris (film), 301
This Man Is News (film), 301-302
This Prize is Dangerous (Hoch & Goulart), 199
This Week (magazine), 87
Thomas, Jameson, 289
Thompson, Jim, 14, 343
Thompson, Wendy, 321
Thoms, Jerome, 319
Thornton, Cyril, 283
"Thou Art the Man" (Poe), 79
Three Coffins, The (Carr), 77
"Three Kills for One" (Woolrich), 70

"Three O'Clock" (Woolrich), 60, 66, 70
Three Star (magazine), 25
"Three's a Shroud" (J.D. MacDonald), 218
Thrilling Detective (magazine), 133
Thrilling Mystery (magazine), 57
Thunder Road (film), 240
Ticker Tape Murder, The (Propper), 153
Tiger Island (Ritchie), 222
Tilbury, Zeffie, 305
Time (magazine), 414
Times Square (Woolrich), 54
"Tin Suitcase, The" (J.D. MacDonald), 217
Tiomkin, Dmitri, 325, 327
"To Slay an Eagle" (Hoch), 200
"Toad Cop" (Nevins), 355
Tomasini, George, 345
Tombes, Andrew, 311, 312
Tone, Franchot, 66, 311
Tonight, Somewhere in New York (Woolrich), 67
"Too Fair to Die" (Adams), 128
"Too Many Have Lived" (Hammett), 356
"Too Nice a Day to Die" (Woolrich), 66
Toomey, Regis, 311
"Top Comes Off, The" (Gardner), 31
Top-Notch (magazine), 25, 27
Torch (Lutz), 213
"Torso Trap, The" (Lawrence), 140
Totheroh, Dan, 293
Touch of Evil (film), 349-350
Tourneur, Jacques, 344
"Traffic in Webs, A" (Hoch), 199
Tragedy of X, The (Queen), 76-77
Tragedy of Y, The (Queen), 77
Tragedy of Z, The (Queen), 77
Train, Arthur, 38, 41
Transvection Machine, The (Hoch), 197
Treacher, Arthur, 293
Tree, Dorothy, 287
Trenholme, Helen, 287, 288
"Trepanned Skull, The" (Keeler), 202
"Trick and Fancy" (J. Phillips), 235

Tropical Heat (Lutz), 213
True Crime Detective (magazine), 102
Truex, Ernest, 303, 304
Truffaut, François, 67, 381
Truman (McCullough), 394
Truman, Harry S., 214, 394-395
Truth of the Matter, The (Lutz), 211
Turkel, Joseph, 342
Twain, Mark, 72
"Twelve Days of Christmas, The" (song), 87
20th Century (movie studio), 285
20th Century Crime and Mystery Writers (Reilly), 114, 232, 248, 406
20th Century-Fox (movie studio), 196, 333
Twilight Zone, The (TV series), 379, 380
Two Complete Detective Books (magazine), 128
Tyler, Harry, 287
Tyler, W.T., 270
Underground Cities Contract, The (J. Phillips), 244
"Understanding Electricity" (Lutz), 210
Underworld Romances (magazine), 132
United Artists (film releasing company), 285, 325, 334, 340, 342
United Progressive News (labor newspaper), 94, 97
Universal Pictures (movie studio), 289, 293, 311, 312, 313, 317, 318, 323, 349, 383
University of California, 91, 415
University of California at Berkeley, 93, 94
University of California at Los Angeles (UCLA), 412
University of California Press, 381
University of Florida, 397
University of Hawaii, 238
University of Michigan, 360
University of Missouri, 232
University of Pennsylvania, 147-148, 214

University of Rochester, 190
University of Southern California (USC), 93
University of Texas, 232
University of Toronto, 132
University of Western Ontario, 359
Up Jumped the Devil (Adams), 114, 123-124, 127
Urge to Kill (Lutz), 213
Utica Free Academy, 214
Valentine, Joseph, 293
Valley of Fear, The (Conan Doyle), 77, 97
Van Cleef, Lee, 338
Van Dine, S.S. (Wright pseudonym), 13, 73, 74, 79, 107, 108, 147, 148, 279, 392, 399
Van Dyke, W.S., II, 283, 284, 303, 304
Van Zandt, Philip, 338
Vance, Cyrus, 257
"Vanished Steamboat, The" (Hoch), 192
Vanishing Gold Truck, The (Keeler), 206-207
Varconi, Victor, 289
Varden, Norma, 327
Vatican Council II, 103
Veiller, Anthony, 297
Velvet Touch, The (Hoch), 196
Vengeance Is Mine (Spillane), 341
Vernon, John, 372
Vernon, Richard, 323
Verral, Jean (Mithoefer), 132, 134, 135, 137
Verral, Charles Spain, 130-139, 146
Vertigo (film), 328, 346, 379, 380
Vice Czar Murders, The (Adams), 125
Vickers, Martha, 347
"Victim No. 5" (Keeler), 201
Vidal, Gore, 398
"Village of the Dead" (Hoch), 192
Vincent, June, 317
Vinson, Helen, 279
Vitagraph (movie studio), 55
Vogel, Virgil W., 349
Voice of the Seven Sparrows, The (Keeler), 202
Vonnegut, Kurt, 19, 208

Vuolo, Tito, 342
Vye, Murvyn, 333
Wadsworth, Henry, 283
Walker, Helen, 338
Walker, Robert, 327
Walker (publishing house), 197
Walking Tall (film), 334
Wallace, Edgar, 121, 359, 393
Wallace, Jean, 338, 339
Wallach, Eli, 351
Waller, Eddy, 334
Wallis, Hal B., 307
Walls Came Tumbling Down, The (Eisinger), 315
Walls Came Tumbling Down, The (film), 315-316
Walsh, Thomas, 387
Waltz into Darkness (Woolrich), 64-65, 67
"Wandering Daughter Job, A" (Hoch), 192
War and Peace (Tolstoy), 15
Ward, Edward, 303
Ward, Jonas (Ard pseudonym), 167, 168, 172, 173, 177
Warner Bros. (movie studio), 161, 279, 280, 287, 288, 289, 297, 307, 327, 345
Warren, Earl, 51
Warwick, John, 301
Washburn, Bryant, 295
Washington, George, 194, 199
Washington Square Enigma, The (Keeler), 203
Waterloo College, 359
Watson, Minor, 289
Waugh, Charles G., 26, 30, 196
Waxman, Franz, 293
"Way Up to Hades, The" (Hoch), 408
Wayne, David, 91
Wayne, John, 177, 186, 237
Webb, Jack, 351
Webb, Roy, 297
Webber, Peggy, 345
Webster, Daniel, 238
Webster University, 274
Weekly Standard, The (magazine), 399
Weingarten, Lawrence, 281
Weird Tales (magazine), 92

Weisband, Edward, 255
Welch, Richard, 262, 265
Welles, Orson, 19, 185, 324, 349, 350
Wendell, Howard, 336
Wendkos, Paul, 347
West (magazine), 25
Western Trails (magazine), 25
Westcott, Gordon, 287
Westlake, Donald E., 19, 222, 371, 373, 374, 378
Westminster Gazette, The, 359
Westminster Review, The, 357
Weston, Garnett, 295
Whale, James, 293, 294
Wharton School of Finance, 214
What About Murder? (Breen), 399
What Price Murder (Adams), 122
When She Was Bad (Ard), 170-171, 175
"When You Got a Pigeon" (J.D. MacDonald), 216
"Where There's Smoke" (Hoch), 192
Whispering Sands: Stories of Gold Fever and the Western Desert (Gardner), 27
White, James Marsden, 95
White, Ken, 138
White, Lawrence, 98
White, Lionel, 342
White, Phyllis (Mary Price), 93, 94, 95, 96, 97, 103, 104
White, William Anthony Parker (Anthony Boucher), 92, 93, 405
"White Eye, The" (Lawrence), 133, 139, 140
White Wolverine Contract, The (J. Phillips), 245
Whitney, Peter, 336
Whittington, Harry, 47, 146
Who Killed the Robins Family? (Chastain), 199
Who's Who, 231
Wichman, Glen, 115
Widening Gyre, The (Parker), 361
Widmark, Richard, 326, 333
"Wife Who Lived Twice, The" (J. Phillips), 240
Wigmore, Dean John H., 41, 47
Wilde, Cornel, 338, 339

Wilde, Oscar, 194
"Will-o'-the-Wisp Mystery, The" (Hoch), 197
William, Warren, 287, 288, 307
Williams, Adam, 336
Williams, Robert, 317
Williams, Robert B., 342
Williams, Sumner, 329, 330
Wills, Thomas (Ard pseudonym), 167, 170, 171, 175, 176, 177
Wilson, Bob, 347
Wilson, Clarence, 277
Wilson, Edmund, 223
Wilson Library Bulletin, 399
Winchell, Prentice, 395
Winchell, Walter, 233
Windsor, Marie, 342
Wisberg, Aubrey, 319
Wolfe, Ian, 329, 334
Wolfe, Thomas, 183, 233
Woman's World (magazine), 198
Wonderful Scheme of Mr. Christopher Thorne, The (Keeler), 203
Wong Howe, James, 283
Woodbridge, George, 321
Woolrich, Claire Attalie (Tarler), 53, 159
Woolrich, Cornell, 14, 15, 16, 18, 53-71, 130, 148, 159, 160, 187, 212, 215, 218, 219, 304, 311, 312, 314, 317, 318, 319, 323-324, 326, 341, 344, 363, 364, 381, 396, 411, 412, 413
World Films (production company), 334
Wrecker, The (stage play), 299
Wrecker, The (film), 299
Wright, Bob, 127
Wright, Lee, 94, 95
Wright, Maurice, 275
Wright, Richard, 59
Wright, Teresa, 331
Wright, Willard Huntington, (S.S. Van Dine), 73, 279
Writer, The (magazine), 119
Wrong Man, The (film), 328, 345-346
Wynn, Hugh, 281
Wynn, Keenan, 349, 372

X. Jones of Scotland Yard (Keeler), 203
X v Rex (P. MacDonald), 281, 282
Yale University, 260
"Ye Goode Olde Ghoste Storie" (Boucher), 92
Year's Best Mystery and Suspense Stories (anthology series), 189
Yordan, Philip, 338
Yost, Robert, 295
You Asked for It (Fleming), 395
"You Pays Your Nickel" (Woolrich), 58
"You Remember Jeanie" (J.D. MacDonald), 219

You'll Get Yours (Ard), 170, 174-175, 179
"You'll Never Escape" (J.D. MacDonald), 220
Young, Loretta, 285
Young, Robert, 293, 294
Young Man's Heart, A (Woolrich), 55
Young's Magazine, 201, 202
"You've Got To Be Cold" (J.D. MacDonald), 216
Zanuck, Darryl F., 285
Zardoz (film), 372

RAMBLE HOUSE's
HARRY STEPHEN KEELER WEBWORK MYSTERIES
(RH) indicates the title is available ONLY in the RAMBLE HOUSE edition

The Ace of Spades Murder
The Affair of the Bottled Deuce (RH)
The Amazing Web
The Barking Clock
Behind That Mask
The Book with the Orange Leaves
The Bottle with the Green Wax Seal
The Box from Japan
The Case of the Canny Killer
The Case of the Crazy Corpse (RH)
The Case of the Flying Hands (RH)
The Case of the Ivory Arrow
The Case of the Jeweled Ragpicker
The Case of the Lavender Gripsack
The Case of the Mysterious Moll
The Case of the 16 Beans
The Case of the Transparent Nude (RH)
The Case of the Transposed Legs
The Case of the Two-Headed Idiot (RH)
The Case of the Two Strange Ladies
The Circus Stealers (RH)
Cleopatra's Tears
A Copy of Beowulf (RH)
The Crimson Cube (RH)
The Face of the Man From Saturn
Find the Clock
The Five Silver Buddhas
The 4th King
The Gallows Waits, My Lord! (RH)
The Green Jade Hand
Finger! Finger!
Hangman's Nights (RH)
I, Chameleon (RH)
I Killed Lincoln at 10:13! (RH)
The Iron Ring
The Man Who Changed His Skin (RH)
The Man with the Crimson Box
The Man with the Magic Eardrums
The Man with the Wooden Spectacles
The Marceau Case
The Matilda Hunter Murder
The Monocled Monster

The Murder of London Lew
The Murdered Mathematician
The Mysterious Card (RH)
The Mysterious Ivory Ball of Wong Shing Li (RH)
The Mystery of the Fiddling Cracksman
The Peacock Fan
The Photo of Lady X (RH)
The Portrait of Jirjohn Cobb
Report on Vanessa Hewstone (RH)
Riddle of the Travelling Skull
Riddle of the Wooden Parrakeet (RH)
The Scarlet Mummy (RH)
The Search for X-Y-Z
The Sharkskin Book
Sing Sing Nights
The Six From Nowhere (RH)
The Skull of the Waltzing Clown
The Spectacles of Mr. Cagliostro
Stand By—London Calling!
The Steeltown Strangler
The Stolen Gravestone (RH)
Strange Journey (RH)
The Strange Will
The Straw Hat Murders (RH)
The Street of 1000 Eyes (RH)
Thieves' Nights
Three Novellos (RH)
The Tiger Snake
The Trap (RH)
Vagabond Nights (Defrauded Yeggman)
Vagabond Nights 2 (10 Hours)
The Vanishing Gold Truck
The Voice of the Seven Sparrows
The Washington Square Enigma
When Thief Meets Thief
The White Circle (RH)
The Wonderful Scheme of Mr. Christopher Thorne
X. Jones—of Scotland Yard
Y. Cheung, Business Detective

Keeler Related Works

A To Izzard: A Harry Stephen Keeler Companion by Fender Tucker — Articles and stories about Harry, by Harry, and in his style. Included is a compleat bibliography.

Wild About Harry: Reviews of Keeler Novels — Edited by Richard Polt & Fender Tucker — 22 reviews of works by Harry Stephen Keeler from *Keeler News*. A perfect introduction to the author.

The Keeler Keyhole Collection: Annotated newsletter rants from Harry Stephen Keeler, edited by Francis M. Nevins. Over 400 pages of incredibly personal Keeleriana.

Fakealoo — Pastiches of the style of Harry Stephen Keeler by selected demented members of the HSK Society. Updated every year with the new winner.

RAMBLE HOUSE's OTHER LOONS

The End of It All and Other Stories — Ed Gorman's latest short story collection

Six Dancing Tuatara Press Books — *Beast or Man?* by Sean M'Guire; *The Whistling Ancestors* by Richard E. Goddard; *The Shadow on the House*, *Sorcerer's Chessmen* and *The Wizard of Berner's Abbey* by Mark Hansom, *The Trail of the Cloven Hoof* by Arlton Eadie and *The Border Line* by Walter S. Masterman. With introductions by John Pelan. Many more to come!

Death Leaves No Card — One of the most unusual murdered-in-the-tub mysteries you'll ever read. By Miles Burton.

The Dumpling — Political murder from 1907 by Coulson Kernahan

Victims & Villains — Intriguing Sherlockiana from Derham Groves

Ultra-Boiled — 23 gut-wrenching tales by our Man in Brooklyn, Gary Lovisi. Yow!

Shadows' Edge — Two early novels by Wade Wright: *Shadows Don't Bleed* and *The Sharp Edge*.

Evidence in Blue — 1938 mystery by E. Charles Vivian

The Case of the Little Green Men — Mack Reynolds wrote this love song to sci-fi fans back in 1951 and it's now back in print.

Hell Fire and **Savage Highway** — Two new hard-boiled novels by Jack Moskovitz, who developed his style writing sleaze back in the 70s. No one writes like Jack.

Researching American-Made Toy Soldiers — A 276-page collection of a lifetime of articles by toy soldier expert Richard O'Brien

Strands of the Web: Short Stories of Harry Stephen Keeler — Edited and Introduced by Fred Cleaver

Through the Looking Glass — Lewis Carroll wrote it; Gavin L. O'Keefe illustrated it.

The Sam McCain Novels — Ed Gorman's terrific series includes *The Day the Music Died*, *Wake Up Little Susie* and *Will You Still Love Me Tomorrow?*

A Shot Rang Out — Three decades of reviews from Jon Breen

Mysterious Martin, the Master of Murder — Two versions of a strange 1912 novel by Tod Robbins about a man who writes books that can kill.

Dago Red — 22 tales of dark suspense by Bill Pronzini

Two Robert Randisi Novels — *No Exit to Brooklyn* and *The Dead of Brooklyn*. The first two Nick Delvecchio novels.

The Night Remembers — A 1991 Jack Walsh mystery from Ed Gorman

Rough Cut & New, Improved Murder — Ed Gorman's first two novels

Hollywood Dreams — A novel of the Depression by Richard O'Brien

Seven Gelett Burgess Novels — *The Master of Mysteries*, *The White Cat*, *Two O'Clock Courage*, *Ladies in Boxes*, *Find the Woman*, *The Heart Line*, *The Picaroons*

The Organ Reader — A huge compilation of just about everything published in the 1971-1972 radical bay-area newspaper, THE ORGAN.

A Clear Path to Cross — Sharon Knowles short mystery stories by Ed Lynskey

Old Times' Sake — Short stories by James Reasoner from Mike Shayne Magazine

Freaks and Fantasies — Eerie tales by Tod Robbins, collaborator of Tod Browning on the film FREAKS.

Seven Jim Harmon Double Novels — *Vixen Hollow/Celluloid Scandal*, *The Man Who Made Maniacs/Silent Siren*, *Ape Rape/Wanton Witch*, *Sex Burns Like Fire/Twist Session*, *Sudden Lust/Passion Strip*, *Sin Unlimited/Harlot Master*, *Twilight Girls/Sex Institution*. Written in the early 60s.

Marblehead: A Novel of H.P. Lovecraft — A long-lost masterpiece from Richard A. Lupoff. Published for the first time!

The Compleat Ova Hamlet — Parodies of SF authors by Richard A. Lupoff – A brand new edition with more stories and more illustrations by Trina Robbins.

The Secret Adventures of Sherlock Holmes — Three Sherlockian pastiches by the Brooklyn author/publisher, Gary Lovisi.

The Universal Holmes — Richard A. Lupoff's 2007 collection of five Holmesian pastiches and a recipe for giant rat stew.

Four Joel Townsley Rogers Novels — By the author of *The Red Right Hand*: *Once In a Red Moon*, *Lady With the Dice*, *The Stopped Clock*, *Never Leave My Bed*

Two Joel Townsley Rogers Story Collections — *Night of Horror* and *Killing Time*

Twenty Norman Berrow Novels — *The Bishop's Sword*, *Ghost House*, *Don't Go Out After Dark*, *Claws of the Cougar*, *The Smokers of Hashish*, *The Secret Dancer*, *Don't Jump Mr. Boland!*, *The Footprints of Satan*, *Fingers for Ransom*, *The Three Tiers of Fantasy*, *The Spaniard's Thumb*, *The Eleventh Plague*, *Words Have Wings*, *One Thrilling Night*, *The Lady's in Danger*, *It Howls at Night*, *The Terror in the Fog*, *Oil Under the Window*, *Murder in the Melody*, *The Singing Room*

The N. R. De Mexico Novels — Robert Bragg presents *Marijuana Girl*, *Madman on a Drum*, *Private Chauffeur* in one volume.

Four Chelsea Quinn Yarbro Novels featuring Charlie Moon — *Ogilvie, Tallant and Moon*, *Music When the Sweet Voice Dies*, *Poisonous Fruit* and *Dead Mice*

Five Walter S. Masterman Mysteries — *The Green Toad*, *The Flying Beast*, *The Yellow Mistletoe*, *The Wrong Verdict* and *The Perjured Alibi*. Fantastic impossible plots.

Two Hake Talbot Novels — *Rim of the Pit, The Hangman's Handyman.* Classic locked room mysteries.

Two Alexander Laing Novels — *The Motives of Nicholas Holtz* and *Dr. Scarlett*, stories of medical mayhem and intrigue from the 30s.

Four David Hume Novels — *Corpses Never Argue, Cemetery First Stop, Make Way for the Mourners, Eternity Here I Come*, and more to come.

Three Wade Wright Novels — *Echo of Fear, Death At Nostalgia Street* and *It Leads to Murder*, with more to come!

Eight Rupert Penny Novels — *Policeman's Holiday, Policeman's Evidence, Lucky Policeman, Policeman in Armour, Sealed Room Murder, Sweet Poison, The Talkative Policeman, She had to Have Gas* and *Cut and Run* (by Martin Tanner.)

Five Jack Mann Novels — Strange murder in the English countryside. *Gees' First Case, Nightmare Farm, Grey Shapes, The Ninth Life, The Glass Too Many.*

Seven Max Afford Novels — *Owl of Darkness, Death's Mannikins, Blood on His Hands, The Dead Are Blind, The Sheep and the Wolves, Sinners in Paradise* and *Two Locked Room Mysteries and a Ripping Yarn* by one of Australia's finest novelists.

Five Joseph Shallit Novels — *The Case of the Billion Dollar Body, Lady Don't Die on My Doorstep, Kiss the Killer, Yell Bloody Murder, Take Your Last Look.* One of America's best 50's authors.

Two Crimson Clown Novels — By Johnston McCulley, author of the Zorro novels, *The Crimson Clown* and *The Crimson Clown Again.*

The Best of 10-Story Book — edited by Chris Mikul, over 35 stories from the literary magazine Harry Stephen Keeler edited.

A Young Man's Heart — A forgotten early classic by Cornell Woolrich

The Anthony Boucher Chronicles — edited by Francis M. Nevins
Book reviews by Anthony Boucher written for the *San Francisco Chronicle*, 1942 – 1947. Essential and fascinating reading.

Muddled Mind: Complete Works of Ed Wood, Jr. — David Hayes and Hayden Davis deconstruct the life and works of a mad genius.

Gadsby — A lipogram (a novel without the letter E). Ernest Vincent Wright's last work, published in 1939 right before his death.

My First Time: The One Experience You Never Forget — Michael Birchwood — 64 true first-person narratives of how they lost it.

A Roland Daniel Double: The Signal and The Return of Wu Fang — Classic thrillers from the 30s

Murder in Shawnee — Two novels of the Alleghenies by John Douglas: *Shawnee Alley Fire* and *Haunts.*

Deep Space and other Stories — A collection of SF gems by Richard A. Lupoff

Blood Moon — The first of the Robert Payne series by Ed Gorman

The Time Armada — Fox B. Holden's 1953 SF gem.

Black River Falls — Suspense from the master, Ed Gorman

Sideslip — 1968 SF masterpiece by Ted White and Dave Van Arnam

The Triune Man — Mindscrambling science fiction from Richard A. Lupoff

Detective Duff Unravels It — Episodic mysteries by Harvey O'Higgins

Automaton — Brilliant treatise on robotics: 1928-style! By H. Stafford Hatfield

The Incredible Adventures of Rowland Hern — Rousing 1928 impossible crimes by Nicholas Olde.

Slammer Days — Two full-length prison memoirs: *Men into Beasts* (1952) by George Sylvester Viereck and *Home Away From Home* (1962) by Jack Woodford

Murder in Black and White — 1931 classic tennis whodunit by Evelyn Elder

Killer's Caress — Cary Moran's 1936 hardboiled thriller

The Golden Dagger — 1951 Scotland Yard yarn by E. R. Punshon

A Smell of Smoke — 1951 English countryside thriller by Miles Burton

Ruled By Radio — 1925 futuristic novel by Robert L. Hadfield & Frank E. Farncombe

Murder in Silk — A 1937 Yellow Peril novel of the silk trade by Ralph Trevor

The Case of the Withered Hand — 1936 potboiler by John G. Brandon

Finger-prints Never Lie — A 1939 classic detective novel by John G. Brandon

Inclination to Murder — 1966 thriller by New Zealand's Harriet Hunter

Invaders from the Dark — Classic werewolf tale from Greye La Spina

Fatal Accident — Murder by automobile, a 1936 mystery by Cecil M. Wills

The Devil Drives — A prison and lost treasure novel by Virgil Markham

Dr. Odin — Douglas Newton's 1933 potboiler comes back to life.

The Chinese Jar Mystery — Murder in the manor by John Stephen Strange, 1934

The Julius Caesar Murder Case — A classic 1935 re-telling of the assassination by Wallace Irwin that's much more fun than the Shakespeare version

West Texas War and Other Western Stories — by Gary Lovisi

The Contested Earth and Other SF Stories — A never-before published space opera and seven short stories by Jim Harmon.

Tales of the Macabre and Ordinary — Modern twisted horror by Chris Mikul, author of the *Bizarrism* series.

The Gold Star Line — Seaboard adventure from L.T. Reade and Robert Eustace.

The Werewolf vs the Vampire Woman — Hard to believe ultraviolence by either Arthur M. Scarm or Arthur M. Scram.

Black Hogan Strikes Again — Australia's Peter Renwick pens a tale of the outback.

Don Diablo: Book of a Lost Film — Two-volume treatment of a western by Paul Landres, with diagrams. Intro by Francis M. Nevins.
The Charlie Chaplin Murder Mystery — Movie hijinks by Wes D. Gehring
The Koky Comics — A collection of all of the 1978-1981 Sunday and daily comic strips by Richard O'Brien and Mort Gerberg, in two volumes.
Suzy — Another collection of comic strips from Richard O'Brien and Bob Vojtko
Dime Novels: Ramble House's 10-Cent Books — *Knife in the Dark* by Robert Leslie Bellem, *Hot Lead* and *Song of Death* by Ed Earl Repp, *A Hashish House in New York* by H.H. Kane, and five more.
Blood in a Snap — The *Finnegan's Wake* of the 21st century, by Jim Weiler
Stakeout on Millennium Drive — Award-winning Indianapolis Noir — Ian Woollen.
Dope Tales #1 — Two dope-riddled classics; *Dope Runners* by Gerald Grantham and *Death Takes the Joystick* by Phillip Condé.
Dope Tales #2 — Two more narco-classics; *The Invisible Hand* by Rex Dark and *The Smokers of Hashish* by Norman Berrow.
Dope Tales #3 — Two enchanting novels of opium by the master, Sax Rohmer. *Dope* and *The Yellow Claw*.
Tenebrae — Ernest G. Henham's 1898 horror tale brought back.
The Singular Problem of the Stygian House-Boat — Two classic tales by John Kendrick Bangs about the denizens of Hades.
Tiresias — Psychotic modern horror novel by Jonathan M. Sweet.
The One After Snelling — Kickass modern noir from Richard O'Brien.
The Sign of the Scorpion — 1935 Edmund Snell tale of oriental evil.
The House of the Vampire — 1907 poetic thriller by George S. Viereck.
An Angel in the Street — Modern hardboiled noir by Peter Genovese.
The Devil's Mistress — Scottish gothic tale by J. W. Brodie-Innes.
The Lord of Terror — 1925 mystery with master-criminal, Fantômas.
The Lady of the Terraces — 1925 adventure by E. Charles Vivian.
My Deadly Angel — 1955 Cold War drama by John Chelton
Prose Bowl — Futuristic satire — Bill Pronzini & Barry N. Malzberg .
Satan's Den Exposed — True crime in Truth or Consequences New Mexico — Award-winning journalism by the *Desert Journal*.
The Amorous Intrigues & Adventures of Aaron Burr — by Anonymous — Hot historical action.
I Stole $16,000,000 — A true story by cracksman Herbert E. Wilson.
The Black Dark Murders — Vintage 50s college murder yarn by Milt Ozaki, writing as Robert O. Saber.
Sex Slave — Potboiler of lust in the days of Cleopatra — Dion Leclerq.
You'll Die Laughing — Bruce Elliott's 1945 novel of murder at a practical joker's English countryside manor.
The Private Journal & Diary of John H. Surratt — The memoirs of the man who conspired to assassinate President Lincoln.
Dead Man Talks Too Much — Hollywood boozer by Weed Dickenson
Red Light — History of legal prostitution in Shreveport Louisiana by Eric Brock. Includes wonderful photos of the houses and the ladies.
A Snark Selection — Lewis Carroll's *The Hunting of the Snark* with two Snarkian chapters by Harry Stephen Keeler — Illustrated by Gavin L. O'Keefe.
Ripped from the Headlines! — The Jack the Ripper story as told in the newspaper articles in the *New York* and *London Times*.
Geronimo — S. M. Barrett's 1905 autobiography of a noble American.
The White Peril in the Far East — Sidney Lewis Gulick's 1905 indictment of the West and assurance that Japan would never attack the U.S.
The Compleat Calhoon — All of Fender Tucker's works: Includes *Totah Six-Pack, Weed, Women and Song* and *Tales from the Tower*, plus a CD of all of his songs.
Totah Six-Pack — Just Fender Tucker's six tales about Farmington in one sleek volume.

RAMBLE HOUSE

Fender Tucker, Prop.   Gavin L. O'Keefe, Graphics
www.ramblehouse.com   fender@ramblehouse.com
228-826-1783   10329 Sheephead Drive, Vancleave MS 39565

www.ingramcontent.com/pod-product-compliance
Lightning Source LLC
Chambersburg PA
CBHW031129160426
43193CB00008B/81